Special Education Considerations for English Language Learners

Delivering a Continuum of Services

Else Hamayan

Barbara Marler

Cristina Sanchez-Lopez

Jack Damico

Caslon Publishing

Philadelphia

Caslon, Inc.
P.O. Box 3248
Philadelphia, PA 19130

Caslonpublishing.com

9 8 7 6 5 4 3 2

Library of Congress Cataloging-in-Publication Data

Hamayan, Else V.
Special education considerations for English language learners : delivering a continuum of service / Else Hamayan . . . [et al.].
   p. cm.
Includes bibliographical references and index.
ISBN 0–9727507–9–7 (pbk. : alk. paper)
1. English language—Study and teaching (Elementary)—Foreign speakers.
2. English language—Study and teaching—Foreign speakers.   3. English language—Study and teaching (Primary)—Foreign speakers.   4. English language—Study and teaching (Secondary)—Foreign speakers.   5. English language—Study and teaching (Elementary)—Foreign speakers.   6. Special education—English language.   I. Title.
PE1128.A2H88 2007
372.65'21—dc22   2006101765

Foreword

Every day, teachers struggle with the decision to refer or not to refer an English language learner (ELL) to special education services. Teachers agonize over whether or not they have made the right decision if they do make such a referral. They want students' needs to be met, and wonder if referral is the most efficacious path. This book exposes the myths and inaccurate assumptions behind the instinctive referral to special education classes and proposes a comprehensive alternative that aids caring educators in reaching their intended goal. As someone who has worked in bilingual/cross-cultural special education for over 25 years and who has encountered thousands of teachers unsure of how best to serve struggling ELLs, I am pleased to see this practical and extremely well-grounded book come onto the professional resource market.

My primary reason for recommending this book, however, is not the analytical component, important as that is. I have argued in many professional venues that the fairest, least biased, and most valid assessment means nothing without follow-up in the form of delivery of quality educational services, and that is my primary interest in recommending this book. The authors understand what matters in serving learners well and the mechanisms to get there.

Special Education Considerations for English Language Learners represents the integration of best practice from the fields of bilingual, multicultural, second language, and special education. Using a research-based approach, it details a step-by-step process for serving all ELLs effectively from the start. Grounded in the paradigm of ecological assessment, the authors identify the essential information that needs to be gathered and the means of gathering that information so that educators can distinguish second language development and learning difference They then show practitioners how to deliver responsive interventions to learners.

Else Hamayan, Barbara Marler, Cristina Sanchez-Lopez, and Jack Damico are deeply familiar with each of the seven learner factors that must be addressed. Where they break new ground is in their discussions of physical and psychological factors, previous schooling factors, and cultural and linguistic factors that affect student performance. They offer sound guidance for conducting comprehensive assessments and recommend effective, research-based interventions for at-risk students. This is precisely what has been missing from the practicum—sound and comprehensive pedagogy for ELLs who are having learning difficulties.

I highly recommend this volume to school-based, collaborative decision-making and intervention-focused teams that aim to serve learners fully and well through informed practice. The many useful tools and resources offered for assessment and the templates and instructional guidelines offered to plan responsive interventions will produce satisfactory outcomes for learners. This welcome resource will engender productive and meaningful conversations among school-based practitioners, and the subsequent actions those professionals take will lead naturally to the delivery of a rich continuum of services for all ELLs.

Nancy Cloud, Ed.D.
Feinstein School of Education and Human Development
Rhode Island College

Preface

English language learners (ELLs) who are having significant difficulties in school present a special challenge to teachers and administrators. Although many of the difficulties are part of the normal process of second language learning, in some schools the difficulties that ELLs have are perceived as inordinate. Often, that perception leads to the conclusion that these ELLs have some exceptional need, and they end up as special education students. Regardless of whether that decision is based on appropriate assessment and regardless of whether the decision to place these students in special education is a valid one, ELLs who are having academic difficulties present a challenge to educators in many schools. This handbook deals with precisely that challenge.

This handbook offers an alternative to the system where struggling ELLs must be identified as having a special education need in order to receive support from a special education specialist. Based on a system of extensive information collection we offer suggestions for interventions that would help support the specific difficulties that ELLs often have in school. Some of these interventions are specific to individual students while others are systemic and would improve the learning context for all ELLs. The interventions we recommend emerge from our knowledge of second language learning as well as special education research and practice. We also recommend a team consisting of teachers, administrators, and specialists that ensures a broad perspective and that a continuum of services are provided to these students.

The genesis of this book lay in a workshop that Jack Damico and I developed years ago in response to requests for assistance from schools. The requests were very similar, and typically took the form of a question: "How can we tell if English language learners have special education needs?" Initially the workshop focused exclusively on the question of how to distinguish between long-term disabilities and normal second language difficulties that ELLs were having in school. In fact, the workshop became known casually as "the LD/L2 Workshop." Over the years, however, we came to understand that the question of is it L2 or is it LD was extremely murky, and probably the wrong question to ask.

Subsequently Barbara Marler and Cristina Sanchez-Lopez of the Illinois Resource Center in Des Plaines began working with schools and school districts on this issue. They began helping schools restructure in fundamental ways the system in place to provide better support for ELLs who are having significant academic difficulties. Cristina also started working extensively with Theresa Young of the Toronto District School Board, and their work began to influence the ideas in this book significantly. We try to move staff away from needing to know right at the beginning whether an ELL has a disability that can be categorized as a special education need. Our work is based on the principle that support is more effective if it is provided seamlessly as part of a continuum that is integrated into the everyday school life of a student or a group of students. Ensuring a continuum of services is of utmost importance to our framework.

The handbook was written with three purposes in mind. First, we wanted to help teachers identify specific difficulties that students encounter in school. Second, we wanted to help educators deduce the source of those difficulties through extensive information gathering, and third, we wanted to help school staff identify interventions most likely to be effective in alleviating these academic problems.

We hope that the handbook also helps educators in deciding whether to pursue special education services for these students at all. Finding assistance that works for any student experiencing academic difficulty is not easy. When those students are ELLs, the challenge is amplified; finding assistance that works becomes much more difficult. We hope that this handbook will help educators better navigate the intervention options. We offer pragmatic and effective interventions that are rooted in the theoretical tenets of second language acquisition and acculturation. They are also firmly based on research on effective educational programs for ELLs and they result from our work in schools. The book can also be used as a professional development tool for professional learning communities, problem-solving teams, and action research groups.

The approach we propose would not work without a strong collaborative model in which professionals with expertise in different areas come together to solve a problem: what to do about a student or a group of students who are having unusual academic difficulty. The approach requires that individuals from different specializations collaborate and share their expertise with one another. In doing so, they must be open to perspectives different from their own. We call these collaborative groups ECOS teams (for Ensuring a Continuum of Services). It is the ECOS team that coordinates the information gathering, the formulation of interventions, and the support of teachers.

The way that the workshop on which this book is based was conceived reflects that collaboration directly. Jack Damico is well versed in special education, and my expertise is in ELL education. We brought our areas of expertise together and created the workshop that eventually led to this book. Later, with the addition of Barbara Marler and Cristina Sanchez-Lopez to the team, new perspectives were introduced. Barbara brought teaching and administrative experience, and Cristina gave us insights from a teacher's perspective. Cristina's work with Theresa Young, a speech-language pathologist from the Toronto District School Board, added yet another perspective. Without this evolving collaboration, the ideas in this book would not be as wide-ranging.

The special features in this book were designed to make it easier for schools to begin offering a continuum of services to ELLs who are having academic difficulties. One or more of the following special features appear in various chapters:

Chronicles: The chronicles are true stories told by different individuals, running the gamut from a parent to a university professor. They illustrate specific points made in the book and are accompanied by questions for discussion.

ECOS Team Activities: This feature serves to set up discussions, challenges, practical activities that will help ECOS teams understand and further investigate issues presented in the chapters. Many of these items would be effective as professional development activities.

Steps for ECOS Teams to Take: Chapters 2 to 4 summarize the steps that ECOS teams need to take to begin the process through which the continuum of services framework becomes part of the everyday working of a school.

Checklists, Rating Scales, Questionnaires: The book offers many tools that can serve to assess aspects of the program or the way that support is provided to students, evaluate the current situation in a school, and develop the process for establishing a continuum of services.

Questions for Discussion: Chapters 5 to 11 include questions that are intended to prompt further discussion of the integral factors that need to be considered in designing interventions for ELLs experiencing academic difficulties. These questions are meant to get teams to think about their own specific setting and to apply the concepts to their student population.

The book also has extensive material in the appendices—open-ended worksheets, an evaluation form, and augmentative information—and a glossary, with definitions of some of the key concepts presented in the text.

We hope that the suggestions in this book are helpful in setting up a system in schools whereby ELLs receive the support they need in a seamless way. We would be gratified if the book also inspired educators to move away from the status quo and join with colleagues to do what is most effective for ELLs who are having more than the average share of difficulty in school.

Else Hamayan

Contents

Chapter **3**   **Describing before Diagnosing: Observation
of Specific Difficulties That ELLs May Experience**   **29**

Chapter **4**   **Delivering a Continuum of Services**   **45**

1

A Framework for Considering the Special Needs of English Language Learners

KEY CONCEPTS

To serve the needs of English language learners who are having significant difficulties in school, a system must be set up that allows support to be provided in a continuum, without interruption, and immediately following the identification of those difficulties.

When English language learners (ELLs), students who are developing proficiency in a second language and who are learning academic content through a nonproficient language, are perceived as having an inordinate amount of difficulty in school, the issue presents a tremendous challenge to teachers, special education specialists, and administrators. Almost immediately the question arises as to whether those ELLs have a long-term disability (Fradd & Weismantal, 1989). More often than not, when a teacher feels that an ELL is having greater than expected difficulty at school, there is an inclination to jump to the conclusion that the student has a special education need.

Historically in the United States, there has been a tendency to refer ELLs inappropriately to special education, which in turn has led to the overidentification of ELLs as having special education needs and a disproportionate representation of these students in special education (Artiles & Ortiz, 2002; Cummins, 1984; Gottlieb & Hamayan, 2006; Ortiz, García, Wheeler, et al., 1986). The overrepresentation of ELLs is particularly acute in programs for the learning disabled (e.g., Jitendra & Rohena-Diaz, 1996; McNamara, 1998; Ortiz, García, Holtzman, et al., 1985). The path to the special education door is well worn because it is a familiar way of getting help for students who are having difficulty in school. Owing to the lack of other effective remedial options, special education may also be perceived as being the only means available to teachers to find help for students experiencing academic difficulties. Teachers are likely to choose special education readily as the source of support for ELLs because it does generate help, funding is still available, and even if they know that it may not be appropriate, it assuages their feelings of guilt and satisfies the need for accountability.

Unfortunately, this perceived solution frequently results in negative consequences. Since most special educators are not well trained in diversity education, second language acquisition, or bilingual education (e.g., Kritikos, 2003; Roseberry-McKibbin, Brice, & O'Hanlon, 2005), their best attempts at assistance often are misdirected and ineffective. Additionally, placing an inappropriate special education label on an ELL results in changed expectations for that student and often provides a convenient if incorrect excuse for the ELL's difficulties (Coles, 1987; McDermott & Varenne, 1995; Ogbu & Simons, 1998; Taylor, 1991). Finally, if the ELL is served in special education, the school system may believe that the student's needs are met and may not provide the minority language education needed by that ELL. It is important, therefore, that this apparent "solution" not be employed inappropriately.

Reasons for the Misidentification of Special Needs among ELLs

To ensure that misidentification does not occur, this manual proposes a different approach to assessment and service delivery for ELLs that can overcome many of the problems in traditional assessment and remediation directed toward this student population. Before highlighting solutions, however, we present three reasons why such misidentification is likely to occur in this population. These reasons are problematic assessment practices, the influence of the medical model when addressing educational issues, and funding biases toward special education. Each is briefly discussed here.

Assessment

The first and most significant reason for the tendency to overidentify ELLs as in need of special education is that the assessment of proficiency and its manifestations among ELLs is fraught with difficulty. Assessment as a process is a complex enterprise that requires consideration of multiple factors, including symbolic proficiency, affect, previous experience, cultural and linguistic learning and application, expectations, and contextual variables (Carroll, 1993; Damico, 1992; Gutkin & Nemeth, 1997; Hamayan & Damico, 1991; Lubinski, 2000; Müller, 2003; Wentzel & Wigfield, 1998). However, this complexity and the methods to address it are not typically considered in school settings. Consequently, a number of biases that orient the assessment process away from the best interests of the ELL become operational. These biases include a focus on superficial behaviors rather than underlying factors as indices of difficulty, the collection of inadequate data—often in the form of norm-referenced and standardized test results—that do not enable sufficient descriptions of proficiency, a lack of recognition of several consequences of bilingualism during assessment, and the application of inappropriate discrepancy formulas for interpretation purposes.

At a superficial level, the way that academic and language difficulties manifest among ELLs is very similar to the way such difficulties manifest among students with long-term disabilities or special needs (Crago & Paradis, 2003; Cummins, 2000; Damico & Damico, 1993a; Salameh, Håkansson, & Nettelbladt, 2004). For example, Paradis (2005) examined English grammatical morphemes in 24 typically developing ELLs and compared their productions with those of monolingual English-speaking children exhibiting specific language impairment (SLI). She found that the ELLs' accuracy rates and error patterns were similar to those reported for same-age children with SLI. Similarly, both ELLs and monolingual English-speaking learning-disabled[1] students may frequently search for words in English even though they have understood the concept. That is not to say that the causes of these difficulties are the same in the two populations. Rather, there are only so many ways that language and learning difficulties manifest behaviorally, despite the underlying causal variables (i.e., disability or difference). It is not enough to focus only on the

---

[1]The term *learning disability* is used in this book to refer to the variety of cognitive, perceptual, language, or mathematical disabilities that lead to difficulties in learning in an academic setting.

superficial indices of difficulty; one must also determine whether deeper or more complex variables are operating (e.g., Ahlsén, 2005; Armstrong, 2005; Damico, Smith, & Augustine, 1996; Holm & Dodd, 1999; Perkins, 2005).

Language and learning disabilities are generally due to factors intrinsic to the learner, such as a neurological impairment or a problem with symbolic processing (Perkins, 2005), whereas second language learning difficulties are typically due to factors extrinsic to the learner, such as the language learning process itself or cross-cultural differences (Damico & Hamayan, 1992). In the case of vocabulary usage, for example, if an ELL frequently forgets a common word that has been taught, it is possible that the visual aid used to represent the concept may have been culturally irrelevant for that student (for example, the Liberty Bell representing the concept of freedom or independence that is specific to American history); hence the visual symbol would not provide any help for that student in learning new vocabulary. For learning-disabled students, the same difficulty—that is, forgetting common words that have been taught—may result from a completely different set of reasons. The student may have oral language comprehension or production difficulties as a consequence of word retrieval problems, or the student may have memory problems. In such cases, the pedagogical needs of the two populations are different: learning-disabled students need support in creating compensations to overcome their problems (e.g., Damico, Smith, & Augustine, 1996; Dunaway, 2004; Genesee, Paradis, & Crago, 2004; Westby, 1997), whereas second language learners need to develop further proficiency in academic language.

Another difficulty in assessment is that the data gathered as part of the referral and evaluation process are frequently inadequate. There is a tendency to rely too heavily on norm-referenced and standardized test scores, which give only a very narrow and potentially quite inaccurate view of what a student is able to do (Flynn, 2000; Gutiérrez-Clellen & Peña, 2001; Laing & Kamhi, 2003; Tetnowski & Franklin, 2003). As discussed by Damico (1991), norm-referenced and standardized tests typically focus on superficial aspects of language structure, have validity and authenticity concerns, provide numbers that have a differentiating function rather than an interpretive function, and focus on identifying students' weaknesses; consequently, these tests do not give us a good sense of what ELLs are able to do. Further, ELLs, who are often unfamiliar with the cultural context of test items, are likely to give the wrong answers not because they do not have the specific skill being assessed but because they do not understand the question. This constellation of factors promotes unreliable test results that give an inaccurate view of the student (Aspel, Willis, & Faust, 1998; Gunderson & Siegel, 2001; Müller, 2003; Portes, 1999).

In addition, norm-referenced and standardized assessment tools typically do not account for the fact that the students being tested are bilingual. Instead, tests designed for monolingual students are developed or translated from one language to another, and different norms are collected. Even assuming that the tests developed are valid and reliable (a dangerous assumption), factors relating to bilingualism as a process are not always carefully considered (Chamberlain & Mederios-Landurand, 1991; Genesee, Paradis, & Crago, 2004; Grosjean, 1998; Oller & Eilers, 2002). For example, although many studies have demonstrated that ELLs are highly variable in their performance, based on individual, contextual, affective, and developmental factors as well as proficiency (e.g., Bialystok, 2001; Genesee, Paradis, & Crago, 2004; Goldstein, 2004; Thordardottir, Rothenberg, Rivard, et al., 2006), these variables are rarely considered in the scoring criteria or in the interpretive instructions for these tools (Damico, 1991, 1992; Lubinski, 2000; Wilson, Wilson, & Coleman, 2000). Similarly, although numerous studies have indicated that an ELL's test performance should be interpreted using both languages via conceptual scoring—that is, scoring the meaning of a response regardless of the language in which it is produced (e.g., Bedore, Peña, García, et al., 2005; Marchman & Martinez-

Sussman, 2002; Oller & Eilers, 2002; Pearson, Fernández, & Oller, 1993, 1995)—this is not typically done. Failure to take into account the complexity of the bilingual process during assessment further reduces the effectiveness of traditional assessment and diagnostic tools when focusing on ELLs.

Finally, the discrepancy model for identifying learning disabilities, which was initially useful as a gatekeeping mechanism, does not serve ELLs well, since it is normal for ELLs to have lower scores on verbal tasks than on tasks that do not require as much verbal processing (Campbell, 1996; Campbell & Kenny, 1999; Cummins, 1996; Kohnert, 2004). This discrepancy may provide an accurate description of monolingual students with a learning disability (Fletcher et al., 1998; Sternberg & Grigorenko, 2002). However, it also describes quite precisely a major characteristic of normally developing ELLs! Perhaps because of these problems, the Individuals with Disabilities Education Act (IDEA) of 2004 has given districts permission to go beyond the discrepancy formula to embrace a model that assesses how students respond to different interventions and instructional activities. This moves the definition of learning disability out of the domain of a discrepancy between performance and potential and into the domain of response to intervention (RTI). The RTI model seeks to improve the learning environment for all students in the classroom by supporting both teachers and students and subsequently keeping track of students who resist these interventions. We discuss the potential advantages and disadvantages of using this model to identify ELLs with disabilities in Chapter 4.

To get a better sense of what an ELL is able to do and what he or she has difficulty with, a considerable amount of information needs to be gathered. In many instances, staff members do not have the time or resources to gather the qualitative information necessary to determine ELLs' needs. Unless they are trained in the process and provided with appropriate tools, gathering accurate and useful qualitative information is a difficulty in many schools. There is often a lack of know-how of how to use ethnographic approaches to collect data in such a way that the information obtained is meaningful and useful. It is important to adhere to certain standards in order to collect qualitative data that are authentic, and to have the conviction that these data are not inferior to data obtained through more standardized means.

Neither can staff always collect the amount of information needed for such a determination. At the end of the assessment process, we are often left with something akin to a huge jigsaw puzzle with several pieces missing. Further, these data are often gathered and interpreted by school personnel who are not adequately versed in ELL education issues, second language acquisition, or cross-cultural education and the implications of these factors for the assessment and instruction of ELLs (Goldstein, 2004; Müller, 2003; Oller & Eilers, 2002; Ortiz, et al., 1986; García & Ortiz, 1988). Often the bilingual or the English as a second language (ESL) specialist is not involved in making sense out of the gathered information, let alone in the data collection (Chronicle 1.1 describes an instance in which language proficiency testing was overlooked completely).

Prevalence of a Medical Model

A second fundamental reason for the tendency to overidentify ELLs as needing special education services lies in the way in which the special education system has evolved in the United States. In the last quarter-century, a medical model has prevailed in the way that many people attempt to understand the special needs that some students have in school. This model is based on the notion that disabilities or challenges can be identified much like the list of ailments that are officially recognized as diseases in the medical field (Coles, 1987; McDermott & Varenne, 1995; Skrtic, 1991; Taylor, 1991, 1993). This tendency to view academic and language learning difficulties from the

CHRONICLE 1.1

Monica Graduates!

By N.B., a parent   *Arlington Heights, Illinois*

When my daughter Monica was in third grade, she was getting C's in every-thing. Monica had been in this school since kindergarten. She arrived from Poland not speaking a word of English. The school did not do anything special for her; they didn't give her any special classes in English. Now I know there is something called ESL for children who come with no English. I thought some-one should be helping her with English, but I also didn't want her missing what the teacher was teaching. She needed a lot of help with English, but I figured the school knew best what to do. A lot of people told us to speak English at home, but my English is not so good, and besides, I wanted her to keep up her Polish. So we stayed speaking Polish at home, and it was difficult for her at school. But we worked hard and I knew she was smart, so at a parent-teacher conference I asked whether the school could give Monica a test to de-termine her level of English proficiency. I was interested in knowing how much English Monica had acquired.

The teachers must have misunderstood. The next thing I knew, we received a "consent to test" permission form to initiate special education testing. I was shocked! I had never imagined that Monica had any kind of learning prob-lems. Here she was learning two languages and doing OK. Sure, it took her a little longer to get things in class, but she seemed to be managing. I have a friend who is a bilingual teacher at another school, so I asked her what I should do. She said not to test her. She said that if they tested her it would probably be in English, and even if it were in Polish, Monica would not do well on the test, but not because she had a learning problem. She said that we should talk to the teachers and see if they would give Monica some more help with English.

The school was not happy that we were not signing the form, and they did nothing to help Monica. They told us to get her tutoring at home. We did that in English, math, and English history. I can't say that it was easy, but we worked at it, and little by little, Monica's English became better and better. When Monica finished grade 8, she graduated with high honors.

Monica is now fully bilingual, and she just graduated from high school and will be starting college in September. I guess we made the right decision, but it was very difficult. What if Monica did have a problem? Well, I don't worry much about it. She did well, and most important, she's going to college, and she can speak and read both English and Polish.

Questions for discussion:

- What beliefs that the parent had are supported by research?
- What misconceptions does the parent have, if any?
- What did the school do that was effective?
- What did the school do wrong, if anything?

perspective of human pathology can be seen in the medicalization of learn-ing problems in the *Diagnostic and Statistical Manual of Mental Disorders* (American Psychiatric Association, 2000) and the tenth edition of the *International Classification of Diseases* (World Health Organization, 2002). Whether these medical designations are defensible or not, they do function to create an explicit grounding for the discipline of special education (Skrtic, 1991).

This prevailing medical orientation has as a result created a set of beliefs about the nature of special education and even about ELLs' role within special education, and these beliefs inform both our perceptions of academic and language-learning problems and our assessment practices (Damico, Müller, & Ball, 2004; Frick & Lahey, 1991; Klasen, 2000; McDermott, 1993; Taylor, 1993). This situation has falsely suggested to educators that disabilities can be easily identified in a valid and reliable manner, which results in misidentification, because the complexity of the phenomenon and the individuality of the ELL are often overlooked.

In reality, exceptionality is not an objective and easily verifiable empirical construct. Rather, it is a social construct, and the diagnostic criteria employed for various exceptional traits have been constructed on the basis of a number of sociocultural factors that mirror whatever ideologies are in vogue at any given time (e.g., McDermott & Varenne, 1995; Reid, Maag, & Vasa, 1994; Skrtic, 1991). These diagnostic categories may be further complicated by ambiguity and subjectivity, and this lack of definitional rigor may result in various types of problems. Indeed, the extreme overidentification of ELLs as learning disabled and language disordered is a clear demonstration of the problems (e.g., Jitendra & Rohena-Diaz, 1996; McNamara, 1998; Ortiz, García, Holtzman, et al., 1985; Stow & Dodd, 2005).

Availability of Categorical Funding

The third reason for the misidentification of ELLs as having disabilities lies in the categorical status of special education. The legal status of special education gives impetus to the tendency to formally identify separate categories of disabilities. When Public Law 94-142 (The Education Act for All Handicapped, also known as the IDEA) passed in 1975, it provided legal support for special education and subsequently created a separately funded category within the educational system. Since then, students have had to be formally identified as having special education needs before funding can be received by the school for that individual student. Thus, the identification of these disabilities is connected with additional funding that gives the school much-needed resources. Having additional funding attached to the categorization of students in special education may make it less objectionable for schools to identify special education needs. The gate or hurdle that would keep students from being needlessly categorized into special education is simply not there. It is too tempting to place students in special education when they are perceived to fall outside of what is considered "normal," regardless of the underlying reasons.

This categorization of special education could also have the opposite effect. In some districts, because of fear of monitoring agencies or potential litigation, the gatekeeping mechanisms are overused. The pre-referral process becomes so complex and time-consuming that students who do need support never get it (Stow & Dodd, 2005). Students have to fail or wait beyond an assimilation period before they are even referred to special education.

The Need to Provide Relevant Services in a Timely Manner

The accurate identification of the special needs of ELLs is important for two reasons. The first reason has to do with the stigma of the label (Cummins, 2000; Goffman, 1964; McDermott & Varenne, 1995). As much as we try to make it sound as though a special education placement is within acceptable limits, the label still carries a certain stigma that will remain with a student, formally and informally, for a long time (Coles, 1987; McDermott, 1993; Taylor, 1991). This stigma is especially problematic insofar as many in mainstream society perceive ELLs as having lower status; many in the general society do not value the languages and cultures that ELLs and their families bring with them. Immigrants and refugees are often marginalized and do not participate fully in what the larger society has to offer. So the added burden of yet another stigmatizing label is not helpful at all (Harry & Klingner, 2006).

The more compelling reason for not erroneously placing ELLs into special education is that we must ensure the most effective learning environment for these students. If an ELL is having difficulties in school because of second language issues, the best support for that student would come from expanding proficiency in English as a second language, and not from special education interventions (e.g., Damico & Hamayan, 1992; Freeman & Freeman, 2001; Genesee, Paradis, & Crago, 2004). Studies have shown that Hispanic students who were classified as learning disabled performed at a lower level after three years of special education placement (Wilkinson & Ortiz, 1986). Thus, these students may not benefit at all from the support they receive in that setting.

Another difficulty with the way special education services are provided to students in general is that it often takes a long time before any additional support is given to ELLs who are having special difficulties in school. Many school districts feel compelled to wait until a full fledged referral has resulted in a formal categorization into special education before providing specialized support. Thus, the student remains without those specialized interventions for too long. This state of affairs is significantly influenced by some myths regarding ELLs in need of special education services.

Some Myths Regarding ELLs and Special Education

Several myths prevail in the area of special education for ELLs. These myths guide us in the way we approach education in general, in the way we interpret students' behaviors, and in how we teach and assess students. The following are commonly held misconceptions regarding ELLs and special education.

Myth 1: If we label an ELL as learning disabled, at least he will get some help.

Response: A special education placement when none is warranted does not serve the student well. First, we are bestowing on the student a stigmatizing label that the student does not need. Second, interventions that are specifically geared to help processing, linguistic, or cognitive disabilities often do not help children acquire second language proficiency. In fact, special education services can limit the kind of learning that ELLs need (Gersten & Woodward, 1994). Special education interventions tend to target a narrow selection of skills to enable mastery, and discrete skills are often practiced out of context (Damico & Damico, 1993a; Westby & Vining, 2002). This complicates the learning process for ELLs, since they need a meaningful context in order to comprehend the language that surrounds them (Genesee, 2006). In addition, special education interventions often use reading materials with controlled phonics and vocabulary, which reduces the meaningfulness of the text. Intervention tasks often revolve around surface structures of language, targeting grammar, syntax, and spelling. This constricts language usage and makes it more difficult for ELLs to understand and retain information (Gersten & Woodward, 1994).

Myth 2: We have to wait five to seven years for ELLs to develop their English language skills before we can rule out language as a cause for the student's difficulty.

Response: Although it is true that ELLs may take five to seven years to develop proficiency in academic language (Cummins, 2006), there is no need to withhold any kind of support services that an ELL might need in the meantime. The timeline suggested by Cummins was meant to give teachers a sense of how much to expect students to learn through a language that was not yet fully developed, especially in abstract academic concepts. Besides, if a student truly has an intrinsic difficulty, then it exists in all the student's languages and in most use contexts. The sooner these exceptionalities are identified and supported, the better opportunity the student has to be successful in school.

Myth 3: When an ELL is identified as having a disability, instruction should be only in English, so as not to confuse the student.

Response: Children with speech, language, or learning impairment can become fully bilingual (Genesee, Paradis, & Crago, 2004; Perozzi, 1985; Perozzi & Sanchez, 1992). There is even emerging evidence that children with Down syndrome can be successfully bilingual and that bilingualism does not disadvantage their language development (Kay-Raining Bird, Cleave, Trudeau, et al., submitted). The majority of people in the world are bilingual, and some of them have disabilities. Disabilities certainly do not arise from being bilingual. They manifest in all or most contexts. The decision to shift to instruction in English exclusively is usually based on lack of knowledge of the research, ignorance of the students' native language, or convenience. Developing the native language can help students with SLI make better progress in the second language. In addition, for ELLs with severe disabilities, it is especially important to maintain the home language, since the students' main caregivers will be their parents well after they have left the school system and have entered adult life. It is important that parents and family be able to communicate with and have close ties to their children.

The Continuum of Services Framework

Because of the tremendous difficulties associated with identifying ELLs as having special education needs, an altogether different approach to the problem is needed. Two major changes must occur in the school culture for this new approach to be implemented. First, the urge to formally and quickly categorize a student into a special education placement must be repressed. Instead, information must be gathered as extensively as possible about the student and his or her surroundings. As more information is gathered, interventions that we believe to be most effective for specific difficulties are introduced into students' everyday routines (Sanchez-Lopez & Young, 2003). As an added advantage of this approach, these interventions may very well be helpful to other students in the classroom, not just the particular ELL in question. Second, the compulsion to provide only the interventions allowed by specific funding sources must be circumvented. Instead, interventions, both systemic and specific, must be introduced independently of the category or the specific funding program that the student is eventually placed in. In fact, we suggest that these interventions be introduced as soon as problematical behaviors are identified as being characteristic of a student.

As interventions are put into practice, an informal evaluation of their effectiveness will guide teachers as to which ones to maintain and which ones to change or omit altogether. Somewhere along this process, the team that is coordinating the interventions and information gathering may decide that a full-fledged referral is needed, and the results of that referral may place the student formally in a special education category. The interventions that are deemed effective will become part of the student's individualized education plan (IEP) and will continue to be used. It is only through such a framework that the needs of ELLs who are having significant academic difficulties can be met in a way that makes sense from the student's perspective.

This framework is supported by the current trend to use an RTI approach in assessing the need for and in providing special needs support to students who are having significant academic difficulties. In this model, specific interventions are made and the student's response to those interventions is used as a base. There are several advantages to an RTI approach with ELLs. First, it encourages a proactive process that does not wait for ELLs to fail but instead provides enhanced instruction in a timely manner across grade levels. It emphasizes high-quality, consistent, and effective instruction, linked to authentic assessment, for ELLs throughout the day. It focuses on students in a very explicit way. Finally, it requires collaboration across disciplines and creates new roles for problem-solving team members.

A Collaborative Model

The continuum of services framework and the process entailed cannot be implemented without a strong collaborative setup within the school. That is the topic of the second chapter of this handbook. It can be subdivided into several parts.

First, the information gathering that is part of the framework requires the participation of everyone who comes in contact with the student in question. Everyone who knows ELLs is a valuable source of information. It is not unusual for different staff members to have quite different perceptions of the same student. The ESL teacher may find a student gregarious and an active participant in classroom work, whereas the physical education teachers may think that the same student is shy and reserved. Yet another teacher may perceive the same student as a troublemaker, and parents may see the student completely differently. It is important for all those individuals to contribute their perceptions and assessment of the student.

Second, since a large body of information is to be gathered from a number of people, there needs to be a team of four or five individuals to process and interpret the information. In many schools, these teams are called Teacher Assistance Teams (TAT). In this handbook, we refer to these teams as Ensuring a Continuum of Services (ECOS) teams. The ECOS team also manages the delivery of interventions and provides support to the teachers, administrators, and parents in making the changes necessary in the student's daily school life. In that capacity, the team suggests interventions and helps the staff and the parents provide the support that the team has determined to be most effective for the student. The team serves as a sounding board for the teachers as they try the instructional strategies suggested. It undertakes the same role with respect to the parents. The team supports administrators in their effort to make the more general systemic changes in the program or at the district level. The team also helps teachers and administrators monitor progress and evaluate the effectiveness of the interventions. Without this collaborative structure, the continuum of services framework will surely fail.

Chapter 2 discusses the makeup of such teams and the roles that various members play. We point to the importance of sharing expertise and building knowledge, and we describe how professional bridges can be built to form a system that serves students better (Sanchez-Lopez & Young, 2003). To establish a smooth collaboration, it is important to pay heed to team dynamics and establish clear interpersonal communication pathways. Ongoing professional development is also a key to the smooth functioning of this team approach. Chapter 2 ends with a discussion of the appropriation and use of resources, materials and support.

Information Gathering

The continuum of services framework is characterized by the constant gathering of information. Rather than attempting to determine immediately whether the academic difficulties of an ELL are due specifically to a long-term disability (that is, something that would lead to a special education designation) or are a normal part of the second language learning process, educators must first acquire extensive information about the student. The questions that need to be asked first are "What specifically is the student having difficulty with?" and "What do we know about this student?" rather than "Why is the student behaving this way?" Answering these two questions entails gathering information about what the student is doing at school, as well as the characteristics that define that student.

The information regarding the difficulties that the student is encountering must be as specific as possible—for example, inability to commit multiplication facts to memory, or difficulty in following directions. It is important to focus observations as much as possible and to try to identify specific academic behaviors or aspects of learning that the student is having difficulty with rather than to claim a more ambiguous "learning problem," as is often the case.

As soon as specific problematical behaviors are identified for a student or a group of students, the ECOS team, which includes experts in both ESL and special education, reflects on possible reasons for that behavior. The ECOS team then pinpoints possible second language development reasons and possible disability reasons for each behavior that has been observed in the student. As soon as that is done, the ESL and special education specialists identify the specific instructional interventions they believe will best benefit that student for that particular behavior. Thus, some of these interventions come from the field of ESL and serve the purpose of strengthening the student's second language proficiency. Others come from the field of special education and serve the purpose of helping the student with processing strategies and retention.

At the same time, more general information is gathered about seven integral factors in the student's home and school life. These integral factors cover both the environment that the student is in as well as the student's characteristics. The seven integral factors are the following:

1. the learning environment created for the student,
2. personal and family factors,
3. physical and psychological factors,
4. previous schooling,
5. proficiency in oral language and literacy in both first (L1) and second language (L2),
6. academic achievement in both L1, if available, and L2, and
7. cross-cultural factors.

This information serves two purposes. It will serve as an important context within which instruction, in general, and interventions, specifically, are given. Having a better understanding of ELLs gives teachers some sense of how these integral factors influence learning and achievement in general, and therefore the information would be valuable for any teacher who came into contact with ELLs. This information may also lead to more general systemic interventions that could be introduced at home or at school. It may not always be possible to change these factors in a student's life. However, if we understand what these factors are and how they influence learning, the information may inform data collection and evaluation. It may suggest ways to modify the learning environment for the student and may suggest ways to help the teacher, the family, and the student surmount hurdles created by these factors. By gathering information about these integral factors and changing the extrinsic environment, schools can anticipate and prevent a great many difficulties that ELLs encounter. In this way, schools can be proactive about ELL issues. For example, if school administrators know the schools is about to receive a group of refugee students, it would help if they researched the refugee experience and prepared their social workers and other school staff to anticipate difficulties that these students are likely to experience.

These seven integral factors are extrinsic in the student's life. It makes sense to concentrate on these extrinsic factors because a vast majority of second language learners experience difficulties in school when they receive instruction through a language in which they are not fully proficient. On the other hand, only a small proportion (in the United States, around 10%) of students have a long-term disability or disorder that could be diagnosed as a learning disability. Since bilingualism, or the development of proficiency in two or more languages, does not itself lead to the creation of a disability, it is much more likely that any difficulties encountered by second language learners can be remedied by changing what can be changed in these extrinsic factors. Thus, we need to eliminate the likelihood of extrinsic factors causing the student's difficulty before we conclude that the student may have an intrinsic disability.

Describing before Diagnosing

In Chapter 3, we describe the first step to be taken once a teacher or another staff member has expressed concern about a student or a group of students: identifying specific difficulties that ELLs may encounter. Specific areas of classroom behavior, performance, or tasks that the student has difficulty with or is likely to have difficulty with must be listed. The chapter provides a limited list of possible difficulties commonly encountered by students with special needs. We show that each of these behaviors can be attributed to either a normal second language learning process or a disability. Thus, it is essential to describe in as much detail as possible what it is that the student is having difficulty with before diagnosing. We also point out in Chapter 3 the importance of addressing extrinsic environmental reasons for ELLs' difficulties first, before intrinsic reasons are considered.

This information about specific difficulties needs to be gathered by all who come into contact with the student, and it must be gathered through a variety of formal and informal means. It is only through a collaborative approach that school staff can come close to having enough of the right kind of information to make an informed decision about the kinds of interventions that may help a student become a better learner in school.

Providing Support: A Continuum of Services

Once the specific behaviors that an ELL has been having difficulty with have been identified, the team discusses possible reasons for those behaviors. They come up with possible second language learning reasons and possible special education reasons. Then the team begins to identify interventions for each behavior based on the team's attribution of that difficulty to normal second language learning challenge or to a long-term disability (Sanchez-Lopez & Young, 2003). These are the strategies that teachers believe would be most effective to cope with and remediate those difficulties. These instructional interventions are introduced as soon as they are identified for a student. We refer to these as specific interventions.

As information continues to be gathered, both about the specific behaviors exhibited by an ELL at school and about the integral factors defining that ELL, the interventions that would be most appropriate to remedy any of the more general integral factors are also determined by the team. We refer to these as systemic interventions. As we begin to learn more about the student and his or her past, home life, and language and academic development, we can begin to introduce specific and systemic interventions that should help the student overcome the difficulties engendered by these factors. For example, if we discover that the parents of a Spanish-speaking ELL do not have reading materials in Spanish at home, we would want to ensure that the school library has a collection of high-quality books in Spanish (systemic intervention), and begin to send home books in Spanish for parents to read with their children (specific intervention). It is not always possible to remediate some factors. For example, some ELLs in the fourth and fifth grades have had a total of one year of formal schooling because of war conditions in their home country, and that fact cannot be changed. What can be changed, however, is the learning environment for students with limited formal schooling (a systemic intervention). As soon as they enter school, these students could participate in an intensive program in which they would learn about school in the United States and would acquire some of the foundation they missed by not attending school the expected number of years. The interventions, both systemic and specific, that seem to be most effective can become part of the student's daily routine.

As the factors in the student's life become clearer to teachers and specialists, the specific instructional interventions can begin to take into account the possible conditions that may be leading to the specific behaviors exhibited by the student. For example, if a student has been observed to consistently forget words that have been taught from one day to the next, and, from the extensive information gathering that is taking place, the teacher realizes that she has been using visual materials that may not be familiar to the student, a possible instructional intervention might be to give explanations in the student's first language. Such explanations could be provided by peers, the parents, or the teacher herself, if she is bilingual. On the other hand, if the parent liaison in the school discovers from talking to the parents that the child often shows memory problems at home and has difficulty recalling words in the native language, the teacher might begin to train the student to use strategies to cue herself by giving the student the first sound, number of syllables, descriptions of the word, or other strategies. This intervention could be provided under the guidance of a speech pathologist, who would consult the teacher as to the best way to use these strategies.

The more general systemic interventions would be introduced as soon as information emerged about an integral factor in the student's life. That same information may also lead to refining the instructional intervention in such a way that it begins to makes more sense within the larger context of that student's surroundings. Thus, the two sets of interventions, one set based on specific observations of the student's behavior in the classroom and the other on information gathered about the seven integral factors, would occur simultaneously and quickly.

The key to providing this support is to begin it immediately, as soon as observable difficulties are identified. There is no need to delay the instructional interventions until extensive information has been gathered about the student's home and school life. In this way the services provided to these students would flow smoothly and continuously.

In Chapter 4, we describe this solution-seeking approach to provide a continuum of services in a timely manner. But this approach is not without its challenges, so we suggest ways to create a structure within the school that would allow teachers to consult one another and to provide the support as needed. To show how this process can be implemented in a real-life setting, we offer a case study of a school we have worked with. We present a step-by-step description of how this process was started and how it was developed.

The Seven Integral Factors

The greater part of the handbook is concerned with the seven integral factors that must be considered in determining how best to meet the needs of students experiencing difficulty. Each chapter begins with a discussion of one particular factor and why it is important, then offers suggestions for assessing the factor and perhaps modifying it. The goal is to help the student learn better. Each chapter ends with suggestions for intervention that would make the factor more effective in helping the student overcome academic hurdles. Resources to implement these interventions are also provided.

Chapter 5 takes up the first factor, the learning environment created for students, particularly the program designed for ELLs. In general, an effective learning environment for ELLs should have an enriching rather than a compensatory or remedial approach. The critical issues to consider here are teachers, resources available, the type of program implemented, and the range of services offered in the school, with special attention paid to the role that the student's native language and culture play in the learning environment. In addition, characteristics of instruction and assessment need to be considered, especially with regard to the use of the student's native language and culture. In the discussion of the adequacy of the learning environment, we provide a rating scale to help determine areas of weakness that need improvement. We also suggest some systemic and specific interventions that could be used, such as changing the program design for ELLs, changing the instructional approaches, and expanding existing programs within the school to better meet the needs of ELLs.

Chapter 6 focuses on personal and family factors. The critical issues to consider here include socioeconomic status, family dynamics and mobility, expectations, the student's interests, and the student's experiential background. We also discuss what parental involvement means and how to foster it. We suggest ways to gather information about an ELL's personal and family background, and we discuss the interpretation of gathered data in the appropriate cultural context. We end the chapter with suggestions for systemic and specific interventions to address potential hurdles in a student's personal and family background.

Chapter 7 focuses on physical and psychological factors. These include posttraumatic stress, impaired vision and hearing, chronic pain, malnutrition, developmental milestones, and special family situations. We suggest ways to gather information in this area and pay special attention to ethical considerations and to ways of interpreting the information that is gathered in a way that makes sense within the cultural context of the students and their families. We then discuss interventions for helping students overcome physical or psychological hurdles in culturally responsive ways.

In Chapter 8, we discuss previous schooling, including the quantity and quality of formal schooling that ELLs received before entering the school they currently attend. We also suggest that the informal education that some ELLs have received be taken into account. We suggest ways of collecting information about ELLs' past educational experiences and of meeting the needs that arise out of insufficient or very different schooling. We pay special attention to strategies that may be helpful to students with limited formal schooling.

Chapter 9 deals with the critical issue of oral language and literacy development, a factor that is central to academic performance. We suggest that information be gathered about oral language and literacy development in both the student's native language and in English, and we emphasize the need to be aware of the complex nature of language proficiency. Here, both social and academic language are important. We also discuss the importance of understanding the relationship between a student's first and second language and of determining language use patterns outside the school The assessment of this critical factor must be as extensive as possible and should include both standardized, quantitative and authentic, qualitative measures. Information about an ELL's oral language and literacy must come from varied contexts and sources. Suggestions are given to ensure extensive, reliable, and valid assessments of this critical factor. Interventions to help support the development of oral language proficiency and literacy are integrated throughout Chapter 9. These interventions address both first and second language development, because one of the basic premises for intervention is that the continuing development of both languages is better for the learner than the loss of the native language.

In Chapter 10 another critical factor, academic achievement, is discussed. We point to the need to take into account all the content areas that students are exposed to in school, and pay special attention to the distinction between social language and academic language. The significant issue in gathering data about academic achievement is that more than standardized tests must yield information about what ELLs can do in different content areas. It is also crucial to keep in mind the fact that it is extremely difficult to separate knowledge of concepts from the language that is used to talk about that concept. We give suggestions for gathering information in both English and the native language, if appropriate. The chapter ends with general strategies to support the academic achievement of ELLs.

Chapter 11 presents the last of the seven integral factors, issues stemming from differences in the cultural norms and values that ELLs bring with them and those that govern the school and mainstream society. Discussions of cultural differences and how they affect learning must be focused on the individual rather than the group. This avoids making overgeneralizations and stereotyping individuals based on notions we have about groups of people. We describe culture as a complex set of norms and values that govern our lives, determine how we approach learning, and determine how we interact with our environment. We discuss the way these norms and values shape learning and play a role in assessment. We also discuss the role of identity as it affects students' potential for learning. ELLs with confused identities cannot learn effectively (Cummins, 1996). We provide suggestions for assessing the student's capacity to function in the school culture and discuss the importance of identifying the student's culture accurately. We suggest ways of using cultural informants and strategies for creating the cultural environment that is most supportive of ELLs.

The continuum of services framework creates an enriched environment for ELLs and, more broadly, is of benefit to all learners. However, it entails a major change in the way we have approached special education in the schools. Advocating change in the system so that it helps all students become more successful in school is a responsibility for all of us. We hope that this handbook helps you attain that goal.

2

A Collaborative Model of Information Gathering and Service Provision

KEY CONCEPTS

To provide a continuum of services, a team consisting of staff with expertise in different areas must collaborate to gather information about the difficulties that the student is encountering, as well as characteristics of the student's home and school life. The team then suggests interventions and monitors the student's progress.

The process of developing a continuum of services to meet student needs relies on problem-solving teams sharing expertise and working within a strong collaborative structure in the school. In both special education and diversity settings, when these structures have been employed, the results have suggested positive and effective innovations (e.g., Bartolo, Dockrell, & Lunt, 2001; Damico & Nye, 1990; Giangreco, 2000; Miramontes, Nadeau, & Commins, 1997; Orelove & Sobsey, 1996). The primary responsibility of the team is to coordinate the gathering of information and the implementation of interventions. The team is ultimately responsible for ensuring that a continuum of services is provided to individual students and to similar groups of students within a school.

In our version of the team approach, we call these collaborative groups ECOS (Ensuring a Continuum of Services) teams. Although the team structure may exist in a school under different names, such as Teacher Assistance Team or Student Services Team, the team may have a different setup and a different set of objectives. Traditional Teacher Assistance Teams, for example, are often designed to create a general educational initiative for teachers who must deal with learning problems in their classrooms or a preventive model of service delivery before referrals to special education (e.g., Chalfant & Pysh, 1989; Kock, 1997; Wiener & Davidson, 1990). When addressing the continuum of services for English language learners (ELLs), a new team may be formed, or an existing team may be modified to fit the parameters of the continuum of services framework presented in this handbook.

Theresa Young, Toronto District School Board, Toronto, Onario, Canada, was a major contributor to this chapter and helped to write it.

Responsibilities of ECOS Teams

To effectively meet the needs of each individual ELL, the ECOS team must obtain sufficient information to determine the needs of the student, the impact of the various contexts on the student's performance, and the strengths and weaknesses exhibited by the student. To accomplish these objectives, the ECOS teams have four major responsibilities: coordinating information gathering, interpreting information, suggesting interventions, and monitoring progress.

Information Gathering

The ECOS team ensures that all the information already available in the school is identified and available to all those who can make use of it. The team then begins coordinating the information-gathering process, once gaps in the data have been identified. Table 2.1 lists some of the data that should be available for making initial decisions regarding ELLs. These data are considered the starting point from which the more elaborate and important data on the seven integral factors will be developed.

ECOS team members do not actually gather all the data themselves. Rather, they contact individuals who have access to the necessary information and ensure that the information is added to the depository. Information

Table 2.1   Checklist for Determining if Sufficient Initial Data Are Available

Have the following data been collected, and are these data available for review by the ECOS team?	Yes	No
1. Has the student's school record been checked?		
2. Have the student's medical records been obtained?		
3. Have any prior assessment findings been obtained?		
4. Are there samples of the behaviors targeted as problems?		
5. Have consultations been held with the teacher about the management of the student in the classroom?		
6. Is someone at the school familiar with the cultural background of the student and the family?		
7. Is there information about the student's country of origin?		
8. Is there information about the student's religious background?		
9. Is a cultural/linguistic informant available if needed?		
10. Is there information about the student's cultural background?		
11. Has the degree of language dominance been appropriately determined?		
12. Has placement in bilingual education or ESL been considered or tried?		
13. Have other remedial instruction measures been tried?		

needs to be gathered about the specific difficulties that ELLs are having in school as well as about the seven integral factors that are described in Chapters 5 to 11. These seven integral factors are (1) the learning environment created for the student, (2) personal and family factors, such as literacy habits at home, (3) physical and psychological factors, (4) previous schooling performance, (5) proficiency in oral language and literacy in both first (L1) and second language (L2), (6) academic achievement in both L1, if available, and L2, and (7) cross-cultural factors.

Interpreting Information

While the information about a particular student or group of students is being gathered, the ECOS team members collaborate with one another to make sense out of the student's difficulties. The difficulties may stem from a host of factors, including experiential differences, instructional practices, materials, second language learning processes, or disabilities. The team starts putting the puzzle together as more information about the student or the group of students comes in.

Suggesting Interventions

As information is collected and as the student's behavior and difficulties are being interpreted, the team begins to identify interventions for each difficulty. Some of these interventions will be based on the interpretation of the reasons for the observed difficulties. For example, some difficulties may reflect a normal second language learning challenge and some may be attributable to an intrinsic disability. Pooling members' expertise, the team suggests interventions to the teachers who work with the student. The ECOS team also recommends ways that teachers can implement the interventions, and if possible, they support the teachers in making these interventions part of the everyday classroom activities. In the case of systemic interventions, the team supports administrators in bringing about a change at the programmatic level (e.g., Hamayan & Freeman, 2006; Miramontes, Nadeau, & Commins, 1997; Winter, 2001).

Monitoring Progress

The fourth responsibility of ECOS teams is to monitor the effectiveness of the interventions and programming they suggest. It is not enough to make suggestions. As advocates for ELLs, and to ensure a kind of intervention fidelity, it is important to determine (1) whether the teachers need training or assistance with the suggested interventions or programming, (2) whether the teachers are able to effectively implement these suggestions in the classroom, and (3) the impact of these suggestions on the ELL's progress behaviorally (e.g., Chalfant & Pysh, 1987; Damico, 1987; Marvin, 1990; Reid, Secord, & Damico, 1993; Thomas, Correa, & Morsink, 1995).

Throughout this handbook, we offer a variety of suggestions for accomplishing each of these responsibilities. The key to success on all four tasks—gathering data, interpreting information, suggesting interventions, and monitoring progress—is to keep the tasks manageable. For example, the methods chosen to monitor progress should not be so cumbersome that no one can implement them. In addition, methods used for assessing the effectiveness of an intervention should not interrupt instruction. Rather, the assessment practices should be embedded in best practices schoolwide and should enhance and enrich rather than constrict what happens in schools. All these tasks should be done collaboratively. The cycle of brainstorming, implementing, assessing, and reflecting will be disrupted if any part of the process is repeatedly delegated to the same person. If ECOS teams suggest interventions, they must support the implementation of those interventions. When a method for monitoring progress is suggested, a plan must be in place for those who will assess to know how often assessment will take place, under what conditions, and how the qualitative and quantitative assessment results will be reported to the ECOS team.

Makeup of ECOS Teams

An important characteristic of these school-based ECOS teams is that they include a diversity of professions. It is important to include professionals who bring multiple perspectives to the task of interpreting information that is gathered about any student, as well as creating and implementing interventions for all students who are experiencing difficulties in school, regardless of their language background (Bunce, 2003; Knoff, 1983; Lacey & Lomas, 1993). However, it is especially important for these teams to come with diverse perspectives when dealing with ELLs who are experiencing academic difficulties (Damico, 1993; Damico & Damico, 1993a; Fradd, 1993; Sanchez-Lopez, 2006; Young & Westernoff, 1999). Bringing diverse perspectives to bear is important because functioning bilingually is a complex process, especially when abstract academic concepts are to be learned (Cloud, 2006; Cummins, 2006).

ELLs are a varied group of students. They enter U.S. schools from countries all over the world and from many regions within those countries. They come from every socioeconomic category, from hundreds of language backgrounds, and with a variety of life and educational experiences. The more professionally and personally diverse the ECOS team, the more likely it is that the team will be able to generate a variety of interventions and creative solutions for implementation. If a more homogeneous team makeup is maintained, with individuals of similar backgrounds, then it is less likely that the team will be able to generate the appropriate interventions needed by the individual student or group of students. A homogeneous team is also less likely to expand team members' knowledge and perspectives, thus making the team less able to keep up with the needs of increasingly diverse student populations. At a minimum, the ECOS team should include ESL/bilingual educators and special educators.

When a team is trying to determine whether the academic difficulties that ELLs are experiencing are due to intrinsic problems, and trying to create the most effective interventions for those students, it is essential to have both the ESL/bilingual perspective and the special education perspective to sort through possible explanations of the difficulties and begin to craft interventions. As discussed in Chapter 1, the process for determining eligibility for special education services for ELLs is fraught with difficulties. No one perspective or piece of information can determine if a student's difficulties are due to English language learning difficulties or to a learning disability or specific language impairment. Only by sharing our professional knowledge and experience with one another can we develop a deeper and broader understanding of possible causes of students' difficulties (Damico & Hamayan, 1991; Damico, Smith, & Augustine, 1996; Friend & Cook, 1992; Giangreco, 1994; Prelock, 2000). Only then can we develop specific interventions and programming options that would be effective for ELLs experiencing academic difficulties. Both ESL/bilingual specialists and special educators bring unique strengths to the problem-solving process.

ESL/Bilingual Specialists

ESL/bilingual specialists bring extensive experience with a range of ELLs from a variety of linguistic and cultural backgrounds. Although there is no normative database with which to construct a profile of the "typical" ELL

(Bialystock, 2001), most ESL/bilingual specialists understand the second language acquisition process. This knowledge may be partially based on teachers' familiarity with research and theories of learning that come from fields as diverse as applied linguistics, teaching English as a second language, social anthropology, educational psychology, and psycholinguistics. These specialists' understanding of ELLs also comes from their observations of second language learners as the students develop proficiency in two languages. Bilingual teachers and some ESL teachers can also draw on their own experiences in becoming proficient in a second language.

The knowledge that may be specific to the ESL/bilingual specialist includes information about characteristic stages of learning a second language. It also includes information about common patterns of errors and typical difficulties that ELLs encounter on their way to becoming proficient in the second language. This knowledge also includes information about the acculturation process and how to use the students' native language and culture in instruction.

Based on their experience teaching a variety of ELLs at different stages, ESL/bilingual specialists also bring a sense of what is typical for ELLs. They have seen a multitude of ELL writing samples, engaged in conversations with students from all over the globe, witnessed how affective issues influence ELLs' performance, implemented and adapted instructional strategies at various levels of language proficiency across content areas, and developed cultural insights from interactions with ELLs and their families. This can enable astute ESL/bilingual specialists to more readily perceive unusual aspects of learning that warrant attention, especially when they instruct the same students over a period of time.

Special Education Specialists

Special education specialists—resource room teachers, learning disability specialists, psychologists, speech-language pathologists and specifically trained social workers—bring knowledge and experience unique to their professions to the problem-solving process. Some of the knowledge available to these professionals may be different from that of the ESL/bilingual specialist. For example, many special education specialists have knowledge about different types of learning disabilities, the range of severity within those disabilities, and how they manifest in both instructional and social interactions. Special education specialists typically know the meaning-making principles and instructional methods that are most likely to help children compensate for a disability. They are also familiar with the written and spoken language of students at different points in their academic development and can recognize the various compensatory adaptations that exceptional learners employ in their attempts to overcome their difficulties (Damico & Nelson, 2005; Perkins, 2005). The range of professionals who come together to serve students with special needs further diversifies the team by virtue of their professional training, unique experiences, and professional perspectives. Thus, collectively, special education personnel can offer a broad repertoire of strategies to use with a range of learners.

These specialists typically have some academic background in neuro-anatomy and physiological psychology, and they are familiar with various working models to aid hypothesis making in the diagnostic problem-solving process (Bartolo, Dockrell, & Lunt, 2001; Benton, 1994). Psychologists bring information from fields such as neurology, neurophysiology, behavioral psychology, and brain research. Speech-language pathologists offer a deep understanding of expressive and receptive first language development in oral and written modes. For example, they can offer insights into a student's oral academic language and how it can be enhanced to support literacy. Special educators bring experience, strategies, and perspectives to the ECOS team as advocates, in that the very nature of their work is to give a voice to students with unique learning needs.

Other Professionals

ECOS teams need, at a minimum, ESL/bilingual specialists and special educators, but even further, teams need to enlist all other professional resources at their schools. These include school administrators, general education teachers, literacy specialists, guidance personnel, and possibly parent liaisons and occupational therapists. Any and all of these professionals can form part of the ECOS teams. In the end, it is to the students' benefit for staff to take the time to build multiperspective teams, which transcend the otherwise compartmentalized nature of schools.

We can no longer afford to imagine we teach in isolation or to think of some students as "mine" and others as "yours." To address the range of learning needs presented by students, we must work across disciplines and across classrooms. By looking at the school community as a whole and pooling our professional and experiential resources, we can address the needs of more students, develop a variety of creative learning environments, and share the responsibility of teaching the diverse range of learners in our schools. All of these outcomes will ultimately serve to prevent difficulties in the long term.

Building Professional Bridges across Specializations

Most teachers can probably remember occasions when they informally consulted a colleague on a particular topic, teaching strategy, or concern. The professional discussions that result from such consultations enrich teaching and significantly expand teachers' ability to help students (Miramontes, Nadeau, & Commins, 1997; Thomas, Correa, & Morsink, 1995). Most teachers probably also remember other occasions in their teaching experience when they wished they could have consulted a colleague, but there was no structured time built into the day for these discussions to occur. Some teachers work in schools where they are not allowed to talk to a particular professional without submitting a written request or getting official permission. Many schools do not have an environment that encourages teachers to talk to one another professionally during the school day.

ECOS team meetings can become a forum for sharing expertise and experiences, asking questions, querying new developments, and clarifying problematic ideas that individual teachers may have. Time spent with the ECOS team is an opportunity to do creative problem solving, develop cross-professional programming, craft short- and long-term interventions, and design creative ways of implementing and documenting the success of these interventions. The potential outcome of effective teamwork is that more students can benefit from appropriate support in a timely manner rather than having to wait until they fail before they receive attention and support. The potential of these teams will be lost if professionals fall back on the familiar model characterized by gatekeeping, lengthy waiting times, and compartmentalized service delivery (Chalfant & Pysh, 1989; Fradd, 1993; Friend & Cook, 1992; Kock, 1997; Wiener & Davidson, 1990).

Characteristics of an Effective ECOS Team

When a group of professionals with different specializations talk to one another, productive interdisciplinary discussions can occur that in turn broaden knowledge and extend collaborative practices. But in order for this to occur, professional bridges must be built across areas of specialization. Building bridges requires the team to have clear and congruent principles, a shared lan-

Table 2.2 Critical Principles That Must Be Shared by ECOS Team Members

- Our policies, programs, practices, and assessments for ELLs have a clear enrichment orientation that sees linguistics and cultural diversity as a resource to develop, not as a problem to overcome.
- Because a strong first language (including first language literacy) provides a solid foundation for cognitive development, academic achievement, and language and literacy development in English, we draw on and support an ELL's first language skills to the greatest degree possible at our school.
- All our staff members share responsibility for the education of ELLs.
- We make sure that parents of ELLs know and understand the school district's or school's policies, programs, and practices regarding their children.

Source: Hamayan and Freeman, 2006.

guage, respect for each other, the ability to pose questions to others, and effective interpersonal and communication skills (Chalfant & Pysh, 1989, Kock, 1997; Marvin, 1990). These characteristics combine to create positive team dynamics.

Clear and Congruent Principles

For an ECOS team to function well, members must share some basic principles and values. These principles, regardless of whether they are verbalized or remain unspoken, form the foundation for interdisciplinary discussions. If there is a serious mismatch among the principles that different members of the ECOS team believe in, conflict and misunderstanding are likely to occur. From our work as members of interdisciplinary teams and from our experience developing a continuum of services framework at various schools, we have found that it is best to talk about the principles that team members adhere to openly and explicitly. We have also found that it is best to have this discussion about principles before a conflict arises. That way, team members can have the discussion with minimal emotional burden.

The principles that are essential for an ECOS team to function within the framework that we are suggesting are listed in Table 2.2 (a more extensive list of principles regarding ELL education in general can be found in Hamayan and Freeman, 2006).

A Shared Language

Conversations have a way of turning into monologues when two professionals use the same term to mean different things (Kock, 1997; Prelock, 2000). For that reason, it is essential that ECOS teams clarify the terminology that is used repeatedly in their discussions to make sure all members have the

ECOS TEAM ACTIVITY

Use the list of four principles in Table 2.2 to generate a discussion by dividing the team into two groups. Assign one group to agree with the principles and one group to disagree with them. Have the groups think of arguments to defend their positions before they begin to discuss the principles. Follow up by having each member reflect privately on his or her own position regarding these principles. End the activity by affirming the importance of adhering to these principles, and invite individuals who are doubtful about their beliefs and the extent to which they are congruent with the rest of the group's beliefs to share their feelings (either privately or, if the person feels comfortable sharing in public, with the rest of the group).

ECOS TEAM ACTIVITY

Have each person on the team bring a list of three or four terms, with definitions, that they think are essential for the team's discussions. Discuss the meanings and possible interpretations of those terms.

same understanding of those terms. For example, a discussion can spiral into chaotic miscommunication when the ESL teacher uses the term *bilingual* to mean any student who has proficiency in two languages but the general education classroom teacher understands the term to mean only those students who are in the bilingual program and who still lack proficiency in English. The ESL teacher will likely refer to the bilingual student as being able to function well in both languages, while the general education teacher will protest that in her class, the bilingual student is not able to do the work in English at all. In turn, the ESL teacher may interpret that remark as prejudicial to all students who come from a language background other than English, and before long the discussion has disintegrated into a heated emotional argument.

This problem is exacerbated by the fact that each area of specialization in the field of education that is likely to be represented on an ECOS team has its own professional vocabulary that nonmembers may misunderstand. Thus, it is essential that a common vocabulary be established among team members.

Breaking Down Disciplinary Boundaries

The disciplinary boundaries delimiting the professions must be breached if effective interaction is to occur. Aspel, Willis, and Faust (1998) and others (e.g., Chalfant & Pysh, 1989; Elias & Dilworth, 2003; Gutkin & Nemeth, 1997; Knoff, 1983; Kock, 1997; Winter, 1999) have demonstrated how the subjective biases, professional orientations, and discipline-specific practices of the members of school-based teams often result in a lack of perspective taking and a breakdown in communication, often to the detriment of the students being considered during the teaming process. Consequently, ECOS teams should attempt to reduce the boundaries that exist between the disciplines.

Perhaps the most frequent practice upholding disciplinary boundaries is the use of norm-referenced and standardized tests (Chandler, Dunaway, Levine, et al., 2005). Each of the various disciplines has typically been trained in the administration and interpretation of skill- or trait-specific tools, and whether it is the speech-language pathologist holding on to a test of language ability, or a resource room teacher guarding his or her *Woodcock-Johnson*, or a psychologist insisting on a concentration on cognitive or processing abilities, each tends to focus on professional turf with respect to assessment practices, interpretation, and recommendations (e.g., Gunderson & Siegel, 2001; Gutkin & Nemeth, 1997; Taylor, 1991). To reduce these boundaries, the team should embrace a more descriptive assessment that focuses on the actual needs of ELLs in their learning contexts. In this way, each of the professionals can collect data on what the student actually does when attempting to learn, and the discussion can focus on authentic evaluations and contextualized behaviors rather than on discipline-specific test scores. In this way the team shifts from defense of professional territory toward aiding the individual student (Anastasi & Urbiba, 1997; Chandler, Dunaway, Levine, et al., 2005).

Respectful Questioning

When building professional bridges and reducing disciplinary boundaries, team members need to feel comfortable to explore other people's perspectives. They need to be able to ask questions freely about what they do not know. This can be a very vulnerable position to take as a professional. However, for productive interdisciplinary interactions to occur—and they are at the heart of the model we propose—it is vital to ask questions (Kock, 1997; Marvin, 1990). Team members should begin with the understanding that no individual has *the* answer as to the best placement choice or type of intervention for any particular student or group of students. Team members should acknowledge that the services that students need may not yet exist in the school system. Then the team can begin to develop creative solutions by blending the individual team members' expertise, knowledge, experience, and resources.

Recognizing that each team member has spent a large portion of his or her adult life studying and practicing in a professional field engenders a respectful approach to others' contributions. However, each team member must understand that he or she comes from a specific framework and has to rely on colleagues for perspectives from other fields of expertise. This requires each professional to use collaborative skills to learn more about their colleagues' contributions and to be open to fitting that knowledge into their existing professional schema. These sorts of exchanges are more likely to take place in an environment in which the primary disciplinary boundaries have been relaxed, where there is a focus on the student, not on discipline-specific practices and biases, where all participants listen to each member's point of view, and where team members feel comfortable seeking clarification on any given point without being viewed negatively (Joyce & Showers, 2002; Prelock, 2000). This allows members of the team to better understand the different needs of the students they serve and to consider different explanations for student difficulties in light of the new information they receive.

Effective Interpersonal and Communication Skills

For respectful questioning to occur, team members need to use interpersonal skills and communication strategies that lead to smooth dialogues. These skills include active listening, clarifying, refining, and summarizing information to understand other viewpoints (Ontario Association of Speech-Language Pathologists and Audiologists [OSLA], 2005). The ability to depersonalize difficult ex-

CHRONICLE 2.1

An Open Conversation Turns Sour

By an administrator member of an ECOS team

I was sitting in on an ECOS Team meeting once and was quite impressed with how well team members were working together. The team had only started getting together a couple of weeks earlier, and it had not been a smooth start. The special education specialists had not been very open to considering the suggestions and ideas put forth by the ESL and bilingual teachers. But that day, the conversation was very balanced—until the ESL teacher started to try to convince everyone else that an ESL strategy she used frequently should be used by every single teacher of the student under discussion. The strategy is called the Total Physical Response, or TPR. Although it is limited in scope, TPR is quite useful for introducing new vocabulary.

The ESL teacher kept using the term TPR without explanation, until one of the special education teachers asked, "What's TPR?" The ESL teacher seemed surprised and said, "You don't know what TPR is?" As soon as the words were uttered, something changed in the group dynamics. The special education teacher, who had been leaning forward, moved back in her chair, crossed her arms, and said, "Obviously not." The conversation went downhill from then on.

It took a lot of mediating to get the group back to functioning smoothly, but I could see that we had to be very careful with how statements were made and how questions were asked.

Question for discussion:

- What assumptions were made by the members of the team in this episode?
- How would one go about "mediating to get the group back to functioning smoothly?"
- What type of activity would be good as a follow-up to this event?

changes that arise by acknowledging emotional comments as a by-product of sharing new and different perspectives is also an important characteristic of effective collaborative exchanges (Chronicle 2.1 provides an example). Efforts to repair communication breakdowns and adapt to others' communication styles and a willingness to modify one's position contribute to positive team dynamics.

To ensure that a newly formed team is off to a good start or to assess how well an established team displays the characteristics discussed above, the checklist in Table 2.3 may be useful.

How to Form Effective ECOS Teams

In many schools, a team already exists that is responsible for special education issues. The existing team can be transformed to work as an ECOS team within the framework suggested in this handbook. Alternatively, the school staff may decide to begin at the beginning and form a new team. In that case, the following steps are likely to happen:

1. The bilingual/ESL director and the special services (special education) director meet to develop a common vision. Administrative support and involvement are essential to tailor the format of the team to meet existing needs and to function well within existing structures.

Table 2.3 Checklist for Assessing the Effective Characteristics of an ECOS Team

Clear and Congruent Principles		
1. I have a clear understanding of the principles we espouse.	Yes	No
2. I agree with the principles we espouse.	Yes	No
A Shared Language		
1. There are very few terms that we use repeatedly that are not clear to me.	Yes	No
2. Whenever someone uses a vague or unknown word, I ask for clarification immediately.	Yes	No
3. If needed, we have a glossary of terms and acronyms that I can refer to for clarification.	Yes	No
Respectful Questioning		
1. I feel comfortable asking for clarification from any member of the team.	Yes	No
2. I feel respected by all members of the team.	Yes	No
3. I know whom to go to for questions about issues I am not an expert on.	Yes	No
4. I feel comfortable answering questions that others ask me.	Yes	No
Effective Interpersonal and Communication Skills		
1. I am able to communicate clearly even about topics that others on the team are not familiar with.	Yes	No
2. I rarely misunderstand something that someone else on the team has said.	Yes	No
3. If a communication breakdown occurs, we are generally able to repair it quickly.	Yes	No
4. When a miscommunication escalates into an emotional argument, we are generally able to step back and start over.	Yes	No

2. The idea of the ECOS team and the philosophy underlying the framework of a continuum of service are introduced to school staff.

3. Staff members begin to consider the following questions: Who will take the initiative to form (or modify existing) teams? Who will constitute the members of the team? What kind of support will the school provide?

4. Each school suggests that a representative group of professionals form the ECOS team. The following professionals must be members: the school psychologist, a speech-language pathologist, at least two bilingual/ESL educators, a social worker, a school administrator, and a special education teacher.

5. Other professionals are encouraged to attend meetings.

6. The ECOS team is introduced to the rest of the school.

7. The team decides on regular times to meet: before the school year begins, regularly at a convenient time while school is in session, and in the spring to attend articulation meetings to anticipate needs that might arise during the next school year.

8. ECOS team members determine their professional development needs in both professional content areas (such as second language learning and the impact of cultural diversity on learning) and procedural aspects (such as problem-solving procedures and interpersonal communication). They make a plan for professional development in those areas.

9. The team plans a schedule for meetings when there are no students to be brought up for discussion and when there is time to share expertise and to brainstorm possible explanations and interventions for typical difficulties that arise each year.

What ECOS Teams Can Accomplish

Several benefits arise from having ECOS teams established as part of the everyday working of the school. One of the most important benefits is the change that occurs in the general school ambiance. A school where ECOS teams meet regularly is likely to be a more collegial place where teachers support each other. It also is likely to be a place where there is an explicit focus on learning rather than on tactical and organizational challenges. Having ECOS teams as part of the everyday working of the school also has specific benefits, as described below.

Professional Reflection

A specific benefit of establishing ECOS teams within a school is that it leads to teachers reflecting on their work with individual students or groups of like students. Since one of the purposes of ECOS teams is to focus on the needs of students, teachers become accustomed to questioning the nature and origin of students' learning difficulties. Additionally, since ECOS team meetings attempt to provide support to teachers by suggesting instructional and programmatic strategies that might alleviate some of the difficulties that students are encountering, teachers are likely to develop the habit of asking why they teach the way they do, or why a program is set up the way it is. By asking these questions, teachers begin to reflect on their practice and on the theoretical bases that define that practice. Teacher reflection has been shown to enhance a teacher's performance and consequently student achievement (Du-Four & Baker, 1998; Freeman, 1998).

Capacity Building

Another specific benefit of having ECOS teams is that teachers learn from one another. By collaborating with one another within the comfortable context of ECOS team meetings, teachers with different specializations can learn each other's skills. This capacity building in both content knowledge and collaborative skills works to the benefit of the team and students. Thus, the ECOS team framework allows teachers to generate unique professional learning opportunities for themselves when they pair up with another teacher with a different area of specialization. For example, if a speech-language pathologist coteaches a unit with an ESL teacher in which graphic organizers are used in oral or written retelling, learning is likely to take place on multiple fronts. The speech-language pathologist may see the value of contextualizing interventions, and the ESL teacher may discover the importance of focusing on specific language aspects within that meaningful context.

A bilingual teacher might team with speech-language pathologists to implement a long-term intervention aimed explicitly at relating students' native language to particular language structures that students are having difficulty with. A middle school team might find it helpful to meet with the school psychologist and the bilingual parent liaison on a regular basis to determine how better to meet the behavioral and emotional needs of the adolescents they teach. After consulting grade-level teams, a school psychologist may see that teen depression is more prevalent among ELLs of a particular language background, and can then work with the team to implement a schoolwide program aimed at addressing this issue in a more systemic and culturally appropriate manner. The goals of this intervention might be to try to prevent difficulties in students who are at risk for depression, as well as to support those students who are currently experiencing significant emotional issues.

Redefining Roles

Cross-professional interactions among ECOS team members can lead to another significant benefit: a redefinition of traditional roles in implementing interventions. Members of ECOS teams may soon realize that their traditional roles—as general education classroom teachers, speech-language pathologists, or ESL teachers—will begin to change. They may see a need to change the way they practice their profession to better meet the needs of students. From this role change, new and innovative programming for students can emerge. For example, through discussions with teachers, the ECOS team may have found that many students were having difficulty keeping up with the literacy demands of their science, social studies, and mathematics classes in the intermediate and middle grades. A school literacy specialist and the ESL teacher may then decide to pool their professional resources and expertise and open a literacy enrichment center in their school. The literacy enrichment center might allow grade 3 through grade 8 students to receive additional literacy support to complement what they are doing in their subject area classes. Another component of this intervention might be that the literacy and ESL/bilingual specialists develop a series of workshops to teach classroom teachers literacy strategies that could be used across the curriculum. The same type of collaboration might take place between the math instructional specialist and a reading teacher to meet the needs of students at all grade levels who need math enrichment activities to strengthen their understanding of mathematical concepts as well as mathematical language.

The Big Picture

The more members of the ECOS team extend their knowledge base beyond their own area of expertise and the more teams collaborate, the more they are able to understand each other's perspective. The more teachers cross professional bridges and add new information and skills to their repertoires, the more likely they are to see how their specific area of specialization fits into the larger context of education and schooling. Thus, another benefit of ECOS teams is that teachers will better understand how their work fits in with everyone else's work. This is true of all the components of instruction that a student gets in one year, but it also applies to how students progress from one year to the next.

Catalysts for Change

One last important point to make about the ECOS teams is that they can become a catalyst for changing how we allocate and distribute human, physical, and fiscal resources. All the creative programming we design requires equally innovative methods of resource use. Proposed changes cannot be implemented if the budget cannot support them. An ECOS team can challenge this situation by suggesting that those with budgetary authority examine whether or not resources have been allocated equitably to the ELLs in the school and in the district. On close examination it is common to find that resources can be redistributed to implement the innovation on behalf of ELLs.

An Innovative Approach

This team approach to gathering information, developing intervention ideas, and implementing both systemic and specific interventions stands in contrast to the traditional gatekeeping model, which can pit one professional against another. In a traditional model, teachers and families may find themselves on the defensive, trying to prove that they have done everything humanly possible to help the students, and only after the situation has significantly deteriorated is the student referred to the team for help. On the other side of the coin, school teams may be under pressure to to discuss only the most severe cases to decide who qualifies for a full case study. In a more collaborative model, the goal is to help many more students in a timely manner.

Team members know that students' needs and abilities are not neatly organized in distinct categories. These teams recognize that there is a broad range of learner needs in our schools that call for an even broader range of interventions and ways of implementing these interventions. Through this collaborative problem-solving approach, where the goal is to prevent academic and linguistic difficulties, students ultimately benefit. Students no longer have to fail and be identified as qualified for special education services before receiving support. Teachers benefit from the collaborative teams because they need not wait for issues and concerns to become overwhelming in their classrooms before getting support for themselves and for their students.

Before these results can be realized, the ECOS team must start at the beginning, by collecting information about the specific difficulties that an ELL or a group of ELLs faces. That is the topic of the next chapter.

STEPS FOR ECOS TEAMS TO TAKE

1. The ECOS team is formed.

2. The team meets for team-building activities, to clarify roles and responsibilities, and to discuss principles.

3. The team is introduced to the rest of the school.

Describing before Diagnosing: Observation of Specific Difficulties That ELLs May Experience

KEY CONCEPTS

The first step in providing a continuum of services is to gather information about the difficulties that a student is experiencing by describing those difficulties as specifically as possible.

Before implementing changes, it is necessary to describe in detail the actual behaviors presented by the students who are experiencing sufficient difficulty to warrant our attention. That is, it is essential that we focus on behaviors that allow us to get to know the weaknesses of the students within the context of the classroom or other learning and social environments before we draw conclusions about the causes of these students' difficulties. The primary reason is that diagnosis, no matter how seemingly straightforward, is a complicated process, fraught with many potential missteps that may lead to inaccurate conclusions. These conclusions in turn may further aggravate the problems faced by the student and his or her teacher. Consequently, we offer a procedural solution that stresses obtaining a sufficient description of the student before assigning causes.

In this chapter, we lay out a process that focuses on difficulties faced by the student and a method by which possible explanations can be considered and accurately assigned for each of these difficulties. Such explanations form the basis for the interventions designed for a particular student or a group of students experiencing similar difficulties. We also present a list of potential difficulties that English language learners (ELLs) often encounter and suggest that the ECOS team, in collaboration with others in the school, generate such an inventory of difficulties for individual students or groups of like students.

The Importance of Describing before Diagnosing

When a red flag is raised, typically by a classroom teacher, about a student or a group of students who are having unusual difficulty at school, there is a tendency to focus on the students' general performance. We hear statements like "They are having trouble learning," "They can't read," or "They can't remember things." Although these statements describe what these students may be

---

Theresa Young, Toronto District School Board, Toronto, Ontario, Canada, was a major contributor to this chapter and helped to write it.

experiencing in very general terms, at least two problems are associated with such general evaluations. First, because they are general ratings of performance, such statements do not help us understand specifically what the student is having difficulty with, which makes designing appropriate interventions quite difficult. Second, these general ratings influence teachers' perceptions of the student's performance in other academic areas as well, even if there are no problems or the problems are of lesser severity, and this further complicates the issue. This tendency, known as the "halo effect" or the "devil effect," has long been recognized by social scientists as a cognitive bias whereby a general evaluation of one attribute, skill, or trait influences the evaluation of other attributes, skills, or traits (such as academic skills) (Cook, Marsh, & Hicks, 2003; Thorndike, 1920; Willingham & Jones, 1958). Consequently, these more broad-brush evaluative statements may inappropriately influence both the evaluations of and expectations for the identified students in areas that may not be as problematic, resulting in undesirable inaccuracy across various dimensions of performance (Feeley, 2002; Freijo & Jaeger, 1976).

In addition, we often find that when an ELL (or group of ELLs) is identified as having difficulties in school, there is a tendency to assume something is intrinsically wrong with the student. We hear statements like "Jorge has problems with math" or "They can't process information fast enough" rather than "The way we teach math doesn't seem to be effective for Jorge" or "The way we present new concepts doesn't make it easy for these students to process the information." The first step that needs to be taken, therefore, is to describe as specifically as possible exactly what it is that the student is having difficulty with, without attributing the difficulty to a specific cause. This requires that the ECOS team get to know the student in terms of the behaviors presented and how they indicate the student's strengths and weaknesses, rather than draw unwarranted conclusions from generalized statements, assumptions, and perceptions. No placement decisions or intervention efforts will be sufficient if the data on which they are based are inaccurate or insufficient.

The ECOS team must urge teachers and everyone who works with a particular student or group of students to answer the question "What?" before attempting to answer the question "Why?" Refraining from asking "why" first is challenging for many teachers, because in an effort to meet the needs of ELLs who experience difficulties, the first question that is posed is "Is it LD or is it L2?" That is, there is a strong tendency to try to determine whether the cause of a student's difficulties is a disability or normal second language learning processes as soon as a problem is identified. Teams traditionally choose one or the other too early in the process.

There are several compelling reasons to reframe the approach to causal attribution and to avoid making a diagnostic decision so early in the process.

Similarity of Surface Behaviors

The difficulties experienced by ELLs in the normal process of learning English and the difficulties experienced by students with diagnosed learning disabilities (LD) and specific language impairment often appear similar, if not identical (e.g., Damico & Damico, 1993a; Paradis, 2005; Salameh, Håkansson, & Nettelbladt, 2004). Because there are only so many ways that difficulties may manifest behaviorally, the mere presence of these behavioral markers is not sufficient for accurate or adequate causal interpretation (Damico, 2003; Damico & Nelson, 2005; Genesee, Paradis, & Crago, 2004; Perkins, 2005). The behaviors don't point directly to the cause or reason. Thus, when viewed superficially, ELLs in the normal process of learning English and students with diagnosed LD may appear to be experiencing the same processes. For example, while ELLs often exhibit what look like language disfluencies associated with disability, disfluencies are a natural part of second language development (Cloud, 1994). Even the ability to perceive and organize information can be distorted when students are learning a second language (Hamayan & Damico, 1991). However, the causes of these difficulties may be quite different for ELLs and for students with disabilities.

Some further examples of difficulties that ELLs might experience that could be misinterpreted as LD include forgetting words that are taught in class from one day to the next, needing extensive wait time to prepare for oral production, understanding more than they can express either orally or in writing, difficulty following spoken directions, experiencing anxiety during the school day, and "freezing" when asked to answer questions in class. Students with the kinds of intrinsic meaning-making difficulties that appropriately identify them as exceptional may demonstrate the same behaviors, but for different reasons. ELLs may have difficulty following spoken directions. Students with diagnosed LD may have intrinsic difficulties with receptive language that would lead to similar behaviors. Another example is that ELLs who are learning academic content in their second language sometimes experience anxiety during the school day and may freeze when asked to answer questions in class. Students with LD may respond in similar ways if they are aware of the difficulties they have expressing themselves. ELLs may also appear distracted at different times throughout the day, and sometimes seem to shut down. Students with learning challenges may perform similarly, given the intrinsic nature of the challenges they experience across learning contexts throughout the school day.

These are just a few of the many possible observable behaviors that ELLs may exhibit to a greater or lesser degree when the extrinsic learning environment is not meeting their learning needs. Students with LD may exhibit some or all of the same behaviors; however, if they are also ELLs, these difficulties will be evident in both languages and across many learning contexts (Crago & Paradis, 2003; Cummins, 1984, 2000; Damico & Hamayan, 1991; Damico, Oller, & Storey, 1983).

The Tendency to Choose Disability

As has been discussed extensively in the literature, when learning problems are initially identified, there is a tendency to locate them in the student rather than in the practices and biases of the schools or school personnel (e.g., Coles, 1987; Cummins, 2000; Delpit, 1988; Erickson, 1987; Ogbu & Simons, 1998; Taylor, 1991). This is likely a primary reason for the overrepresentation of ELL students in some aspects of special education (Artiles & Ortiz, 2002; McNamara, 1998). Because of the overrepresentation of ELLs in special education programs, we suspect that a team of teachers is more likely to come up with a disability explanation than a second language learning process explanation. Since most assessments of ELLs are done primarily if not exclusively in English (Gunderson & Siegel, 2001; Roseberry-McKibbin, Brice, & O'Hanlon, 2005), educators may initially misinterpret the ELLs' behaviors as reflecting LD. School staff may be more accustomed to associating the difficulties they observe in ELLs with students who are in special education programs, especially because the difficulties exhibited by the two groups of students may appear very much alike on the surface.

The tendency to choose an intrinsic disability as the cause of ELLs' difficulties may also be based on the assumption that the source of all educational difficulties is related to causes that are intrinsic to students (Carroll, 1997; Gutkin & Nemeth, 1997). This assumption is exacerbated by general education teachers' lack of familiarity with the principles of second language acquisition and its impact on academic contexts. School staff may not be as familiar with typical difficulties that ELLs experience in the normal process of learning in a second language and how these difficulties can look like LD. Chronicle 3.1 provides an account of one such situation.

The Tendency to Choose Intrinsic Explanations

By a bilingual coordinator

A kindergarten teacher asked me to observe a student in her class. She was concerned that this child was not able to discriminate initial consonant sounds in words. When I arrived, I was impressed with her class. All the students were very engaged in learning, and she made instruction comprehensible through the use of visuals, manipulatives, pictures, and many gestures and facial expressions to accompany what she said. I noticed that the children had dictated a language experience story about their school routines, and the teacher had written out the entire story on large chart paper. The dictated story was being used as a meaningful context to teach some skills to the students.

The day I visited the class, the teacher concentrated on initial consonant sounds so that I could observe the ELL student in question. She asked the students to think of words from the story that started with the /t/ sound. The students "read" aloud the story they had dictated and stopped when they heard words that started with the /t/ sound. She asked what that word meant, and the students took turns answering orally or with gestures, then they moved on to the next example. It was great to hear the students read their story. I was watching the ELL student in her class. He seemed very attentive and paid close attention to everything in the lesson.

Afterward, she asked different students to tell the class a word that started with the /t/ sound. The native English-speaking students gave examples: "tooth, treat, tower," they yelled. Finally the ELL child raised his hand. The teacher asked if he had a word that started with the /t/ sound, and he nodded yes. "*Maestra*" he blurted out confidently. She looked at me with a great deal of concern. She asked him if he was sure, and he said yes. She gently pointed out that the word he had mentioned started with the /m/ sound. The ELL student seemed confused, and looked down at the carpet.

After the lesson, the teacher and I had an opportunity to talk about what happened. She was glad that I had witnessed the student's difficulty. When I told her that *maestra* was Spanish for "teacher," her eyes opened wide and she shook her head. We realized that the student had understood exactly what the teacher was asking of him, but he didn't speak enough English yet to say all the words he understood. I assured her that it is common for second language learners to have a larger receptive vocabulary than expressive. The teacher's face lit up with this realization. She had thought that she was not getting through to the student and didn't know what else to do. She was beginning to doubt herself and started to think that his difficulties must be due to something intrinsic. I told her it is always a good idea to get support from ESL/bilingual staff when she had concerns about any ELL student. I suggested that she continue to find ways to assess what her students knew separately from their ability to tell her in English. She immediately thought of an example. "What if during that exercise I had given the students visuals to use in supporting their oral answers? Also, I could have allowed them to share their answers through gestures." Even if her ELL had answered in his native language, she would have known that he understood because he would have shown her a picture of a teacher or pointed at her when he said *maestra*.

Questions for discussion:

- In this example, how could knowledge of the second language acquisition process inform instruction?
- What else could the teacher do to assess the student's knowledge of concepts and skills?
- How could the native language be used to validate the difficulty that the student was having?

The Nature of Second Language Acquisition

Because ELLs are not proficient in the language of instruction, they usually experience difficulty learning the content. This is part of the normal development of proficiency in an additional language (Bialystok, 2001; Genesee, Paradis, & Crago, 2004; Hamayan & Freeman, 2006). Interpretation of academic difficulties experienced by ELLs is further complicated by the fact that students may sound proficient in some contexts, misleading teachers to believe that these students can process the language of textbooks and lectures in all academic content areas. ELLs master social language, which is more concrete, much earlier than they master the abstract academic language that is necessary to succeed in an academic setting (Cummins, 2000, 2006; Genesee, Lindholm-Leary, Saunders, et al., 2006).

Because of these confusions, it is essential that the diagnostic decision be made after some information regarding the specific behaviors that ELLs are exhibiting is collected. That is, it is essential to answer the "what" question before we drift into the vicinity of the "why" question. The process of data collection and explanation discussed in the next section will assist the ECOS team in meeting these responsibilities.

The Process of Data Collection and Explanation

The ECOS team process is intended to execute four responsibilities, and two of these address the issues linked to the "what" and "why" questions. The collection of information about ELL behaviors that reveal difficulty at school as specifically as possible addresses the "what" question and is the first responsibility of the ECOS team; the possible explanation for these difficulties focuses on "why" and completes the second responsibility. To effectively meet the needs of ELLs and their teachers when suggesting interventions, these two responsibilities must be met.

However, since the primary concern when conducting assessments of ELLs as opposed to other students involves how the issue of diversity is handled, there must be a framework built into the assessment process that allows an accounting for this diversity. It is not enough to recognize that poor performance may be due to differences as well as deficits; the ECOS team must be able to systematically account for this possibility in a way that is institutionalized. That is, an expected phase of each evaluation and diagnosis should involve first a focus on the "what" and then on the "why"—an attempt to both describe and then determine how many of the specific difficulties can be explained as a result of the ELL's linguistic diversity, an intrinsic impairment, or a combination of the two.

This ECOS diversity framework can be achieved by employing a kind of two-stage process. Described elsewhere as a *bi-level analysis paradigm* (Damico & Hamayan, 1992; Damico, Smith, & Augustine, 1996), this framework incorporates an initial descriptive analysis of the difficulties exhibited by the ELL in the contexts of interest, followed by a detailed explanatory analysis.

The first stage of analysis in this ECOS framework is a *descriptive analysis.* At this descriptive level, the ECOS team collects information on the specific difficulties exhibited by the ELL. There are two ways of accomplishing this task, which we discuss later. The purpose, however, is to ask and answer the "what" question: What behaviors cause this ELL to have problems in the classroom? Either by generating the problematic behaviors or difficulties from scratch or by employing an inventory of difficulties, the ECOS team acquires data that document the ELL's weaknesses, the ELL's overall success or failure in the classroom, and even the ELL's progress over time (when pre- or postanalyses are conducted). At this level of analysis, the ECOS team functions primarily as an agent of the school and even the mainstream culture to determine what types of difficulties the ELL exhibits.

The second stage of the analysis in this ECOS framework involves an *explanatory analysis* and directly addresses the "why" question. This process seeks to determine the causal factors for the difficulties noted in the descriptive analysis. At this analytic level, the examiner notes the ELL's difficulties or weaknesses in the context of interest and seeks to determine why these behaviors occurred. At this time, the ECOS team directly addresses the diversity issues and functions more as an advocate for the ELL than as an agent of the mainstream culture.

The explanatory stage of the ECOS framework typically does not involve additional data collection. Rather, this level involves a deeper interpretation of the data collected in the descriptive stage. The ECOS team attempts to explain how variables such as aspects of the context, the student's sociocultural experience, or the student's cognitive abilities or linguistic proficiency can account for the described difficulties. Specifically, there are seven integral factors to be addressed at this level. Each is discussed below and in some detail in subsequent chapters. The stages of the diversity framework are detailed in the following sections.

Stage 1: Generating an Inventory of Specific Difficulties

The ECOS team must begin to elicit from all those who come in contact with the student in question a list of specific difficulties that the student is exhibiting. There are two ways in which this task can be accomplished. One way is to generate the list of difficulties from scratch. ECOS team members urge staff to observe the student in question closely and to submit brief descriptions of behaviors or examples of tasks that the student has difficulty with. An inventory of difficulties (IOD) is then compiled by putting all the observations together. Another way of obtaining a list of specific difficulties that a student is encountering is to start with a previously constructed list. ECOS team members then ask staff to check off those behaviors that they observe in their contact with the student in question.

Generating an Independent Inventory of Difficulties

Generating an IOD from scratch is the more valid way to identify difficulties. The observations are not tainted by someone else's suggestions, and the observers must pay close attention to what the student is doing and then construct the behaviors themselves. There are two keys to this process of generating a specific IOD. The first key is to ensure that the focus is on actual behavior, not on generalized statements or inferences about behaviors. Such generalizations or inferences about behavior typically result in inappropriate or inaccurate data. The easiest way to determine whether the data collected are behaviorally specific enough is to employ the following strategy:

Once a statement is provided, read that statement and ask yourself, "As evidenced by what?" If the answer to this question seems circular, then the difficulty that you have been given is an actual behavior. For example, if the teacher states, "She cries when she has difficulties," and you ask, "As evidenced by what?" and the teacher answers, "Well, she is crying" or "Tears fall from her eyes," then the difficulty is an actual behavior. However, if the answer to the question is not circular but provides another behavior, then it is likely that the original difficulty as stated was an inference. For example, if the teacher states, "She is sad," and you ask, "As evidenced by what?" and the teacher answers, "Well, she is crying," then the crying is the behavior and the sad state is an inference.

The second key to good data collection is to triangulate the data obtained. That is, once a teacher has provided a set of behaviors that serve as indices of difficulty for the ELL, that set should be cross-checked against a second person's set of observations, and if possible a third. Employing triangulation as a verification strategy helps ensure the accuracy and appropriateness of the data (e.g., Damico & Simmons-Mackie, 2003; Fielding & Fielding, 1986; Flick, 1992). By collecting data using different methods and over different sampling periods, then combing and comparing data from different sources, the ECOS team can estimate how similar the data are and whether or not a particular collection procedure or contextual variable affected the representativeness of the data.

To assist in focusing on actual behavioral statements of difficulty, the ECOS team should employ the following process when obtaining the data:

1. Explain to all potential data collectors or contributors to the IOD the importance of observing and describing the difficulties manifested by the ELL.
2. Provide the data collectors with instructions to observe and code. For example, "Over the next week or so, if Lydia does or says something that catches your ear, grabs your eye, or gets your attention *and you have the time*, write it down," or "Over the next several days, watch Lydia and see what kinds of problems she seems to have. Notice especially her attempts to work on academic subjects, her reactions, and any attempts to problem solve. It is important to jot these behaviors down so we can get a feeling for the kinds of difficulties she has."
3. Give the data collectors time to collect the data.
4. After they have turned in a list of difficulties, determine whether the data are sufficient.
5. Contextualize the behaviors by asking follow-up questions if the data provided are not sufficient. Two types of questions enable contextualization: *experience questions* ("Can you tell me about an instance when you saw this behavior in Peter?") and *example questions* ("Can you give me an example of what he actually does when he is doing *x*?").
6. If at all possible, verify the accuracy of the behavioral difficulties by triangulation.
7. Compile this unique and individual IOD for this ELL.

Working with a Predetermined Inventory of Difficulties

Although working from a predetermined list or IOD may predispose to inaccurate observation of a given behavior in a student, such may sometimes be necessary. Opportunities for direct observation in classrooms may be limited, and it is more time-consuming to generate a list from scratch than to work from an existing list. Moreover, our experience suggests that many teams resist generating the IOD themselves. Thus, we offer a preconstituted list that

Table 3.1 A Partial List of Potential Difficulties That Students May Encounter in an Academic Setting

1. Omits words or adds words to a sentence. Forgets names of things that he or she knows. Has to describe them.

2. Is easily distracted.

3. Has trouble following directions.

4. Can do rote arithmetic problems on paper but has difficulty with math word problems.

5. Avoids writing.

6. Does not transfer learning from one lesson to another, has to relearn each concept from scratch.

7. Very literal: misses inferences, subtleties, nuances and innuendoes.

8. Often understands concepts but cannot express this understanding in written symbolic form with paper and pencil or on multiple-choice tests.

9. Learns from watching, not listening.

10 Can't categorize, classify, or summarize.

11. Can't provide an oral narrative of a story just heard real aloud.

12. Low frustration tolerance. Gives up easily or explodes.

can serve as a starting point for generating a school-specific or even student-specific IOD.

Lists of academic difficulties can be found in many introductory special education textbooks. We have compiled a list of the most common difficulties that are brought up when we work in schools and during our workshops with teachers and special education specialists. A partial list is given in Table 3.1. This list consists of the academic difficulties most commonly identified for ELLs who are having a particularly challenging time in school. A more comprehensive list is provided in Appendix A. If educators decide to use a preconstituted list like the one in Table 3.1, we recommend starting with that list and adding one's own observations to it rather than using initially a more comprehensive list that someone else has generated. It is too easy to imagine problems where none exist.

Once a list like the one in Table 3.1 has been generated by all who come in contact with the student and the ECOS team has turned the list into an IOD by culling items and removing repetitions, the next phase begins. In fact, this next phase, coming up with possible explanations for the difficulties, can begin as soon as any difficulties have been identified.

Stage 2: Explaining the Difficulties

Although on the surface, ELLs in the process of learning academic English and students with diagnosed disabilities may look very similar, the causes of these difficulties differ (Damico, 1991; Damico & Hamayan, 1992; Genesee, Paradis, & Crago, 2004; Perkins, 2005). Different causes require different educational programming, depending on whether the difficulty arises from normal second language learning needs or from an intrinsic learning, perceptual, or processing disability. Exploring whether the causes are extrinsic, intrinsic, or a combination is critical to providing appropriate programming for these students.

There are always underlying causes that are extrinsic to ELLs that could lead to academic difficulties, such as cross-cultural differences and lack of proficiency in the academic language used in a specific content area. If an ELL (or a group of ELLs) is encountering academic difficulties, these extrinsic factors must be addressed, regardless of whether or not the student has an LD.

Even though the difficulties that ELLs experience may be normal manifestations of learning another language, they might be intensive enough that the students are still very much in need of programming to address their unique needs and circumstances. These are students who are challenged by being ELLs but who are not disabled; they are in the category of ELL minus the disability (ELL – LD). It is also possible that the difficulties that some ELLs experience are indicative of an underlying intrinsic LD in addition to being a normal manifestation of learning another language. These students are challenged through both extrinsic (L2) and intrinsic (disability) factors; that is, they are in the category of ELL plus LD (ELL + LD).

Difficulties in ELLs' second language may be due to any of the seven integral factors discussed in this handbook:

1. the learning environment created for the student,
2. personal and family factors,
3. physical and psychological factors,
4. previous schooling performance,
5. proficiency in oral language and literacy in both the first (L1) and the second language (L2),
6. academic achievement, and
7. cross-cultural factors.

Each of these factors can be complex, multilayered, and different for each group of students the team works with. ELLs are a heterogeneous group of students; there is no "typical" ELL student to use as the norm. Finding the causes of ELLs' difficulties begins by considering these seven extrinsic factors before one can assume the existence of intrinsic causes due to LD. ECOS teams can expand their vision of the types of difficulties ELLs encounter when learning in English environments by becoming more familiar with the seven integral factors.

To illustrate the different causes that may underly the same apparent difficulty, Table 3.2 contrasts possible causes for a specific behavior, difficulty retelling a story in sequence. The left column lists possible reasons why an ELL with no LD (ELL – LD) might have these difficulties; the right column lists possible underlying reasons why an ELL student with LD (ELL + LD) might exhibit the same problem. The more specific the difficulty, the easier it will be to generate ELL – LD and ELL + LD explanations for it. It also helps to discuss the circumstances and the various contexts in which the difficulty is observed to occur. The example in Table 3.2 was used to explore a teacher's concern about a particular student. The teacher initially said that the student had "no reading comprehension." A few probing questions were asked:

- Does the difficulty occur in the first language or only in the second language?
- What is the student's academic English proficiency level?
- Is the difficulty observed in oral language, written language, or both?
- When does the difficulty occur?
- Is the difficulty apparent with fiction only or with nonfiction texts as well?

Only after such questions were asked did a specific description of the difficulty emerge. It eventuated that when the student heard a story in English, he could not retell it in English. It was critical to get that very specific information before proceeding to the next steps of generating possible explanations and then creating interventions in all of the student's languages.

The teacher's first comment was a diagnosis: "He has no reading comprehension." The subsequent description uncovered precise observable behav-

Table 3.2 Possible Explanations from Different Perspectives for a Student Who Has Difficulty Retelling the Events of a Story in Sequence

Possible ELL – LD Explanations (Observed in English)	Possible ELL + LD Explanations (Observed in English and the Native Language, and in Several Contexts)
Listening: • The student may not understand stories because they are in English or because the cultural context of the stories or events was irrelevant or unfamiliar.	**Listening:** • The student may not understand the vocabulary (either the content or organizational words such as *first, next, last*), story events, inferred information, or narrative structure in L1 and L2. • The student may have auditory memory difficulties, making it difficult to retain lengthy information.

Speaking:
• The student understands stories told in English, but does not feel sufficiently comfortable with English-speaking abilities to retell stories.
• The student may have developed skills in social English but may not have been taught the academic language of sequence (*first, then, next*) to be able to retell stories smoothly.
• The student may be able to retell stories in the student's native language after hearing a story in English.
• The student's primary language has a different structure for telling stories, so the student's retelling in English sounds "out of order/out of sequence."
	Speaking:
	• The student may have oral expressive difficulties in both languages with:
	  - formulating ideas into sentences that clearly relay the meaning of the story,
	  - the concept of sequencing in a variety of contexts, not just in story retelling,
	  - the use of cohesive devices (conjunctions and pronoun references) to connect the story information,
	  - organizing information into a story structure.

Reading Comprehension: • Stories are not at the student's instructional level in English, so the student does not understand enough of the story to retell. The student could recount some details that correspond to pictures if the student has acquired the vocabulary.	**Reading Comprehension:** • The student may have weak decoding skills in all languages. • The student may not understand the vocabulary (either content or organizational words such as *first, next, last*), story events, inferred information, or narrative structure in L1 and L2.

Writing:
• The student may be in the early stages of English language acquisition and is still developing writing skills.
• The student may be using first language structures to negotiate writing in the second language, which can make the written text sound "out of sequence" in English.
• The student may need to develop writing in his or her first language.
	Writing:
	• The student may have difficulty spelling in all languages.
	• The student may have difficulties in oral language production that are also evident in written expression, including:
	  - sentence formulation.
	  - sequencing in a variety of contexts. including stories,
	  - use of cohesive devices in both languages (e.g., conjunctions, pronoun references),
	  - organizing the information into story structure.

Cultural Impact: • The cultural context of the story may be wholly unknown to the student; for example, the student may come from a culture where people do not keep animals in their houses as pets, and the student may be appalled and distracted by a story about pets. This makes it difficult to concentrate on comprehension and on the sequence of the story. • Different languages may have storytelling structures that differ from English.	

ECOS TEAM ACTIVITY

With members of the ECOS team, use the chart in Appendix B to generate additional or other observable difficulties that students may exhibit in the school setting. Next, practice generating possible explanations for each behavior from contrasting perspectives.

---

iors and the context in which they occurred. The latter approach is much more useful because it provides specific information to guide the problem-solving process.

Benefits of Discussing Possible Causes

The ECOS team benefits from doing this exercise as a team because the members learn from each other about their differing perspectives and areas of experience and expertise. Team members can clarify what different professionals mean when using certain terms, thus generating a shared vocabulary. Although there are tremendous long-term benefits to having this discussion and engaging in the negotiations that ultimately result when a diverse group of professionals tries to find a solution to a puzzle, many teams are reluctant to explore causes of difficulties completely on their own and request guidance, a facilitator, or an example they can follow. Table 3.3 provides such an example for the 12 sample difficulties listed throughout this chapter.

The examples given in Table 3.3 are merely examples. They are by no means definitive and final answers to the question, what could be the causes (ELL – LD and ELL + LD) of each difficulty? The explanations were generated by a school district we worked with. ECOS teams should use the examples in Table 3.3 as a springboard for developing their own explanations for difficulties observed in their students, and remember that the exercise is just an exercise. Chronicle 3.2 recounts the experience of one teacher who used the list in Table 3.3 in a way that limited her analysis of a student's performance rather than helping her explore possible reasons for the student's difficulties.

Working in a Timely Fashion

The process of exploring reasons for the specific difficulties encountered by students must happen as soon as a difficulty is identified. In the interest of providing students with the most effective interventions as quickly as possible, the team must formulate hypotheses regarding the causes of difficulties in order to determine the specific and the more general systemic interventions they want to see in place. The extrinsic factors, discussed in Chapters 5 to 11 as the seven integral elements in a student's school life that can account for ELL difficulties, can be addressed explicitly by the ECOS team from the outset. Interventions that would help alleviate any negative effects of

(text continues on page 42)

ECOS TEAM ACTIVITY

Using Table 3.3, generate discussion among team members regarding the validity of the causes attributed to each of the 12 difficulties. Assign one of four roles to team members: (1) *Critic:* find something wrong with the explanation(s); (2) *Supporter:* come up with ideas to support the explanation(s); (3) *ELL – LD Developer:* find additional ELL – LD explanations; (4) *ELL + LD Developer:* find additional ELL + LD explanations. The four groups develop their ideas and arguments, and the whole group reassembles to discuss.

Table 3.3 Possible Explanations for Typical Academic Difficulties Encountered by ELLs

Observable Behavior	Possible ELL – LD Explanations	Possible ELL + LD Explanations
1. Omits words or adds words to a sentence. Forgets names of things that he/she knows. Has to describe them.	- Word not in L2 vocabulary yet - Word/concept not learned in L1 - Word retrieval problems	- Memory/oral language processing difficulties
2. Is easily distracted.	- Doesn't understand - No visual/concrete support - Child mentally exhausted	- Auditory processing - ADHD - ADD
3. Has trouble following directions.	- Doesn't understand L2 - No demonstrations or context given for directions/procedure	- Sequencing problems - Processing—attention - Memory
4. Can do rote arithmetic problems on paper, but has difficulty with math word problems .	- Language-based - Currency different - Different experience	- Processing—abstract reasoning - Lack of generalization - Can't hold information in head long enough
5. Avoids writing.	- Most difficult aspect for ELLs - Afraid of making mistakes	- Fine motor difficulties—expressive language, can't expand - Frustration from overcorrection - Expressive language difficulties
6. Doesn't transfer learning from one lesson to another. Has to relearn each concept from scratch.	- Forgets English words learned orally with no context	- Memory - Language processing
7. Very literal: misses inferences, subtleties, nuances, and innuendoes.	- Difficult to express/represent abstract concepts (teacher and child)	- Abstract reasoning difficulties
8. Often understands concepts but cannot express this understanding in written symbolic form with paper and pencil or on multiple-choice tests.	- Writing is most difficult task	- Difficulty expressing and organizing thoughts on paper
9. Learns from watching, not listening.	- Does not understand L2 - Needs physical model	- Attention deficit - Auditory processing
10. Can't categorize, classify, or summarize.	- Doesn't understand topic - Needs model	- Organizational issues
11. Can't retell a story in sequence or summarize.	- Can't in L2 but may be able to in L1 (orally).	- Organization - Processing - Auditory sequencing
12. Low frustration tolerance. Gives up easily or explodes.	- Doesn't understand content - Tired - Doesn't feel successful	- Doesn't understand - Student conscious of falling behind

CHRONICLE 3.2

Digging Deeper for the Cause: The Dangers of the List

By an ECOS team leader

An ESL teacher approached me about a student who was having significant difficulty in her class. She pulled out a chart we had used for discussion at a recent meeting of our ECOS team. The chart listed possible explanations for typical academic difficulties encountered by ELLs (see Table 3.3). I was surprised to see the list in her hands, since it had not been intended for distribution to staff. At first I was glad to see something that we had found quite useful in our team meeting being used by one of the teachers, but later I regretted not having made it clear to everyone that this list was not to be distributed and used by others until we had had a chance to discuss it with them and to do some professional development on the topic.

As soon as the teacher started telling me about the student, she pointed to two items on the list. She said, "We think that Andreas has either memory processing or word retrieval problems. Or it could be some kind of language processing issue," pointing to numbers 1 and 6 on the list. She was certain he had some sort of disability, and she had already begun the process to have him evaluated. She felt that he could not retain concepts once he learned them and had difficulty acquiring them in the first place. He was quite proficient in academic English even though he had been in the United States only since the summer. I asked her for an example of what he was having difficulty with. She told me about the first social studies unit they were studying. It was focused on the colonial period in U.S. history. This is when she began to suspect his difficulties were due to intrinsic causes. She noticed a few times during this unit that this student was not able to grasp concepts. One example came with the concept of *antique*.

I asked her to describe the strategies she had used in teaching the student this concept. It seemed to me that she had done everything right. She had brought in real objects. She showed the student antiques that would have been used in colonial times in the United States, such as a stovetop iron for clothes and a bed warmer. She had shown the student pictures and discussed each item and compared them with what is in their home today. She even asked the child to find out what each of these items was called in his native language. I was stumped. She seemed to have done everything right, and the child seemed to follow her, but he just couldn't explain to her what an *antique* was. I asked her what the special education teachers had suggested, and she said they could help him with memory and word retrieval strategies and some expressive language exercises, but he would first need to have a full case study done to see if he qualified for their services.

I was not convinced. Very little information had been collected. We were still in the early stages of trying to change the school so that our ECOS team could process requests for intervention from teachers, and we did not have a system in place yet. Before we ended our conversation, I asked her to keep in touch with me about what happened with this student. As an afterthought, I asked her where the student had come from. She told me he had moved from Greece the past summer. I couldn't believe I hadn't thought to ask that question before! That changed everything! I told her that his background gave him a much different notion of what is old or antique than what we have here in the United States. He came from the land of the Acropolis and the Parthenon. It was quite possible that the objects the teacher brought in to illustrate the

continued

concept of antique were still being used in homes in Greece today. I told her that perhaps a referral to special education was not yet called for. The teacher could try some other interventions first. One example I suggested was that they build a timeline comparing the history of his country and the history of the United States, and then study the influences of Greece on other civilizations around the world. This might be more relevant to him and even quite interesting to the other students in the class.

I realized that we needed to use tools, such as the list of difficulties, very carefully to avoid a situation like this one. This very good teacher and her caring special education colleagues had made the mistake of using the ELL/LD possible causes chart as if it were an exhaustive list. Since the child did not respond to the interventions for the ELL causes provided in the chart, they assumed that they should jump over to the LD possible explanations. This is the danger of assuming that any student will fall neatly into a particular category or will exhibit the traits on a predetermined checklist of characteristics. We must dig below the surface to find out what might be causing an ELL's difficulty. Finally, we must collect as much information as possible as quickly as possible.

Questions for discussion:

- What are some procedural errors that might exist in this school's process for referring students to special education?
- What could have been done to prevent this situation from going as far as it did?
- What other pieces of information about this student would you like to gather?
- What is the specific difficulty that this ELL is exhibiting? List other interventions that the school could implement to support this student and to capitalize on his linguistic and cultural resources.

(text continued from page 39)
these integral elements can be established while the team analyzes the difficulties to see if they cut across contexts and languages. If the team finds that to be the case, then the difficulties may be caused by factors that are more intrinsic in nature. During this process, it is critical to keep in mind the various myths introduced in Chapter 1 and summarized in Table 3.4.

Remembering the Myths

Remembering the myths about ELLs and special education keeps the ECOS team from misconceptions at this critical moment of the team's work and will ensure that effective interventions are crafted for ELLs according to whether or not they also have a disability. Whether or not an LD is present, there is no need to withhold support services that an ELL student might need while developing proficiency in English. If these students are normal ELLs without disabilities, it is imperative that they not be directed into special education, as these programs are unlikely to meet their language learning needs or help them achieve their academic potential.

The perspective that "at least they will get some help in special education" is dangerously misinformed, because the nature of the support typically provided to students with disabilities can disadvantage ELL learners. For example, traditional special education programming tends to target specific

---

Table 3.4 Commonly Held Myths Regarding ELLs and Special Education

Myth 1: If we label an ELL as learning disabled, at least he or she will get some help.

Myth 2: We have to wait five to seven years for ELLs to develop their English language skills before we can rule out language as a cause for the student's difficulty.

Myth 3: When an ELL is identified as having a disability, we need to shift instruction so that it is only in English, so as not to confuse the student.

---

skills that are often practiced without a meaningful context. The acontextual language use makes it more difficult for ELLs to understand and retain information (Gersten & Woodward, 1994). In the case of an ELL with LD, all the student's linguistic resources should be tapped to support learning. Limiting the student to one language is a common approach that is misinformed and straitjackets ELLs by limiting them to using only some of their language skills during the school day. As Genesee, Paradis, and Crago (2004) have observed, children are capable of learning two languages even under conditions of impairment.

Reframing the Issue: ELL ± LD

The question of whether an ELL's academic difficulties are due to the second language learning process or to a disability (L2 versus LD) is no longer useful formulation. The answer is rarely neat enough to be useful. The cause of some difficulties in English will, for a great part of ELLs' school careers, be due to the normal process of learning academic content in a nonproficient language. It is difficult to attend to both language and academic content when one is not proficient in the language of instruction, or when one knows the language of instruction conversationally but not in the academic realm. This distinction between academic and social second language proficiency is discussed in Chapter 9. A more useful approach in this problem-solving process is to reframe the question as one of whether the difficulties the ELL is experiencing are indicative of an underlying intrinsic LD in addition to normal manifestations of the problems of learning another language or just the usual difficulties related to working in the second language that must be addressed differently (ELL with or without LD).

In Chapter 4, we look at a process for verifying whether the observed difficulties are occurring in just the academic English setting or in both of the student's languages, and across social as well as academic settings. If the difficulty manifests in all settings and across languages, then the team can begin to explore underlying learning difficulties. In the case of ELL + LD, the team would have the task of addressing the student's second language needs, as well as providing the student with specialized support specific to his or her learning disabilities. If the student's difficulties are observed only in English language contexts and not in the home language and not in all settings, it is more likely that the student is experiencing the typical challenges that arise in learning academic content through a second language (ELL – LD). However, the student may need more support and intervention than other ELL students who are making steady progress in an ESL/bilingual program.

We have proposed a process for ECOS teams to describe students' difficulties specifically rather than broadly diagnosing them from the outset. The collaborative process asks team members to generate lists of possible causes of the difficulties from their various perspectives by considering possible extrinsic and intrinsic causes. Because of the nature of second language learning, it is critical that the team first address the possible extrinsic causes for the difficulties by looking at the seven integral factors to guide them. In Chapter 4, we continue this problem-solving process by showing how teams can create interventions that address both the extrinsic and intrinsic causes for ELL difficulties. We also show how to document students' progress and assess their response to these interventions.

STEPS FOR ECOS TEAMS TO TAKE

1. The ECOS team is formed.

2. The team meets for team-building activities, to clarify roles and responsibilities, and to discuss principles.

3. The team is introduced to the rest of the school.

4. The team asks all those who come in contact with the student in question to write down a list of specific difficulties that the student is exhibiting, describing rather than diagnosing.

5. Using the list in Table 3.1, the team suggests other behaviors to add to the list. This will become the inventory of difficulties (IOD) that serves to generate interventions.

6. Using the evolving IOD, the team elicits from every person an assessment as to whether the student in question shows a particular behavior on th IOD.

7. As soon as one or two items are established as part of the IOD, the team begins to discuss possible causes from an ELL perspective and contrasts these causes with possible disability causes.

4

Delivering a Continuum of Services

KEY CONCEPTS

As soon as a difficulty is identified for an English language learner or a group of English language learners, interventions drawn from English as a second language and special education must be put in place both at an individual (specific) level and at a general, schoolwide (systemic) level.

Creating an effective program for students experiencing academic difficulties means providing support in a timely manner as soon as specific needs are identified. Although the natural acquisition of skills and knowledge is never truly sequential and time-linked (Wells, 1990), learning as dictated by a curricular approach is coupled to schedules, timetables, and calendars, and students who for whatever reason cannot benefit according to the designated sequences and timetables are at a disadvantage. Consequently, rapid response in terms of identification, planning, and implementation should be a priority if the ECOS team is to have a real impact.

In light of the information presented in the first three chapters of this book, two facts should be clear. First, the traditional service delivery methods employed for English language learners (ELLs)—particularly when they hinge on traditional components and phases of special education—are not sufficient to meet the needs of these children. In the traditional service delivery system, the time between the appearance of difficulties and the implementation of an intervention can be quite long, and additional problems arise for ELLs in this traditional system (such as the inappropriate use of standardized tests, resulting in overidentification). Other approaches or strategies are needed. Second, it should be recognized that the ECOS team approach provides a viable alternative to the traditional approaches and, if employed appropriately, will meet the needs of ELL students.

This chapter presents a collaborative solution-seeking approach to providing a continuum of services to meet the range of difficulties that students experience in the classroom, and one that can be implemented in a timely manner. The approach described is an alternative to traditional practices employed in special education service delivery, which typically require referrals and standardized assessment to determine eligibility for service before interventions can be put into place.

The collaborative solution-seeking approach we describe may be viewed as a hybrid of several previously described approaches to addressing the needs

Theresa Young, Toronto District School Board, Toronto, Ontario, Canada, was a major contributor to this chapter and helped to write it.

of struggling learners (e.g., Chalfant, Pysh, & Moultrie, 1979; Chandler, Dunaway, Levine, et al., 2005; Damico & Hamayan, 1992; York-Barr & Rainforth, 1997), but it is uniquely linked to ELL students. Further, this approach can be utilized in a way similar to a response to intervention (RTI) approach while avoiding some of the potentially problematic practices currently suggested by some RTI advocates (e.g., Fuchs, Mock, Morgan, et al., 2003; Justice, 2006; Wright, 2005). To demonstrate how this may be accomplished, we explore the similarities to RTI approaches that are currently evolving in the field of special education. Much of our framework depends on the creation of a forum within schools to allow ESL/bilingual and special education teachers the opportunity to consult one another and provide support across their professions. We discuss the challenges involved in shifting from current models to this more responsive one, along with related legal and fiscal issues. We argue that by intervening across languages and contexts, the ECOS team can bring to light difficulties related to English language learning. We also show how important it is for the home language and culture to be engaged as resources in the ELL's school environment.

Providing Support in a Timely Manner

Once the ECOS teams begin to discuss possible causes for the variety of ELL difficulties on the inventory of difficulties (IOD), a logical next step is for teams to generate a variety of interventions that will provide support for the ELLs. A solution-seeking framework can be used to determine the best possible interventions for specific difficulties. It is important that support be provided as soon as or even before difficulties arise. Rather than waiting for problems to occur, a proactive rather than a reactive stance should be taken. ECOS teams can strive to anticipate and prevent difficulties rather than intervene only after difficulties have become manifest. In this way the ECOS team can build capacity for addressing the needs of future ELLs and can establish an effective working relationship with other teachers at the school. Taking a proactive stance to address the needs of ELL students is necessary, given the various problems and expectations that often arise through a lack of information about second language acquisition and bilingual education (e.g., Roseberry-McKibbin, Brice, & O'Hanlon, 2005; Samway & McKeon, 1999; Wiley & Wright, 2004).

Getting a Head Start

ECOS teams have at their disposal a variety of options for getting a head start in addressing student needs (e.g., Miramontes, Nadeau, & Commins, 1997; Stevenson, 1995; Woodward, 1994). For example, team members could attend and facilitate spring articulation meetings at the different grade levels in their school. The information presented by teachers after an entire year of teaching can help the next grade teachers and the ECOS team anticipate difficulties that may arise. The team can start planning interventions and procedures to be implemented during the summer and the following school year, and can suggest professional development activities that would help staff meet the incoming students' needs. This strategy is extremely effective for systemic interventions that involve more than one teacher's instructional strategies and plans for one classroom (Lucas, Henze, & Donato, 1990). For example, if a middle school administrator knows that her school will be receiving a group of refugee students from the elementary school, it would be very beneficial to find out as much as possible about this group of students, their culture, how individual students responded to their first year in the U.S. school system, and other information related to the seven integral factors discussed in this handbook. Why wait for difficulties to arise when they can be anticipated, especially since these systemic interventions will only improve the school environment and expand the staff's expertise?

In another situation, school administrators might approach the ECOS team to discuss the rapidly changing demographics in their districts and try to figure out ways to anticipate some of the special needs of a wide range of language and socioeconomic groups. The ECOS team may recommend that a particular emphasis be placed on hiring teachers and other staff members who share the language and cultural backgrounds of the incoming students (Coelho, 1994). They might also ask library or media center personnel to order books in the languages of the students (Krashen, 2004). The team might contact a university nearby and organize university teacher candidate students to support ELLs during the school day and receive clinical credit toward their credentials for the time they spend in the schools. This type of "university in-reach" may also help build various types of collaborative programs across academe and within the schools themselves (e.g., Welch, Sheridan, Wilson, et al., 1996; Wiener & Davidson, 1990).

Another approach that the ECOS team can take is to gather information from teachers once school has been in session for a month or two. The earlier in the school year that the ECOS team meets with groups of teachers and surveys them for potential difficulties, the sooner the team can generate interventions, both systemic and specific, that would be effective for those anticipated difficulties (Duckworth, 1997; Graves, 2002). During these meetings, ECOS team members and teachers can view students' portfolios and see examples of progress or lack of progress from the beginning of the school year (e.g., O'Malley & Valdez-Pierce, 1996; Shea, Murray, & Harlin, 2005). Teachers might also share their concerns about disruptive classroom behavior, and the team could help these teachers establish classroom procedures to run things more smoothly. If these procedures proved successful, the teachers might in turn share the strategies and procedures with the rest of their colleagues in a school staff meeting. In this case, the specific intervention may become a general intervention that is implemented throughout the school, and the students will benefit by experiencing consistency throughout their day and across grade levels. Teachers will be glad that a team exists in the school to listen to their concerns about how to best address ELLs' needs before these concerns become crises.

This approach is in contrast to the more traditional models that exist in many schools. The traditional models often pit one set of professionals against another and one professional's judgment against another's. This contentious environment puts professionals on the defensive and leads them to rely heavily on objective test scores rather than on their own professional judgment (Kohn, 2000; McNeill, 2000; Sacks, 1999). It may also put teachers on the defensive for needing or wanting assistance for their students. On the one hand, teachers feel they have to prove they have done everything possible before asking the team for help. On the other hand, the team is under great pressure to reduce the number of students served in special education and to prove definitively that the difficulties are due to intrinsic factors and not to other possible causes (Chalfant & Pysh, 1989; Gutkin, 1990).

As was discussed in Chapters 1 to 3, it is very difficult to definitely diagnose a disability in an ELL and to sort out which difficulties are typical manifestations of learning a second language and which are related to disabilities. In more traditional models, the system has become so cumbersome that only the most persistent teachers get instructional support in the classroom and support for their students and their families (Five, 1995; Penfield, 1987; Taylor, 1991). Many teachers remain silent out of concern that their inability to deal with a particular student's or group of students' challenges reflects poorly on their skills as a teacher. If in addition to that pressure the system makes teachers feel even more vulnerable by questioning their motives and abilities, they are more likely to remain silent about students' difficulties in the future.

The ECOS team has the ability to pull resources, ideas, and creative solutions together to support students and teachers in a timely manner. The ECOS team can also be a place where teachers come to propose ideas they have about innovative and creative programming that could be implemented in their school to address the constantly changing needs of their students. Once ECOS teams have gathered information about the needs of ELLs in their schools, they can begin the process of generating interventions for those specific needs. This process is in some ways analogous to aspects of the RTI approach that is becoming increasingly popular in the field of special education.

Response to Intervention

Response to intervention or responsiveness to instruction (RTI) provides an alternative to the typical practices currently employed in many schools to provide support to students who experience academic difficulties (Ehren & Nelson, 2005; Fuchs, 2003; Fuchs, Mock, Morgan, et al., 2003). Traditional practices evolved out of special education approaches that assumed academic difficulties to be due to disabilities intrinsic to the student. These approaches have required students to be diagnosed with an identifiable categorical disability such as a learning disability, reading disability, specific language impairment, or developmental delay before the student could receive the necessary support.

However, the identification, assessment, and placement of students into such categories are problematic on all counts, and especially so when the students are ELLs. When traditional assessment procedures are employed and then fit into the "test-score discrepancy models" that have been employed for three decades in special education (e.g., Coles, 1987; Fletcher, Francis, Shaywitz, et al., 1998; Flynn, 2000), several limitations to this approach to assessment and placement become obvious. First, the student must demonstrate chronic academic failure to be referred for assessment and eventual placement. Second, the decisions about identification and placement frequently depend on test scores and discrepancy formulas that provide no information on why a child is performing poorly. Finally, this approach provides little or no information to assist in determining what might be done to overcome the problems (Gunderson & Siegel, 2001). These last two limitations are especially problematic when addressing the kinds of diversity issues seen with ELL students, since test scores and discrepancy formulas fail to consider variables external to the child, such as experiential and linguistic differences.

With the revised Individuals with Disabilities Education Improvement Act (IDEA) of 2004, however, there has been a shift in focus regarding the identification of students for special education services. Primarily, there has been a shift away from the use of discrepancy models to identify exceptionalities, particularly learning disabilities. According to federal regulations, state departments of education can no longer force school systems to use a severe discrepancy between intellectual ability and achievement as the litmus test for determining whether a child has a specific learning disability. Instead, it is suggested that the schools employ a process that determines whether the child responds to scientific, research-based intervention by using a "dual discrepancy model"—in other words, RTI.

When the dual discrepancy model (Fuchs, 2003; Fuchs, Mock, Morgan, et al., 2003) is used to identify problems, including exceptionalities, the student is provided with actual interventions, and changes in the student's performance are documented (Fuchs, 2004; Stecker, Fuchs, & Fuchs, 2005). In this model, the first indication of discrepancy is the finding that the student is performing academically at a level significantly below that of his or her typical classroom peers, regardless of the suspected reasons. That is, the student exhibits a discrepancy in initial skills or performance that is important in the context of interest, the classroom. At this time, various levels of intervention or instruction may be employed, and any changes that occur are documented. If despite the implementation of one or more well-designed, well-implemented interventions crafted to overcome the student's difficulties the student fails to reduce the performance gap between him- or herself and classmates, then the second and more specific discrepancy in the rate of learning relative to classroom peers is noted and may be sufficient reason for placement into special education services.

With this reorientation, the dual discrepancy model has been employed to create more recent assessment processes that have evolved from the understanding that the source of academic difficulties for some students can be the quality of the instruction they have experienced rather than an intrinsic disability (Vaughn & Fuchs, 2003; Wright, 2005). To address this possibility, RTI takes a different tact to address the broad-ranging academic challenges that students face in the general education classroom. This approach is based on a tiered model of high-quality instructional support, with ongoing assessment to determine which students respond to the instruction. When the students respond to the interventions by making progress, it is assumed that the instructional support that is provided at this tier is sufficient to meet their learning needs (Fuchs, Fuchs, & Compton, 2004; Kame'enui, Fuchs, Good, et al., 2006; Vaughn & Fuchs, 2003).

In the RTI approach, Tier I is considered the level of *universal intervention*, at which the instruction employed is available to all students. An example is additional classroom writing instruction in the form of several dedicated mini-lessons. This level of instruction is provided for all students in the general education classroom, with ongoing curriculum-based assessment. Students who do not respond or who are *resistant to instruction* are then provided with a second tier of support. Tier II, *individualized intervention*, is intended for students who need additional support. These students are typically given individualized intervention plans. This level of support may take the form of specialized, small-group, intensive instruction for nonresponsive students. This might involve, for example, direct one-on-one shared reading with a teacher or trained aide or supplemental peer tutoring to increase fluency during reading. As this level of intervention is employed, ongoing assessment is used to determine which students continue to resist intervention and thus require a third tier of support. When required, Tier III is the level of *intensive intervention*. This level of support may entail specialized individualized interventions for students with significant needs (Fletcher, Denton, Fuchs, et al., 2005; Fuchs, 2002). This level of support may involve special education services or may be employed as the last set of interventions before placement into special education. Tier III is employed differently in various locales.

Potential Benefits of RTI for ELLs Experiencing Difficulties

RTI approaches can benefit all students by providing timely support in the classroom as needs are identified. If employed appropriately and carefully, RTI can also introduce high-quality instruction into general educational classrooms across the grades. Ideally, a student with academic delays can be provided with one or more effective interventions, and, because the response to the intervention is monitored, appropriate changes and additional support or placements (if needed) may be provided. Using RTI, then, educators can avoid placement decisions on the basis of formalized tests, which are often problematic in relation to accurate prediction, and the results of RTI can be used to document those specific instructional strategies found to be effective for a particular student (e.g., Aspel, Willis, & Faust, 1998; Cloud, 1994). In such cases the students, teachers, and parents all benefit.

This approach can be especially beneficial for ELLs who experience a normal level of difficulty, as they often need enhanced instructional support to make progress in bilingual, ESL, or general education classrooms (e.g., Collier & Thomas, 1997, 2002; Lucas, Henze, & Donato, 1990; Saenz, Fuchs, & Fuchs, 2005; Ukrainetz, 2006). The flexibility that RTI provides is important in that ELL difficulties may arise at any grade level and can be as varied as the number of ELL students enrolled in the school. There is no single intervention, program, strategy, or resource that will address all ELLs' needs.

This new approach provides the context for the sort of creative problem solving that addresses students' needs in our schools. As discussed in Chapter 3, although ELLs with academic difficulties may appear similar to students with intrinsic disabilities and are often referred to special education when difficulties arise, typical ELLs do not require special education interventions to learn effectively. In fact, they can be disadvantaged by traditional special education approaches (Cloud, 2006; Gersten & Woodward, 1994; McMaster, Fuchs, & Fuchs, 2006).

An RTI approach can be employed proactively to address the needs of ELL students across grade levels throughout the school, without students having to wait for referrals for assistance. If properly implemented, RTI promotes high-quality, consistent, effective instruction in general education settings for ELLs, which can prevent failure and frustration. Another potential benefit of this approach is that it includes assessment that can be designed to be closely linked to instruction, so that assessment provides diagnostic information and also functions to guide instruction. As well, assessment can be embedded in instruction, making it less disruptive to the learning process. Appropriately employed, RTI approaches shift the focus to more authentic assessment and away from overreliance on standardized measures, which are often administered acontextually (Damico, 1991; Gottlieb, 2006). In this way, intervention that can improve students' academic performance from the outset can be introduced without waiting for students to experience significant failure first. An RTI approach also provides opportunities for collaboration across disciplines to plan and implement classroom interventions. An increased focus on intervention can provide expanded or new roles for problem-solving team members to co-instruct with colleagues, demonstrate strategies, or model lessons in the classroom.

As discussed in greater detail in the section titled "Challenges to This Continuum of Services Framework," however, it is important that innovations like RTI be, in fact, innovative. There is a tendency to use the RTI framework, the tiered system, but to do so with decontextualized, fragmented, and artificial interventions and with monitoring and assessment tools that can easily subvert the process (e.g., Fuchs, 2003; Justice, 2006; Shinn, 1989; Vaughn & Fuchs, 2003). The great advantage of RTI approaches hinges on the application of authentic innovative teaching and remedial strategies and descriptive and authentic monitoring and assessment. Using decontextualized phonemic awareness activities or highly suspect tools such as the Dynamic Indicators of Basic Early Literacy Skills (DIBELS) does not benefit ELL students (e.g., Goodman, 2006; Wells, 1998).

A Solution-Seeking Approach

In our continuum of services framework, the ECOS team takes a solution-seeking approach to create the best possible interventions for specific difficulties that students are experiencing. The ECOS team begins by describing observable difficulties experienced by ELL students as specifically as possible. This constitutes the descriptive phase of the bi-level analysis paradigm. Then the team enters the explanatory phase of the paradigm by generating the possible causes from both an extrinsic (ELL) and intrinsic (disability) perspective. Once this is accomplished, it is time to craft interventions based on the causes identified. It is essential that the team first address the extrinsic causes

(Damico, Smith, & Augustine, 1996). In our model of ELL ± LD, we begin by assuming that the student who is having difficulties is a typical ELL, without a disability. It is much more likely that this is the case than that the student has a disability. The goal is to first address all possible causes that may lead a typical ELL to encounter difficulties in school. These possible causes can result from any of the seven integral elements listed in Chapter 1.

There are a number of reasons for beginning the process of determining interventions from the ELL perspective rather than the disability perspective. By implementing ELL interventions first, one can observe how these ELL students respond when their learning environment is enriched and their difficulties are specifically addressed. In keeping with the mediational and constructivist approaches to learning that have been addressed throughout this book (e.g., Krashen & Terrell, 1983; Lightbown & Spada, 2003; Vygotsky, 1978; Wells, 1998), prioritizing the ELL perspective will determine whether the contextualized mediation is all that is required. If what these students need is a learning environment that is more effective for learning a second language and learning through that second language, their performance will improve quite readily when interventions and programming address their ELL needs (e.g., Chalfant, Pysh, & Moultrie, 1979; Echevarria & Short, 2003; Freeman & Freeman, 2002; Genesee, Lindholm-Leary, Saunders, et al., 2006; Wells, 1998). Intervening in all of the students' languages and in as many academic contexts as possible often yields dramatic results for typical ELLs (Lindholm-Leary, 2006).

This brings us to a second reason for creating and implementing ELL interventions first. If the difficulties are truly related to learning English, there will be a clear contrast between what is observed in English and what is observed in the student's home language and familial context. Later in the chapter we elaborate on this process of using students' responses to these interventions to validate that the observed difficulties are normal manifestations of learning a second language and are to be expected for them as ELLs.

Seeking ELL Educators' Expertise to Generate ELL Interventions

At this point in the problem-solving process, the ELL experts may take the lead in generating and vetting ideas for the interventions that are to be implemented. The ELL educators on the team can filter each of the suggestions made by team members through an ELL perspective. They do this using what they know about second language learning and second language learners. This includes their knowledge of how ELLs learn (Bialystock, 2001), research on ELL reading and writing (Genesee, Lindholm-Leary, Saunders, et al., 2006), cross-cultural education (Banks, 2005), second language acquisition (Lightbown & Spada, 2003), linguistic and literacy transfer (Cummins, 2000), and research on bilingual education (Genesee, Lindholm-Leary, Saunders, et al., 2006). Although suggestions for interventions are welcomed from all ECOS team members, at this end of the continuum of services the team typically defers to the members with the most experience as well as theoretical background in teaching ELLs. If teams fail to listen to these professionals, they will tend to jump to intrinsic, special education approaches and strategies that should begin to appear only in the second half of the continuum.

The interventions that will most likely be discussed at this stage include instructional strategies and activities that address extrinsic factors in ELLs' learning environment that typically account for the difficulties. They are introduced as soon as they are identified for a student, as there is no need to put off interventions until extensive information has been gathered about the more general aspects of the student's home and school life. Thus, the services provided to these students flow smoothly and continuously. Who is to implement the strategies, in what contexts, toward what goals, and according to what timelines are also matters determined by the team.

As information continues to be collected, both about the specific behaviors exhibited by an ELL at school and about the integral factors defining that ELL's circumstances, the systemic interventions that are most appropriate to remedy any of the more general factors are also considered by the team. These interventions are discussed in greater detail in subsequent chapters.

After the ECOS team members help teachers implement specific interventions and accompanying ongoing, *authentic* assessments for a period of time, perhaps two to four weeks, the team reconvenes to examine the outcome. ECOS team members then examine the qualitative and quantitative information that was collected before and during the interventions. If the ELL's difficulties have resolved with specific and systemic interventions, plans need to be put in place to ensure that these interventions become part of the student's daily learning environment. Table 4.1 lists interventions considered most effective by the ECOS team for a student who was experiencing difficulty providing an oral narrative of a story that had just been read to him. The interventions listed in Table 4.1 are a limited set provided for exemplary purposes and may not be appropriate for all ELLs.

Using the chart in Appendix C, the ECOS team works together to generate a set of ELL interventions for each possible explanation that was generated earlier.

Seeking Special Educators' Expertise to Generate Special Education Interventions

When students' difficulties do not resolve with specific and systemic extrinsic interventions, the ECOS team continues to seek solutions. Revising or modifying the initial interventions may accomplish this objective. In addition, the team takes the next step of revisiting the specific difficulties from the perspective of any new information that has been added about the student, this time considering possible causes from a special education perspective. That is, what could account for this specific difficulty if it were related to an intrinsic condition such as a learning or reading disability or a specific language impairment (ELL + LD)?

When an individual has an intrinsic condition such as a learning disability or a language disorder, that individual exhibits both similarities to and differences from normal learners (Damico, 2003; Damico & Nelson, 2005; Perkins, 2005). In terms of similarities, both possess the species-specific capacity that Vygotsky referred to as "semiotic ability" (1978). Consequently, both are meaning makers and must adhere to the primary principles of meaning making (Bruner, 1990; Cambourne, 1988; Smith, 2004; Wells, 1986, 2003). This means that regardless of the differences due to the intrinsic impairment, effective and efficient acquisition and use of any of the meaning-making manifestations (for example, oral language, literacy, cognition, memory, intelligence) depend on immersion in a meaningful context where the individual has an opportunity to observe and actively engage in the process of meaning construction. In the contexts of language use or learning, there is always the need to create practical or pragmatic maps of the world by combining one's semiotic capacity with the linguistic conventions of one's language commu-

---

ECOS TEAM ACTIVITY

Using Table 4.1, generate discussion among team members regarding the effectiveness of the interventions listed. Assign one of three roles to team members: (1) *Critic:* finds something wrong with the intervention(s); (2) *Supporter:* comes up with ideas to support the effectiveness of the intervention(s); and (3) *Interventions Developer:* finds additional ELL interventions. The three groups develop their ideas and arguments and return to the whole group to discuss.

nity, so that meaning is constructed as an emerging phenomenon (Damico & Nelson, 2005; Perkins, 2005). This is accomplished through social interactions with more competent meaning makers who serve as models, guides, and mediators (Cambourne, 1988; Vygotsky, 1978; Wells, 1986, 2003).

As a result of the intrinsic impairment, however, the individual with the exceptionality also exhibits some differences from the normal learner and language user. For example, the individual with an intrinsic disability does not acquire skills or knowledge as easily, efficiently, or quickly as the normal individual. Second, this individual requires more focused mediation from more competent meaning makers in order to acquire new knowledge. That is, it is important to carefully tailor input and activities to the individual's zone of proximal development (Vygotsky, 1978). Sufficient and appropriate mediation is crucial when working with individuals with exceptionalities (Wells, 2003). Third, owing to the intrinsic impairment, the individual with the exceptionality does not easily create independent strategies to help him- or herself overcome the difficulties. Rather, more competent mediators must provide these strategies to the individual. Finally, the exceptional individual often exhibits difficulty in extending what he or she has learned from one context to another. Consequently, it is best to work on effective and needed meaning-making strategies within the authentic contexts of usage.

In reality, the difference between general education and special education does not rely on specialized techniques and strategies. Regardless of one's intrinsic capacity, the same meaning-making principles apply. When working with the exceptional individual, however, the teacher or interventionist must have more patience, must more carefully plan and implement appropriately targeted mediation, and must directly model and teach effective strategies to help the exceptional individual overcome the difficulties, and these activities should be accomplished in the contexts of need.

Given this understanding of the similarities and differences, to provide a continuum of interventions, the ECOS team then generates interventions from this perspective. Special education and ESL/bilingual professionals both contribute their experience and knowledge to this discussion. Just as with ELL specialists, special educators can generate interventions employing appropriate mediational techniques and beneficial strategies that will best meet the needs of these students if intrinsic difficulties exist (e.g., Cloud, 1994; Damico & Hamayan, 1992; Dunaway, 2004; Genesee, Paradis, & Crago, 2004; Westby & Vining, 2002). They can lend their experience to the ECOS team in working with students' disabilities while ESL/bilingual educators continue to remind the team that as an ELL, the student brings resources from the student's first language and can benefit from continued interventions in this language. All too often, once a disability perspective is taken in meeting student needs, the native language is viewed as unnecessary or even as a barrier to progress in the second language, despite current knowledge that this is not the case (Genesee, Paradis, & Crago, 2004). Questions of who is to implement the strategies, in what contexts, toward what goals, and according to what timelines are also determined by the team. Precise documentation of the interventions, their implementation, and the results can add qualitative information to the assessment data for diagnostic purposes. Table 4.2 lists special education interventions regarded as most effective by an ECOS team for a student who was experiencing difficulty providing an oral narrative of a story that had just been read to him. The interventions listed in Table 4.2 are a limited, exemplary set. It should be remembered that the strategies selected and the mediational level employed should always be tailored to the needs of the specific ELL and his or her disability.

Using the chart in Appendix D, the ECOS team works together to generate a set of special education interventions for each possible explanation that was generated earlier, and fills in the empty cells with these interventions.

(text continues on page 57)

Table 4.1 Generating ELL Interventions in Listening, Speaking, Reading, Writing, and Cultural Impact

---

Difficulty: Student cannot provide an effective oral narrative of a story just read to him (observed in English)

| | ELL Interventions | |
Possible ELL Explanations	In L1	In L2
Listening The student may not understand many stories because they are in English or because the cultural context of the stories or events is irrelevant or unfamiliar to him.	• Have the student listen to stories in his primary language. • Have parents tell stories to their child on a regular basis.	• Provide graphic aids during the storytelling. • Do some prelistening activities to prepare the student for comprehension. • Make certain the story or text is at the student's instructional level and that the classroom instruction is highly contextualized and comprehensible, with many visuals and much modeling or demonstration.
Speaking The student understands stories told in English but does not feel comfortable enough in his English-speaking abilities to create a narrative. The student may have developed his social English skills but may not have been taught the academic language of temporal organization (*first, then, next*) to be able to effectively narrate stories. The student may be able to tell stories in his native language after hearing a story in English.	• Provide parents with a schedule of daily school routines and request that they ask their child to retell the events of school in the primary language every day for a period of time. • Ask the parents to tell their child stories from their culture and then have the child narrate the stories to them on different occasions. • Once the practice is established, ask parents what they observed about the narratives. • Provide the child with pictures and a sequence graphic organizer during a storytelling, then have the child retell the story, event, or procedure in the primary language with the visual supports. • More directly focus on organizational language with a writing workshop approach that focuses on structural organizers during writing in the child's primary language. Have the parents, L1 tutors, and primary language volunteers practice retellings with the student, first with speaking prompts and graphic organizers and eventually without these supports. • Have the student retell interesting events from the news, from his past, or from the movies.	• Provide a graphic organizer during the story retelling. • Use a dialogic narrative format to create a short play (Paley, 1994). • Provide opportunity for the child to practice this language orally. • Model this language by incorporating it into a Language Experience Approach activity. • Allow the child to retell the event, story, or procedure with visuals, pictures, or manipulatives, by pointing, sequencing the pictures, or by recreating the event. • When appropriate, conduct a mini-lesson on various story structures used in Western literature or storytelling. • Provide a word bank of the key terms and verbally scaffold language needed to recount.

continued

Table 4.1 *continued*

Possible ELL Explanations	ELL Interventions	
	In L1	*In L2*

Reading

The story was not at the child's instructional level in English, and so he did not understand enough of the story to retell. He could recount some details that correspond to pictures if he has acquired the vocabulary.

Perhaps the child's primary language has a different structure for telling stories, and so his retelling in English sounds "out of order/out of sequence."

- If the student is literate in the native language, provide ample opportunities for reading stories in that language.

- Provide a sequence graphic organizer during the reading.
- Do some prereading activities to prepare the student for comprehension.
- Make certain the story or text is at the student's instructional level and that the classroom instruction is highly contextualized and comprehensible, with many visuals and much modeling or demonstration.

Writing

The student may be in the early stages of English language acquisition and is still developing his writing skills.

The student may not have been explicitly taught to write in English by someone who knows ESL strategies.

The student may be using his first language structures to negotiate writing in the second language; this may make the written text sound "out of sequence" in English.

The student may need to develop his writing skills the native language on which to build writing in English.

- Teach the student the specific sequential vocabulary to use when writing in his own language.
- Ask family members and others who know the student's language to incorporate sequential writing into daily events at home.
- Create Language Experience Approach stories in the student's L1 to model the sequential nature of a story or event.
- Contrast how storytelling or retelling differs in L1 and L2.

- Provide a sequence graphic organizer during the writing task.
- Provide the language of sequence in English in writing.
- Model this language by incorporating it into the writing of a Language Experience Approach story.
- Allow the child to "write" the event, story, or procedure with visuals, pictures, or manipulatives, by pointing, sequencing the pictures, or recreating the event.
- Explicitly teach the story structure used in Western literature or storytelling.
- Provide a word bank of the key terms and the sequential language needed to recount.

Cultural Impact

The cultural context of the story may be wholly unknown to the student. For example, the student may come from a culture where people do not keep animals in their houses as pets, and he may be appalled and distracted by a story about pets. This makes it difficult for him to concentrate reading comprehension and on the sequence of the story.

Different languages may have storytelling structures that differ from English.

- Ask the student to tell stories he knows from his home culture, and discuss similarities or differences.
- Use books and events from the student's native country to practice retelling in L1.
- Have the student bring in materials, books, and oral legends in his own language and from his own culture, and ask him to retell them and become comfortable in L1 before doing so in L2.

- Use books in English that relate to the student's native language or culture.

Table 4.2 Generating Special Education Interventions in Listening, Speaking, Reading, and Writing

Difficulty: Student cannot provide an oral narrative of a story that has just been just read to him

Possible Disability Explanations (Observed in student's two languages in academic and social contexts)	Special Education Interventions in L1 and L2
Listening The student may not understand the vocabulary (content or organizational words such as *first, next, last*), story events, inferred information, or narrative structure in L1 and L2. The student may exhibit distractibility.	• In each of these activities, ensure that each activity is contextualized and that the interactions between student and teacher provide the appropriate level of mediation (Crowe, 2003; Wells, 2003) so that when you present a story in L1 to practice oral retelling, it will be comprehended. With effective modeling and interspersed mediation (Damico & Damico, 1993), transfer the process to oral retelling in L2. • Use L1 to mediate and reduce overload when appropriate (Crowe, 2003; Johnson, 2004). • With appropriate mediation during shared reading activities (Dionysius, 1994), teach balanced comprehension strategies (Damico & Damico, 1993b). • Present the story with visual support (pictures, book) or dramatically (voices, demonstration, sound effects).
Speaking The student may have oral expressive difficulties in both languages with: • formulating ideas into sentences that clearly relay the meaning of the story, • the concept of sequencing in a variety of contexts, not just in story retelling, • the use of cohesive devices (e.g., conjunctions and pronoun references) to connect the story information, • organizing information into story structure.	• Rehearse a well-organized scene from a book or story that is rich in the needed vocabulary. This should culminate in a performance in front of other students. Provide appropriate verbal support and mediation, and any necessary visual support (2 to 8 picture cards). Transfer to L2 using the same events, then extend the process to stories presented auditorily of increasing length. • Employ appropriate exposure to necessary vocabulary and utterances of different length and complexity using communicative reading strategies (Norris, 1988) • During story telling activities provide sufficient modeling and then retelling of personal narratives employing interspersed retelling techniques (Koskinen, Gambrell, Kapinus, et al., 1988). • Employ targeted conversational intervention with a conversational format (Brinton & Fujiki, 1994). • Target specific grammatical and cohesive devices and provide contextualized exposure via modeling and then interactional commentary during representational play activities (Culotta, 1994). • Provide parents with a schedule of daily school routines and request that they ask their child to tell them about events at school in the primary language every day for a period of time. • Ask parents to tell their child stories from their culture and then have the child tell the stories to them on different occasions. • Once the practice is established, ask parents what they observed about the narratives. • Ask the student about interesting events from the news, from his past, or about a movie he saw recently.

continued

Table 4.2 *continued*

Possible Disability Explanations (Observed in student's two languages in academic and social contexts)	Special Education Interventions in L1 and L2
Reading Comprehension Poor comprehension due to inability to employ predictions and efficiently use background information.	• During shared reading, use mediational techniques like modeling, rereading, foreshadowing, characterization, and synopsis to weave meaning into the text when fluency changes suggest the child has lost comprehension (Damico, 2006).
	• Provide ample practice retelling orally with L1 partners, such as volunteers or parents for homework.
	• Activate background knowledge and ensure vocabulary and cultural references are understood with activities prior to and during story reading. Ensure that necessary mediation strategies are used during teachable moments (Dionisio, 1994; Wells, 2003).
	• Check comprehension frequently to prompt explanation or demonstration of vocabulary, events, and reasoning.
	• Use books with visual support to aid comprehension.
	• Provide ample practice retelling orally with L1 partners, such as volunteers or parents for homework, before the written retelling is sought.
Writing The student may have difficulty spelling in all languages.	• Develop spelling skills in the context of writing a story retelling in L1.
The student may have difficulties in oral language production that are also evident in written expression, including:	• Edit together for sentence and overall organization to ensure that it clearly relays what the student has understood; if easier, practice in L1.
• sentence formulation,	• Support decoding skills in context of story reading in L2.
• sequencing in a variety of contexts, including stories,	• Activate background knowledge and ensure vocabulary and cultural references are understood with activities prior and on-line discussion during story reading.
• use of cohesive devices in both languages (e.g., conjunctions, pronoun references),	• Use frequent comprehension checks that prompt explanation or demonstration of vocabulary, events and reasoning.
• organizing the information into story structure.	• Use books with visual support to aid comprehension.
	• Explicitly teach story structure, parts, and organization.

(text continued from page 53)

Challenges to This Continuum of Services Framework

Changing perspectives and practices presents challenges for professionals in all contexts, but when the changes involve the public domain (that is, public education), there may appear to be even more barriers to implementation (Parish & Arends, 1983). In this section we discuss several of the more salient challenges to the effective implementation of the ECOS framework. For some of the perceived challenges, the barriers are surprisingly minimal. For others they may be deceptively complex. We discuss these potential barriers in three primary groups: barriers created by a shift in practices, barriers created by regulatory and fiscal constraints, and barriers due to inertial expectations and tendencies.

ECOS TEAM ACTIVITY

Using Table 4.2, generate discussion among team members regarding the effectiveness of the interventions listed. Assign one of three roles to team members: (1) *Critic:* finds something wrong with the intervention(s); (2) *Supporter:* comes up with ideas to support the effectiveness of the intervention(s); and (3) *Interventions Developer:* finds additional special education interventions. The three groups develop their ideas and arguments and return to the whole group to discuss.

Shifting Practices

The first set of perceived barriers emerges with the necessity of altering one's practices to accommodate a more effective framework. Changing practices, whether it involves procedural modifications, test selection, interpretative notions, or intervention approaches, is never easy. We all have a tendency to employ practices that we are comfortable with and that appear to have met our professional needs in the past. These familiar routines and practices give us confidence and enable us to operate with less cognitive effort when we are implementing them. Once it has been shown that these practices are not effective and not the best approaches to service delivery, however, we must strive to adapt if we are to maintain our professional integrity. This means learning new frameworks, methods, strategies, and knowledge bases if necessary. For illustrative purposes, we will mention several important changes we may be expected to make in implementing the ECOS framework.

When school problem-solving groups such as ECOS teams shift their focus toward anticipating and preventing difficulties rather than taking a "wait-and-fail" attitude with the student before assessment and placement, many things must change. Most obviously, teams will have to resist the impulse to label before programming. The team—and the individuals that make up the team—must not indulge the initial temptation to try and localize the problems within the child (Cummins, 1984). Rather, the immediate orientation should be to assume the child's intrinsic competence. This individual should be considered initially as a normal learner who has merely fallen prey to external variables that interfere with learning (e.g., Damico & Hamayan, 1992; Fradd & Weismantal, 1989; García & Ortiz, 1988). If this shift in practice occurs, energy spent on finding definitive diagnoses can be redirected toward finding creative ways to intervene while identifying the causes of the ELL's difficulties and the effectiveness of interventions through the student's responses to those interventions. With this shift in both perspective and practice, the localization of problems within the student should occur only after multiple attempts to identify the external operational variables have proved unsuccessful and only after reasonable and appropriate interventions to overcome external variables have been tried and have failed.

Second, collaboration should increase in schools as professionals realize that no one professional perspective can address all ELLs' needs. These collaborative relationships will require professionals to step outside their traditional roles and share their perspectives, knowledge, and experiences with their colleagues through creative programming. In fact, this is one of the primary foci of the ECOS teams, a primary reason for this book, and why many implementation exercises have been provided in these pages. This process, however, may not be easy to accomplish. When changing to more collaborative practices, the professional pairings that may emerge as a result of collaborative interventions may be foreign to the school setting and to the work habits of the involved individuals. Initially a new collaboration may feel threatening to the individuals involved, and the arrangement may seem cumbersome. However, with some experience working together and with the successes obtained through collaborative efforts, any initial awkwardness can be overcome.

One reason that an honest attempt at collaboration will work is due to the complexity of service delivery to ELLs. Any professional who has worked with this population knows that many variables and complicating factors must be addressed, and it is rarely possible to face these issues alone. Consequently, while team building, the school personnel will face challenges, but they also will observe that many of these challenges and the complexities wrapped in ELL service delivery become more effectively and efficiently addressed as the collaborations within the ECOS team improve. Success is typically the watchword as team members acquire new information for their professional knowledge bases in areas that may be completely outside their previous experience. Honing collaborative practices, understanding the skills and expertise of other professionals, and building trust occur over time with ongoing teamwork (Bahr, Fuchs, & Fuchs, 1999; Chalfant & Pysh, 1989; Fradd, 1993).

A third example of changing practices involves a direct collaboration of a different kind: collaboration with the appropriate administrative personnel. When modifying practice to improve service delivery, it is not sufficient that only the team members change. They must secure the assent of the classroom teachers and the parents of the students they serve if the changes are to be successful (Blosser, 1990; Damico, 1987; Gutkin, 1990; Marvin, 1990; Montgomery, 1990). To gain that kind of support, it is often necessary to secure administrative support as well. Administrative support is necessary to initiate and sustain the level of systemic change required to shift to a more proactive framework. Inadequate funding for personnel and resources to support ECOS team involvement in the classroom strains the system and sets the team up for failure if these needs are not addressed. However, these issues are not within the bailiwick of most team members. Rather, they are the purview of administrators, and therefore collaboration with principals, supervisors, and coordinators is needed to address these issues. Chronicle 4.1 describes a remarkable program that takes a proactive stance and involves the collaboration of professionals with different areas of expertise.

The approach described in this handbook encourages all educators in a school to develop and modify their practices accordingly, to build professional bridges with others outside their field, to consult their colleagues regularly, and to work collegially to address the needs of their students. There will always be students who need the very specific services of a particular professional in a particular program, but we believe that the learning environment for all students is enriched when the professionals in the school collaborate and are encouraged to consult one another outside of a formal protocol. The recognition that changing practices presents opportunities rather than barriers should help overcome potential challenges.

Regulatory and Fiscal Constraints

When ECOS teams and the ECOS continuum of services are discussed on school sites, especially when special education is involved, some of the challenges most frequently mentioned are the regulatory and fiscal constraints placed on school personnel. Professionals are often concerned that the various innovations suggested are not consistent with federal regulations or guidelines and that the fiscal constraints are insurmountable (e.g., American Federation of Teachers, 1994; Bhat, Rapport, & Griffin, 2000; McLaughlin, Fuchs, & Hardman, 1999; Murphy, 1996; Parrish & Chambers, 1996; Tomlinson, 1985). In the case of the suggestions for the ECOS team and the continuum of services framework, this is more a perception than a reality.

In remedial public education in the United States, the major regulatory instrument is the Individuals with Disabilities Education Act. First formulated

A Proactive Program through Cross-Disciplinary Collaboration

By a speech-language pathologist

The Toronto District School Board in Toronto, Ontario, Canada, provides a remarkable example of interdisciplinary collaboration in their Kindergarten Early Language Intervention (KELI) Program. The goal of this innovative program is to provide early oral language intervention for young students from schools in low socioeconomic areas as a way of preventing or alleviating later challenges with academic, literacy, and social skills. Kindergarten teachers from general education classes nominate students who appear to be learning language differently from other students. It is important to note that the Toronto District School Board is one of the most multicultural and diverse education systems in the world. Based on the experience that these general education teachers have in working with many students from different language backgrounds, the teachers nominate students who appear to be learning language differently from other ELLs as they progress through their junior kindergarten year.

The speech-language pathologist and KELI teacher combine information from classroom observations, language and academic screening activities, and nomination checklists from general education teachers to come up with specific criteria for selecting students for the KELI program. The selected students attend a special program that is designed to provide supplementary instruction rather than supplant the time these children spend during the regular school hours. In this program, students attend school for two half-days in addition to the five half-days of their regular kindergarten program at their neighborhood schools.

In the KELI classes, a speech-language pathologist and kindergarten teacher, with special education qualifications, co-instruct classes of eight students to provide them with rich learning opportunities to use oral language, literacy, and social interaction skills. The speech-language pathologist provides interventions that are completely contextualized, so that children are never given language tasks that are not meaningful and relevant. So that these students can build meaningful connections, each unit of instruction is designed around a theme, with five to seven related stories. The activities in the unit, for example story retelling, dramatic play, and snack preparation, all relate to the vocabulary, events, and messages in the stories. In this model, the expertise of the speech-language pathologist and of the kindergarten teacher are combined in ways that support students in developing their expressive and receptive language and early literacy skills.

The teacher and speech-language pathologist have incredible learning opportunities on a daily basis as they blend their roles and share responsibilities through planning and co-instructing all aspects of the lessons together. Administering assessments collaboratively and reporting results to parents and administrators, offer further opportunities for these professionals to learn from one another.

Questions for discussion:

- What would it take for your district to set up a similar program that offers intervention proactively, offers instruction to a group of students beyond the school day, and entails interdisciplinary collaboration?
- Describe some of the potential benefits of this professional collaboration for these students.
- What professional strengths and resources does each professional bring to the classroom?

in 1975 as PL 94-142 and reauthorized several times since then, IDEA is the congressional act that results in the Regulations Governing the Assistance to States for Education of Children with Disabilities Program and the Preschool Grants for Children with Disabilities (2006). In the most recent reauthorization of IDEA, the 2004 Individuals with Disabilities Education Improvement Act, PL 108-466, some rather significant changes were introduced that support the need for and implementation of frameworks and processes like the ECOS team.

Because of continued disenchantment with the traditional approach to special education, the 2004 reauthorization of IDEA discussed several obstacles to implementing effective special education services. Among the obstacles cited were that implementation of the act had been impeded by (1) low expectations for the students, (2) an insufficient focus on applying replicable research involving proven methods of teaching and learning for students with disabilities, (3) a disproportionately high number of referrals and placements of "minority children" in special education, and (4) the application of discrepancy models that used inappropriate tests, which often led to disproportionate placements. To address these and other concerns, the 2004 act requires a number of innovations that provide the opportunity for local educational agencies (LEAs) and individual schools to implement programs like the ECOS approach. For example, the reauthorization requires states to submit a plan that provides assurances of policies and procedures designed to prevent the inappropriate overidentification or disproportionate representation by race and ethnicity of children as children with disabilities. In effect, this provides an opening for innovative programs like ECOS to be suggested as ways to meet the federal plan requirements.

Additionally and significantly, the document provides for more specific incorporation of "early intervention services" rather than the use of discrepancy models to place students in special education programs. The phrase "early intervention services" refers to exactly what ECOS is designed to do: address the needs of students and determine the need and eligibility for special education services on the basis of pre-referral interventions rather than assessments. In reality, this was also the intent of the last reauthorization of IDEA, in 1997. However, the phrase used in that document was "pre-referral intervention," and it was merely recommended. In the 2004 version, the focus shifts from evaluation to intervention as the primary determinant of placement. Although the 2004 act does not directly mention RTI or any other specific approach, the phrase "early intervention services" points toward such approaches. In fact, the document also authorizes the appropriation of federal special education funds to implement an early intervention process to try and bolster academic achievement before referral to special education; the monies that may be used for such an approach may be as much as 15% of the IDEA funding in some states.

The new reauthorization of IDEA and the regulations that implement it (2006) have also required other changes that provide an opportunity for innovations such as ECOS teams. For example, with regard to the category of learning disabilities, the regulations state that an LEA may use a process that determines whether the child responds to scientifically based intervention and that state education agencies may not require the use of discrepancy models. Rather, LEAs may use alternative research-based procedures to determine classification as learning disabled. Finally, the new documents (as with the 1997 reauthorization) do not require test scores to make placement decisions into special education. In fact, in the 2004 version, references to tests have been changed to "assessment materials," thus downplaying the more traditional testing paradigm.

It should be pointed out that these regulatory changes reduce other concerns as well. For example, concern has often been expressed about collecting information on children with suspected difficulties. In many LEAs, certain kinds of data cannot be collected for special education considerations unless parents sign a consent form. Although there has always been disagreement as to whether this was necessary or not, a focus on early intervention services *before* placement reduces this concern. Procedurally, then, the ECOS team does not need consent to do a formal observation or classroom-based assessment of a student under the law's new reauthorization.

The fiscal constraints suggested as reason to refrain from implementing innovations such as ECOS teams is also more of a perceived challenge rather than a real one. These perceptions typically result from an inaccurate understanding of special education funding issues. For example, there is a misconception on the part of many professionals that the bulk of financing for special education comes from the federal government and that regulations governing those monies are highly restrictive. This is not the case. Current IDEA monies may be used for early intervention innovations (up to 15% of total IDEA Part B funds in some states). Especially in kindergarten to third grade, such expenditures are encouraged. In fact, the federal regulations *require* several states to use monies for early intervention services. Second, although Congress was authorized by PL 94-142 to provide as much as 40% of the average per-child expenditure for special education in public schools by 1982, this has never occurred. Currently, the federal government provides less than 10% of the funding to states for special education, and the state and local governments provide more than 90% of the average per-child expenditure for special education in public schools (Murphy, 1996; Parrish & Chambers, 1996). Finally, since state and local governments provide most of the funding, and since the current reauthorization of IDEA encourages innovations such as ECOS or RTI, there is an opportunity to influence state and local regulations and practices. Insofar as the average per-pupil cost of special education is is estimated to be twice as great as that of regular education (Chaikind, Danielson, & Brauen, 1993) and these costs are escalating (Murphy, 1996; Parrish & Chambers, 1996; Tomlinson, 1985), local agencies should be willing to support any innovations that provide better services at a more affordable price.

The Challenge of Inertial Concepts

The last barrier to implementation of the ECOS team and the continuum of services framework may be the most problematic. That is the tendency toward inertia in professional matters. In physics, inertia is the tendency of a body to remain at rest or to stay in motion unless acted on by an outside force. We can employ that concept metaphorically to describe the professional tendency to resist action or change.

Although it is sometimes the case that defensible innovation is recognized and implemented, too often when innovations are suggested there is a reaction against them that may be traced to sheer inertia. That is, the resistance is determined less by the difficulties that might accompany such an innovation and more by reluctance to change. Inertia may manifest in one of two forms. The first is direct opposition to the innovation by teachers and other professionals involved in its implementation. These confrontations often take the form of objections to innovation for a variety of reasons. Often cited in this context are regulatory and fiscal constraints, refutations of the theoretical, empirical, or clinical basis for the proposed changes, or the dramatization of barriers to implementation. These arguments are advanced in such a way as to stop the innovation. Examples of this type of overt resistance have already been discussed: the increased effort and training needed to shift practices and the claim that such changes are too expensive. However, these often are not legitimate barriers but tactics employed because of the inertial tendencies of professionals.

Another example is the frequently cited claim that the federal government allows only "scientifically based" assessment and intervention practices when discussing regulatory or funded activities or initiatives. The claimants then quickly assert or assume that this means practices based on experimental research. This is not the case. Scientific research is not limited to the experimental paradigm. Rather, scientific research includes any practices reported and documented in research articles published in peer-reviewed professional journals, and this includes all forms of naturalistic and observational research as well (Cronbach, 1957; Lum, 2002; Wright, 2005). Indeed, much of what we know about human development and learning is the result of research that is not experimental in nature (Simmons-Mackie & Damico, 2003). To presume that the demonstrations of efficacy and effectiveness must hinge on experimental research that often does not enable the appropriate investigation of real learning and meaning making is not defensible (e.g., Allington, 2002; Bruner, 1983; Cronbach, 1975; Pearson & Samuels, 1980; Strauss, 2001). Challenges to innovation based on this claim are most likely an overt reflection of the inertial tendency.

The second form the inertial reaction may take is more subtle and therefore more problematic. It involves a superficial adherence to the innovation while the agent continues to employ traditional or non-innovative components, activities, or practices that may actually subvert the innovation. A single illustration should suffice. Over the past few years, there have been many attempts to apply RTI approaches using the three tiers of intervention that quickly disintegrated into discrete, fragmented, and decontextualized interventions or tests rather than contextualized, authentic, meaning-based interventions and assessment as documentation. For example, the professional may employ decontextualized phonemic awareness drills or activities as the well-designed and well-implemented intervention in order to determine the learning responses of the students. The problem is that in the case of ELLs (and many other learners), such decontextualized activities are not effective teaching or intervention strategies (e.g., Freeman & Freeman, 2001, 2002; Krashen, 2001; Wells, 2003). A poor response to intervention, then, is likely to be an indictment of the method and not the child. Further, the measures employed to assess change might also be less innovative. Documenting change by using tools such as the DIBELS measure (Kaminski & Good, 1998) further subverts the excellent goals of the RTI approach because this tool is less innovative and is problematic as a measure of authentic literacy skills (e.g., Goodman, 2006; Manning, Kamii, & Kato, 2005). Consequently, while the framework and the emphasis on placing intervention before evaluation are positive, using the same tired, ineffectual teaching strategies and assessment procedures will significantly dilute the effectiveness of RTI. In effect, because of the tendency to inertia, we merely see old wine in new bottles, and the needs of the children are not met.

It should be stated, of course, that the tendency to inertia is often unconscious and the individuals who exhibit these reactions may not recognize this tendency. Tom Skrtic (1991b) has written very persuasively that the real reason for reluctance to change—that is, the tendency to inertia—is an under-

---

ECOS TEAM ACTIVITY

Become experts in the laws that govern special education. Assign pairs of ECOS team members different sections of the law. Each dyad's task is to scrutinize a section of the law with the purpose of figuring out how a continuum of services framework could be created within the legal parameters.

lying culture of the schools that has been assimilated by the teachers and other professionals. As with other cultural knowledge systems, this cultural system creates expectations and places various boundaries on the awareness and behaviors of those who interact with it. Unless the professionals are inherently reflective or are given explicit reasons to change, the tendency is to change only superficial mechanisms, and not the underlying knowledge system. This is why the overt or subverting reactions occur. Real change, according to Skrtic, depends on changing both the superficial operational mechanisms and the underlying cultural expectations. In this book, we have designed procedures and exercises that will assist in these changes. We describe some efforts and discuss the tremendous need for advocacy as a catalyst for additional change in the last chapter.

A Forum for Crafting Interventions

The challenges just described are also what make this approach such a potential catalyst for change and growth in addressing the diverse needs of students. The ECOS team could become the structure within a school that promotes creative programming, fosters innovative collaboration, and provides a forum for crafting both specific and general interventions for ELLs and for all students. This could also mean that when systemic interventions are implemented, general education students could also benefit, by being exposed to the same good practices designed for ELLs (Chalfant & Pysh, 1989; Friend & Cook, 1996; Maeroff, 1993). The approach to teaching and learning in these schools will broaden, and they will be better able to accommodate the diverse linguistic and cultural backgrounds and academic needs of students who enter through their doors every day.

The success of this approach would be drastically diminished, however, if ECOS teams relied on one-size-fits-all programming. Taking a "cookbook" approach to crafting interventions can only lead to failure, as each ELL or group of ELLs that is experiencing difficulties comes with a different set of circumstances that warrants careful consideration. The process described in this handbook requires significant creativity: it requires ECOS teams to assess students' and teachers' needs, generate reasonable explanations for a host of difficulties, elicit ideas, and devise interventions and programming. For this process to work, ECOS team members should have due regard for a few key principles.

Key Principles for Crafting Interventions for ELLs

Often, the interventions suggested and implemented for ELLs are those that have traditionally worked for monolingual English speakers. In the school, staff members who are not familiar with ELL education assume that these interventions will work similarly with ELLs. However, some strategies that were designed for native speakers of English are not effective for ELLs. Sometimes the intervention proves successful in the short term but not in the long term. Lack of success can also lead the team to erroneously assume that the difficulties are related to intrinsic disabilities. Adapting evidence-based interventions developed for one population for use by another ignores the learning principles known to be true for the second population. Although no one solution can address the needs of all ELLs, there are some key principles that should be followed in designing interventions and support services. The key principles discussed in this section have been derived from research in general and bilingual education, sociolinguistics, social second language acquisition, natural learning theory, and social action theory. ECOS teams that allow these principles to guide the creation of interventions for ELLs rather than imposing prepackaged programs will have more success.

Principle 1: *Second language input must be made comprehensible for proficiency to develop.*

The language that surrounds an ELL must be contextualized and presented with a physical or visual referent so that it is meaningful; this is a necessary requirement for successful language acquisition (Krashen, 1982). This principle, often referred to as the *comprehensible input hypothesis*, should remind the ECOS team that most of what people hear in their non-native language is incomprehensible noise, and whatever interventions the team devises should work toward making meaning out of this noise. Thus, interventions in English should always be accompanied by a visual or physical context such as a graphic representation, pictures, photographs, physical models, manipulatives, or realia, to help ELLs makes sense of the words or the text.

Principle 2: *A second language develops more easily when learners are actively engaged in authentic use of the language.*

When learners are focused on using the second language for meaningful communication, proficiency in that language develops more efficiently (Smith, 2006). ELLs need authentic reasons to communicate. They need to listen to understand, they need to say things they want to say, they need to read to gather information (hopefully about something they are interested in), and they need to write about things they want to write about. When communication is authentic, learners also become actively involved in the interaction and use of language, and this helps push the language learning forward significantly as well. The implication of this principle for ECOS teams is that the interventions they recommend must have authentic communication at their base. Classroom tasks must require listening for understanding, oral explanations or summaries, reading to collect information, and writing to inform others.

Principle 3: *Because of a common underlying proficiency, concepts and structures that are learned in one language have the potential to transfer to the other language that the student is learning.*

There is a common underlying proficiency that is the basis for learning and producing any language (Cummins, 2000). This underlying proficiency allows for strong cross-language relationships that help the learner. This principle suggests using the first language as a resource for developing the second language, as well as a means for learning new concepts. Any concept can be previewed and learned in ELLs' native languages first to facilitate learning in the second language. The concepts do not have to be re-taught in the second language if they have been established in the first language. Interventions should be implemented in both languages as a way to check for understanding and progress. This principle also implies that past experiences must be used to scaffold comprehension by building connections with existing knowledge and skills.

Principle 4: *When you learn a second language in an additive bilingual context, you are more likely to reach high levels of proficiency in both languages than if you were learning the second language in a subtractive bilingual context. In the latter situation, not only is the native language likely to be sacrificed but the second language may not develop to an optimal level of profiency.*

In an additive bilingual situation, an individual adds proficiency in a new language without losing proficiency in the native language. In contrast, in a subtractive bilingual situation, as the individual becomes more proficient in the new language, proficiency in the native language diminishes, or worse, is lost altogether (Lambert, 1974). ELLs' loss of the native tongue in the course of acquiring English can have severe social, cognitive, and academic consequences for the students and their families. For this and other reasons, team members should never implement an intervention or programming that will cause ELLs to lose their first language, identity, culture, or will cut them off from their families and communities. Chronicle 4.2 gives an example of a simple strategy that brings in students' native languages and helps make the classroom more effective for both ELLs and monolingual English-speaking students.

Principle 5: *Second language acquisition occurs in predictable stages.*

The stages of second language acquisition are generally defined as preproduction, early production, speech emergence, intermediate fluency, and fluency (Krashen & Terrell, 1983). Although there is little consistency in the time it takes individual learners to go through the stages, the order is quite well defined. This has some implications for what to expect from learners in different stages (Hamayan & Freeman, 2006). It also means that the interventions devised must be appropriate for each particular stage of second language acquisition. An intervention is more likely to be effective if it accords with the particular stage of second language acquisition that the learner is passing through.

Principle 6: *To succeed at school, ELLs must develop conversational fluency as well as academic proficiency.*

It is not enough for students to develop everyday conversational skills in English. Academic proficiency, which is quite different from conversational fluency, is key to academic achievement (Cummins, 2006). In addition, students need to develop a third aspect of language proficiency, discrete language skills that help them learn about language. This principle reminds ECOS team members that ELLs may sound proficient in English but may still be lacking the language skills necessary for success in school. Thus, any assessment of ELLs' second language proficiency must address all aspects of language, and gaps in any of the three aspects of language proficiency must be addressed with specific interventions.

Principle 7: *Some ELLs may take more than five years to develop a high enough level of academic proficiency to survive in a classroom where abstract concepts are taught in English.*

Although many ELLs develop fluency in social English, they may take five to nine years to catch up to native English speakers in academic English (Cummins, 2006). Most ELLs are not given this long to develop the language skills they need to survive in an academic setting where English is the medium of instruction. ELLs must have repeated opportunities to use language in a

(text continues on page 69)

ECOS TEAM ACTIVITY

Discuss these principles during an ECOS team meeting by posing the question, "What evidence of the application of these principles do we see in our school?" If a principle seems to be lacking, then ask the question, "What needs to be done for this principle to be in effect in our practice?"

Viewing Students' Languages as Resources

By a monolingual English speech-language pathologist

I co-teach a kindergarten classroom with a general education kindergarten teacher. We have children from many different language backgrounds, including English, and for a while I felt the need to incorporate the students' native languages into classroom work. I felt it would help the students, some of whom seemed to be having significant language difficulties. I had read about the academic advantages for ELLs when they continue to use and develop their native languages while learning English, even when they may have specific language impairments. So it seemed logical to use all the students' linguistic and cultural resources in school.

Two strategies that were already in place were interviews with parents about their child's L1 use that we did during the intake process, and the use of multilingual greetings as part of our daily entry process with the children. Both practices provided a great deal of insight into the children's languages and cultures and allowed us to connect with the families of these students even though we didn't speak their languages. Our students' families appreciated the fact that we wanted to know about their cultural and linguistic backgrounds.

When we started using the multilingual greetings at school, some children found it strange to hear their language in that context. Somehow these very young children had already got the message that school was the English domain and their home languages were not welcome there. I even heard one five-year-old advising another child against using her native language in class. We continued to remind the children that we wanted to learn about their languages and they were welcome to speak their other languages in our classroom. I would tell them how fortunate they are for knowing how to speak many languages. Eventually, with all the encouragement, the greetings began to take off, with the students participating more freely and using different languages. Monolingual English speakers were encouraged to try each others' greetings, and everyone seemed to like using Dora the Explorer's "hola" on a regular basis!

I felt it was time to extend the use of students' native languages in class. I did this by taking the step of previewing important vocabulary for each unit in their home languages before reading the related stories. The Family and Friends unit was next, so I made up a homework assignment for students to do with their parents or other family members (Table C4.2). I wrote out some of the important vocabulary that the students would be hearing in English over the next weeks—for example, *mother, father, sister, brother, grandmother, grandfather, aunt, uncle,* and *cousin.* Those words were listed in the first column. In the next column, parents were asked to write the name of their language and how each word is written in their language. In the last column parents wrote phonetic versions of how the words are pronounced, using the English alphabet. In this way we could attempt to approximate the spoken words if the students were hesitant to say them, so that they could 'teach' us. Examples of a few words were provided in French.

The results were truly amazing! I wasn't certain how clear the directions I had given were, but I guess they were clear enough. Every student brought the homework back! I made transparencies so that I could share them with everyone. That year we had approximately 17 languages represented in the class, and it was beautiful to see all these written out. The students were very proud to share the homework they had completed with their parents and to

continued

Table C4.2 Homework: Family and Friends

We are collecting different ways of saying these words in English and in other languages. Please help your child teach us how you say these words at home in your language.

Example:

Word	Language	How you write it	How you say it (i.e., how it sounds)
Mother Father	French English	*mere* *papa*	*mair* *papa*

Name: _____ Home Language:_____

Word	How you write it	How you say it (i.e., how it sounds)
Mother		
Father		
Sister		
Brother		
Grandmother		
Grandfather		
Aunt		
Uncle		
Friend		

help us pronounce the words we couldn't say very well. Even students who had previously indicated they didn't speak another language willingly demonstrated what they knew in their language in this activity.

From this simple activity, we all gained a great deal of linguistic and cultural knowledge. The students began seeing similarities and differences between their languages. We also learned that in some languages different words are used when referring to an aunt who is your mother's sister and your father's sister; the same was true for grandparents and cousins. We learned that in some languages there are different words to indicate you are referring to older or younger siblings. When reading a story that featured a grandfather, we made a word web with all the different ways we knew to say grandfather.

continued

It was fascinating and encouraging to continue to find ways to incorporate students' native languages into instruction even at this young age for children who experience challenges in both languages.

Questions for discussion:

- What knowledge and beliefs were required to implement these L1 activities and practices? What are some potential long-term benefits of these practices?
- How could teachers at other grade levels adapt these L1 strategies and routines for use in their classroom instruction?
- How could the ECOS team support English-speaking teachers who want to begin incorporating ELLs' native languages into their instruction?

(text continued from page 66)
variety of meaningful contexts. The ECOS team must pay close attention to the opportunity that an ELL has had to develop academic language proficiency. The team must advocate for the best learning environment that would promote the development of academic proficiency among ELLs.

Validating Difficulties and Intervening across Contexts

By observing the seven principles, ECOS teams can design interventions based on the hypothesized causes of specific behaviors. It is critical that these interventions be implemented across contexts and in all of the ELLs' languages (Goldstein, 2004). By monitoring the progress of ELLs in both of their languages, the team can identify the contexts in which difficulties occur. Expanding on the hypothesis of a common underlying language proficiency that gives rise to all meaning-making manifestations, including language, cognition, memory and intelligence, we think it unlikely that an individual with a true disability would express that disability in one language but not another (e.g., Carroll, 1993; Cummins, 1984; Damico, 1992). If the difficulty is intrinsic to the individual, it would be expected to manifest in all the ELL's languages and in all the contexts that lead to its use. Here is another excellent reason to maintain learning in both the native language and English: once ELLs begin to lose their home languages, as may occur in a subtractive school environment, it is very difficult to uncover an intrinsic disability as the cause of the students' difficulties (Cummins, 2000).

An Example of Validating the Source of Difficulties

In the example we are using in this chapter, a student experiences difficulties retelling a story that has just been read to him. A possible ELL explanation for this difficulty is that the student is in the early stages of second language acquisition (see Table 4.1). If so, there are a number of ways that his limited English proficiency may become manifest. For example, the student may understand a story read in English or a procedure presented in class but may not have enough oral English to provide a sufficiently well-organized and coherent narrative about the story or procedure. Further, he may not have much experience with narratives, so the problem becomes one of experiential diversity in addition to the linguistic diversity (McCabe, 1989). To understand this complex situation, ECOS team members need to find out the source of the difficulty. Does the difficulty come from the student's poor comprehension of the story told in English? Does he understand the story because the teacher has made it highly comprehensible, but not speak English well enough to supply a coherent and appropriate narrative in front of his teacher or peers in English? Has he not had experience using narratives? Has he not been encouraged to employ different types of narratives so that he can relate his various experiences? Or is the difficulty due to an intrinsic problem that affects his entire meaning making process so that he has difficulty no matter what language or context is asked of him?

ECOS teams may suggest that classroom teachers provide contextualized models, demonstrations, and mini-lessons on the uses of narratives during storytime and storytelling activities (Paley, 1994), in critical literacy activities (Edelsky, 1999), and during writing workshops (Freeman & Freeman, 2002). However, this should always be done within context. The team will want to know if the student can employ narratives in any circumstance and if the student can benefit from various types of cross-modality scaffolds when attempting to create a narrative (e.g., Alvermann, 1991). The ECOS team will also ask the teacher to provide contextualized assignments using dialogue journals (Bode, 1989) and by making narrative construction the focus of that week's homework for everyone. The teacher may have students go home and narrate the events of the day to an adult throughout the week. With young children, teachers may place a name tag on each child (in the child's native language) that reads, "Ask me about science today." Older students may have to practice narrating the events of a procedure in their native language to an adult or volunteer in the room before retelling and reporting to the class (Wells, 1990).

After a couple of weeks of this practice and support in hearing and employing various types of narratives across languages and contexts, the team reconvenes to discuss how ELLs responded to the interventions. It is important for the team to contrast what happened in various language contexts as well as in nonverbal settings. It is also important to note whether the students were able to use their social language to construct narratives in either language but were not able to use their academic language to narrate more abstract concepts. With the recommended interventions implemented, ELLs who do not have intrinsic difficulties with sequencing should be able to show progress in at least one of the contexts and languages and would typically benefit from various contextual and interactional scaffolds (Trousdale, 1990; Wells, 1998, 2003). ELLs who show the same difficulties across contexts and in all their languages, even in enriched, highly contextualized learning environments, must proceed to more intense intervention. This process of validating difficulties emphasizes the need to look at ELLs' performance in as many contexts as possible. If teams looked only at ELLs' performance in English (such as work samples, oral or written output, or performance on standardized measures), they would never develop a complete profile of the students and would not be able to confirm with any certainty the source of the students' difficulties (Sanchez-Lopez, 2006).

Home Language and Culture as a Resource

Viewing the home language and culture as resources is a key precept for the ECOS team in planning and implementing interventions for ELLs. First, the home language and culture serve as a crude gauge to assess whether the difficulties that a learner is experiencing are due to an intrinsic disability. By intervening in both languages, it becomes apparent whether the difficulties experienced by the ELL exist in the home language as well as in English. Assessment in two languages across contexts provides invaluable diagnostic information, as it is generally accepted that difficulties resulting from intrinsic disabilities would be evident in both languages and in multiple contexts. If an ELL's difficulties are evident only in English and are not present in similar activities when the student is using the native language, it is likely that they are simply manifestations of second language learning. However, if the difficulties appear in both languages, the ECOS team reconvenes for further data collection and to plan interventions from a special education perspective. The results of these interventions can also provide qualitative information to aid in assessing students who are referred for special education services.

Second, the home language and culture serve as a basis for learning new concepts, as well as for developing proficiency in the second language. It is much easier to acquire language forms when contextual scaffolding is available and background information or experiences can be drawn on to aid in processing or novel information (Bruner, 1990; Smith, 2004, Wells, 2003).

Bilingualism and Disabilities

In many academic settings, once it has been determined that an ELL does indeed have an intrinsic learning disability, use of the home language often falls by the wayside, owing to the common misconception that students having significant difficulties should use their "limited language learning" resources to focus on one language (Damico & Hamayan, 1992). As Principles 3 and 4 suggest, however, research shows exactly the opposite: maintaining ELLs' first languages "is beneficial for psychosocial, cognitive, educational reasons and dual language skills need to be viewed and developed as positive personal, social, educational, vocational assets especially in subtractive bilingual environments" (Genesee, Paradis, & Crago, 2004, p. 151).

A growing body of evidence supports the hypothesis that work in the first language helps second language development. For example, when normally developing bilingual preschoolers were taught one set of words in their first language followed by the same words in their second language and another set of words only in their second language, they demonstrated understanding of words in the first condition with fewer trials (Kiernan & Swisher, 1990). The results of similar studies have shown that the first language supports learning a second language even among children with specific language impairment. When bilingual preschoolers diagnosed with specific language impairment were presented with one set of words in their first language followed by the same words in their second language, and another set in the second language followed by the same words in their first language, they took fewer trials to understand words that were presented initially in their first language (Perozzi, 1985; Perozzi & Sanchez, 1992). Evidence continues to emerge indicating that the faculty for bilingualism is adequately strong and that more than one language can be learned even under conditions of language impairment (Paradis, Crago, Genesee, et al., 2003).

If ELLs are found through this process to have intrinsic learning disabilities (ELL + LD), these students should receive all the interventions and support at the ELL end of the continuum, as well as the specialized support that special education can provide in both of the ELL's languages. In practice, this means that although many of the same meaning-based and contextualized activities and teaching approaches may be employed, the mediational techniques, contextual scaffolds, and strategies and contexts within which interventions occur will be carefully planned and implemented (e.g., Culotta, 1994; Crowe, 2003; Kasten, 1998; Norris, 1988). In this way, students with exceptionalities gain the benefits of the principles of meaning making while still getting the appropriate accommodations for their specific levels of disability.

Monolingual Educators in Multilingual Settings

One of the major challenges in creating this bilingual intervention environment is the lack of resources: staff members remain mostly monolingual, despite an increasingly linguistically diverse student population. The obvious solution is for administrators to try to fill positions with personnel who speak and have literacy in the languages of their ELL population. The goal in a multilingual school should be an additive environment for all ELLs, regardless of their language background. However, given the increasing range of linguistic and cultural diversity found in schools, this is not always possible, and more often than not, monolingual educators and service providers must somehow provide support in languages they do not know. Some publications address specific languages that could provide useful information to speech pathologists and special educators (Cheng, 1991; Coehlo, 1991; Goldstein, 2004; Swan & Smith, 2001).

Innovative projects and materials available on the Internet can provide models and resources in just such a situation. These linguistic and cultural resources that educators, students, and families can use to actively promote additive bilingualism in multilingual schools are listed in Table 4.3. More extensive examples of how these resources have been used across grade levels are discussed in Chapter 9.

Even with these resources, monolingual teachers need to forge alliances with speakers of their students' native languages in the community. They may be fortunate enough to work with bilingual educators or teacher assistants who speak some of these languages. Educators need to enlist parents, university students, older students, and volunteers as resources to support the native language and provide cultural information relevant to ELLs in the classroom.

A Sample Process

The following is a description of the process of developing the continuum of services framework in two districts that we will call District A and District B.

In District A, the process started when the ESL director and special education director began discussing about how they could better support ELLs in their district who were having academic difficulties. The ESL director and a speech-language pathologist started a district think tank, with participants from various fields in the district asked to review the literature in the field of both ESL and special education. The think tank made some recommendations at the district level for professional development and suggested ideas for how to proceed.

The ESL director and special education director arranged a day for special education staff and ESL staff in the district to become familiar with the seven integral factors. There were representatives from each school at this larger meeting. Participants engaged in different activities that facilitated cross-professional conversations. The participants shared some of their concerns and questions in this large group and made further suggestions to the district personnel, who worked with building administrators to improve the program and other aspects of the learning environment for ELLs. These representatives returned to their schools and shared what they learned with their home schools. School administrators scheduled short meetings at their schools where information about the seven integral factors was shared so that all would have a common base of knowledge with regard to ELLs.

District A then brought the professionals together again for a day to go through the solution-seeking process described in this chapter, using examples of difficulties that ELLs exhibited in their schools. In this district, after reviewing the seven integral factors, the schools identified very specific areas that should be improved to help improve ELLs' academic progress.

District B was in a little different situation when they approached the process. They had a very well-established infrastructure for addressing the needs of ELLs in all seven areas. What they had not done was to initiate conversations between ELL and special education. Over a three-year period, multi-

Table 4.3 Linguistic and Cultural Resources

Multilingual Resources

http://thornwood.peelschools.org/Dual/index.htm	Online dual-language literacy project, with a link to dual-language resources.
http://www.bbc.co.uk/worldservice/index.shtml	World news headlines in 33 languages.
http://www.icdlbooks.org	International Children's Digital Library provides free access to children's books from around the world with texts in 34 languages.
http://onlinebooks.library.upenn.edu/archives.html# foreign	
www.EnchantedLearning.com	Resource for content area graphics, word banks, and some downloadable bilingual books.
http://www.google.com/language_tools?hl=en	Search any topic in students' primary languages.
http://www.childrensbooksonline.org/library.htm	Children's Books Online: The Rosetta Project, PO BOX 808; Searsport, ME 04974 USA.
http://www.glencoe.com/sec/math/mlg/mlg.php	Math concepts translated into various languages are listed alphabetically, with short explanations in English.
http://www.wikipedia.org	Free access to online encyclopedia articles in many different languages.
http://www.wwf.org	World Wide Fund for Nature: science information in many languages, representing 43 countries.
http://www.multiliteracies.ca//index.php	Showcase of multilingual projects at different grade levels.
http://209.161.219.123/Default.asp	Far Eastern Books: dual-language books as well as *Star Children's Picture Dictionary* in multiple languages. PO Box 846, Adelaide Street Station, Toronto, Ontario, Canada M5C 2K1.
www.home.comcast.net/~bilingualslp	Web site regarding communication disorders and bilingualism. It has some translated material that could be useful in describing disorders to parents.
Talk With Your Child in Your First Language	A series of videos and brochures for parents to help prepare the young child for school success, translated into multiple languages. Ottawa-Carlton District School Board, Ottawa, Ontario
http://www.todaysparent.com/lifeasparent/parenting/article.jsp?content=20040402_150336_3232&page=1	"Tongue Tied" (article in *Today's Parent* magazine regarding raising bilingual children).
http://www.cplol.org/eng/posters.htm	Posters about language development in different languages (Danish, Dutch, Estonian, French, German, Greek, Irish, Italian, Latvian, Russian, Slovenian, Spanish, Swedish, Turkish, Welsh).
http://www.ldonline.org/features/espanol	Information about learning disabilities for parents in Spanish.

Language- and Culture-Specific Resources

Cheng, L. L. (1991). *Assessing Asian language performance: Guidelines for evaluating limited-English-proficient students* (2nd ed.). Oceanside, CA: Academic Communication Associates.	Historical, linguistic, and cultural background information, as well as phonological and linguistic comparisons of Asian languages.
Coelho, E. (1991). *Caribbean students in Canadian schools: Book 2.* Markham, ON: Pippin Publishing.	Historical, cultural, and linguistic information pertinent to students from the Caribbean.
Goldstein, B. A. (Ed.). (2004). *Bilingual language development and disorders in Spanish-English speakers.* Baltimore, MD: Paul H. Brookes.	Compilation of information about development and disorders for bilingual speakers of Spanish and English.

continued

Table 4.3 *continued*

Multilingual Resources	
Haghighat, C. (2003). *Language profiles.* Vols. I-III. Toronto, ON: World Languages Publishing House. Also available at http://alphaplus.ca.	Historical, linguist and cultural background information as well as linguistic comparisons for 67 languages.
Swan, M., & Smith, B.(Eds.). (2001). *Learner English: A teacher's guide to interference and other problems* (2nd ed.). Cambridge: Cambridge Handbooks for Language Teachers.	Examples of interference from various languages when learning English.
www.settlement.org/CP/english/index.html	Cultural profiles of different groups of people speaking different languages. Mentions some pragmatic rules and customs that could affect speech and language services.

perspective teams met to review information related to each of the seven integral factors. This served to remind everyone of the areas that had to be addressed to prevent a wide range of ELL difficulties. On two occasions, teams met to go through a sample process of crafting interventions. The emphasis in those meetings was on professional bridge building, collaborative problem solving, and listening to each other's perspective. Today, the bilingual/ESL director and the special education director are in frequent communication about their individual program needs and responsibilities and the areas where they can collaborate and share services in this new approach to address and prevent difficulties for all students. Both the bilingual/ESL program and the special education program have undergone dramatic changes to implement innovative programming for ELLs.

An Introduction to the Seven Integral Factors

While school-based ECOS teams work on making progress in implementing the solution-seeking approach presented in this chapter, the school district as a whole must take time to study and reflect on each of the seven integral factors presented in this handbook. The source of most extrinsic difficulties can be found and explained when we fail to fully address any or all of these factors:

1. the learning environment created for the student,
2. personal and family factors,
3. physical and psychological factors,
4. previous schooling performance,
5. proficiency in oral language and literacy in both the first (L1) and the second language (L2),
6. academic achievement, and
7. cross-cultural factors.

When considering ELLs who are experiencing difficulties, schools are too quick to ask, is it an ELL difficulty or is it a learning disability problem? A more productive conversation can begin once schools start to consider a broader range of sources of difficulties.

STEPS FOR ECOS TEAMS TO TAKE

1. The ECOS team is formed.

2. The team meets for team-building activities, to clarify roles and responsibilities, and to discuss principles.

3. The team is introduced to the rest of the school.

4. The team elicits from all those who come in contact with the students in question a list of specific difficulties that the students are exhibiting, describing rather than diagnosing.

5. Using the list in Table 3.1, the team brainstorms other behaviors that need to be added to the list. This will become the inventory of difficulties (IOD), which will serve to generate interventions.

6. Using the evolving IOD, the team elicits from every person an assessment as to whether the students in question show that behavior.

7. As soon as one or two items are established as part of the IOD, the team begins to discuss possible causes from an ELL perspective and contrasts these with possible disability causes.

8. The team begins to gather information on the seven integral factors.

9. Using the key principles, the team starts generating specific and systemic ELL interventions for each difficulty in all of the students' languages.

10. The team determines who implements the strategies, in what contexts, toward what goals, and on what timelines.

11. The team implements, assesses, and documents ELL interventions.

12. The team reconvenes to evaluate ELLs' responses to the interventions in many contexts and all languages.

13. If ELLs respond to interventions in either language and any context, the team will:

    a. Document progress and develop programming that incorporates these interventions as a normal part of the ELLs' learning environment.

13. If ELLs do not respond to interventions as expected, the team will:

    a. Note that the difficulties seem to be manifest across social and academic contexts in all of the ELLs' languages.

    b. Continue to use ELL interventions and supports and move across to the disabilities explanations.

    c. Implement special education interventions in addition to ELL interventions in all of the ELLs' languages and across contexts.

    d. Reconvene to evaluate ELLs' progress.

    e. If ELLs do not make significant progress in either language with ELL + LD support, then the team must document this programming and begin more extensive assessment as part of a case study evaluation.

14. The team attends and facilitates spring articulation meetings at the different grade levels.

15. The team starts planning interventions and procedures to implement immediately in the summer and in the following school year.

5

The Learning Environment Created for ELLs

KEY CONCEPTS

The first characteristic of students' home and school life that should be considered in understanding the difficulties these students encounter is the learning environment. "Learning environment" is a broad term that encompasses teachers' preparation and presentation of materials, the resources available, the program design, the range of services offered, the value placed on the native language and culture, and characteristics of instruction and assessment. The interventions developed from this integral factor are systemic and may improve the learning environment for all students.

The learning environment created for English language learners (ELLs) is one of the most critical factors influencing academic achievement and language acquisition. The environment should have an enriching rather than remedial or compensatory quality, and the enrichment should be apparent and experienced in every aspect of school life. The ELL should feel supported both affectively and cognitively. There are few places as exciting, as hopeful, or as motivating as a supportive academic environment. Students in such an environment can focus on acquiring new ideas and skills that also enhance their understanding of the world and their confidence in dealing with it. Academic success requires a supportive learning environment. We present this element first, because school staff should systematically attempt to improve the learning environment for ELLs as soon as a challenge is identified.

Before we discuss the specific aspects of the learning environment that is created for ELLs, it may be helpful to consider the findings in the 1981 Supreme Court case, *Casteñeda v. Pickard.* This case established a three-prong test for determining whether a school district is adequately serving limited-English-speaking students. First, the program must be based on theory or practice recognized by experts in the field as legitimate. Second, the district must provide adequate resources to implement the program. Third, the district must periodically evaluate the program. In recognition of the importance of this legislation, we base our discussion of the factors defining the learning environment for ELLs on theory and practice that is supported by research. It is up to the school to fulfill the remaining two requirements, providing adequate resources to implement a sound educational program and assessing the quality of that program on an ongoing basis.

Key Factors in the Learning Environment

A number of factors have a demonstrable impact on the creation of a strong and supportive learning environment. Each of these factors should be considered important to structuring an academic environment that supports rather than conflicts with the goals of academic success for ELLs. The following factors contribute the most to the learning environment of students: teachers, resources, the design of the program (in terms of implementation and configuration), the range of services offered, the role of native language and culture in instruction and assessment, and characteristics of instruction and assessment. Each of these items is discussed separately here.

Teachers

Qualified teachers are essential to ELLs' academic and linguistic success, yet the schools with the neediest students are staffed by teachers who are either novices or not skilled in the area of instruction (Haycock, 1998). *"Children in the highest poverty schools are often assigned to novice teachers almost twice as often as children in low poverty schools. Similarly, students in high minority schools are assigned to novice teachers at twice the rate as students in schools without many minority students. Classes in high poverty and high minority schools are likely to be taught by "out-of-field" teachers (those without a major or minor in the subject they teach). The situation in grades 5-7 is even worse"* (Jerald, 2003). ELLs need to be instructed by teachers who know how to teach linguistically and culturally diverse students. Teachers of ELLs must have received training in the basic tenets of second language acquisition, the process of acculturation, effective instructional and assessment methods, and cross-cultural issues, in addition to acquiring basic instructional competency and subject area expertise.

General education teachers without specialized training in ESL/bilingual education cannot by themselves provide the enriching instructional learning environment ELLs need. In some cases they may make the ELL learning environment worse by setting inappropriate expectations, assigning tasks that are beyond the ELLs' linguistic capabilities, or using teaching strategies that do not benefit ELLs because they were designed and implemented with monolingual English speakers in mind. Teachers may also misinterpret ELLs' performance and arrive at flawed judgments of ELLs' progress. On the other hand, ESL/bilingual teachers may understand second language learning, but without subject area expertise in the intermediate grades and at the middle and secondary school level, they too are unable to provide the needed enriched learning environment by themselves. Chronicle 5.1 describes the dilemma many teachers of ELLs face at the middle or secondary school level. Most ESL/bilingual teachers are language development experts, not content area specialists, while most middle and secondary school teachers are content area specialists, not language development experts. The school district should try to remedy this situation rather than hold on to the expectation that the ESL/bilingual teacher will provide instruction in all subjects at all grade levels.

If their teachers lack the necessary depth and breadth of subject area knowledge, ELLs will get a watered-down version of the curriculum at best, and little or no access to the academic curriculum at worst. The effect in either case is to create gaps in learning that will be harder to address later and increasingly difficult to distinguish from intrinsic learning disabilities (LD) as the student continues in school (Crago & Paradis, 2003; McDermott, 1993; McDermott & Varenne, 1995). Most states in the United States offer separate endorsements for ESL/bilingual education, in some cases for pre-service teachers and in other cases for in-service teachers.

Being a Language Development Specialist (as a Bilingual/ESL Teacher) versus a Content Area Specialist at the Junior High Level

By a junior high bilingual/ESL teacher

Initiating a transfer from the elementary level to the middle school level was something I wanted to do to widen my teaching experience to include more grade levels after teaching for seven years at the elementary level. I certainly widened my experience, but not in the way intended. I found myself trying to teach biology without specimens, chemistry without chemicals, and U.S. history without original source documents to ELLs. Additionally, I tried to help students study for vocabulary tests in elective courses, for example in sewing class without benefit of access to sewing machines, and in computer drafting and design class without benefit of access to computer drafting/design software. The materials unique to core and elective content areas were not available to me as a bilingual teacher either on a sign-out basis (because there was always a section of the course running) or in my classroom (because I was not assigned to a science lab or the darkroom or the life skills room).

My ELLs were assigned to one team at each grade level. Fortunately, I worked with a great group of teachers who were willing to work with me. My teaching responsibilities were clarified to be restricted to the realm of native language literacy instruction, ESL instruction, and literacy development, particularly vocabulary development, within the content area. The core academic teachers were obligated to obtain training in ESL methodology and assessment, foundations of language minority education, and issues in cross-cultural education (the ESL approval/endorsement). Additional staff members were recruited with target language fluency and/or bilingual endorsement/approval and content area endorsement to provide math, science, and social studies classes in the native language.

Questions for discussion:

- Did the school do the right thing and improve the learning environment for ELLs?
- Is the new arrangement more manageable for staff?
- Do ESL/bilingual teachers face a higher burnout rate than other teachers?
- Are other student population groups subject to similar configurations?

Because of the importance of having the right mixture of knowledge and experience in both general education and language diversity education, a focus on the training and employment of both types of teachers might be expected. However, there is often a paucity of ESL/bilingual teachers, and if the district cannot recruit teachers with ESL/bilingual training, it must strive to provide existing staff with the requisite training through incentives to enroll in graduate programs, supplemented by in-service staff development opportunities. Additionally, the district can establish mentoring and coaching programs, pairing veteran staff with novice staff and ESL/bilingual staff with general education staff. Another possibility is to organize the teaching staff into grade-level or cross-disciplinary teams. That is, groups of teachers would be configured into teams that would include ESL/bilingual teachers. This approach establishes a natural context for educators to share their expertise, plan, learn, and prepare instruction together, get to know all the students on their team, and provide input on how to address individual students' needs. The ECOS team and the framework described in this book are geared toward the construction of these types of service delivery options. However, ongoing professional development is also needed to ensure that all staff working with ELLs stays abreast of developments in the field and changes in the law. For a detailed description of the knowledge and skills that teachers and staff need to qualify for working with ELLs, see Crandall, Stein, and Nelson (2006). Table 5.1 is a checklist based on that document.

The practice of assigning program assistants to provide initial instruction to ELLs is all too prevalent and results in a weak, ineffectual educational program. ELLs who have had instruction initiated predominantly by paraprofessionals are at considerable risk for academic difficulties (Haycock, 1998). ELLs who have been in an oversized class or part of a teacher's heavy caseload may not have received appropriate or sufficient instruction to ensure their academic and linguistic success. Self-contained classes for ELLs should be at 90 percent of the average district class size to ensure that teachers are able to differentiate instruction according to both content-area skill levels and language proficiency levels as needed. Caseloads for pullout and resource ESL/bilingual teachers should be comparable to those of teachers of other pullout and resource programs in the district. Administrators' tolerance of large class sizes for language minority students and heavy caseloads for pullout and resource ESL/bilingual teachers results in an unproductive learning environment for ELLs (Miramontes, Nadeau, & Commins, 1997).

When ELLs receive instruction from unqualified or inappropriately certified teachers, there is a negative cumulative effect on their educational experience that isolated instances of good instruction cannot overcome. ELLs must receive enriched, accelerated instruction from highly motivated and talented teachers over their entire school experience to keep pace with their native English-speaking peers. If this does not occur, a host of potential reactions may result. First, and critically, they may never close the gap between themselves and their mainstream peers. The kinds of instruction and the actual instructional format play a significant role in this case (e.g., Collier & Thomas, 2002; Echavarria & Short, 2003). Second, students may simply become less responsive to the teaching strategies and the acceptable expectations of the classroom. Since they have not been able to receive effective assistance from teachers and educational support staff, they may create other types of strategies that result in marginalizing them within the classroom context, and the ELL may simply opt out of the process (Sinclair & Ghory, 1987). Third, the student may be inappropriately placed in special education, where the student's needs cannot be effectively met and the expectations of the student's learning potential will be greatly reduced (Cummins, 1984; Damico & Damico, 1993; García & Ortiz, 1988). Finally, the ELL may simply drop out of school when that option becomes available. No individual chooses to remain in a situation of struggle or failure when other options are available.

ECOS TEAM ACTIVITY

Using the checklist in Table 5.1, have different individuals in the school check the extent to which general education teachers, ESL teachers, and bilingual teachers meet the qualifications suggested by Crandall, Stein, and Nelson (2006). This activity should be completed for the group of teachers known as general education, ESL, or bilingual teachers. It is not meant to evaluate individual teachers.

Table 5.1 A Checklist for Assessing the Qualifications of Groups of Teachers

General Education Teachers

☐ Know how ELLs acquire and develop their first and second languages.

☐ Know how ELLs develop first and second language literacy.

☐ Know cross-cultural differences in communication.

☐ Can adapt instruction to accommodate students with different levels of English proficiency.

☐ Can provide instruction that is appropriate for different learning styles.

☐ Know how to confer with parents who may not speak English and who may have different expectations about the appropriate roles and responsibilities of parents and teachers in the education of their children.

☐ Know how to assess by providing ELLs with an opportunity to demonstrate their understanding in a variety of ways, without relying on oral or written English that is above the level of the proficiency of ELLs.

☐ Know the types of ESL or bilingual programs and services offered to students and can work collaboratively with ESL and bilingual teachers in co-planning or co-teaching lessons.

ESL Teachers

☐ Know the structure of English and how to teach that English structure to ELLs.

☐ Know how to help ELLs develop oral and written proficiency in English.

☐ Know first and second language acquisition and how to teach English, through English, to ELLs with different English proficiency levels.

☐ Know cross-cultural communication and differences in learning styles and be can create lessons for learners with diverse learning styles.

☐ Know the basic laws and regulations governing the education of ELLs.

☐ Know the policies and procedures related to ELLs in the school and district.

☐ Know their specific responsibilities, including whom to report to.

☐ Know state or district curriculum and standards related to ELLs.

☐ Know the content taught in mainstream classes and can integrate academic concepts, texts, tasks, and tests into the ESL classroom.

☐ Can work collaboratively with mainstream teachers in co-planning, co-teaching, or previewing and reviewing content in ESL instruction that effectively integrates academic content into the language focus.

☐ Know the resources available to ELLs and their families and how to access these resources.

☐ Can manage classes with a seemingly continual intake and outflow of students.

☐ Can work with students who have experienced severe shock or trauma from revolution or war.

☐ If applicable, can function without the support of a school or even a regular classroom.

☐ If in an elementary school, know scheduling and can negotiate time for pulling out ELLs for ESL instruction.

☐ If in a middle or high school with ELLs who have limited prior schooling or literacy, can teach initial literacy in English.

Bilingual Teachers

☐ Know the policies and procedures related to ELLs.

☐ Know state or district curriculum and standards related to instruction of bilingual students.

☐ Can work collaboratively with ESL and mainstream teachers ,especially in transitioning students from bilingual classes to ESL, sheltered, or mainstream classes.

☐ Know the bilingual resources available in the community and can help families, the school, and the district access these resources.

☐ Can help serve as a cultural interpreter for other school personnel.

☐ Can manage classes of students with diverse backgrounds, including differences in proficiency in the home language and English.

☐ Can work with students who have experienced severe shock or trauma from revolution or war.

Resources Available

An abundance of high-quality, age-appropriate academic content area materials is essential for an effective learning environment for ELLs. These materials should be at a variety of language proficiency and reading levels. In addition to English, these academic materials should reflect the languages and cultures of the students in the school. In Chapters 9 and 10 we present ideas on how to integrate these multilingual and multicultural materials throughout the curriculum. Sufficient teacher resource materials, including teacher manuals for any series the district has adopted, must be provided. Curriculum guides in all content areas and copies of content area standards are also required. Additional teaching materials such as trade books (in both the native and second languages), realia, manipulatives, software, and access to all materials available to every teacher in the district should also be part of this environment. An abundance of leisure reading materials should be available to students in the classroom library, the school library and the community library (Krashen, 2004). Instruction without sufficient learning and leisure reading materials in both languages renders the instruction less accessible for ELLs and therefore compromises the learning environment.

ELLs need to interact with other students using academic language in order to practice newly learned language skills. ELLs also need to have access to peer language models in both nonacademic classes (such as physical education, music and art) and planned, structured academic activities. One-on-one instruction does not provide an optimal level of interaction, as learners need rich and varied opportunities to communicate with peers and adults (Coelho, 1994; Duckworth, 1987; Genesee, 2006; Lave & Wenger, 1991). The district should provide physical classroom space sufficient to accommodate group sizes of 5 to 20 students. The school must provide, within the scheduling process, opportunities for ELLs to attend nonacademic classes with their native English-speaking peers. Additionally, schools must support the integration of ELLs with monolingual peers in structured academic activities by providing ESL/bilingual teachers and general education teachers time for collaborative planning and team teaching. Chronicle 5.2 is the account of an ESL teacher who not only works under dire conditions but also provides instruction isolated from the general education teachers. ELLs who have had the bulk of their language assistance in a one-on-one configuration or who have not experienced integration in nonacademic classes are less likely to develop their language and academic skills at the same rate as those who have had many opportunities for group interaction in an instructional setting.

In the interest of equity and protection from discrimination, classrooms for ELLs should not be isolated in a remote location or differ in quality from the classrooms the school provides for monolingual English-speaking students.

ECOS TEAM ACTIVITY

Assign students and teachers from each grade level and each classroom the task of taking four photographs of their room, two of spaces or things they like and two of those they do not like. Include common spaces as well, such as the library, the lunchroom, and central office, if you wish. Make copies of the list in Table 5.2, and rate each classroom as to the quality of resources it offers. The photographs serve as reminders of how different classrooms look, but they also give the team a sense of students' own perspective of their own environment. You can make the activity more interesting by not indicating which photographs were positive and which were negative. Ironically, this activity will be much more difficult for schools that do not have adequate resources and where taking photographs and making prints or slides on the computer will be more complicated than in a school where resources are abundant.

Dealing with Heavy Caseloads

By an ESL teacher

Last year was crazy, and given the bumps in enrollment, this year promises to be even crazier! I am an ESL teacher in a small, rural school district. The school board tells us that money is tight, but I feel that in my efforts to serve ELLs, I am actually doing them a grave disservice. I have teaching responsibilities at four different schools—two elementary, one middle school and one high school. My caseloads at each school range from 6 to 30 ELLs. The students span the range of English language proficiency from the preproduction level to nearly fluent.

There is no way I can be at each school each day—the schools are at least 10 miles apart, and because my schedule is so erratic I cannot participate on grade-level teams at any school. The physical space I have to teach varies at each building, depending on how much space the principal can spare. In some buildings I have to work at a table in the library, in others I may be given be a small classroom. Most of my teaching materials are in the trunk of my car.

I cringe when I hear that a student needed my help with a project or a parent dropped by the school to speak with me and I missed the opportunity to clarify, explain, or reassure because I was at another school. There is no continuity in my instruction. Pretty much, I can only manage to help ELLs with their homework or projects, many of which are inappropriate. I feel that I am not providing the high-quality instruction I know my students need. More important, my body and my mental health may not withstand yet another crazy year.

Questions for discussion:

- What assistance do you imagine is in place for ELLs when this teacher is at another building?
- What does this learning environment communicate about the value the district places on the ELLs it serves? What assumptions are being made?
- What must be done to improve the learning environment for ELLs in this school district?

Instruction in the hall, on the stage, in mobile units on the playground, or in the lunchroom is not acceptable. Student desks, classroom furniture, and other equipment should be on par with what all other children in the school are using. ELLs should have equitable access to all resources that are available to every other general education student in the building, even if it means providing those resources in the students' native languages. ELLs and their families are very aware of substandard room assignments, poor-quality equipment, and barriers to educational programs that preclude their participation. Such situations send a clear message that often results in lower self-esteem and pessimism, which in turn influences academic and linguistic achievement negatively. Table 5.2 is a checklist that can be used to rate the adequacy of resources for ELLs.

Program Design

The creation of an effective and efficient program design is no small endeavor. It requires an understanding of the law (to establish minimum requirements), a needs assessment (to establish the needs within the district), and a review of the research (to establish which pedagogical practices should be replicated).

Table 5.2 Rating the Resources in the School

	1 = Hardly	2 = Somewhat	3 = Mostly	4 = Very much so

There are sufficient age-appropriate student materials in the content areas in L1 and L2.	1	2	3	4
There are sufficient student materials at different levels of ESL proficiency.	1	2	3	4
There are sufficient teacher resource materials.	1	2	3	4
There are adequate and useful curriculum guides in all content areas.	1	2	3	4
There are sufficient supplementary books in both L1 and L2.	1	2	3	4
There are abundant supplementary materials, manipulatives, etc.	1	2	3	4
The library has sufficient leisure reading materials in both L1 and L2.	1	2	3	4
Classrooms are set up in such a way that ELLs are constantly interacting with English-speaking peers.	1	2	3	4
Classrooms provide comfortable space for the number of students they hold.	1	2	3	4
Classrooms for ELLs are in the midst of all other classrooms.	1	2	3	4
ELL classrooms are equipped just as adequately as classrooms for English-speaking peers.	1	2	3	4

Many districts maintain a language assistance program for ELLs that was formally established years ago and may now be based on outdated research and practices. Just as demographics change (through changes in immigration patterns, numbers of newly enrolled students, and native language backgrounds), so too new research continues to emerge and laws or regulations change to meet new needs. Often the basic design is kept, with small changes made to meet immediate needs on a short-term basis. Over time, staff members realize that the current program design no longer works efficiently and effectively. Staff may recognize the desirability of modernizing the program design to meet new needs.

At the very minimum, the program design for a district's language assistance program must conform to statutory demands delineated in both federal and state laws. The design must satisfy court case precedents as well (Crawford, 2006). In the United States, federal laws regarding the education of ELLs have their roots in the Fourteenth Amendment to the Constitution. The Fourteenth Amendment guarantees that no state can make or enforce any law abridging the privileges or immunities of citizens or deprive any person of life, liberty, or property without due process of law; nor can a state deny equal protection under the law. Title VI, Section 601, of the Civil Rights Act of 1964 prohibits discrimination on the basis of national origin in federally funded programs. The Bilingual Education Acts of 1968 and 1974 (formerly known as Title VII) provided supplemental funding for school districts interested in establishing programs to meet the distinct needs of large numbers of ELLs in need of language support in the United States. The Equal Educational Opportunity Act (EEOA) of 1974 provided definitions of what constituted a denial of equal educational opportunity. Among them is "failure by an educational agency to take appropriate action to overcome language barriers that impede equal participation by students in an instructional program."

Notable court cases related to ELLs include *Lau v. Nichols* and *Casteñeda v. Pickard*. In *Lau v. Nichols*, the Supreme Court ruled in favor of the plaintiffs and reaffirmed the 1970 Memorandum[1], stating that identical education does not constitute equal education under Title VI of the Civil Rights Act of 1964:

---

[1]An interpretation of the Title VII regulations that prohibited denial of access to educational programs because of a student's limited English proficiency issued by the Department of Housing, Education and Welfare.

There is no equality of treatment by providing students with the same facilities, textbooks, teachers and curriculum, for students who do not understand English are effectively foreclosed from any meaningful education. Basic English skills are at the very core of what public schools teach. Imposition of a requirement that, before a child can effectively participate in the educational program, he must have already acquired those basic skills is to make a mockery of public education. We know that those who do not understand English are certain to find their classroom experiences wholly incomprehensible and in no way meaningful.

The Supreme Court recognized the authority of the Office for Civil Rights (an office within the U.S. Department of Education) to establish regulations for compliance with the 1964 Civil Rights Act.

Casteñeda v. Pickard has special relevance, since it established important criteria for determining a school's degree of compliance with the Equal Educational Opportunity Act of 1974. Although the decision was rendered by the Fifth Circuit Court of Appeals, which has jurisdiction over Texas, Louisiana, and Mississippi, many courts and auditing agencies across the country have applied its three-pronged approach across the United States. Compliance requires the satisfaction of the three criteria described earlier in this chapter and listed in Table 5.3.

State and federal legislation and court cases set the minimum standard for ELLs' learning environment. Ignorance of the law is no excuse for a school's failure to meet the requirements of the law. ELLs who have not participated in a language assistance program that satisfies the letter of the law are truly at a disadvantage and will not make typical progress.

The use of a needs assessment serves to document perspectives from different constituent groups, changing demographics within the ELL population, and local circumstances that may be unique. Addressing the needs of different constituent groups at the beginning of the process of program design ensures that the design has broad-based appeal and remedies missing components or services identified by ESL/bilingual teachers, general education teachers, administrators, parents, and ELLs. The completed needs assessment not only serves as the foundation for the program design but may also indicate where other systemic interventions are warranted. Appendix E shows a sample needs assessment that may be modified to fit the specific circumstances of a school.

Research on program effectiveness, along with the minimal requirements

---

Table 5.3   Criteria Established by *Casteñeda v. Pickard*

1. **Theory:** The school must pursue a program based on an educational theory recognized as sound or, at least, as a legitimate experimental strategy.

2. **Practice:** The school must actually implement the program with instructional practices, resources, and personnel necessary to transfer theory into reality.

3. **Results:** The school must not persist in a program that fails to produce results.

ECOS TEAM ACTIVITY

Have team members focus on the first part of the requirements of *Casteñeda v. Pickard.* Using the following sentence from those findings, have team members write down what they think the theory is behind the program designed for ELLs: "The school must pursue a program based on an educational theory recognized as sound or, at least, as a legitimate experimental strategy." Ask team members to respond to the following question: "What is the educational theory (or experimental strategy) that is reflected in the way we teach our ELLs?" Have individuals write down their thoughts, discuss with a partner, then hold a group discussion.

of state law, should inform decisions regarding the suitability of the English as a second language (ESL) program, transitional bilingual education program, maintenance bilingual program, or dual-language program in a particular district. Miramontes, Nadeau, and Commins (1997) assert that crucial decisions should be made regarding a program of language support; specifically, the instructional emphasis of that program should be determined and decisions should be made as to whether the program focuses on content area instruction, literacy instruction, or both. As Nguyen (2006) and de Jong (2006) suggest, decisions regarding program design should be made by administrators and staff based on the real needs of the population and the long-term goals for the students. Districts and schools need to take a flexible approach in their program design to be able to meet the diverse needs that exist in the community that the school serves.

We have strong evidence regarding two general aspects of the program for ELLs: the use of the native language and culture, and the approach to developing proficiency in English as a second language. As far as the first aspect is concerned, there is a considerable body of research that points to the desirability of bilingual instruction where both the native language and English are used (Collier & Thomas, 2002; Genesee et al., 2006; Lindholm-Leary, 2006). The International Reading Association adopted a resolution in 2001 advising educators to teach initial literacy skills in students' first language whenever possible to prevent reading difficulties in the future. A child who never learned to read in his native language is at a distinct disadvantage when compared with an ELL peer who did. A child who never had subject area instruction in his native language is also at a disadvantage when compared with an ELL peer who did receive such instruction. More will be said regarding the importance of the native language and culture later in this chapter.

As for ESL instruction, since the early 1990s, research-based instructional approaches that integrate language and content to foster the academic progress of ELLs have been widely advocated (Chamot & O'Malley, 1994; Echavarria, Vogt, & Short, 2004). ELLs who received traditional ESL instruction as opposed to content-based ESL instruction will likely experience more academic difficulty (Thomas & Collier, 2002).

Although program design is important and necessary, it is not sufficient. Consideration must also be given to the actual program configuration. That is, one must consider the manner in which the teachers and students are organized within the classroom so that the actual interactions and teachable moments may occur. This consideration is essential because it helps specify the actual implementation of the program design. Examples of the different configurations that may be chosen include self-contained classes, pullout programs, and resource rooms. All of these configurations may produce solid results, but they must be implemented properly. If not implemented properly, ELLs may not have sufficient amounts of comprehensible instruction, nor will they have sufficient peer interaction, and consequently they will experience academic and linguistic difficulty.

Additionally, if school districts are engaged in some other type of programmatic reform, such as comprehensive school reform, implementation of professional learning communities, or another systems model, care must be taken to ensure that ELLs are taken into account and their strengths and needs are incorporated into the action plan.

Regardless of the specific program design, Commins (2006) suggests seven critical features that can guide educators' efforts to address the needs of ELLs adequately. These critical features are included in the checklist in Table 5.4.

Range of Services Offered

Once the program design has been determined and the instructional emphasis decided, the range of services must be considered. Decisions need to be made about the frequency and duration of instructional services offered to

Table 5.4 A Checklist for Assessing Whether the ELL Program Meets the Critical Features.

We have created a climate of belonging by:

☐ Utilizing materials that value students' home language and culture.

☐ Reaching out to parents and community members.

☐ Encouraging parents to interact with their children in their strongest language (usually not English).

We have implemented standards-based instruction by:

☐ Organizing instruction around a common body of knowledge, with attention to differentiation in the methods of delivery.

☐ Identifying enduring understandings and essential vocabulary and highlighting them in instruction.

☐ Gathering curriculum materials at a wide range of reading levels.

We use data to inform and shape instruction by:

☐ Finding out who the learners are and what they bring to instruction.

☐ Assessing students' academic and literacy skills in their primary language, whether or not it is used in instruction.

☐ Using multiple forms of assessment to documents students' progress, as well as attainment of benchmarks.

We elevate oral language practice by:

☐ Providing constant opportunities for interaction in order to increase student talk and decrease teacher talk.

☐ Determining the language structures required for participation in instructional activities, and providing students with opportunities to practice them aloud.

We deliver meaning-based literacy instruction by:

☐ Using text to represent ideas and concepts that students understand and can say.

☐ Incorporating language experience approaches.

☐ Making conscious connections between the big ideas from the content areas and what students will read and write during literacy instruction.

We prepare the physical environment to tie meaning to text by:

☐ Using every inch of the classroom as a resource for students in their independent work.

☐ Making it apparent through words and pictures posted on the walls what students are learning about.

We collaborate with our professional colleagues by:

☐ Taking a schoolwide perspective on meeting students' needs.

☐ Working as part of grade-level or content area teams.

☐ Finding time to articulate across grade levels: topics, and genres, enduring concepts, shared resources, expectations, and assessments.

Source: Adapted from Commins (2006).

ELLs at all levels of English language proficiency. The possibilities extend from the minimal to the optimal. Some language assistance programs offer a minimal amount of services: one period of ESL instruction each day or allowing ELLs to participate in language assistance programs for only one year. Other programs provide a full day of comprehensible instruction and allow ELLs to participate at all levels of English language proficiency until they are able to compete academically in a general education classroom with their native English-speaking peers. ELLs who received minimal instruction provided by an ESL/bilingual teacher are more at risk for academic difficulty than ELLs who were provided language assistance program services designed to meet the students' academic and linguistic needs during the five to seven years they were acquiring English (Genesee et al., 2006). School staff members need to remind themselves that it takes quite a long time for ELLs to catch up to their English-speaking peers (Collier & Thomas, 2002; Cummins, 2006).

Role of the Native Language

In quality programs for ELLs, the role of the native language in instruction is never left to chance. When ELLs have the opportunity to acquire literacy in their native language first, the probability of future academic and linguistic difficulties diminishes (Elley, 1997; International Reading Association, 2001; Krashen, 2003). In addition, use of native language instruction is essential for building on ELLs' strengths, activating prior knowledge, and assisting with the transfer of knowledge to the second language (Genesee et al., 2006). Structured and deliberate decisions are made at the programmatic and curricular level and guidelines are developed to help teachers make decisions at the classroom level. This process is called language allocation (Hilliard & Hamayan, 2006).

Educators are urged to guard against the token use of the native language in instruction. For example, offering ELLs verbatim translation of instruction or bringing in a teaching assistant whenever possible to help small groups of students in the classroom is not effective native language instruction. This short-term and haphazard approach limits language proficiency and skill development (Miramontes, Nadeau, & Commins, 1997). Failure to make these decisions about native language use at the programmatic or curricular level results in ELLs being subjected to the personal philosophies and competencies of each ESL/bilingual teacher they encounter in their educational career and makes for an uneven learning experience in the program. ELLs with such uneven experiences with native language in instruction are likely to experience both academic and linguistic problems (Crawford, 1994; Genesee, 2006).

The role of the native language is discussed in greater detail in Chapters 8, 9, and 10.

Role of the Native Culture

A culturally responsive curriculum is critical to ELLs' academic and linguistic success because learning is an interaction between individual learners and an embedding context (Bruner, 1996; García, 2006; Rogoff, 2003; Wells, 1986). We often forget that in addition to the challenge of learning new and abstract concepts in a language they are not proficient in, ELLs have to overcome the hurdle of learning in an unfamiliar context. This is true even for ELLs who were born in the United States if their home culture is different from the school's culture and the culture of the textbooks. Thus, if a school does not have a culturally responsive environment, it will be more difficult for ELLs to reach optimal levels of achievement in the content area curriculum. Without the support of their native cultural contexts, ELL will not have the sufficient contextual scaffolds to overcome their second language limitations; without the familiarity of their native cultural contexts, additional learning must occur that will only exacerbate their differences from the mainstream educational context (Agar, 1994; Bunce, 2003; Damico & Hamayan, 1992). Curricula can be culturally responsive in many different ways (Banks, 2005). A good foundation includes infusion of the history and culture related to students' native country into the social studies curriculum. Instructional teaching strategies, student learning activities, and assessment tasks should be carefully chosen in all content area subjects to activate prior knowledge and to illustrate concepts and skills in a way that is familiar to the participating ELLs. Resources integral to instruction, as well as those selected to provide enrichment or extension, should be reflective of ELLs' background and previous experiences to promote optimal learning and reduce cultural bias.

Meaningful cultural learning begins with allowing all students to view the curriculum from multiple perspectives. This enriches the school experience for everyone, not just ELLs. Presenting history, science, literature, and mathematics from multiple viewpoints opens a window for all students and allows each student to be better prepared to live in the world they will encounter when they leave school (Gilbert, 2005). Making certain that ELLs see themselves reflected in the curriculum is critical in keeping these students motivated and involved in school. Stereotypical cultural experiences presented in school that promote caricatures of different ethnic groups can make students ashamed of their ethnic identity, language, families, and community. This separation may lead to other difficulties. Cultural relevance goes beyond school and into the extracurricular activities. More often than not, ELLs do not take advantage of all the activities that the school offers. As Chronicle 5.3 illustrates, a little effort goes a long way toward increasing the integration of ELLs in all aspects of school life, including extracurricular activities. The role of the native culture is discussed in greater detail in Chapter 11.

Characteristics of Instruction

The quality of instruction influences the learning environment for ELLs. Regardless of the specific instructional strategies or approaches used in the classroom, three principles of effective instruction for ELLs must be applied. These three principles are: increased comprehensibility, increased interaction, and the promotion of higher-order thinking skills (Miramontes, Nadeau, & Commins, 1997). Approaches that increase comprehensibility include sheltered English instruction (Echavarria, Vogt, & Short, 2004), balanced literacy instruction (Pearson & Duke, 2000), content-based ESL (Chamot & O'Malley, 1994), and interdisciplinary and thematic units. Approaches that increase interaction for ELLs include cooperative learning, cross-age and peer tutoring, opportunities for integration with native English-speaking peers, and use of hands-on manipulatives.

ELLs should be exposed to higher-order thinking skills instruction from the very beginning of their educational career; there is no need to postpone this instruction until they are fluent in English. A focus on content area skills and concepts with an emphasis on academic language development contained within thematic and integrated units of instruction is essential. Familiarity with the process of second language acquisition and English as a new language standards, native language standards, and content area standards will allow teachers to align these standards and in the process set high yet reasonable expectations for ELLs. All teachers should be encouraged to differentiate their instruction to meet the range of academic and linguistic skills found in the groups of ELLs they serve.

ELLs exposed to poor instruction or instruction that does not incorporate best-practice as outlined in the research on ELS/bilingual education are likely to have their academic and linguistic growth stifled and hindered. Instruction is discussed in greater detail in Chapter 10.

Characteristics of Assessment

For an assessment to be comprehensive enough to serve its purposes, this task should involve both formative and summative measures and should include qualitative and quantitative data. This will ensure that both the process and the product of meaning making may be addressed and that both rich descriptions of strengths and weaknesses and numerical data for comparison purposes will be available. Assessment should be embedded in instruction

CHRONICLE 5.3

A Small Effort Has a Long-Term Effect

By an ESL/bilingual junior high teacher

My principal called me into his office one day and said that he was bothered by the fact that ELLs were not participating much in extracurricular activities. He asked me why the ELLs were not attending the basketball games and the dances and said that he wanted to increase their participation in these and other extracurricular activities. I asked him the following: How many ELLs were on the team? How many ELLs were cheerleaders? How many songs played at the dances appealed to the ELLs?

Clearly, these questions had never crossed this man's mind. And this principal was someone who bent over backward to help students. He was a true advocate of preteens. He just had never contemplated the situation from the perspective of these students. He and I hatched a plan to begin working with all the coaches and club sponsors to be sure the gatekeeping mechanisms did not exclude ELLs and that ELLs were actively recruited to participate in extracurricular activities. We also made sure that the school provided support for ELLs who wanted to participate but did not have adequate support from their families (such as money for uniforms, transportation, and someone to help the kids practice before tryouts). All the staff members were enthusiastic about the endeavor. Slowly, we saw participation increase. I left the school at the close of the school year to take another position.

About 10 years later, I was sitting in a conference session on the topic of extracurricular involvement when a man sitting behind me raised his hand and shared with the group the incredible statistics he had regarding extracurricular participation of minorities at his middle school. Everyone in the audience wanted to know the name of the school that had achieved such tremendous success. It was the same school in which the principal and I had hatched our plan. It is gratifying to know that even with changes in personnel and leadership (the principal had since retired) the goal of ELL participation in extracurricular activities was still being implemented and pursued.

Questions for discussion:

- Many changes that are made at the programmatic level do not survive beyond the tenure of the individuals who initiated the change. What could have contributed to the long life of this change?
- How would you approach coaches, club sponsors, and volunteers who help with extracurricular activities with a challenge like this one?

and student centered. Assessment should span all four language domains—listening, speaking, reading, and writing—and should measure progress in all content areas. Self and peer review should be integral components. Evaluations of student work samples should be made against clear and understandable rubrics. Specifically for ELLs, assessment should be conducted in both the native language and the second language (Gottlieb, 2006a; Oller & Eilers, 2002).

Traditional assessment is not sufficient for ELLs. Standardized and multiple-choice tests tend to have several problems that make them ill-suited for ELLs. First, these tools typically focus on superficial aspects of language structure (vocabulary, verb tenses) and learning (such as informational comprehension that only requires repeating brief facts) rather than on more complex and authentic aspects of texts (Wells, 1998). Second, they are language dependent, which makes it difficult to ascertain whether the student does not know the content being assessed ordoes not know the language needed to express knowledge of the content. Third, they are primarily dependent on acquisition and use of knowledge within a particular cultural context—one that does not incorporate the ELL's cultural knowledge system. Alternative assessment (also known as authentic assessment) is often promoted in the field of ESL/bilingual education as a mode of assessment that must be paired with traditional assessment measures to obtain valid and reliable student profiles. Alternative assessment consists of any method of finding out what a student knows or can do that is intended to show growth and inform instruction and is an alternative to traditional forms of testing (O'Malley & Valdez-Pierce, 1996). Educators should be wary of drawing conclusions about student progress solely on the basis of standardized test scores; alternative, authentic assessment results should also be considered. The characteristics of effective assessment are discussed in greater detail in the remaining chapters.

Suggestions for Information Gathering and Evaluating the Adequacy of the Learning Environment

An accurate and comprehensive picture of the ELL's learning environment must be assembled to determine if ELLs are being given the best opportunities to learn. The current learning environment must be evaluated, but in addition, for older students, some information must be obtained about the learning environment that surrounded ELLs in the past. An evaluator may be able to determine an ELL's current level of functioning within a particular context of interest, but unless information is available regarding previous opportunities to learn, the pedagogies used, and the mediations attempted when difficulties arose, accurate interpretation of these data is not possible (Hamayan & Damico, 1991). Consequently, the ECOS team should have some idea as to whether and how ELLs were taught the skills and concepts they are experiencing difficulty with and how successful the teaching practices were in those instances of instruction. The team needs to determine whether the instruction ELLs have received has been quality instruction. Longitudinal data are also important to determine whether instruction has followed a developmental plan. Review of the student's cumulative records may yield limited information about the subject areas that he or she received instruction in.

Information that is more illustrative will likely come from interviews or surveys conducted with current teachers, former teachers, and administrators. Teacher observations and anecdotes may also provide insight into the ELL's learning environment. Information about the learning environment can be collected in this informal and qualitative manner, or alternatively, ECOS team members may choose to use a more standardized tool to obtain evaluations of the different aspects of the learning environment (see, for example, the tool presented in Appendix F).

Suggestions for Systemic Interventions

Table 5.5 lists some suggestions for interventions that would have an impact systemwide at the school or district level. Since the ECOS team is intended to serve an advocacy role in addition to a pedagogical role, it is important to build capacity at a level broader than the individual student or a specific classroom or school. Without such capacity building, the same procedures will likely have to be reestablished over and over again at different locations or with different ELLs. This will result in inefficiency at best and a systemic failure at worse. These systemic interventions are likely to take time and will need extensive planning for them not only to take place but to succeed.

Table 5.5 Systemic Interventions for the Learning Environment Created for ELLs

Teachers	• Use a plan for recruiting, hiring, and retaining teachers that would reflect the student population, based on historical and projected demographics.
	• Post job vacancies in publications that ESL/bilingual teachers read.
	• Partner with universities that have pre-service programs in ESL/bilingual programs.
	• Work with local high schools and Future Teachers of America to help "grow your own" teacher candidates.
	• Start a graduate-level cohort of teachers who would receive training that leads to ESL/bilingual certification.
	• Design and implement a long-term professional development plan that includes all staff that interact with ELLs and would focus on ELL education.
	• Institute a mentoring or coaching program.
	• Resolve large class sizes, reduce ESL/bilingual teacher caseloads.
Resources	• Ensure that ELLs receive an appropriate allocation or percentage of the entire district or school budget.
	• Incorporate resources needed to teach ELLs in all grant budgets, not just those focused on ELL education.
	• Inventory the native language materials in the school library, classroom libraries, and classrooms. Students can do this as a project.
	• Inventory all teaching materials to be sure everyone has what they need.
	• Audit use of space in the building and make changes to ensure that ELLs have instruction in equitable instructional areas.
	• Revamp the building scheduling process to allow ELLs to participate in nonacademic classes with their monolingual English-speaking peers.
Program Design	• Have individuals who play different roles in the school evaluate the effectiveness and efficiency of the existing program design.
	• Investigate clustering ELLs in mainstream homerooms.
	• Make sure that the various programs established in the school flow into one another and are coordinated with one another rather than having separate programs that students enter and exit.
Range of Services Offered	• Increase the weekly frequency of specialized support that ELLs receive.
	• Extend specialized support that ELLs receive for a longer period of participation.
Role of Native Language	• Provide native language instruction. If formal instruction in the native language is not possible (for example, if only two students in the school have the same L1), ensure that native language support is set up outside of school.
	• Create a district and curricular plan for language allocation.
	• Examine the native language support that is given to each group of students over the entire range of grades to ensure that it makes developmental sense.
	• Ensure that the support that is given in the native language is well integrated with the rest of instruction that the student receives.
Role of Native Culture	• Complete a cultural responsiveness audit of the existing curriculum.
	• Evaluate the extent to which the cultures represented within the school are visually and orally reflected in the daily functioning of the school.
Characteristics of Instruction	• Ensure that all teachers who work with ELLs are using strategies (such as SIOP) that make the language of instruction more comprehensible.
	• Assess the extent to which there is interaction that helps reach curricular goals among students in the classroom.
	• Evaluate the curriculum and classroom activities to make sure that they promote high levels of thinking skills.

continued

Table 5.5 *continued*

Characteristics of Assessment	• Make sure that performance-based assessment is used and that the results of such assessment play a significant role in the evaluation of the student.
	• Ensure that teachers embed assessment in instruction.
	• Assess in both the first and second language whenever possible.
	• Distinguish between assessment of language proficiency and academic achievement.
	• Distinguish between social or conversational language proficiency and academic language proficiency.

Suggestions for Specific Interventions

Since there is a primary concern with how problems affect individual ELLs, there is typically a question of whether (and how) the implementation of any of the procedures or strategies presented in this chapter can be modified to help a specific student. Teachers are ultimately concerned about the student who sits in the classroom every day: how can they best assist this individual? As teachers ourselves, we have discussed strategies and procedures that are based on our own experiences and those of other teachers. Each of these procedures or ideas has been employed with individual students and, although oriented to general concerns in this chapter, any of the previously mentioned systemic interventions can be adapted or modified to suit the learning environment needs of an individual ELL experiencing academic or linguistic difficulty.

Questions for Discussion

1. What are the strengths and needs of the learning environment that we provide for all of the ELLs we serve?
   1.1. How do we mitigate differences in SES groups?
   1.2. How do we enhance or support the family dynamics?
   1.3. Are our expectations reasonable? How are these expectations communicated?
   1.4. How do we tap into students' interests and experiences? How do we incorporate them into the curriculum?
   1.5. Are our plans for advancing student motivation culturally responsive?
   1.6. Do we regularly activate and build students' prior knowledge?
2. Is the learning environment responsive to changes in our demographics?
3. Is the learning environment working for all groups of ELLs?
4. Are ELLs included in each and every policy or practice implemented at the building and district level?
5. What changes to our policies and practices should we seek to implement?
6. What systemic interventions are needed?
7. How is the learning environment meeting the needs of the ELLs who are currently experiencing difficulty in school?
   7.1. Is it sensitive to the differences in SES groups?
   7.2. Is it supportive of family dynamics?
   7.3. Is it based on reasonable and communicated expectations?
   7.4. Does it incorporate the student's interests and experiences?
   7.5. Does it utilize culturally responsive techniques of motivation?
   7.6. Does it build on and activate the student's prior knowledge?

6

Personal and Family Factors

KEY CONCEPTS

The second factor to be considered is personal and family characteristics, including socioeconomic status, family dynamics, expectations, the student's interests and motivation, experiential background, and parental involvement. If these factors are creating challenges, interventions may be needed to support or mediate events occurring in the home.

Personal and family characteristics have a tremendous influence on every aspect of our lives, including success in school. For this reason, when students are experiencing academic difficulties, we need to find out as much as we can about their life outside of school. Knowing something about the personal and family background can help educators target students' needs and understand students better, which can in turn guide educators to devise and implement appropriate interventions to support the students most effectively. Knowledge of the student's home life and personal circumstances can also aid in evaluating students' progress more accurately by illuminating the larger context within which the student functions. For some students, certain factors will figure prominently in their successes. For other students, these factors may not come into play at all. Depending on the individual's particular situation, some factors may exert more influence than others (Dudley-Marling, 2000).

In this chapter we discuss the student's personal and family characteristics that are likely to play a significant role in the academic achievement of English language learners (ELLs). The list is by no means exhaustive, but it is a good start. The chapter ends with suggestions for gathering information about these aspects of personal and family life, as well as suggestions for interventions to help ameliorate any negative influences these characteristics might have on academic achievement.

Key Factors in the Student's Personal and Family Background

Numerous variables play an implicit or explicit role in orienting a student toward learning. Among the key personal and family variables are socioeconomic status (SES), family dynamics, expectations, the student's interests and motivation, experiential background, and parental involvement.

Socioeconomic Status

Considerable research has focused on the impact of SES on academic achievement (e.g., Arnold & Doctoroff, 2003; Brooks-Gunn & Duncan, 1997; White, 1982). In fact, SES is the family characteristic that most powerfully predicts school performance. In general, the higher the SES of the student's family, the higher the student's academic achievement is likely to be. Although SES is a complex and fluid construct whose actual influence is quite variable (Bolger, Patterson, Thomson, et al., 1995; Bradley & Corwyn, 2002), this relationship has been demonstrated in countless studies and seems to hold no matter what measure of status is used—occupation of the principal breadwinner, family income, parents' education, or some combination of these (Boocock, 1972; Ollendick, Weist, Borden, et al., 1992). In the case of ELL families, the family's current SES may have nothing to do with their SES in their home country. Many immigrant parents who were professionals in their home country and provided a high level of income find themselves working in menial jobs in the United States. Educators should keep this in mind when obtaining information about the SES of an ELL's family because it may account for the lower correlation between SES and academic achievement among immigrant families (Sirin, 2005).

With respect to the strong correlation between SES and academic achievement, we must make it clear that coming from a family with a lower SES almost always means going to a school that does not meet high standards with regard to quality of teachers and the quality of instruction (Haycock, 1998). Thus, the issue is muddied by the fact that lower SES children typically end up in ineffective schools and therefore show lower academic achievement (Sirin, 2005). However, coming from a lower SES home does present some challenges for students.

Research has demonstrated that the SES of families is highly correlated with the amount of talking parents do to children. The verbalizations of the children are also significantly different as a result of the verbal input they receive. In their extensive research, Hart and Risley (2003) studied 42 American families from three widely different social strata (professional families, working-class families, and welfare families) and attempted to determine the amount and kinds of language exposure the children received in their homes from age 13 months until about age 36 months. Using a sophisticated research paradigm, they found that the children in welfare families received less than half the language experience of working-class children in each hour of their home lives (in terms of words heard per hour), and nearly 3.5 times less than children in professional families. In professional families, children between the ages of 13 and 24 months heard an average of 2,150 words per hour, in working-class families the average was 1,250 words per hour, and in welfare families the average was 620 words per hour. There were also some differences in the quality of input, such as greater richness of nouns, modifiers, and past tense verbs in professional families, but even when the quality of input did not vary, the *amount* of input provided the children from higher SES backgrounds was significantly greater. Not surprisingly, Hart and Risley's research and subsequent follow-up with 29 of the children at nine years of age found strong correlations between the verbal input received and the verbal output produced at 36 months of age, and the amount of language growth and usage (as measured on standardized tests) at nine years of age. One can only speculate about the additional differences noted when there are also linguistic and cultural diversity variables within the homes. However, differences in verbal input and its consequences are not the only issues. Many other variables are also involved when SES is considered.

Maslow's hierarchy (Maslow & Lowery, 1998) helps to clarify these other challenges since it provides a useful way of thinking about the factors that motivate the everyday activities of human beings (Covington, 1992). The first human needs are physiological or biological, such as the need for food, water, or shelter, followed by the need for safety, followed by the need to belong and to be accepted. After that, the needs include esteem and self-actualization. Maslow's hierarchy prioritizes the necessities of life and asserts that individuals are able to advance to the next level once needs have been satisfied at the previous level. Following Maslow's theory, the lower SES family's ability to focus on their children's education may prove to be quite difficult until more basic needs are provided (Kozol, 1988; Taylor, 1983).

It is natural for families to focus on the basic needs before directing their attention to higher level needs. Meeting the families' physiological needs depends on employment and income. Many immigrant families are employed in lower-paying jobs, and therefore the immigrant family striving to meet the physical needs of all its members must expend significant effort at this lower level of the hierarchy of needs, at least for an initial period of time. In some families both parents work long hours, in other families parents stagger their shifts in order to have one parent at home when the other is at work, and in many families older children are expected to work and contribute a paycheck. Often the work is physically exhausting or dangerous. Meeting the family's basic needs can be so all-consuming that other needs go unmet. Chronicle 6.1 describes such a situation. If the family is able to provide the necessities of life for itself, students are better able to get down to the business of learning.

Safety needs also figure prominently for immigrant families, particularly those in lower SES groups. Newly arrived immigrant families often first settle in poorer neighborhoods, many of which have a high crime rate. Parents, fearing for their children's safety, may institute household rules for their protection. For example, parents may forbid their children to play outside. In areas with a history of drive-by shootings, parents may instruct their children to lie on the floor when they do their homework. If the family is able to mitigate such safety concerns, students are more likely to be able to concentrate on their studies.

Many immigrant families live in cramped quarters where it may be difficult to find a quiet space for the children to do their homework. In general, children from lower SES homes do not have easy access to resources such as crayons, magazines, books, encyclopedias, or the Internet. Having all these resources at home gives higher SES children a tremendous advantage over their peers, who have to share a few crayons with siblings in order to complete an assignment and who cannot look up information they need for a report right in the comfort of their home.

Family Dynamics

Immigration, especially when it is by limited choice, can wreak havoc on the family structure. Children's separation from their parents and the change in family dynamics because of immigration to the United States can play a big

---

ECOS TEAM ACTIVITY

In many schools, teachers do not live in the neighborhood of the school, and thus do not know the comings and goings of the community. How familiar is the ECOS team with the neighborhood of the school? For those members who are not residents of the school neighborhood, assign a simple everyday errand to each staff member, such as borrowing a book from the local branch of the public library, buying a carton of milk from the local grocery store, mailing something from the local branch of the post office. Have each person jot down notes so that they can tell others about their experience and about their impressions of the neighborhood.

Laundry Takes Precedence

By the director of a suburban bilingual program

It seemed simple, really: my request of parents to spend an hour with their child every weekday assisting them with their schoolwork. These were students whose parents were employees of a racetrack. My request did not meet with much of a response. I didn't begin to understand why until I was able to venture onto the racetrack grounds and speak with the moms. They told me that they only had one day off from working every week and that day is Monday (the only day that horse races are not run). Saturdays and Sundays are long workdays for both moms and dads, and Mondays are laundry days.

Since there are no laundry facilities on the racetrack property that are available to back stretch workers, women must take the family laundry to the nearest laundromat. Jockeys, groomers, and trainers have laundry facilities, but most backstretch workers (those who walk the horses after their runs and clean their stalls) are considered the lowest of the low in the pecking order of the racetrack industry.

Getting to the nearest laundry facility is a challenge. Most women (and many men) working at the racetrack do not hold a driver's license, and if they do, they do not own a car. That means they must walk. The closest laundromat was at least two miles away, off the expansive racetrack property. Women would commandeer a shopping cart from the local grocery store and push it back over gravel roads to their living quarters on the backstretch. They would load the dirty laundry into the cart and push it the two miles to the laundromat, wash, dry, and fold the clean clothes, load them back into the grocery cart, and then push the cart back over the gravel roads to their living quarters.

The entire process easily took seven hours on their only day off from work each week. Once I understood their situation, I realized how silly my request was. Once I began to tailor my requests for parent involvement to what the parents could actually do, the parents were thrilled to give support to their children.

Questions for discussion:

- How can visiting children in their homes and speaking with parents in their environment help teachers create a better learning environment?
- How can the teacher's ignorance influence the learning environment?
- How can teachers use the reality of family living situations to foster learning?

role in ELLs' success in school by adding to the anxiety level that many ELLs experience. The family's degree of mobility can also play a role. As a result of the ways that immigration unfolds, many ELLs may be separated from their parents for long periods. Parents may have left their children in the care of grandparents or other relatives while they immigrate to the United States, with the intention of sending for their children once they have secured jobs and housing. In other situations, one parent may come to the United States with older offspring while leaving younger children back home with the other parent. In still other situations, parents may send their children to live with relatives already established in the United States. Parents' work schedules once they get to the United States may preclude much contact with their children during the workweek. The lack of regular and routine parent contact over months and even years may prove stressful for some students and may devastate the family dynamics.

Upon arrival in the United States, families may experience outside cultural and linguistic influences that also change family dynamics. For example, as children acquire English proficiency at a faster rate than their parents, the school and, in some cases, the parents themselves tend to rely on the children to provide translation services. Whether children are translating for their parents in a doctor's office, in the used car lot, or at a parent-teacher conference, such situations can affect the balance of power in the family structure, yielding more power to the child and less power to the parent. This imbalance of power is often called *parentification* in the literature and can affect children and parents negatively. Parentification refers to children or adolescents assuming adult roles before they are emotionally ready and at the expense of their own developmentally appropriate needs and pursuits (Chase, 1999).

In addition, if children have been discouraged in school to continue to develop their native language, they begin to lose fluency in that language. Besides the negative effect that native language loss has on cognition and academics (Cummins, 2000; Lambert, 1974), the ties that bind parents to their children weaken. This will have significant effect on the strength of the family unit and will certainly affect the students' well-being.

The family may also have a gender role structure that is different from that of the community to which they have immigrated. The original family structure may change once the family immigrates, and this might result in added stress. For example, the original family structure may have been more patriarchal in the native country, but in the United States, mothers may feel pressured to have a stronger voice in decision making. Such situations can create conflict in the family.

Immigrant families, possibly as a result of tenuous employment status and strained family ties, may also move frequently. These moves may interrupt the children's instruction, whether they move across the United States following agricultural crop schedules or industrial plant openings or move between neighboring school districts in pursuit of more affordable housing or higher wages. Feelings of homesickness and a desire to stay connected to the native language, culture, and friends and relatives left behind can fuel the desire to return to the native country for long trips. Such trips, if not handled properly by the school, can exacerbate the effects of the family's mobility and the amount of interrupted education the student experiences, and thereby may hinder the ELL's progress in school.

High levels of stress are not atypical in immigrant families. Even when parents are able to secure employment, such employment may be erratic or undependable, causing stress in the family. Immigrant parents may be ill-equipped to deal with such stress, and this situation can lead to depression, verbal abuse, physical abuse, or substance abuse. When these symptoms of stress emerge, parents may have little knowledge of support systems within the community they can turn to for help. Community support systems may or may not be culturally and linguistically responsive, thereby limiting the effectiveness of treatment.

Although the discussion so far has considered the negative effects of the family stressors associated with immigration, many immigrants are able to situate themselves in appropriate communities, get the help they need, and adapt quite well to their new surroundings (Portes, 1999; Stanton-Salazar, 1997; Trueba, 1988). However, school staff must be aware of the stressors that may be affecting some families of ELLs, and must be sensitive to the issues that may be causing a challenge for these ELLs at school.

Expectations

Parents' and their children's expectations of education and their attitudes toward it are an influence on ELLs' school success. Few parents would argue that education is not valuable for their children. Exactly why it is valued may differ for different immigrant families and differ from the school's perspective. Some parents from different cultural backgrounds may view education as the path to upward economic mobility and a way to gain entry into the workforce as soon as possible. Others may view education as a top priority for their sons but of less importance for their daughters. Still others may push the oldest child to pursue higher and higher levels of education, with younger siblings expected to help support the eldest in his endeavors. Parents, students, and educators may find themselves at cross-purposes if the views of the parents and children are not consonant with those of the school system.

Student Interests

Students' interests include their past, their current life outside of school, their hobbies, and their passions. Much has been said about the importance of a culturally responsive curriculum that taps into ELLs' interests in academic areas and extracurricular activities (see, e.g., Banks, 2005). These curricula incorporate the students' cultural backgrounds as integral elements during learning activities rather than trivializing or negating them. As a result, culturally responsive curricula capitalize on ELLs' interests. When students are provided with tasks and activities that are inherently engaging, their motivation rises (Marzano, 2003; Portes, 1999). Schools should play close attention to the interests of ELLs to create thematic topics, instructional and assessment tasks, and school activities that extend beyond the school day that tap into the interests of the ELLs they serve.

ELLs contribute the added advantage of bringing with them interesting and often exotic experiences that mainstream students can only read about in stories or encyclopedias. When the curriculum integrates these different perspectives and experiences into the everyday working of the classroom, it is not only the ELL who benefits from the added familiarity but the mainstream student who is enriched by learning about these experiences.

Student Motivation

The link between student motivation and achievement is straightforward. If students are motivated to learn the content in a given subject, their achievement in that subject will most likely be good. If students are not motivated to learn the content, their achievement will be limited (Marzano, 2003). Motivation deals with why people behave in a certain way. While there are many theories that attempt to explain how motivation works, it would be wise to use these theories with the specific needs and wants of typical ELLs in mind (Suarez-Orozco, 1995). For example, according to attribution theory (Heider, 1958), success is attributed to one or more of the following four causes: ability, effort, luck, and task difficulty. The perception of one's ability is tainted for ELLs by a constant struggle to express what they know in their second language and constantly making mistakes and not being understood by others. As for effort, when ELLs spend hours each night doing homework that takes monolingual English students a fraction of the time, it gives them a skewed concept of what level of effort is rewarded and produces results. When teachers give ELLs assignments that are beyond their capabilities, student motivation wanes.

Self-worth theory is based on the premise that the search for self-acceptance is one of the highest human priorities (Lareau, 1987; Marzano, 2003; Stanton-Salazar, 1997). Self-acceptance or acceptance into one's peer culture can be very hard to come by for an ELL. If academic achievement is a criterion for acceptance, ELLs may not experience that acceptance for years on end. If adeptness in social interactions is a criterion for acceptance, ELLs may also wait years to experience the English language fluency such social interaction demands.

Mawi Asgedom (2003) has said that while growing up in suburban Illinois as an ELL, he sat through many awards ceremonies and never received any kind of acknowledgment for his efforts or his successes in learning English. Many awards were given—for perfect attendance, for honor roll achievement, for sports performance, for volunteering—but because he had limited English proficiency he was precluded from being considered for those awards (except for perfect attendance). If we never celebrate or reward the effort and diligent work it takes to learn English as a second language, might we be diminishing students' to advance their learning?

Experiential Background

There is a common misperception that ELLs lack the background knowledge essential to academic success. It may be the case that the ELL's background knowledge simply does not conform to the school's expectations. ELLs may have not participated in the obligatory field trips to the pumpkin farm and the zoo or have familiarity with the supermarket or the post office, experiences that mainstream children pick up along the way. However, ELLs enroll in our schools with a wealth of background knowledge that may be completely foreign to the mainstream students. They may have had firsthand experience raising chickens to sell at a market or building the family home with adobe bricks or watching their parent serve as a scribe for their village.

ELLs coming from war-torn areas or extreme poverty may have developed street smarts in their struggles to survive in their native country. Such background knowledge, while perhaps not part of the school's expectations, can prove to be a valuable resource in instruction if the teacher knows how to access it and help the child use the resulting skills to focus on academic learning (see Chronicle 6.2 as an illustration).

ECOS TEAM ACTIVITY

Start an inventory of interesting experiences that students in the school have had. Be sure to include ELLs in the list. The inventory can be built by word of mouth or by students themselves contributing essays about their experiences. The inventory can serve as a "speakers bureau" type of resource, where students can be called on to showcase their experiences for other students during assembly or special events.

Is That What She's Talking About?

By an ESL teacher

I was trying to teach vertical and horizontal axis and points on a grid (typically taught in sixth-grade math) to my ESL students. My three students were boys from Vietnam. They spoke limited English and I spoke no Vietnamese. I had tried everything to make the concepts comprehensible—visuals, games, simulations, and manipulatives—all to no avail. After many excruciating attempts and failures to get the concept across, I had just about given up. All of a sudden, one of the students said to me, "Oh, I know—same same you drive a boat!" This child had helped his uncle navigate a raft, using the stars, when they were fleeing Vietnam trying to make it to the refugee camps in Thailand. He began explaining to the other two boys in Vietnamese, using gestures and drawing on the board. I could see that the two boys also knew what he was talking about. I felt so humble. These boys knew a lot more about math than I had given them credit for. I had failed to activate their prior knowledge, and in the process had almost given up.

Questions for discussion:

- How can a teacher learn about her students' previous experiences?
- How can the teacher connect these experiences to the curriculum?

Parental Involvement

Parents' expectations of what their role should be in the education of their children varies significantly among immigrant families who are used to educational systems other than the United States. In their childhood or as a parent of a schoolchild in their native country, they may have experienced a clear divide between home and school, with the school system actually discouraging their involvement in their children's education. In some countries, parents are not expected to play a visible role inside the school. When their children enroll in a school in the United States, ELL parents may find the school's requests for input into decision making, volunteering in the classroom, help with homework in the evenings, fundraising assistance, and field trip chaperoning quite perplexing. Based on their prior experiences and education, parents may view themselves as ill-prepared for such work and therefore are reluctant to participate. Thus, if parents of some ELLs are not seen as being "involved" in their children's education, it may be because of divergent expectations.

Parents' ability to participate in the education of their children can be affected by their employment. The jobs immigrant parents have may be quite restrictive in allowing workers time off. Even a phone call from the school that pulls a parent off the assembly line can result in a disciplinary action initiated by the employer.

Parents may see their roles and that of school staff as clearly divided, with parents responsible for providing children with the necessities of life and moral education and the teacher responsible for providing instruction in the basic subject areas. Some parents may view the school's requests for their parental involvement as an indication that the schools have abdicated their responsibility to educate children. Still other parents may have had uncomfortable experiences during their own schooling and therefore feel incompetent when asked by the school to become involved.

CHRONICLE 6.3

Cutting into My Weekend

By the director of a bilingual program

I had to get creative. Attendance at my parent meetings was abysmal. A handful of parents were attending meetings intended for the parents of 2,000-plus ELLs. I surveyed parents as to when they wanted to meet, willing to forgo my preferred times if it meant greater attendance. The parents asked for meetings on Friday nights and Sundays after church. While these times certainly cut into my weekend, I realized I was getting nowhere fast by scheduling meetings on Thursdays at 7 p.m.

I implemented the new schedule, which alternated between Friday nights and Sunday afternoons. I was astounded—attendance was over 90%. Trying something so unconventional as weekend meetings emboldened me. I began to try new things: substituting the never touched cookies and coffee with potluck suppers, incorporating opportunities for adult socialization into the meetings, offering door prize items deemed desirable by the families (such as 25-pound turkeys right before the holidays, gift certificates to indoor playgrounds, and amusement parks) scheduling meetings in apartment community rooms rather than always on school grounds, establishing a crew of fathers who worked the swing shift to serve as field trip chaperones, creating a drop-in parent center with a computer lab for parents.

Doing all those things, I had the most supportive and active set of parents I had ever imagined.

Questions for discussion:

- Why is it important to think nontraditionally about parent involvement?
- Why is it important to think about what parents need in addition to what the schools need from parents? How does one do that?

Epstein (2001) distinguishes between parent support and participation as two components of parent involvement, asserting that parent support influences student achievement more significantly than parent participation. The constraints many immigrant families face in terms of their job schedules, their lack of familiarity with the school system, and a possible limited command of English may render parent participation (volunteering, helping with homework, participating in decision making at the school level, and collaborating with the community) difficult if not impossible (but see how these hurdles can be overcome, in Chronicle 6.3). Whereas a parent's ability to provide support need not be compromised by any extrinsic factors, school systems that place their emphasis on helping parents support their children's education rather than demanding that parents participate through volunteering during school hours on school premises will likely see more return on their efforts.

Suggestions for Information Gathering

How should educators go about gathering information about ELLs' personal and family factors? In two words: very carefully. We should be sensitive to ELL families' need for privacy, just as we are with mainstream families. We need to be clear to parents and children what kind of information we want and why. We must assure parents that the information will be used to create a better learning environment for their children, and we need to show them the specific aspects of everyday school life that will change as a result of the information gathered. We need to be aware of the fact that parents, especially those who have an undocumented status in the United States, may be extremely reluctant to give any kind of information that they perceive as threatening to their existence in the country. If an interpreter is used to obtain information in the parents' native language, that person must be carefully chosen. The interpreter must be someone with whom the parents feel comfortable and someone they can trust.

Both historical and current information should be deemed important in understanding the student's personal and family background. Information gathering in this area will likely require staff to interview the student and the student's family, siblings, teachers, and community members that interact with the student, such as coaches and ministers. Because much of the information obtained is of sensitive nature, schools should build trust, establish a relationship with the family, and seek the cooperation of the parents at the very beginning of the process, keeping in mind the precautionary notes in the preceding paragraph.

Since many ELL parents are not proficient speakers of English, an interpreter who can conduct the interviews in the parents' native language can work in collaboration with staff. How to conduct the interviews has to be determined on an individual basis, depending on the relationship the staff and the interpreter have with the student and the family. Table 6.1 lists a series of questions that may be used to guide the conversations that take place with students and family members. It is not recommended that questions be posed one after the other. Rather, an informal, open-ended conversation can take place in a low-anxiety setting, preferably in the home. Staff can determine, again depending on the level of comfort with the family, whether to write notes on the spot or to do so later.

Another way to gather information is by using teaching strategies that inform us about students' lives while serving an instructional purpose. One of the most effective ways of finding out about students' lives is through dialogue journals (Peyton & Staton, 1993). Dialogue journals are written conversations that take place between student and teacher. The teacher writes a brief message to the student and the student writes back; the teacher responds, and so on. The "conversations" reveal much about the student, but a significant added bonus is that ELLs' language proficiency blossoms through these dialogue journals (Hamayan, 1994).

Schools may also review past school records. However, the parents may have left the records behind, or the previous school did not provide the records. Calls to the student's previous school or the teacher may prove fruitful. Some information may be gleaned from the district's database, such as lists of students eligible for free and reduced lunch, though most districts have placed restrictions on who can and cannot view those lists. For families who have just arrived in the United States, it may be difficult to come by any kind of records, but this should not be perceived as the parents' fault. Even under the best of circumstances, if the family had time to prepare for their journey, immigration is a confusing process that could easily result in lost or misplaced papers.

The questions in Table 6.1 can serve as a guide for the kind of information to glean from these sources of information and a way to organize this information.

While information is being gathered, educators should consult with someone who can serve as a cultural broker or liaison. This person may or may not be the same as the interpreter who conducted the interviews in the native language. This cultural broker assists with the interpretation of the gathered information. This person should be someone who is both familiar with the native culture of the student, the immigrant experience in the local com-

(text continues on page 105)

Table 6.1 Possible Questions to Consider for Getting a Sense of the Student's Personal and Family Background

SES	• What job(s) does the father hold?
	• What job(s) does the mother hold?
	• What shift(s) does each work?
	• What job did the father or mother hold in the home country?
	• How safe is the block on which the family lives?
	• What kind of living space did the family have in the home country?
	• Does the student have a quiet space for doing homework?
	• Are magazines, paper, and writing tools available in the home?
	• Does the family have access to a computer?
Family Dynamics	• What is the family's immigration story?
	• How did the family get here?
	• Did everyone come together?
	• Is there still family in the native country?
	• Who is at home when the student returns from school?
	• What responsibilities do the children have at home?
	• How do the children help their parents?
	• Who translates for the parents?
	• How smoothly do the children communicate with elders in the home in the native language (if that is the parents' and grandparents' more proficient language)?
	• If the mother works, does that add stress to the family dynamics?
	• How often has the family moved?
	• What type of a formal support network—such as church or a social services organization—does the family have? How about an informal support network, such as relatives or close friends or neighbors?
Expectations	• What do the parents want for their children's education?
	• What role does education play in the family's long-term plans?
	• What is the highest level of education that parents would like their children to attain?
Student's Interests	• How does the student spend his or her free time?
	• Does the student have any hobbies?
	• What is interesting about this student's current or past life?
	• What curricular or extracurricular activities is the student good at?
Motivation	• How motivated is the student at school?
	• How clear is it to the student that his or her advances in English and in academic performance are something to be proud of and to celebrate?
	• How clear is it to the student that his or her efforts to complete assignments are appreciated?
Experiential Background	• What U.S.-American school experiences that the student missed might be contributing to confusion, lack of understanding, or a sense of not belonging?
	• What interesting experiences did the student have before arriving in the United States?
Parental Involvement	• What is the parents' understanding of their role vis-à-vis the school?
	• What was the parents' role in the school in their native country?
	• How comfortable do parents feel playing an active role in the school?
	• How welcoming is the school to ELL parents?
	• How easy is it for parents to come to school during school hours?
	• What kind of support do parents provide for their children's learning at home?

Table 6.2 Systemic Interventions That Can Help Overcome Challenges Stemming from Personal and Family Issues

SES	• Establish a parent drop-in center with links to information provided by community agencies. • Create a toy or book or software lending library. • Open a computer lab that is available for parents and students. • Operate a food pantry and a clothes closet that accepts donations and allows parents to select needed clothing and food for their family. • Offer adult ESL and GED courses, community job training sessions, job searches and career planning, training on the topics of budgeting, insurance, financial planning, effective parent involvement, and avenues for financial assistance for postsecondary education. • Start breakfast and lunch programs as well as in-school snack programs. • Run afterschool homework centers and district- or state-sponsored early childhood programs. • Make refurbished school computers available for parents to purchase or lease. • Open a school store for school supplies available at wholesale cost. • Establish a scholarship fund for school field trips. • Provide safe transportation for afterschool programs.
Family dynamics and mobility	• Set up a network of culturally and linguistically responsive counseling services. • Establish a group of trained translators and interpreters, at least for the most popular languages. • Craft a district-wide policy for assignments when students take long trips back to the native country.
Expectations	• Maintain ongoing communication with all the communities the school serves, to incorporate parents' expectations into policies and practices designed and implemented by the school. • Offer parent training workshops that demystify the school's expectations of parents. • Offer workshops that suggest clear and pragmatic strategies to parents for supporting their children's education. • Establish explicit strategies to honor and value the parents' perspective.
Student Interest	• Design interest surveys to be included as a part of the registration process. • Carry out a summer project to incorporate student background, culture and interest into the curriculum and instruction for all students. • Monitor artifacts of student interest, such as attendance sheets for school clubs and intramural activities. • Analyze lists of those who try out for different sports, theater productions, and other competitions. • Note teacher observations as to who attends school dances and sporting events.
Student Motivation	• Develop a checklist or rubric by which teachers can evaluate the appropriateness of the assignments they give ELLs. • Tailor incentive programs to variables over which ELLs have control. • Institute celebrations and awards for accomplishments unique to ELLs. • Implement mechanisms that ensure ELLs receive meaningful feedback from the teachers on their academic and linguistic progress.

continued

Table 6.2 *continued*

Experiential Background	• Build prompts to activate experiential background into the curriculum. • Budget for field trips to provide students with many meaningful life experiences. • Provide more instances of hands-on instruction.
Parent Involvement	• Create policies and practices that emphasize and value parental support over parental participation. • Make the school more welcoming to ELL parents. • Provide training to all who work with ELLs including PTA/PTO board members. • Establish a buddy system for newly arrived parents. • Establish a friendship network that pairs immigrant parents with others like themselves and with parents from the monolingual English parent group. • Help parents to establish a car pool or bus transportation to school events. • Provide child care at school events. • Help parents establish a cooperative for child care needs. • Host some school events in the community rooms of the apartment complexes where ELLs live. • Provide a line item in the budget for district training and paying of translators and interpreters, establishing a preference in hiring procedures for individuals in the immigrant community the school serves or at the very least establishing as a qualification for employment as a school clerical worker the ability to speak more than just English.

(text continued from page 102)

munity, and the culture of the school. Educators who know and understand the factors of SES, family dynamics, mobility, expectations, student interest, student motivation, experiential background, and parent involvement as they appear in the student's life in the native country can then compare and contrast how those same factors play out in the family's experience in the United States. With the insight of the cultural liaison, the ability to make accurate comparisons is enhanced, providing context to the educator's assessment of the student's situation and clarifying which personal and family factors are currently playing a role in the ELL's success in school.

Suggestions for Systemic Interventions

If the school or district notes that significant numbers of their ELLs are impacted by one or more of the previously mentioned personal and family factors, systemic interventions are warranted. Systemic interventions address the needs of current students and may serve to proactively prevent similar needs for future students. Some examples are listed in Table 6.2.

Suggestions for Specific Interventions

If the school notes that some of these factors affect only a handful of students, the school can implement nearly all of the previously mentioned interventions, but on a more limited scale. For example, instead of providing a clearinghouse of information to all parents, one staff member could sit down with the family and direct it to linguistically and culturally responsive community agencies that can help the family with specific concerns. A teacher could help one family resolve transportation issues by providing a bus schedule for the area or connecting the family with another parent who lives nearby and is willing to carpool or provide a ride.

Questions for Discussion

1. What do we know about the personal and family factors affecting the ELLs we serve?
   1.1. Are the demographics changing? If yes, how?
   1.2. Are certain groups of ELLs subject to different factors?
   1.3. Are the families of ELLs in our community well connected to community service agencies and other support networks?
   1.4. Does the impact of these factors on ELLs' success change over time?
   1.5. Are the district and school policies and practices responsive?
   1.6. What changes to our policies and practices should we seek to implement?
   1.7. What systemic interventions are needed?
   1.8. How will we document the effect of these interventions?
2. What do we know about the personal and family factors affecting the ELL student who is currently experiencing difficulty in school?
   2.1. How can we find out more?
   2.2. How should we interpret the data we collect?
   2.3. Which factors are having the most pronounced impact on the student?
   2.4. Are the district and school policies and practices responsive to the student's needs at this time?
   2.5. What specific interventions are needed?
   2.6. How will we monitor the ELL's progress during the intervention?
   2.7. How will we determine the success of the intervention?

7

Physical and Psychological Factors

KEY CONCEPTS

The third integral factor to be considered consists of physical and psychological factors, including medical conditions, impaired vision or hearing, malnutrition and chronic hunger, chronic pain due to untreated medical conditions, posttraumatic stress syndrome, fear, psychological stress, social and emotional development, and feelings of belonging. If challenges are emanating from this factor, physical and psychological support needs to be offered.

Physical and psychological factors can play a crucial role in classroom learning. As discussed by Jack (2000) and others (Blackburn, 1991; Rutter & Madge, 1976; Werner & Smith, 1992), good (or at least neutral) physical and psychological contexts are the foundation on which the ecology of an individual's development and knowledge acquisition is constructed. Learning requires a physical readiness void of illness and pain and an affective context that is relatively free of intervening variables. The presence of a physical malady or too many affective barriers—such as stress, apathy, anxiety, and perplexity—results in inefficiency or even inability to learn. However, the relationship between physical and psychological factors and academic success is complicated by the diversity issues that define English language learner (ELL) populations, and these complications must be addressed.

Educators are undoubtedly aware of the influences of physical and psychological factors when they are working with monolingual English students. However, if they have limited training in ESL/bilingual education, they may not be able to identify how these influences and the resulting dynamics may play out in the lives of the ELLs they teach. Similarly, ESL/bilingual specialists may not realize how closely some physical and psychological factors resemble the effects of a physical disability. Knowledge of these factors and of the learning and performance dynamics that can result will help educators in assessment, for this knowledge permits more accurate data collection and interpretation, so that effective diagnosis and intervention can occur. As with personal and family factors, the role of physical and psychological factors in academic success is highly variable, and their influence varies with each individual student's circumstances and ability to meet challenges.

In this chapter we describe some essential factors in ELLs' physical and psychological situation that can affect their performance at school. We then present ideas for gathering information about these factors. Finally, we suggest systemic and specific interventions to help students with physical or psychological issues that might be impeding optimal learning.

Key Physical and Psychological Factors

The following physical and psychological factors can play key roles in the way ELLs learn in school, so any consideration of behavioral data and their interpretation must also closely consider the role of these factors. Although there is a wide range of factors to consider, the following seem especially important in working with ELLs: disease or medical condition, impaired vision or hearing, malnutrition and chronic hunger, chronic pain due to untreated illness, posttraumatic stress syndrome/disorder, fear, current psychological stress, social and emotional development, and feelings of belonging to the school and the wider community. Any of these factors can interact with language and learning processes in unpredictable ways.

Disease or Medical Condition

As a result of poverty, limited access to health care in their native countries and in the poorer neighborhoods in the United States, stress, and other living conditions affecting health, such as, poor nutrition, close living arrangements, and perhaps less knowledge of good health practices, that tend to co-occur with immigrant, refugee, and other diverse populations, the possibility of disease or a medical condition that results in poor cognitive performance is much more likely in ELLs than in the general population (Blaxter, 1990; Smaje, 1995; Stern, Pugh, Gaskill, et al., 1982; Weissbourd, 1996). For example, the U.S. Department of Education records for 2001 indicate that Hispanics experience a higher than normal incidence of obesity, hypertension (Cousins, et al., 1993) and diabetes (NIH, 2004) and records show that more than 25% of the students in the Other Health Impaired (OHI) category who are covered under special education regulations are from "culturally different" groups. Insofar as the percentage of culturally different students was about 20% of the total school population in 2001, this figure suggests a greater number of identified OHI students in the culturally different population than in the general U.S. population.

Not only is the incidence of disease and other medical conditions likely to be higher in culturally diverse populations, the reactions to these health problems are often different in the families of ELLs. These differences appear to reflect unique cultural beliefs and practices. In some cultures, for example, there are cultural practices and expectations, such as retaining personal control over one's treatments or placing control in the hands of another or the state, a distrust of Western medicine, shamanism, and the use of alternative medical treatments, that result in disinclination to seek Western-style medical help (e.g., Cousin, Power, & Olivera-Ezzell, 1993; Fadiman, 1997; Lau, 1982). In such cases it may be difficult to identify a medical condition and gain compliance with a physician-recommended course of treatment (Bussing, Schoenberg, & Perwien, 1998; Weisz, Suwanlert, Chaiyasit, et al., 1988).

For the purposes of the ECOS team, however, the fact that many ELLs are at greater risk for disease or a medical condition has a practical impact that must be considered. In academic contexts, students learn best when their physical status is unproblematic. When poor nutrition, fatigue, pain, illness, or other negative physical conditions exist, learning takes a back seat to resolving these problems. People in pain or discomfort do not learn well. It is necessary for the ECOS team to try to account for the possibility of disease or a medical condition that is not always obvious and to try to help eliminate or reduce the impact of this health condition.

Impaired Vision or Hearing

Many immigrant children have not had the benefit of periodic and sustained medical attention. In such circumstances, allergies, middle ear infections, and diseases caused by exotic pathogens like bacteria and parasites may be present during development and may cause medical conditions leading to visual

---

ECOS TEAM ACTIVITY

Have the nurse or health aide do a vision/hearing screening test on a member of the ECOS team, but without using language of any kind. How might pantomime be used? Can gestures be used to replace the words *yes* and *no?* Can pictures that are free of cultural bias be incorporated? Discuss ways to make screenings friendlier and yield more valid results for ELLs.

---

or auditory impairments. Even when these conditions occur, the limited access to medical care means that the necessary screenings for these conditions may not occur. Consequently, ELLs may arrive in U.S. schools with undiagnosed vision or hearing problems. There may be several explanations for this situation, including scarcity of medical personnel in refugee camps or during wartime, lack of insurance, or inability to pay for services. Regardless of the cause, it is important for educators never to assume that an ELL who is experiencing difficulty in school has perfect hearing and vision. Sometimes these students fall through the cracks of our own system. Nurses may be unable to communicate sufficiently with a child to complete the vision or hearing test accurately, a child may enroll in school after the schoolwide vision or hearing screenings are completed or a child may have had a vision or hearing problem diagnosed but fails to wear the corrective glasses or hearing aid. Chronicle 7.1 tells the story of a child who would have been misplaced into special education for the want of a vision test.

Malnutrition and Chronic Hunger

In a country as rich as the United States, it is a tragedy that so many children suffer from malnutrition and chronic hunger. However, this problem is evident in all industrialized countries (e.g., Blaxter, 1990; Jack, 2000; Seccombe, 2002; Steinhauer, 1998), particularly among immigrant families (Schiller, 2001; Smaje, 1995). Immigrant children may experience malnutrition and chronic hunger because of poverty or a paucity of fresh fruits and produce in their neighborhood market. Some immigrant families struggle to prepare healthy foods in the cuisine of their new country and may have to travel great distances to purchase foodstuffs used in their native cuisine. Some children must prepare food for themselves while their parents are at work, and the children may not make the healthiest of choices. When malnutrition and chronic hunger exist, steps should be taken to account for their impact during assessment, and any resources available in the community and appropriate to the ELL's family circumstances should be employed to break the cycle of hunger and malnutrition. A growling stomach, low blood sugar, or nutrient deficiencies will influence a student's academic success.

Chronic Pain Due to Untreated Illness, Disease or Condition

Although many ELLs may traverse the U.S. school system with undiagnosed vision or hearing problems, others may have an undiagnosed illness, disease, or condition that is allowed to extend beyond the limits of tolerance. When

---

ECOS TEAM ACTIVITY

Assign team members to visit a grocery store that caters to a target ethnic group. The task is to purchase treats or ingredients to make treats for the next ECOS team meeting that are healthy and new to the group. Have the team members report to the group on their shopping and treat preparation experiences and have the group discuss the nutritional aspects of the treats provided. Relate these conversations back to the experiences immigrant families might have when they arrive in the community.

CHRONICLE 7.1

BD? No! Blind!

By a case manager at a school with a large population of ELLs

I was called in by the ESL teacher to provide my "rubber stamp" of approval to what she described as a classic case of behavioral disorders. On the phone she described Igor's behaviors as problems with buttoning and zippering his clothes, inability to retain information from one day to the next, severe problems with reading, and very inappropriate social behaviors, such as being to close to peers and teacher (to the point of irritation). Igor was a fifth-grade student from Ukraine.

When I entered the room for the meeting, there were 12 building staff members (from the child study team) and an English-speaking psychologist from the district. The team members and the psychologist had reputations of superior professionalism and attention to detail. This was in a wealthy suburban district with all sorts of resources at their disposal.

To start the meeting, one person read a report of Igor's current functioning and restated the behavioral descriptors the ESL teacher had previously shared with me. I listened until she finished reading. Then I asked if anyone had checked Igor's vision. Jaws dropped around the table. No, they replied, they had not because his English was too limited and they did not have anyone who spoke Ukrainian. Fortunately, the decision was unanimous: Igor's vision had to be checked before we could proceed any further. I suggested that the nurse give the vision test with help from the ESL teacher, who would use ESL sheltering strategies to make the test more comprehensible. As it turned out, Igor was legally blind! Even his mother did not know this, as they had lived in rural Ukraine and Igor had not attended school regularly.

We connected Igor to a teacher of the blind and sought to find him large-print materials and glasses. Igor began to make progress after that. In fact, in sixth grade he was recommended for placement in the district's gifted and talented program. I read about Igor six years later in the local paper. He had graduated from high school with honors and had been given a four-year scholarship to a prestigious university!

Questions for discussion:

- What preliminary work had this team failed to do?
- How can you feel comfortable asking a question of the team that on the surface may insult team members' professionalism yet is essential to ensure that a student's needs are accurately diagnosed?
- What if no one on the team had expertise in the area of bilingual/ESL education?

this occurs, the existing disease state or medical condition is greatly exacerbated by the onlay of unremitting pain, which serves as a harbinger of more serious medical status. Some children may suffer from chronic mouth pain resulting from untreated dental caries or "baby-bottle mouth." Other children may suffer from lead poisoning or from exposure to contaminated well water. Still others may experience the side effects of exposure to chemicals such as DDT, DEET, and dioxin. School nurses and health aides need to get involved and work side by-side with ESL/bilingual teachers to learn the hazards and conditions many immigrant families face.

ECOS TEAM ACTIVITY

Have team members contact various cultural or community associations and support networks to determine if any illnesses, diseases, or conditions are prevalent among immigrant groups in their area. Obtain information as to how such instances are dealt with in the native country and relate that information to the current situation in the local community.

Posttraumatic Stress Syndrome/Disorder

Some ELLs come from countries that have seen much violence. They may have aspects of if not full-fledged posttraumatic stress syndrome/disorder (PTSD). PTSD is a psychiatric disorder that can occur following the direct experience with, or witnessing of life-threatening events such as military combat, natural disasters, terrorist incidents, serious accidents, or violent personal assaults. Many survivors of trauma return to normal given time and a different perspective on their experiences. However, some people have stress reactions that do not go away on their own or may even worsen over time. The variables that cause one individual to develop PTSD and another to move beyond the traumatic experience are complex and involve the kinds and severity of the trauma, the age of the individual, personality traits, gender, and support provided in response to the trauma (Macksoud & Aber, 1996). When some individuals develop PTSD, the symptoms can be severe enough and last long enough to significantly impair the person's daily life (U.S. Department of Veteran Affairs, 2006).

As designated by the *Diagnostic and Statistical Manual for Mental Disorders (DSM IV-TR)* (American Psychiatric Association, 2000), the diagnosis for PTSD requires four criteria be met: (1) precipitation by a stressor; (2) reexperiencing of the trauma through dreams, nightmares, or compulsive memories triggered by evocative stimuli; (3) experiencing two or more of a group of symptoms, which include irritability, depression, anxiety, aggressive and impulsive behavior, emotional instability, memory impairment, startle response, and sleep disturbance; and (4) development of a sense of detachment and loss of interest in the current life situation. Of course, any combination of these symptoms could drastically affect academic and social functioning.

The existence of PTSD has been somewhat controversial and was primarily applied to veterans returning from the Vietnam War (Berger, 1977; Walker & Cavenar, 1982). However, Owan (1985) reported that a growing number of Southeast Asian refugees were suffering from severe mental health problems, including what appeared to be PTSD. In 1987, August and Gianola linked the growing number of refugees and their symptoms with the similarities seen in Vietnam War veterans and made a strong case for diagnosing the refugees with PTSD as well. Since that time, PTSD has become a recognized psychiatric disorder that is not linked solely to combat experience but to any number of traumatic events.

Educators throughout the United States report that many more newly arrived immigrant students have borne witness to military conflicts than in previous years (Garbarino, Kostelny, & Dubrow, 1991; Gibson, 1989; Macksoud & Aber, 1996; Potocky-Tripodi, 2002). Still others report that many more newly arrived immigrants coming from the lowest socioeconomic groups in some rural areas of Mexico have experienced stress because of extreme poverty (Huyck & Fields, 1981; Potocky-Tripodi, 2002; Ruiz-de-Velasco & Fix, 2000; Quinn, 2001). Many immigrants, such as the Sudanese and Darfurians, arrive having been exposed to both war and extreme poverty, and may have spent time in a refugee camp before coming to the United States (Mendez, Henriquez, & Aber, as reported in Macksoud & Aber, 1996; Potocky-Tripodi, 2002).

ECOS TEAM ACTIVITY

Have team members view a film together that shows some of the reality of the problems faced by immigrants or individuals who are outsiders trying to assimilate to the mainstream. Pick out five problems that occurred for these individuals and note the responses to these problems by the characters in the film. Several films that might be viewed are *The Fringe Dwellers, Bread and Chocolate, El Norte, In America,* and *Dirty Pretty Things.*

PTSD that is undiagnosed and therefore untreated will surely influence academic achievement. Since social workers may or may not have had training in this area, it is important to ask. If no one in the building has training in working with individuals with PTSD, the school or district should provide staff development opportunities. Systemic or specific interventions may be required, depending on the school's or district's immigrant enrollment patterns. Chronicle 7.2 is an account of an almost undiagnosed PTSD in a young child.

Fear

PTSD can result in the development of fearful reactions based on the recall of trauma that may have paralyzing effects. However, fear may arise from other less severe sources as well. In a discussion of the vulnerabilities of childhood, Weissbourd (1996) observes that many less traumatic circumstances that may cause various forms of apprehension even in psychologically healthy children. This apprehension can be broadly classified as social anxiety (Leary, 1990) and can result in affective experiences such as uneasiness, perplexity, and even fear (Whitmore, 1987). The consequences of these reactions—especially fear—are that the individual may have feelings of tension and discomfort in the context of focus, a tendency toward more negative self-evaluations, and a tendency to withdraw in the presence of others (Schwarzer, 1986). Among the documented cognitive effects of this fear and anxiety are problems in learning a second language (MacIntyre & Gardner, 1991), a decrease in cognitive processing ability (Wine, 1980), inhibited actions, and attempts to escape the situation (Levitt, 1980).

When these apprehensive extenuating circumstances are linked with variables such as cultural diversity, linguistic differences, relocation or resettlement, social or cultural isolation, and other issues that must be addressed by many ELLs (Huyck & Fields, 1981; Portes, 1999), then it is little wonder that fear and anxiety may be present and interfering with learning in these students. A new school environment that is perceived as hostile by the student can cause ELLs to experience panic and create affect and mood problems. The lack of a welcoming and nurturing learning environment can also cultivate anxiety about school attendance, which may grow into chronic avoidance of school or certain learning situations. Fears resulting from the environment can influence students' academic success. No one can learn to his or her full potential in an uncomfortable environment; rather, we learn to escape an uncomfortable environment as quickly as possible.

Current Psychological Stress

Stress influences the ability to learn and retain information (Alsop & Mcaffrey, 1993; Education Alliance at Brown University, 2006; Johnson, 1989; Smith, 1998). All students experience some degree of stress in their lives. However, as newcomers to a culture that is not always hospitable, immigrant students and their families may find many daily situations particularly stressful (Huyck & Fields, 1981; Portes, 1999). For example, ELLs may experience anxiety or panic when struggling to navigate the new, non-native culture. They may feel additional stress as a result of not being able to communicate with

A PTSD Almost Misdiagnosed

By an ESL teacher

Hue was a little girl, seven years old, from Vietnam. She arrived one day in my ESL classroom in the middle of winter, speaking no English and looking forlorn in her thin coat, unsuitable for Chicago winters. Hue was quiet and shy in my room and appeared terrified to leave the room for other classes like gym, music, and art. I decided to postpone that type of integration until she had a bit more English and a bit more self-confidence. She was staying with relatives in the United States. No one could find out what had happened to her parents.

One day, while the children were doing independent work at various centers around the room, Hue began screaming at the top of her lungs. She stood in the middle of the room screaming and twirling in circles with her arms outstretched. The rest of the class, all ELLs, simply stopped what they were doing and watched. Afraid that Hue would get dizzy from twirling and might fall and hit her head on the desk, I went to her on my knees (at her height) and approached her with my arms outstretched. As I got close to her, she fell into my arms. The minute I closed my arms around her, she started thrashing her arms and kicking. I began to rock her in my lap. The other students in the room were wonderful: they said nothing and did nothing. Gradually, she calmed down, snuggled in on my lap, and began to suck her thumb.

The buzz traveled all around the school and staff was unanimous in their unofficial diagnosis: the child had severe behavioral disorders and was emotionally disturbed. Fortunately for Hue and for me, the social worker did not accept the unofficial diagnosis. He worked with me to find out more about Hue's background. After much sleuthing and several interviews with Hue's relatives, we found out that Hue's mother was Vietnamese and her father was American. The father had been an American soldier and his whereabouts were unknown. Hue had been living with her mother in a small Vietnamese village, where they endured discrimination and racism because Hue's father was an American. Unable to tolerate being a pariah of the village, Hue's mother committed suicide. Hue had walked in on her mother while she lay dying from a gunshot wound to her head.

The social worker and I were able to apply a diagnosis of PTSD, rather than emotionally disturbed or behavioral disorder, and we secured the services of a Vietnamese social worker through a Vietnamese community agency in Chicago to begin treating her for PTSD. While things were not easy for Hue for several years, each year brought with it more progress in all areas—emotionally, linguistically, academically, and socially. By the time Hue was in fifth grade, she was well on her way to managing her memories in a healthy way, had made many friends, and was progressing quite nicely in her studies.

Questions for discussion:

- How might some behaviors exhibited in the classroom or on the playground be misinterpreted or misunderstood?
- What can you do if you are the only staff member who disagrees with the consensus of the group?

peers and adults. As social creatures, we are all oriented to a kind of *social-ness* (Collins, 1998) that helps define who we are and how we fit within our social sphere; when communication is reduced for ELLs who are already different, they may view themselves as more different than they truly are and will become more isolated. When this occurs, stress often ensues.

Given their lack of familiarity with the culture and the language, ELLs may suffer from their inability to do even basic everyday tasks. Like all other students, ELLs face pressures about grades and peer interactions. However, for ELLs these pressures may be compounded by feelings of diminished status, overly taxed coping mechanisms, insufficient support systems, and acute homesickness.

The extent to which stress affects an individual depends largely on the individual's access to effective resources and strategies to deal with that stress (Garmezy, 1991; Lareau, 1987). Immigrant families may not have access to support systems, and culturally sensitive social, psychological, and psychiatric services may be inadequate or unavailable (e.g., Magnuson & Waldfogel, 2005; Miech, Essex, & Goldsmith, 2001). Educators should be knowledgeable about how stress and circumstances in the lives of ELLs interact and how the interaction can potentially help or hinder the students' success in school.

Social and Emotional Development

The timeline for social and emotional development is quite different among families from various countries and social strata. What one family considers precocious may be perceived as developmentally late in another family. Developmental milestones are culturally specific.For example, the expectation that a child will sleep alone by about age 13 months in Anglo families in the United States is quite different from the expectation of sleeping alone by about age 39 months in Filipino families. In U.S. American families, children are expected to play alone at 25 months of age, whereas in a Filipino family the expectation is at about 12 months (Carlson & Harwood, 1999; Schulze, Harwood, Goebel, et al., 1999).

Thus, the inability of some young immigrant children to perform many self-care tasks such as buttoning, zippering, and tying shoelaces is generally indicative of a childrearing practice that emphasizes parental control over the dressing of the child, rather than a developmental delay. This childrearing practice reflects a cultural norm that a child's appearance reflects back on the parents and the family. In another example, many immigrant children at the preschool level have difficulty using scissors. Some educators may erroneously conclude this is because of delay in the development of fine motor skills. It may well be because the children have had no experience with scissors.

This makes it essential for educators to become familiar with the characteristics of the immigrant culture and of the specific student's family. These characteristics are likely to influence a student's social and emotional development and will significantly inform the observer's opinion of the student's development. Without this understanding and knowledge, educators may jump to wrong conclusions about the student's progress.

Feelings of Belonging to the School and Wider Community

Alienation is often cited as a significant contributing factor to ELLs' decision to drop out of school (e.g., Brophy & Good, 1974; Entwisle, Alexander, & Olson, 1997; Katz, 1999; Rist, 1970; Ruiz-de-Velasco & Fix, 2000; Sinclair & Ghory, 1987). Feelings of alienation persist beyond the first generation of immigrants in a family, often extending into the second and third generation. These feelings of alienation can be accompanied by a sense of purposelessness stemming from a lack of standards, values, or structure—something akin to the state of anomie described by Durkheim (Durkheim & Coser, 1984). ELLs are likely candidates for these feelings because of their struggle to participate in a new culture and incorporate new norms and values into their existing cultural identity. They may be getting less parental guidance than they need simply because their parents are not familiar or comfortable with the new cultural norms that they are immersed in. ELLs may also experience dissonance when they feel conflict between the norms of their native culture and the non-native culture.

Educators should carefully examine the school and classroom climate to ensure that it promotes inclusion and acceptance. Educators need to ask themselves tough questions. Do teachers relegate ELLs to the back table for instruction? Does the school's curriculum ignore the perspectives and contributions of ELLs' native cultures? Does the staff welcome and promote ELLs' participation in all aspects of schooling and extracurricular activities? Do staff and the student body celebrate and honor ELLs' successes in the same way the accomplishments of general education students are recognized?

Suggestions for Information Gathering

The same prudence that we suggested be taken in gathering information about personal and family background in the preceding chapter must apply to gathering information about physical and psychological factors. We need to adhere to strict privacy standards, we need to be careful in our choice of interpreters, and we need to tread very carefully and with the utmost respect for the student and family. Once again, historical and current information regarding physical and psychological factors should be considered when gathering information in order to understand the student more completely and accurately. A cultural liaison can provide insights into the cultural context of these factors. Educators may have to get training in the factors discussed in this chapter from a professional to better understand how these factors might play out in the lives of ELLs. This knowledge and understanding provide a context to the educator's assessment of the student's situation and recommendation for meaningful and appropriate interventions.

As with personal and family factors, information gathering in the area of the physical and psychological factors will likely require staff to interview the students, their families, their siblings, their teachers, and community members who interact with the students. A trusting relationship must precede such interviews. Confidentiality needs to be maintained, as much of the information gathered will be of a sensitive nature. As mentioned in Chapter 6, dialogue journals can also be a source of considerable information about the students, as can previous school records.

Table 7.1 lists a series of questions that may be used to guide the conversations that take place with students and family members. As with interviews for gathering information on personal and family background (see

(text continues on page 118)

ECOS TEAM ACTIVITY

Team members are to recall an instance where they felt terribly out of place and not welcomed. Perhaps they have experienced ostracism by a clique or the oppression of the glass ceiling as females, or other instances where they were on the outside looking in at another group that was not welcoming. Team members should then attempt to remember and write down as many details as possible: their emotional response to feelings of alienation, the strategies they chose to utilize in those situations, the success or failure of those strategies, and lessons learned from the experience. Team members then discuss and reflect on ways their own experiences with these situations can help build empathy for their students and help students design effective coping tools.

Table 7.1 Possible Questions to Consider for Getting a Sense of the Student's Physical and Psychological Issues

Disease or Medical Condition	• Is there any indication of a possible medical condition? • Has the student had the expected level of medical care for his or her age?
Impaired Vision or Hearing	• Has the student had vision and hearing tests? • If so, have the records been checked?
Malnutrition and Chronic Hunger	• Does the student show signs of hunger frequently? • Is the family comfortable with food preparation routines? • Who is responsible for preparing food in the family?
Chronic Pain Due to Untreated Illness, Disease, or Condition	• Has the student had a general checkup recently? • Is there any suspicion of chronic pain? • Could the student have been exposed to toxic chemicals?
Posttraumatic Stress Syndrome/Disorder	• Did the student experience military combat or a terrorist incident? • Did the student witness a natural disaster? • Did the student experience a serious accident or violent personal assault? • Did the student come from extreme poverty? • Did the student spend time in a refugee camp? • Does the student show any signs of recurring nightmares or flashbacks? • Does the student show any signs of having difficulty sleeping?
Fear	• How comfortable does the student seem at school? • Does the student show any signs of avoiding certain situations at school? • Does the student seem to be particularly anxious in certain contexts at school?
Current Psychological Stress	• Does the student show signs of higher than expected levels of stress (such as headaches, nervous tics, trouble sleeping)? • Has the student been able to form a network of friends in school? • Does the student seem to be under pressure? • Does the student enjoy a status of privilege within at least one aspect of school life? • Does the student express feelings of homesickness? • Does the student or his family have easy access to a support network, formal or informal?
Social Emotional Development	• Has the student reached the developmental milestones that are expected within the student's family?
Feelings of Belonging to the School and Wider Community	• Does the student keep to him- or herself or does he or she have a group of friends to spend time with, both in and out of school? • How is the student dealing with possibly conflicting norms and values in the mainstream and native cultures? • How is the student's new cultural identity developing?

Table 7.2 Systemic Interventions That Can Help Overcome Challenges Stemming from Personal and Family Issues

Disease or Medical Condition	• Let teachers and other staff be aware of the possibility of medical conditions.
Impaired Vision or Hearing	• Implement culturally and linguistically responsive vision and hearing tests beginning in preschool and extending through 12th grade. • Provide for the administration of vision and hearing screenings for ELLs who enroll after schoolwide screenings have been completed. • Cultivate partnerships with agencies that advocate and provide for those with visual or hearing impairments. • Establish a process for obtaining vision and hearing assistive devices, materials, and services at reduced cost for those families with lesser means.
Malnutrition and Chronic Hunger	• Provide parent education, including connecting them with groceries that cater to members of their own community if they are not familiar with the existing community. • Run breakfast, lunch, or snack programs. • Establish school or community food pantries.
Chronic Pain Due to Untreated Illness, Disease, or Condition	• Establish collaborative partnerships with medical and dental agencies in the community to provide families with affordable access to diagnostic and treatment services. • Connect families with free or reduced-fee vaccination clinics, school physicals, and dental clinics.
Posttraumatic Stress Syndrome/Disorder	• Implement a multimethod screening tool used upon enrollment to diagnose this syndrome quickly. • Create a continuum of services for students suspected of experiencing some level of PTSD, ranging from one-on-one counseling to support group activities. • Familiarize staff with the causes, characteristics, and treatment of PTSD. • Provide staff development and parent education opportunities.
Fear	• With the help of a native informant, analyze aspects of the school that may be perceived by someone from that culture as hostile and change it to make it less so. • Set up a buddy system in which students are paired with an older peer who has adapted successfully to the school milieu.
Current Psychological Stress	• Implement educational programs that teach children coping and cultural navigation skills. • Provide easy access to resources that are culturally and linguistically responsive. • Cultivate partnerships with community agencies that provide resources. • Ensure that resources used by ELL families are culturally and linguistically responsive.
Social and Emotional Development	• Provide staff development opportunities that facilitate the integration of information specifically related to immigrants into what educators already know about social and emotional development within the general student population. • Provide staff development opportunities that help staff to understand how culture influences child rearing practices and parental expectations.

continued

Table 7.2   *continued*

Feelings of Belonging to the School and Wider Community	• Does the school and classroom climate promote inclusion and acceptance of diverse cultural norms and values?
	• Do teachers relegate ELLs to the back table for instruction?
	• Does the school's curriculum ignore the perspectives and contributions of ELLs' native cultures?
	• Does the staff welcome and promote ELL participation in all aspects of schooling and extracurricular activities?
	• Do staff and the student body celebrate and honor ELLs' successes in the same way the accomplishments of general education students are recognized?

(text continued from page 115)

Chapter 6), we do not recommend that questions be posed one after the other in a formal manner. In addition, the questions in Table 7.1 can serve to guide and organize all the information gathered in the area of physical and psychological factors.

Suggestions for Systemic Interventions

If the school or district realizes that more than a few students are experiencing academic difficulties because of one or more of the physical or psychological factors discussed in this chapter, systemic interventions are warranted. Some examples of systemic interventions are listed in Table 7.2.

Suggestions for Specific Interventions

If the school or district notes that the physical and psychological factors are affecting only a few students or if ELL enrollment is no more than a few students, the previously mentioned systemic interventions can be implemented but on a more limited basis.

Questions for Discussion

1. What do we know about the physical and psychological factors affecting the ELLs we serve?
    1.1. What are the stresses ELLs and their families are experiencing?
    1.2. Are these factors predictable, or do they seem to arise randomly within the immigrant community?
    1.3. Are certain groups of immigrants subject to different factors?
    1.4. Are the families of ELLs in our community well connected to community service agencies and other support networks?
    1.5. Is the service provided by community service agencies and support systems culturally and linguistically responsive?
    1.6. Does the impact of these factors on ELLs' success change over time?
    1.7. Are the district and school policies and practices culturally and linguistically responsive?
    1.8. What changes to our policies should we seek to implement?
    1.9. What systemic interventions are needed?
    1.10. How will we document the effect of these systemic interventions?

2. What do we know about the personal and family factors influencing the ELL student who is currently having trouble?
    2.1. How can we find out more?
    2.2. How should we interpret the data we collect?
    2.3. Which factors have the most pronounced impact on the student?
    2.4. Are the district and school policies and practices responsive to the students at this time?
    2.5. What specific interventions are needed?
    2.6. How will we monitor the ELL's progress during the intervention(s)?
    2.7. How will we determine the success of the intervention?

8

Previous Schooling Factors

KEY CONCEPTS

The fourth integral factor to be considered is the amount and quality of previous schooling in both English and the student's native language, as well as the congruence of educational approaches that the student has experienced. Interventions developed from examining this factor try to take advantage of prior experiences, as well as make up for gaps in students' previous schooling.

The fourth integral element to be considered when an English language learner (ELL) experiences academic difficulty is the previous schooling that the student has had. Knowledge of this factor is crucial to interpreting the student's current performance, because the ability to perform an academic skill or demonstrate a knowledge set is highly dependent on whether the student has actually had the opportunity to learn that skill or knowledge set. Berliner and Biddle (1995) have stated that opportunity to learn is the single factor that best predicts one's knowledge of specific subjects. In fact, they stated this principle of prior exposure as Berliner and Biddle's Student Achievement Law: "Regardless of what anyone claims about student or school characteristics, *opportunity to* learn is the single most powerful predictor of student achievement" (italics theirs).

This focus on previous schooling to determine opportunities to learn seems logical, but assessment teams all over the country routinely make placement decisions without adequate data on previous schooling factors. For example, if an assessment team focuses primarily on achievement test and language test scores and does not incorporate the prior teaching and curricular content that a student has had into the interpretation of the numbers, it is not observing the Student Achievement Law. Teachers should try to determine whether the difficulty can be traced back to insufficient, interrupted, infrequent, inconsistent, or inferior previous schooling that students have had in the United States or in their native country. Such information can help educators determine the cause of an ELL's difficulty in school by providing answers to the following questions:

- Is the difficulty due to a lack of sufficient instructional exposure to particular skills or concepts?
- Is the ELL's limited success due to a lack of repeated and sustained practice?
- Is the difficulty due to poor-quality instruction or to a mismatch in level of rigor?

- Is limited success due to difficulties in transitioning to a new and unfamiliar educational approach?
- Is the ELL functioning academically at grade level?
- Has the ELL attained age-appropriate literacy skills?
- What skills and knowledge base did the student develop from previous schooling, formal and informal?

Answers to these questions can help educators develop a more comprehensive picture of the student's educational career to date and can inform decision making as to appropriate interventions.

In this chapter, we discuss key factors related to previous schooling, illustrate examples of common situations hinging on schooling history, provide suggestions for information gathering and evaluating the adequacy of previous schooling, begin a list of possible systemic interventions, offer recommendations for applying systemic interventions to individual ELLs experiencing difficulties, and present questions for discussion.

Key Factors in Previous Schooling

The amount and quality of instruction in both the first and second language and the extent to which similarities or differences existed in the educational approaches are key factors of the schooling history to consider. These factors should be investigated for the educational system in the student's country of origin and any other countries the family has passed through en route to the United States, as well as the for ELL's participation in other U.S. schools prior to arrival in the current school where the student is experiencing difficulty. Although these data may be difficult to obtain, a complete and sufficient picture of the ELL's learning aptitude and how to proceed with remediation is not possible without this information.

The amount of instruction refers to both the frequency and the duration of instructional services. How many years of schooling? On average, how many instructional days occurred within those years? Were there patterns of absences due to issues such as working on the harvest or inclement weather? Did events such as fighting or strikes reduce instructional time? The quality of instruction includes the level of rigor (in terms of difficulty and thoroughness) of the teaching and curricular content, staff qualifications, utilization of effective teaching strategies, and the scope and sequence of the curriculum. If the student has had any type of bilingual education, the type of language allocation the student has experienced is important when assessing both the quantity and quality of instruction. Language allocation refers to structured and deliberate decisions made at both a programmatic and a curricular level as to how the first and second languages are to be distributed or apportioned in instruction. The consistency among educational approaches that the student has been exposed to is important to consider as well. Too often, inconsistent methods and approaches to instruction can hinder a student's ability to learn, since these methods often operate at cross-purposes (Damico, Damico, & Nelson, 2003).

As with any element that involves what ELLs bring with them from their past, it is essential to avoid dismissing what is different as worthless. In many countries the approach to learning and schooling may be different from what is expected in the United States (Anderson-Levitt, 2003; Rogoff, 1990; Spindler, 1997); however, the objectives and the accomplishments may be similar. ELLs may have gone to a very different kind of school than one in the United States, but while in that school they learned skills and built a body of knowledge, even if the skills and knowledge are not those taught in U.S. schools. ELLs may be missing years of formal schooling, but perhaps they learned through a more informal setting such as an apprenticeship with an expert or an internship with a mentor. It is important to find out just what the student has come with and not to write off past experiences that can be used as building blocks for learning additional skills and a new body of knowledge.

Amount of Formal Schooling in the First or Native Language

The amount of formal schooling in the first language is the leading predictor of ELLs' success in U.S. schools (Collier & Thomas, 1997; Genesee, Lindholm-Leary, Saunders et al., 2005; Greene, 1997). The degree of children's native language proficiency is a strong predictor of their English language development (August & Hakuta, 1997). Students who have had the benefit of formal schooling in the native language beginning with kindergarten or preschool and continuing without interruption up to and including the period of time during which they immigrated to the United States have a much stronger foundation on which to build. This is especially true for those students who have achieved literacy at grade level in their first language.

Unfortunately, not all ELLs arrive in the United States with the expected number of years of formal schooling. There are many possible explanations for less than optimal frequency and duration of instructional services in a student's native country. The family's socioeconomic status may have limited the number of years the student had access to public education. Family poverty may have necessitated children leaving school and entering the workforce at a young age. Civil war or foreign occupation may have interrupted schooling, an administrator or teacher may have cancelled school sessions, students may have been afraid to attend school, or children may have been drafted into military service at a young age. Agricultural community needs, such as planting and harvesting, may have taken precedence over school attendance. Discrepancies in the quality of public education afforded to students in remote locations as a result of difficulty recruiting teachers to serve there may have led to interrupted schooling as well. Differences in gender expectations may have led to girls stopping schooling to stay home and care for younger siblings.

There are also many possible explanations for less than optimal frequency and duration of instructional services in the first language in U.S. schools. Some of those explanations may arise from variances in the educational infrastructure in the United States, others may come from family circumstances. In the United States, not every school offers bilingual education (instruction and instructional support in the first or native language). In some cases this is because the low numbers of students in a particular target language group do not economically support the employment of a bilingual teacher. In other situations, even where numbers of students in the target language are sufficient to support the employment of a bilingual teacher, school officials may decide not to offer bilingual education. This happens because of the misconception that it is better to immerse students in English rather than allow them to learn new concepts through the student's stronger language and to continue developing in that language so that it forms a strong base on which English proficiency is built. In U.S. schools, there is a prevalence of site-based management, which allows building administrators to set the parameters of educational programming according to local community needs or personal ideology. This means that even if students stay within the same school system, district, parish, or corporation but change schools, the educational programs they encounter may be substantially different from school to school. Lack of bilingual education can hinder both academic and linguistic/literacy development (Lindholm-Leary, 2006).

Even when a school system or school does offer bilingual education to ELLs, services may be delivered in ways that do not ensure optimal duration and frequency. Students who participate in late-exit bilingual programs are more likely to experience academic success than those who participate in early-exit bilingual education programs (Collier & Thomas, 1997; Genesee, Lindholm-Leary, Saunders, et al., 2005). For example, students can be participants in an early-exit bilingual education program where ELLs are typically exited after three or four years of program participation, regardless of whether or not they have achieved academic English fluency. The cessation of services is prompted by a time limit rather than by attainment of any standards (Christian, 2006).

In other cases, ELLs may participate in a bilingual education program where no one has addressed the issue of long-term language allocation. In such cases ELLs may experience inconsistent distribution of the first and second language in instruction. This inconsistency may compound as they advance through the grade levels. ELLs in this situation may attend a kindergarten where most of the instruction is in the first language, with only a small portion of the instruction time allotted to ESL instruction, then advance to first grade and face an abrupt switch to instruction mostly in the second language, with little instruction in the first language. This change and inconsistency will often cause multiple problems—not only confusion regarding comprehensibility but confusion regarding the sociopolitical and psychosocial considerations of the two languages and those who speak them (Delpit, 1988; Hakuta, 1986). Exacerbating the problem at the second-grade level is the teacher who reverts to the language allocation used in kindergarten. Any student would be confused by such inconsistencies in instruction, which serve to decrease the duration of native language instruction. In still other cases, parents may refuse bilingual education services because they lack information regarding the benefits of bilingual instruction.

In terms of frequency of native language instruction, ELLs may be offered only a single period of first language instruction each school day or, worse, only one period per week. In resource programs, time spent with the bilingual teacher may not be valued and therefore not protected. Students may miss instruction because the homeroom teacher chooses not to release them to the resource teacher because he or she feels that instruction in the homeroom is more important.

Family circumstances that contribute to a lower or disrupted rate of occurrence of first language instruction in U.S. schools typically arise from conditions of poverty, where parents are struggling to make ends meet. Changes of residence can mean that ELLs are moving from school to school. Children of migrant workers are the most obvious example of this situation. They may travel in a predictable pattern, based on the schedule of planting and harvesting certain crops, from one state to another state. However, many families may move from residence to residence within the same general geographic area due to rent increases or job changes or the purchase of a new home. ELLs in the United States as well as in their country of origin may face the need to help with child care responsibilities or to secure some type of employment to help with the family's expenses. ELLs' parents may need their older children to watch younger siblings who are sick if the parents cannot take time off work to care for them. Others may work long hours after school helping in family businesses, which in turn may lead to increased school absenteeism.

Sometimes ELLs are prevented from receiving strong support in their native language at school because the family is under the misconception that the sooner the children learn English, the better off they will be. There is strong evidence to the contrary (Genesee, 2006), which is why parents are encouraged to use the native language at home as much as possible (Yturriago, 2006a). Parents need to be educated about the important role that the native language plays in developing proficiency in the second language. They need to be shown that bilingual instruction is not only at least as effective as

English-only alternatives but it tends to be more effective than the English-only programs (Rolstad, Mahoney, & Glass, 2005).

Quality of Formal Schooling in the First or Native Language

Quality of instruction is at least as important as the language of instruction (Slavin & Cheung, 2003). The quality of formal schooling in the first language can vary significantly among ELLs, depending on what the student's current school offers and what the child has experienced in the native country as well as in previous U.S. schools. It is not enough that the student has had continuous instruction in the native language. The level of rigor in previous schooling experiences when compared to that of the current learning environment is important to know. This information allows us to better understand expectations and level of ease or difficulty that the student might be having.

In addition to level of rigor, educators should consider the scope and sequence of the curriculum in the student's previous schooling. Fractions may be introduced later in the previous curriculum than the current one. Other skills and concepts may have not been introduced at all. Failure to master skills and concepts before they have been taught is no fault of the student but rather a mismatch in the scope and sequence of the two curricula.

The qualifications of staff delivering the native language instruction are another important consideration when assessing the quality of the education that the student received in the first language. In the student's country of origin, teachers may or may not have had the extensive postgraduate training that is prevalent in some parts of the United States. In U.S. schools, teachers working in bilingual education programs may have been hired provisionally to remediate chronic teacher shortages. In these cases, the teachers are in the process of completing their basic teaching endorsement and the specialty courses in bilingual/ESL education while teaching ELLs. In some schools, bilingual education teachers are not hired at all. Instead, noncertificated staff, namely professionals and volunteers who happen to be bilingual in English and the first language of the students, provide first language instruction. Instruction of this type should not be expected to yield the same results as that provided by certified bilingual teachers.

Old-fashioned traditional teaching techniques and outdated instructional approaches will not produce student achievement and progress at the same rate as strategies and approaches that have proved effective when used with ELLs. Educators familiar with the research as it relates to ELLs will be able to judge more accurately the effectiveness of approaches and strategies that the student has been given.

Additionally, educators should determine ELLs' first language with accuracy. Many countries have a multitude of indigenous languages. Thus, the fact that a student comes from Mexico does not necessarily mean that the student speaks Spanish fluently or at all. UNESCO has identified 62 living indigenous languages in Mexico, 56 indigenous languages in China, and 65 in India (UNESCO, 1996). Thus, many students from the state of Oaxaca, Mexico, do not speak Spanish as their first language. Rather, they arrive at school in Mexico speaking their native indigenous language and participate in bilingual education programs where Spanish is their second language. According to the Instituto Lingüistico de Verano, 2,563,000 speakers of Nahuatl, 1,490,000 speakers of Maya, 785,000 speakers of Zapoteco, and 764,000 speakers of Mixteco reside in Mexico (Gordon, 2005). When these children enter U.S. schools, English is their third language.

After considering both the amount and quality of previous instruction in the first language, educators should be able to answer with more accuracy the following question: Is it reasonable to expect the child should have attained grade-level competency in literacy and core academic areas in the native language?

Amount of Formal ESL Instruction

ELLs who enter U.S. schools with English foreign language instruction provided either by their country of origin's public school system or through private tutoring enter English as a second language (ESL) classes in U.S. schools with an advantage over those ELLs who have not had the benefits of such instruction. ELLs who transfer into a new U.S. school from another U.S. school may or may not have had the benefit of formal ESL instruction, as the availability of such programs varies greatly across the nation and even in neighboring districts. The frequency and duration of ESL instruction are as important as the frequency and duration of instruction in the first language. ELLs who receive only a period a day of ESL instruction are at considerable risk for academic failure (Collier & Thomas, 1997, 2002).

In circumstances of less than ideal language instruction and the resultant compromises involving frequency and sufficiency of students' experience with comprehensible instruction that is targeted to their needs, students receive appropriate and effective instruction for only a fraction of the school day. Similarly, ELLs who exit ESL instruction prematurely, before they have achieved academic fluency in English, are at risk for academic failure because of diminished duration of service. Failure to address the issue of language allocation can also hinder English language acquisition, as there is no consistent plan for the development of proficiency in the second language.

Quality of Formal ESL Instruction

Exemplary ESL instruction is based on the notion that individuals learn a language when using it to communicate rather than from studying it in isolation. This implies that the methods and curriculum used to develop proficiency in the second language must incorporate the functional uses of language in meaningful contexts (McLaughlin & McLeod, 1996). When meaning and function are the basis of instruction, it follows that the topic of lessons is something other than language itself. Language proficiency is best developed when the focus of instruction is on topics such as history, science, or social studies—that is, academic content areas. Research strongly suggests that content-based ESL instruction produces greater student growth in English language acquisition than ESL instruction that utilizes a traditional approach that focuses on aspects of language such as grammar and vocabulary (Collier & Thomas, 1997).

Exemplary ESL instruction is flexible because it has to meet the needs of ELLs with different levels of fluency. The teacher needs to be able to adjust the curriculum and to be cognizant of the students' first language. Additionally, the transition from first language or sheltered language classes to mainstream classes is gradual, carefully planned, and augmented with support activities to ensure students' success (Echevarria & Short, 2003). While it is often neglected in diversity education, the transition periods or phases between shifting from one type of instruction, intervention, or support to another is a crucial consideration in successful language planning. Criteria for effective ESL instruction are discussed in Chapters 9 and 10.

Congruence of Educational Approaches

Another key question for the ECOS team to consider is how the educational experiences of the ELL fit together to create the student's educational ecology. Just as Bronfenbrenner (1979) advocated a services model of social and psychological development, we should also view the educational experience of the student from a more systems model. That is, we should ask whether the approach to education in the country of origin or in previous U.S. school was similar to or different from the approach the student is currently experiencing. Some approaches may be radically different. For example, in some

ECOS TEAM ACTIVITY

Invite someone who knows about the educational system of another country to have an informal chat about how schools work in that country. Preferably, the country of choice would be one that many ELLs come from. The informant could be a teacher who has recently come from that country, a parent who has recently had a child in a school in that country, or an ELL who has recently arrived from a school in that country. Ask the person to talk about what children learn, how the grade levels are set up, what grading system is used, how students are assessed, what role parents play in the school, and how classrooms are set up. Discuss differences and similarities with the current school system.

schools instruction is highly teacher-directed, whereas in other schools students manage activities that are set up and simply guided by the teacher. When students move from one approach to another, they may have trouble with the transition. Thus, a student who has spent six years in an educational system that emphasizes learning through observation and apprenticeship may feel overwhelmed with an educational approach that stresses hands-on learning and student-to-teacher interaction. In another example, a student who has participated in an educational approach that emphasizes rote memorization and strict absorption of the teacher's opinions may not have developed the skills of independence to allow him to function well in an environment that stresses essential concepts over facts and values problem solving and creative thinking.

Suggestions for Information Gathering and Evaluating the Adequacy of Previous Schooling

At least some of the information about the student's past learning environment or previous schooling may be gathered and compiled at the same time that information is being gathered about the student's current learning environment. However, getting any information about the student's past can be difficult. Although records and documents regarding previous schooling provide useful information, such records may not be available. An interview with the student and the family (parents and siblings) may yield more information that is useful. Table 8.1 offers some questions that may be used to structure the conversation. However, the questions should not be posed one after another. Rather, an informal conversation should take place.

Educators must be aware of the need for privacy with ELL families and the need to explain how the information will be used to improve the educational program for the student having trouble. If an interpreter is needed, that interpreter should be selected carefully. The ECOS team can enlist the help of a staff member knowledgeable about the previous education systems in which the ELL has participated to provide context for the gathered information.

Suggestions for Systemic Interventions

If educators notice that a significant number of ELLs in their school have had similar previous schooling experiences, systemic interventions should be implemented to address the needs of current students and those likely to arrive in the future. Older students who enter U.S. schools having had their formal schooling interrupted need special attention because their needs are significant. These students may not have had opportunity to develop even basic lit-

Table 8.1 Possible Questions to Consider for Getting a Sense of the Student's Previous Schooling Experiences

Amount of Instruction in the First/Native Language	• How often were school sessions scheduled? How often did the child attend school? Did any circumstances prevent the child from attending school (farm work, employment, child care responsibilities, fear, etc.)? Was the teacher always present during scheduled school sessions?
	• Was instruction in the first language available?
	• What language or languages were used for instruction? In which subjects?
	• If two languages were used, was there a plan to manage their use?
	• How long did the child receive instruction in the first language?
	• What grades did the child receive in classes where first language instruction was provided? Test scores?
	• Was age-appropriate literacy development achieved?
	• Was age-appropriate subject area progress made?
Quality of Instruction in the First/Native Language	• What subjects were taught in the previous school?
	• What was expected at each grade level?
	• Were there materials for learning such as books, technology, etc.?
	• What is the typical level of training for teachers at the previous school?
	• How do you think the new school compares with the previous school? Do you think it is very different or similar? Do you think it is harder or easier?
	• How do you feel you your child did in the previous school?
Amount of ESL Instruction	• How often were ESL classes scheduled?
	• For how long did your child receive special ESL instruction?
	• Did anything prevent your child from attending ESL classes?
Quality of ESL Instruction	• Who provided ESL instruction, a special teacher with training in ESL, the classroom teacher, a volunteer, or a paraprofessional?
	• What were the expectations?
	• What grades did the child receive in previous ESL classes? Test scores?
	• How do you feel your child did in previous ESL classes?

eracy skills in their native language, let alone in English. In fact, for many of them, literacy may not have played a major role in their lives. This is quite a drastic difference from life in a school in the United States. These students are also likely to be missing school skills that even young children develop naturally by participating in school life continuously (Freeman & Freeman, 2002).

Like other ELLs, students with limited formal schooling need to be taught social and academic proficiency in English as a second language and the content of the curriculum, but they also need to develop basic literacy skills (see Chronicle 8.1 for an example of basic literacy skills missing from an otherwise extremely clever child), preferably through their native language, and they need to learn the culture of the school (Hamayan, 1994). Some of these students may not have much experience with writing utensils, scissors, or staplers. They may not understand the use of lockers and how cafeterias work. Many districts establish Newcomer Centers for students with limited

A Picture Is Worth a Thousand Words

By an ESL teacher

I was teaching a group of Southeast Asian refugee students who were being prepared at a school in a refugee camp in the Philippines to be resettled in the United States. This was a group of adolescents from Vietnam and Cambodia who spoke very little English. On average, they had had a total of two years of formal schooling over their seven to nine years of school life.

I had set up a library in our classroom, and among the many projects involving literacy that we did, one involved each child producing a book of his or her own, which would then be added to our collection. Some children were able to write original books themselves. Others, like Lathikhone, would copy by hand the big book we had read as a group and draw pictures in the blank space above the writing. The children enjoyed finishing books and seeing them in our library. Even the students who simply copied a story would be listed as an additional author by saying "Rewritten by."

Lathikhone, who had never been in a school in his life, finally finished copying a story that took place in a jungle. He was very excited to start drawing pictures in the space allocated for illustrations. Each page had a sentence or two to illustrate. The story that Lathikhone had chosen was one we had read and acted out, so he was quite familiar with the content and clearly understood the story. Out of the corner of my eye, I saw him go over to the library, pick a book, and bring it to his desk. He was completely engrossed in the drawings, looking up at the book he had borrowed once in a while as though checking his work.

When I passed by his side a little while later, I was dismayed to see that the book he had picked and was copying was about Eskimos! The beautiful drawings he was making had nothing to do with the text he had written! I had surrounded this student, who had not had a chance to learn about different aspects of literacy (such as the structure of illustrated children's books) naturally, over the years, with a literacy-rich environment. I had assumed that he would naturally pick up the notion that illustrations "illustrate" the text that they accompany. But I realized that this was still a foreign notion to him. It was one of the aspects of literacy, school life, and books that probably needed to be taught more explicitly. It was an aspect that does not have to be taught explicitly to children who are introduced to books early on, and who, naturally and gradually, go from books that are primarily picture books to books that have illustrations for every one or two sentences to books that have an illustration every chapter, and finally to books that have only one illustration, on the cover.

Questions for discussion:

- If Lathikhone had had the normal number of years of schooling and had lived in a highly literate society all his life, what would have been possible explanations for his behavior in this narrative?
- How would you explicitly teach the notion that illustrations illustrate the text they accompany? How would you do it after you'd seen that Lathikhone had already finished one or two drawings in his book?

Table 8.2 Suggestions for Systemic Interventions

Insufficient or Poor Quality of Instruction in the First/Native Language	• Newcomers' programming • Before- and afterschool tutoring • Cross-age peer tutoring • Staff development in the area of task analysis • Staff development in the area of differentiation for ELLs • Staff development in the area of building and activating prior knowledge and prior experiences • Staff development in the area of discerning student learning styles and increasing repertoire of teaching styles • Curriculum alignment or backward mapping that takes into account the scope and sequence of the curriculum as taught in other countries • Implementation of linguistically and culturally responsive pedagogy • Establishment of appropriate expectations and benchmarks • Provision of resources to meet students' needs
Insufficient or Poor Quality of ESL Instruction	• Provision of additional ESL instruction • Provision of targeted ESL instruction to remedy gaps in language acquisition • Allowing children more time to acquire English • Abandonment of traditional ESL approaches in favor of content-based ESL instruction • Staff development in effective instructional strategies for ELLs • Staff development in adaptation and modification of assignments

formal schooling. Students receive intensive instruction in identified areas for a limited period of time, typically before they join their peers in the main section of the school (Marler, 2006).

Some examples of other systemic interventions are listed in Table 8.2.

Suggestions for Specific Interventions

If factors related to past schooling are not influencing the academic and lin-guistic progress of groups of children but are of concern for only a few ELLs experiencing difficulty, the interventions listed in Table 8.2 can be imple-mented on a more limited scale. For example, a scaled-down version of a Newcomers Program could be offered to the individual ELL whose formal schooling has been interrupted and who is not at grade level in core academic areas. As well, arbitrary deadlines for program exit can be modified to pro-vide the ELL who is not experiencing success more time to acquire English.

Questions for Discussion

1. What do we know about the previous schooling factors influencing the ELLs we serve?
    1.1. Are groups of ELLs entering our school system from specific coun-tries?
    1.2. If we have clusters of ELLs arriving from specific countries, are they coming from specific areas in those countries? From specific areas in other parts of the United States?

     1.3. If groups of ELLs are coming from specific areas, what do we know about the educational systems and practices common to those areas?

     1.4. Are significant numbers of ELLs coming to school with evidence of interrupted or inconsistent schooling?

     1.5. Are significant numbers of ELLs coming to school without having achieved grade-level competency in core academic areas? In literacy skill development?

     1.6. Do groups of ELLs share similar family circumstances? For example, are many of the ELLs children of migrant workers?

2. What do we know about the previous school factors influencing the ELL who is currently having trouble?

     2.1. Has the student's previous schooling been of the quality and quantity that can be expected to facilitate grade-level achievement in academic areas? In literacy development?

          2.1.1. Has the student participated in quality first language instruction for a sufficient period?

          2.1.2. Has the student participated in quality ESL instruction for a sufficient period?

9

Oral Language and Literacy Development Factors

KEY CONCEPTS

The fifth integral factor to be considered is the student's oral language and literacy development in both the native language and the second language. Because of the nature of bilingualism and language development, interventions that focus on oral language and literacy must be contextualized in a way that is meaningful to the student, must make developmental sense, and must support literacy in the student's native language.

The fifth integral element to be considered when English Language Learners (ELLs) experience linguistic or academic difficulty is their oral language and literacy development. In this chapter we look at the characteristics of oral language and literacy for ELLs in both (or multiple) languages in social as well as academic settings. We describe principles for appropriate ELL language and literacy instruction and discuss the external barriers that may inhibit optimal language and literacy learning for these students. We discuss the importance of gathering information about language use patterns and how this information helps the ECOS team and others assess oral language and literacy across various contexts in all of the ELLs' languages. We look at the advantages of promoting ELLs' native language in the larger context of school for their own benefit and as a critical diagnostic resource. Rather than ending with a separate section on interventions, this chapter presents suggestions for intervention throughout the text. Many of the interventions for oral language and literacy are closely tied to information gathering and assessment and therefore are difficult to separate from one another, so we simply offer a summary of intervention strategies at the end of the chapter.

Oral language is discussed separately from literacy so that we can focus attention on specific issues relevant to each of those areas; however, the separation is artificial, because the two areas of language are interdependent (Cambourne, 1988; Clay, 1991; Geekie, Cambourne, & Fitzsimmons, 1999).

Key Factors in Oral Language Development

Oral language development is a critical factor in ELLs' long-term success in school. Since oral language proficiency is a complex configuration of abilities (Bialystock, 2001; Perkins, 2005), there are many aspects of oral language learning to consider. We start by examining briefly the processes of first and second language development.

First Language Acquisition

Children develop their first language (L1) in highly contextualized interactions they have with their caregivers and immediate family members (Bialystock, 2001; Bruner, 1981). By age four, young children have acquired a great deal of vocabulary and grammar in their native language. They understand many more words than they can produce orally and are able to process adult grammatical structures, although they still make errors in producing those structures. Though there is some variation in the ages at which children pass through the linguistic developmental stages, these stages seem to be universal (Brown, 1973; Pinker, 1994): children babble, they utter one word at a time, they move on to two-word sentences, and then their productions begin to reach adult grammar and vocabulary.

ELLs are no different than anyone else with respect to L1 acquisition. They go through the same process as their English-speaking peers, so that by the time they enter prekindergarten or kindergarten, these students have gone through the expected stages of L1 acquisition in their native language. ELLs who enter U.S. schools at a later age will have developed the expected skills in their oral native language unless they had some disruptive experiences such as war or extensive migration (see Chapter 8 for information on students with limited formal schooling).

Even if schools have not formally instructed ELLs in their native language, there is much insight to be gained from looking at their oral L1 development (Genesee, Paradis, & Crago, 2004; Smith, 2006). Since all children go through similar stages of L1 acquisition regardless of the language they are born into, we can learn about any unexpected developments during those early years even if there are no specialists at school who speak the ELL's native language. Although allowances must be made for individual and experiential variation, finding out when ELLs reached certain linguistic milestones in L1 may provide insight into any possible underlying language or cognitive difficulties or early hearing loss. On the other hand, a child may be quite advanced in L1 development and only begin having difficulties upon entering school in English, or if the parents are discouraged from using their native language at home by the school. Schools should do the opposite: they should encourage parents to use their proficient language, the native language, as extensively as possible at home (Genesee, Lindholm-Leary, Saunders, et al., 2006; Hakuta, 1986; Yturriago, 2006a). This will provide children with the rich and solid foundation on which to build the second language (L2).

Second Language Acquisition

Just as in L1 acquisition, children who learn a second language go through predictable stages of language proficiency development (Genesee, 2003; Hakuta, 1986; Krashen & Terrell, 1983). And just as in L1 acquisition, learn-

---

ECOS TEAM ACTIVITY

Have team members complete a survey about ELLs' native languages. Here are some sample questions:

1. What are the languages spoken by the ELLs in your school?
2. Approximately how many students, teaching staff members, nonteaching staff members, and parent volunteers speak each of the languages?
3. Have school staff members developed language surveys to use in class to highlight all the different languages the students speak?
4. Does the team regularly ask about L1 development when discussing ELLs who are experiencing difficulties?

ers pass through the different stages at very different rates. Some may spend months in the first stage, while others do so for only a few weeks or even days. The typical stages of second language acquisition that most learners go through are described in Table 9.1.

At the beginning of the process of L2 acquisition, learners say very little. This is known as the *preproduction stage.* Students remain in the *silent period* for varying lengths of time, depending on their individual personality, how safe they feel in taking risks and making mistakes, how comprehensible the new language is to them, and other reasons related to the affective environment (Krashen & Terrell, 1983). Teachers often worry that the silence of their newly arrived ELLs indicates a selective mutism. They should be reassured

Table 9.1 Learning English: The stages (Illinois Resource Center [1999]; adapted from Krashen and Terrell [1983]).

Level of English Production	Student Characteristics and Needs	How Students Learn	Most Effective Language for Instruction
Preproduction	Silent period: no speaking Responds to instructions and commands (e.g., "put on your coat") Needs environments where they can understand teachers and peers	Learns by listening and watching Points, gestures, draws, or recreates something to show understanding	First language
Early Production	Speaks using one or two words Gives "yes" or "no" answers May mix languages (this is a normal part of language development) Needs environments where s/he can understand teachers and peers	Learns by listening, watching, and speaking using one or two words Points, gestures, draws, recreates, or responds to questions with one or two word answers to show understanding	First language
Speech Emergence	Speaks using more than one or two words to express a thought and can retell a story or event Responds to open-ended questions Ready for formal reading and writing instruction in English Needs environments where s/he can understand teachers and peers	Begins to ask questions Utilizes basic literacy skills Participates in discussions and responds to questions using emerging syntactic structures (grammar)	First language
Intermediate Fluency	Ready for more advanced reading and writing instruction in English Needs considerable help with vocabulary development in math, science, social studies Needs environments where s/he can understand teachers and peers	Utilizes more advanced literacy skills Builds on content learned through discussions using more advanced syntactic structures	Sheltered English and first language
Fluency	Language and learning skills are comparable to those of a native English speaker		English and first language

ECOS TEAM ACTIVITY

Team members can experience a simulation of the speech emergence stage. Ask pairs to chat with each other for about two minutes about something they did the past weekend. The only stipulation is that they may not use the letter "t" in any of the words in their speech. For example, they are not allowed to say, "I went to my friend's house to eat dinner on Saturday." Rather, they could say, "I go my friend's house for dinner on a day before Sunday." After the two minutes are up, ask each pair to discuss how they felt. What communication strategies did they use? What would have made the task easier? What are the implications for ELLs at this stage of L2 acquisition for assessing their language proficiency? For their knowledge of academic content? For the role of the native language?

that most learners need to spend quite a bit of time processing the new language without having to perform in it.

The next stage is the *early production stage.* In this stage ELLs may begin to use one- or two-word utterances, "Yes, please," "Thank you," and "Go now?" They can understand more of their friends' conversations on the playground, at lunch, and in the school corridors. Then comes *speech emergence,* which can be an exciting time for ELLs as they realize that they can understand a great deal more of what their peers are saying and see that their own oral language is much more developed. Peers may begin to interact with them more, and adults may praise their English production. At this stage, ELLs can string together a list of words or say short phrases. Though exciting, this can also be a frustrating time for ELLs. They are not fully proficient in the L2 but are very eager to converse with their English-speaking friends and classmates, especially in social settings. When they realize they do not have the exact words or enough words in English to express everything they want to say, they may get angry or withdraw from interaction.

Another cause of frustration is that ELLs at this stage of proficiency rehearse and practice their utterances before they try them out with their peers or teachers. This constant practice and rehearsal requires a great deal of effort, concentration, and persistence. If after all that effort their message is not fully understood, ELLs may get discouraged. At this stage, ELLs' oral expressive language in English typically does not correspond to their receptive language in English. This situation can be frustrating for students, because after they produce a rehearsed a phrase or sentence, they may not understand what the other person says in response. In Chapter 11 we discuss the culture shock that often corresponds to this stage of second language acquisition and how it may add even more frustration and emotional stress to ELLs' experience.

Eventually, ELLs reach the *intermediate fluency* stage. At this level of proficiency they have much more oral fluency, with fewer telegraphic-type utterances. They still need more time and a great deal of vocabulary to engage in conversations with their friends or to understand subtleties of their new language, such as humor or figurative language. This will lead to the *fluent* stage of L2 acquisition. After years, some ELLs eventually develop native-like proficiency in their L2.

Conversational Fluency and Academic Language Proficiency

One often overlooked aspect of oral language is the difference between conversational and academic language. A crucial first step in examining oral language proficiency is to understand that distinction (Cummins, 2000, 2006). As Figure 9.1 shows, oral language proficiency may develop for students in at least four areas: social language in L1, academic language in L1, social lan-

Social Language	L1	L2
	Social language in L1 (native language)	Social language in L2 (English)
Academic Language	Academic language in L1 (native language)	Academic language in L2 (English)

Figure 9.1 Areas of oral language development for ELLs.

guage in English, the L2, and academic language in L2 (Gottlieb, 2006). The category of social language includes, but is not limited to, the language of everyday interactions with peers, the language of joking and apologizing, and the language of speaking with strangers. In the category of academic language development we can distinguish between the language ELLs may need in mathematics, science, social studies, language arts, fine arts, and physical education (Snow, Met, & Genesee, 1989).

In L1, academic language typically emerges as a result of exposure to formal education. Thus, for ELLs who have had poor-quality or limited formal schooling, academic proficiency, even in their more proficient language, may be lacking (Freeman & Freeman, 2002; Hamayan, 1994). In L2, social language takes less time to develop than academic language. It usually takes about two years to become proficient in the everyday concrete language of social conversations, whereas it might take ELLs five or more years to develop academic English (Cummins, 2000, 2006). Conversational fluency develops more quickly than academic language because it is contextualized in meaningful real-life communication. For example, with the visual context of a television program, ELLs are better able to understand the language; in oral exchanges with classmates on the playground and at lunch, ELLs have the added support of facial expressions and gestures as clues to what is being said. This comprehensible context allows ELLs to understand some of the language they hear, and it helps them make themselves understood as well.

Academic oral language, on the other hand, is often highly decontextualized and becomes more abstract as students progress through school. Over the last few years, there have been many efforts to develop guidelines (or standards) to help teachers figure out what kind and level of language proficiency to expect from ELLs at different grades. Appendix G shows an example of such a set of standards developed by the World-Class Instructional Design and Assessment (WIDA) Consortium (see *www.wida.us* for the complete set of standards).

A common misconception is that once ELLs are speaking English, they should begin having success in school. Once school staffers understand the difference between social and academic oral language, they are less likely to make such statements. Proficiency in conversational fluency is not necessarily a good predictor of academic language proficiency or academic success. It is a place to begin for ELLs, as they will use their social language to navigate communication in their academic classes. But if they are not given guidance on the English needed to communicate their mathematical or scientific ideas, for example, they will continue to use their conversational fluency to talk about topics that require technical vocabulary and specific procedural language. Chronicle 9.1 shows the importance of the academic language and how it can be promoted in the classroom.

ELLs who have opportunities to engage in academic conversations and have access to books in their native language will find it easier to use academic language in English. These students are likely to become academically

"The glass thing": When Conversational Language Just Won't Do

By a consultant who observed a grade 6 classroom

I was observing a grade 6 science class and saw a teacher do a brilliant job getting the ELLs to use academic language. An ELL was using conversational language, which tends to be inadequately vague to describe knowledge about an academic topic. The following conversation took place:

Teacher: After you have summarized the procedure we used in this experiment, we will share them out in class.
Group 1: (After about 10 minutes) We're ready!
Teacher: Let's have your first step.
ELL (with conversational fluency in English) in group 1: We put some water in the glass thing.
Teacher: Good. How much water? (She writes the student's sentence on the overhead projector, beginning with the word *First.*)
ELL: This much (showing the amount by the distance between his fingers).
Teacher: How much is that in scientific language?
ELL: (Turning to a neighbor) 50 millie-leeters.
Teacher: Correct. 50 milliliters
ELL: Milliliter (he practices pronouncing the word softly to himself). That's the same in my language!

The exchange continued as the teacher asked for clarification on what "the glass thing" was called. She found that many students in the class had used an informal term rather than the actual name of the object, *graduated cylinder.* She also modeled writing procedural language about every specific step that was taken and each piece of equipment that was used and why. She emphasized that scientists need to be very specific and accurate in what they write so that others can replicate their experiments.

The teacher gave many examples, making the students realize that "the glass thing" could be misleading and was too generic a phrase. This was a very receptive and motivated group of students. They did not have to be asked to repeat the word to internalize it and to make it part of their linguistic repertoire. Many students could be seen practicing saying "graduated cylinder," some of them even writing it down in their notebooks.

Question for discussion

- What does it take for a student to make something like the term *graduated cylinder* part of his or her language repertoire?

proficient sooner, closer to five years from when they begin learning the new language. Later in the chapter we discuss the connections between ELLs' L1 and L2 that allow such cross-language development to occur.

Evidence of Instruction in Oral Academic Language

Some parents support their children's academic language learning through outside experiences, travel, and discussions, but for many children, the opportunity to develop academic oral language comes primarily at school. How easily and how quickly the ELL develops academic language proficiency will de-

ECOS TEAM ACTIVITY

This activity is a follow-up to the previous one where team members experienced a simulation of the speech emergence stage when talking about a concrete social event. For this activity, show team members a visual aid from a science or social studies textbook. Again, ask team members to talk about the concept represented in the visual without using any words that contain the letter "t." This simulates what ELLs might experience when using their oral language in an academic context.

After the two minutes are up, ask each pair to discuss how they felt. What communication strategies were they using? What would have made the task easier? How was this experience different from the activity using social language? What are the implications for ELLs at this stage of L2 acquisition for assessing their language proficiency? For their knowledge of academic content? For the role of the native language?

pend on factors such as level and quality of previous formal schooling, how physically and psychologically fit they are, and so on. But ultimately, it is the opportunity we provide these students to learn academic content and the way we prepare them linguistically to make sense of that instruction that determines to a large extent how well ELLs do in school (Bruner, 2006; Smith, 1998).

Teachers need to prepare students for academic content learning before they get to the actual presentation of a lesson. ELLs need to be introduced to the specialized vocabulary that is essential for the topic to be presented in class. As Snow, Met, and Genesee (1989) point out, to study the Civil War, ELLs need not only the content-specific language such as the words *revolution*, *arms*, and *battle* (what Snow and colleagues call *content-obligatory* language), they also need the more nonessential language, such as the past tense, the words *belong* and *carry*, and so on (what Snow and colleagues call *content-compatible* language). (More examples and a discussion of this pre-lesson preparation can be found in Chapter 10.) In addition, teachers need to use sheltering strategies when using academic language so that meaning can be constructed without having to depend solely on language (see Echevarria, Vogt, & Short, 2004, for a detailed description of the Sheltered Instruction Observation Protocol, or SIOP).

It is also important that ELLs have opportunities to engage in oral academic language practice throughout their day across various contexts. Since learning is a social process, ELLs will co-construct meaning when they engage in dialogue with others (Gutiérrez, Baquedano-Lopez, & Tejeda, 1999; Perkins, 1999; Vygotsky, 1978; Wells, 2003). If the instruction ELLs are given consists of doing silent work at their desks hour after hour, or if they are in groups in which one or two students dominate the discussion, or if they are sitting at a computer listening to a digitized voice through earphones, these students are not getting the opportunity to learn and use academic oral language. Teachers must create activities and circumstances that motivate students to use their academic and social oral language with one another. Typically, one does not hear students at lunch, recess, or in the hallways using academic oral language, so it is imperative that teachers orchestrate these opportunities within the classroom. In this chapter and further in Chapter 10, we introduce ideas for how to design lessons and units that allow ELLs to develop their academic listening, speaking, reading, and writing across the curriculum.

When gathering information about ELLs who may be experiencing difficulty progressing in their oral language (for example, not talking during literature circles, refusing to present in science class), it is important to determine how much opportunity students have to use their oral language. The

Table 9.2 A Checklist of Classroom Groupings, Activities, and Environments That Promote Oral Language Practice

Flexible Grouping	• Interest groups
	• Pairs
	• Grouping by language proficiency levels
	• Grouping by language background
	• Expert groups
	• Long-term project groups
	• Research teams
	• Grouping by gender (same and opposite)
	• Triads
Instruction	• Small-group presentations, museums, and mini-conferences
	• Preparing students for group work
	• Thematic content area word banks
	• Active learning
	• Project-based learning
	• Service learning
	• Problem-based learning
	• Product-based learning
	• Shared experiences
	• Individual conferences with students on their reading and writing
	• Students talking at home in L1 about what they learn in school
Affective Environment	• Collaboration
	• Students' languages actively engaged in the classroom
	• Ongoing team-building
	• Students and teachers learning each other's languages
	• Collaborative structures used
	• Sharing materials and responsibilities
	• Established procedures for group work, presentations
	• Students sharing their own experiences
	• Time to think and plan

checklist presented in Table 9.2 may be useful to gauge the extent to which groupings, activities, and environments that promote oral language use by students are evident in the classroom (see also Vogt, 1991). Teachers may either use this checklist for self-assessment or pair up with a colleague to observe each other's classrooms.

Reinforcing Academic Language at Home

Besides the quality of instruction that develops academic language among ELLs, we also have to take into account what happens in this domain outside of school. The families and communities of ELLs can provide a rich opportunity for oral academic language development when it is done in a language that the adults are proficient in, which for most students is the native language. ELLs' native language serves as a very important base on which to build English language proficiency (Bialystock, 2001; Genesee, 2006; Smith, 2006).

ECOS TEAM ACTIVITY

Team members can start to explore what the general feeling is regarding oral language use by students. First, let team members reflect on what it was like for them as students (or what it is like, if they are currently enrolled in a graduate program of study): Were they encouraged to talk in class? What do teachers think of colleagues who allow their students to talk in class? How are "loud classrooms" regarded? What do teachers think when ELLs use their native language in class? What do teachers do to make it likely that students are on task when they are using the native language?

Moreover, much of the proficiency that develops in the native language transfers to L2. Thus, students who have their academic language reinforced at home in the native language are better able to tackle new concepts in English.

Many cognitive, academic, linguistic, and socioemotional benefits result when ELLs are encouraged to talk with family members in their native language about what they are experiencing and learning at school (García, 2005; Wells, 2003). Children learn about the adults in their lives, and this fosters respect and admiration among family members for what they know and have experienced. Thus, it is critical that schools do all they can to elevate the prestige of ELLs' native languages and to encourage parents and other caregivers to continue using their native language with their children as long as possible. The following are ways in which academic language development can be encouraged in the home:

- Parents are informed in the native language, through either a bilingual teacher or bilingual aide or volunteer, what students are studying, in a way that allows parents to support the learning even if they do not speak English.
- At home, students review the events of the day at school and what they understood from the day's learning; parents ask questions, even if they are not familiar with the content of the lesson.
- At home, students generate questions to ask their teachers the next day.
- Parents provide their own perspective on the topics students are studying that could be shared in class the next day (such as different historical perspectives, L1 equivalents of academic terminology, personal experiences, or expertise with the topic in question).
- Parents are given guidelines to model L1 procedural language of sequencing, cause and effect, predicting, elaborating, asking questions, storytelling, and so forth.

When the native language is used freely and extensively in the home, not only does it help build language proficiency in general, it also gives staff another

ECOS TEAM ACTIVITY

Based on the material presented to this point, ask pairs of team members to write out what they consider critical components of oral language development. Compile a list from the whole group, then decide which components team members believe are already taken into account when looking at ELLs who are experiencing difficulties. Which components are not considered? This exercise can lead to topics that the team feels need to be emphasized more at school. The team can make recommendations for professional development to help staff learn about these components and to keep them in mind when trying to figure out how best to help students with difficulties.

opportunity to confirm whether a difficulty that an ELL is having goes beyond the challenges of L2 learning. As mentioned in Chapter 4, we must have access to various contexts to be able to validate the source of an ELL's difficulty. If we notice that a group of ELLs is having difficulty using oral narratives effectively, we must validate whether this difficulty occurs only in English at school or whether it occurs at home as well. We need to confirm, for example, whether a child is having difficulty narrating events from the school day to his or her parents. If the behavior is observed across contexts and languages, interventions that support the students may begin immediately at home in L1, and at school in both languages.

Key Factors in Literacy Development

Many of the challenges that students encounter in school can be attributed to difficulties in reading and writing grade-appropriate texts. Literacy is one of the strongest predictors of academic achievement and therefore of success in school (Clay, 1998; Cummins, 2000; Goodman, 1982; Krashen, 2004; Smith, 2004). School staff often jump to the conclusion that these difficulties are due to reading disabilities, especially if the ELLs have gone through a school system and received the same literacy instruction as their native English-speaking peers. To read and write efficiently and well, however, ELLs need specialized instruction that takes into account specific issues pertaining to bilingual literacy development.

The issues in literacy development as they relate to academic difficulties encountered by ELLs are similar to those already discussed for oral language development. These issues include how literacy develops in L1 and L2, the distinction between conversational and academic language as it applies to literacy, the quality and amount of literacy instruction students have received previously and are receiving presently, and literacy in the home.

Literacy Development in L1 and L2

Three principles embody what is most important to remember about literacy development in ELLs.

Literacy Principle 1: *The most important thing about reading and writing is comprehension, not decoding letters or words or calling out words on a page (Cambourne, 1988; García, 2003; Goodman, 2001; Smith, 2004).*

The first thing we need to keep in mind in literacy development is that reading and writing are complex processes that go far beyond decoding words, copying letters or calling out words on a page. Whether it is in the student's native language or second language, the purpose of any literacy act is to either get or send meaning (Smith, 2003, 2004). For any student, it is far more important to understand what a text says rather than to be able to read the same passage aloud. For an ELL, it is even more essential that reading and writing in L2 be focused and based on meaning, because it is easier to read and write something one understands when using a language one is not very proficient in.

Implications for the classroom: Any interactions ELLs have with print, whether in reading or writing, must be embedded in meaningful contexts to be useful to these students (Dudley-Marling & Paugh, 2004; Edelsky, Altwerger, & Flores, 1990). Thus, phonics practice that is devoid of meaning is not effective as an intervention for young ELLs who are in the preproduction or early production stage of L2 acquisition (Dahl, Scharer, Lawson, et al.,

1999; Freppon & Dahl, 1991). Students would only be repeating meaningless sounds without actually using any of their cueing systems. Too often, teachers give ELLs certain literacy tasks because they have inherited a reading or writing program or were given a particular strategy or a set of materials, or because of a district or state mandate. However, it is important that whatever ELLs are given to read and write stimulates them cognitively and allows them to imagine, think, visualize, and connect what they are reading and writing to other topics and to life experiences (Freeman & Freeman, 2003). When designing literacy instruction or interventions for ELLs, we must check the effectiveness of what we are asking ELLs to do. The following questions must continuously be asked at every opportunity:

- Is the text that students are reading or writing at the level of their oral language proficiency?
- Have we given the students enough background information and experiences for them to understand the text?
- Are students engaged in cognitively demanding literacy activities in which they are reading and writing to solve problems, to express themselves, to put forth their perspective, to communicate with others, or to effect change in the world?
- What is the degree to which we view ELLs' native languages as resources?
- Do we choose materials that reflect ELLs' sociocultural and linguistic backgrounds, as well as those of all the students in our schools and communities?

Literacy Principle 2: *There is a strong connection between oral language development and learning how to read and write (Genesee, Lindholm-Leary, Saunders, et al., 2005; Krashen, 2004).*

Literacy and oral language are closely related in two aspects. First, the development of literacy proceeds in predictable stages, much as oral language does, although with the help of instruction. Second, oral language reinforces the development of literacy and is itself reinforced by reading and writing.

Implications for the classroom: It is essential for teachers to base their literacy interventions on what they know about L1 and L2 acquisition, and they must make the connections between the student's oral language and literacy. Teachers who understand the discrepancy between receptive and expressive skills in the early stages of L2 acquisition will use interventions that allow students to use visual aids, illustrations, and other physical means to complement their oral or written expression and to help in assessing comprehension. Strategies such as the Language Experience Approach (LEA; McCormick, 1988; Nessel & Jones, 1981) or the Scaffolding Reading Experiences Framework (Graves & Fitzgerald, 2003) can be used across content areas to help ELLs use their oral language to connect to literacy. In the LEA approach, for example, teachers plan a shared experience, such as an experiment or a field trip. In small groups, students discuss the experience, take notes, rehearse, and then report to the class. The teacher acts as scribe to capture the students' utterances on chart paper or projected onto a screen. In the process, the teacher models writing for the students. Chronicle 9.2 describes how one teacher took an LEA story and focused on a specific language structure that many students needed help with.

Literacy Principle 3: *Students' native language is a resource for developing literacy in English, not a hindrance (Genesee, Lindholm-Leary, Saunders, et al., 2006; Krashen, 2004).*

It's Just a Few Steps from Oral Language to Literacy

By a consultant who observed a sheltered science class

This is an excerpt from a short Language Experience story that ELLs dictated in a sheltered science class near the end of their unit on the life cycle of amphibians. ELLs in this class had experienced, read, and learned a great deal about amphibians. In this lesson they could concentrate on expressing themselves orally in English without the added strain of putting these thoughts into writing. It was evident also that the teacher had asked the students to talk at home in their native language about what they were learning. The teacher modeled writing for students, as well as some conventions such as spelling and capitalization.

> We saw frogs go through their lifes (lives). First they were so little like balls of jelly. They were like that for a while. They were wet and had different sizes. Then they were like fish. We saw the frogs grow legs, and it was weird to see them like that. We could see through their bodies still. Miss Winters said that they were tadpoles. We had to ask our fathers (parents) how to say that in our language for homework. We had vacation(s) and one frog died. The frogs were bigger now and could breathe the air. They are green and brown. . . .

The students copied this text into their science learning logs and then took turns reading the text to a peer. After they had read the passage a few times, the teacher told them that for homework they should add more sentences to their story. She had time before the end of the period, so she took the opportunity to practice a bit with graphophonemic connections. She started asking students to point to a word in the LEA text that contained the /z/ sound. She was going from the sounds to the text that the students had generated. She knew it would be okay to work on these skills because in was in a meaningful context with words she already knew were in the ELLs' oral expressive language. Students began reading through the text again to listen for the /z/ sound:

> *One student:* Frogs.
> *Teacher:* Yes. Very good. Does everyone hear it? (Everyone says yes.)
> *Another student:* Legs.
> *Teacher:* Yes. Everyone say *legs* and listen for the /z/ sound. What are *legs?* Point to your legs. (Everyone points to their legs.) Where are the frog's legs? (All the students point to the legs on a picture of a frog in their open text.)
> *Teacher:* Another word with the /z/ sound?
> *Student:* Sizes.
> *Teacher:* Yes. Everyone tell your partner what you noticed about the /z/ sound in the word *sizes.*

The teacher in this situation capitalized on ELLs' oral proficiency to act as a bridge to literacy. Together, students and teacher worked on various literacy skills: writing (ideas and conventions), reading comprehension, oral reading fluency, and graphophonemic connections, all in a meaningful, content-based, cognitively demanding context.

Questions for discussion:

- How would the exchange between teacher and students focusing on the /z/ sound be different if the words did not come from the LEA text?
- Would it be fruitful for educators to create LEA stories with students in their native languages? How?

It is clear from the research that literacy in L1 supports English literacy development, regardless of the L1 (Corsaro & Nelson, 2003; Krashen, 1996; Lanauze & Snow, 1999; Lightbown & Spada, 2003). Later in the chapter we look at specific areas of literacy that transfer across languages, but in general, the meaning-making aspects of literacy, such as drawing inferences, comparing and contrasting information, understanding main ideas and details, and recognizing propaganda, transfer broadly across languages. Once students have experience being literate in one language, they have the potential to transfer those skills and approaches to literacy into any additional languages they learn.

Implications for the classroom: ELLs must learn to read in their home language first whenever possible. Reading instruction in L2 can begin when the student has some oral language proficiency in L2 (Freeman & Freeman, 2003; Krashen, 2004; Snow, Burns, & Griffen, 1998). When it is not possible for a school to provide high-quality instruction to ELLs in reading and writing in their L1, these students' native language literacy must be reinforced at home or in the community by means of a tutoring program that the school sets up (Tett & Crowther, 1998). The multilingual resources listed in Table 4.5 in Chapter 4 could be useful for setting up libraries of multilingual materials in school, as well as for parents and children at home. Of special consideration are sites that provide free multilingual books in multiple languages, such as the University of Maryland's International Digital Children's Library (*http://www.icdlbooks.org/*), and the Children's Books Online Rosetta Project (*http://www.childrensbooksonline.org/library.htm*). When older students, parents, or volunteers read these books aloud to younger ELLs, they model fluent reading, help students develop pride in the native languages, and reinforce home-school connections (Trelease, 2001). If it proves difficult initially to find volunteers to read in the different languages, there are many benefits to be had when ELLs read aloud to family members in English or in their native language. The impact on ELLs' reading is positive even when parents do not understand the language of the books or if the parents are illiterate (Damico, Nelson, & Bryan, 2005; Tizard, Schofield, & Hewison, 1982).

ELLs who do not have opportunity to develop literacy in L1 should be introduced to literacy in English through meaningful activities rather than tasks that are devoid of context and meaning (Freeman & Freeman, 2003; Genesee, 2006; Routman, 2003).

An example of how schools can address these three principles successfully is what Cummins describes as *identity texts* (Chow & Cummins, 2005; Schecter & Cummins, 2003). Staff at the Thornwood Public Schools in Mississauga, Ontario, with support from parents, older students, volunteers , and peers, asked students to create dual-language stories, texts and projects in their native languages and English. What began in a few classrooms has now spread throughout the school. These projects and stories are available to view and use online at *http://thornwood.peelschools.org/Dual/*. They provide meaningful literacy activities that connect oral language with reading and writing. Not only do they allow ELLs to develop literacy in both languages, they raise the status of literacy in all ELLs' languages to a high level. Some school prin-

ECOS TEAM ACTIVITY

In small groups, examine the Thornwood Dual Language Showcase Web site and assess how the three literacy principles discussed in this section are applied. How can identity texts support literacy instruction for ELLs? What is the diagnostic potential of this approach for identifying exceptionalities in ELLs? How can this approach be used in different grade levels and across content areas? How could a project like this one be initiated in your school?

cipals have begun similar dual-language projects in their multilingual schools as a way to increase the involvement of language minority parents. Some teachers have inherited ELLs with limited to no literacy development in either language and have used the dual-language projects as a bridge to literacy in both L1 and L2, with remarkable results.

Social Language and Academic Language

Just as in oral language development, it is important to make a distinction between ELLs' social literacy and academic literacy. And just as in oral language development, social literacy is easier to master, because it deals with more concrete ideas and has referents that are usually quite accessible to the learner. The popularity of electronic devices that allow social messaging might suggest that these social literacy skills are being developed quite early and are being put to use quite often. However, just because an ELL is able to send emails, join chat groups on the Internet and send text messages does not mean that he or she is able to handle complex and abstract literacy tasks. Academic texts tend to be more cognitively demanding because of their abstractness, and they also adhere to more rigid rules of accuracy. Table 9.3 shows a partial list of social and academic reading and writing practices that students should be engaging in.

The standards movement, for all its limitations, has produced some guidlines about the types of literacy that can be expected from ELLs for various content areas at different grade levels. Appendix H shows a set of guidelines from the WIDA Consortium for grades 6 to 8 in social studies.

Evidence of Appropriate Literacy Instruction in L1 and L2

At this point it is important to determine whether ELLs who are experiencing difficulties are receiving appropriate literacy instruction in both L1 and L2. Just because they have spent a few years in U.S. schools does not necessarily mean they have received the specialized literacy instruction they need. This issue is important because the greatest predictor of a student's achievement in any skill or ability is the opportunity to learn that skill in a sufficient and appropriate manner (Berliner & Biddle, 1995). When we provide ELLs with exactly the same literacy instruction at the same time in the same way that we provide native English speakers with literacy instruction, we are not offering ELLs the most effective path to literacy.

Effective literacy practices apply the three principles discussed earlier, in the section entitled "Literacy Development in L1 and L2." To summarize, reading and writing have to be taught in ways and contexts that are meaningful to the student. Students should rarely be assigned text to read that is not meaningful to them. Even further, whatever text students read should clearly relate to their daily lives. (See Chronicle 9. 3 for an illustration of a

---

ECOS TEAM ACTIVITY

Using the list of literary activities in Table 9.3, have individual teachers or pairs of teachers check the tasks and activities that their ELLs engage in. Encourage them to think about ways to incorporate some of the activities that are not checked into their daily classroom routines. If there are no bilingual teachers or aides and the classroom teacher is not proficient in the native language of the students, how would teachers go about incorporating more L1 literacy activities into their classroom?

Table 9.3   Checklist of Literacy Practices That Students Engage In

	L1	L2		L1	L2
Social Reading • Notes to and from parents • Comic books and magazines • Books • Internet sites • Instant and text messaging • Emails • Notes in class • Advertising • Closed captions on TV • Song lyrics			**Social Writing** • To-do lists • Internet blogging • Instant and text messaging • Emails • Notes in class • Personal journal or diary • Letters to friends and family		
Academic Reading • Textbooks • Literature • Biographies • Peer review of written work • Oral reports • Encyclopedia entries • Internet or magazine articles • Math problems • Instructions			**Academic Writing** • Essays • Research papers • Learning logs • Lab reports • Reflections • Poetry • Goal sheets • Bibliographies • Homework • Question-and-answer text • Outlines • Notes • Summaries • Paraphrasing		

lost opportunity to relate text to students' lives.) Instruction must take into account the oral language proficiency level of each student and use that oral language to build literacy. Thus, a teacher who understands that a group of ELLs are at the speech emergence stage of oral language proficiency will encourage these students to use content-specific word banks and will give them key words that are about to appear in a lesson before the students even see the text or hear a lecture on the topic (e.g., Allington, 2001; Graves & Fitzgerald, 2003). Literacy instruction in English must also be founded on whatever literacy exists in the students' native language, and for young children embarking on the task of learning how to read, the introduction to literacy must be done in a language the students can understand—their native language (Freeman & Freeman, 2002, 2003; Genesee, Lindholm-Leary, Saunders, & Christian, 2006; Krashen, 2004).

It is never acceptable to establish remedial literacy programs for ELLs or those that reduce reading to its smallest elements, graphemes and phonemes. Teachers must apply these principles to develop literacy in these students in its most extensive definition, including social as well as academic tasks.

Romeo and Juliet: A Lost Opportunity

By a consultant who observed a high school ESL English class

This was one of the toughest high schools in the city, clearly dominated by two opposing gangs. It was also one of the lowest-performing schools in the state. I was asked to observe the ESL English class. I walked in just as the students were entering the classroom in pairs and small groups. The teacher was already in the classroom, organizing his papers. As I settled in at the back of the classroom, I noticed the loud banter going on between the students. Some very sophisticated insults were being exchanged in a mixture of English and Spanish, most in good humor, and all of them very clever. In fact, some of the insults were so funny I wrote them down! I guessed it was members of the two gangs who were hurling insults at each other.

The students settled in, and the class began. They were reading *Romeo and Juliet*. And, wouldn't you know it—They happened to be reading the fight scene between the Capulets and the Montagues. I found it ironic: a group of adolescents from two opposing families who had entered a scene "fighting" with each other were reading their actions mirrored in the same scene in a play. I was hoping that the teacher would bring the relevance of this classroom activity to the students' lives, but he didn't. (I probably would have failed to do so as well had I been teaching the class instead of just observing it!)

The teacher asked individual students to read different roles in the scene. The reading was flat and emptied of meaning, and soon many eyes, including mine, wandered away from the page, away from the rich language, and away from the tense situation unfolding in the play. If only the teacher had pointed out the irony that here was a play, written centuries ago, about something these students were still doing in 2005! If only the teacher had brought the relevance of this scene and the whole play to students' lives, this class would have been about the students themselves, rather than about some fictitious characters in a play written by a dead poet ages ago.

Questions for discussion:

- How would the learning have been different for these students had the teacher pointed out the relevance of the scene to the students' lives?
- In the larger picture of school life in general, what are some likely consequences of the cumulative effect of being taught things that have little relevance to one's life?

Literacy in the Home

ELLs' home literacy experiences are very important, both for reinforcing the development of literacy in general and for supporting reading and writing in the native language. ELLs' native languages and cultures are tremendous resources, since a high level of literacy in L1 positively influences literacy in L2. When ELLs begin to have significant difficulties in school, we need to ascertain the home literacy environment. It would be helpful to know, for example, whether ELLs' families have access to native language books and other written materials in community public libraries, in neighborhood bookstores, in the school library, and in their homes. This information is especially important for older students with limited formal schooling, whose exposure to literacy is typically more limited than that of students who have had the expected amount and type of schooling.

Understanding the Relationship between Students' L1 and L2

The close relationship that exists between a bilingual person's two languages is hypothesized to be based on a common underlying proficiency for language (Cummins, 1981). This common underlying proficiency makes it possible for much to be transferred between the learner's two languages. Evidence of transfer between ELLs' languages can be seen in literacy as well as in oral language. While ELLs are in the process of developing proficiency in one or both of their languages, it is normal, for example, to see instances of L1 syntax appearing in L2 speaking and writing, or for L1 phonology to leave its impact on L2 speaking and listening comprehension.

Transfer from one language to another happens in general areas of language no matter the languages in question. The fact that both English and Spanish express the plural of nouns by adding a morpheme at the end of the noun is something that learners will automatically carry from one language to the other. Language-specific transfer also happens in aspects that are unique to particular languages. The clearest specific transfer is between cognates; an example is *electricidad* and *electricity.* Many low-frequency academic words in English are similar to words in other languages. For example, biography in English is *biographie* in German, *biografía* in Spanish, *biographie* in French, *biografía* in Italian, and *biografiska* in Swedish. This similarity can be particularly helpful in reading in the content areas.

In literacy, research shows both general and specific transfer. Examples of general transfer are in reading comprehension and strategy use. Examples of specific transfer are in word recognition, vocabulary, and spelling. Research also shows both positive and negative transfer (Jimenez, García, & Pearson, 1996; Lanauze & Snow, 1999; Nagy, McClure, & Mir, 1997; Reese et al., 2000), similar to the findings from oral language. August (2006) has summarized the research on transfer in literacy, as shown in Table 9.4.

When there are similarities between the learner's two languages, the transfer is positive and is helpful to the learner, as in the example of the cognates just discussed. This is called positive transfer. However, transfer can also be negative and can result in errors or interference. This frequently happens with false cognates, words that sound similar in different languages but do not have the same meaning. For example, Spanish-English ELLs often mistakenly

Table 9.4 Summary of Research on the Transfer of Literacy between Two Languages

- Word recognition skills acquired in L1 transfer to L2.
- Vocabulary knowledge transfers for words that are cognates.
- Children use spelling knowledge in L1 when they spell in L2, and errors associated with L1 disappear as students become more proficient in L2.
- There is evidence of cross-language transfer of reading comprehension in bilingual persons of all ages, even when the languages have different types of alphabets.
- There is transfer of comprehension from students' L2 to L1. Bilingual students who read strategically in one language also read strategically in their other language.
- There are cross-language relationships for writing, but levels of L1 and L2 proficiency may mediate these relationships.

Source: August (2006).

use the word *library* to mean *bookstore* because the word for bookstore in Spanish is *librería*. Another example of negative transfer or interference is the transfer of grammatical structures from one language to the other, resulting in confusion. For Spanish-English bilinguals, word order is often a common source of interference. For example, it is not uncommon to hear ELLs say "the chair red," following the adjective-noun order in Spanish (*la silla roja*).

Because of this phenomenon of negative transfer or interference, ELLs of similar L1 backgrounds make similar errors in English. Thus, it is important to understand what typical and predictable transfer errors in English are to be expected from a group of ELLs of the same language background. This knowledge would help teachers recognize what is part of the normal L2 development process and what might be unusual and a possible area of concern that would require further investigation and assessment.

The close relationship between a bilingual person's two languages may also be observed in code-switching. Code-switching is generally defined as the alternating use of two languages within the same conversational event (Poplack, 1980). This can happen in the same sentence (*I washed mi mano*) or between sentences (*I did that already. Ahora voy a ir a jugar*). Code-switching occurs during early stages of bilingual language acquisition, but it also happens with individuals who are highly proficient in multiple languages.

It is important to distinguish between these two contexts for code-switching because it is important to know whether the learner is alternating between languages out of necessity, as in the case of the former, or by choice, as in the case of the latter. If ELLs code switch frequently, they may be drawing words and phrases from their native language to fill in for vocabulary they do not yet possess in English. However, as ELLs become more proficient in both languages, it is normal to code switch for social communicative reasons.

Language Use Patterns

Gathering information on how ELLs use their two languages and how they started learning each of their languages is helpful for determining the interventions that are needed. The linguistic resources students bring with them in both L1 and L2 are the place to begin when creating interventions for whatever difficulties the students may be experiencing. This foundational building block, especially in the native language, is often overlooked, since most teachers are concerned with English language development.

More often than not, ELLs' other languages are not considered from the beginning. Sometimes teachers report that ELLs do not like using their native language in school, so the child study team does not pursue it. This raises the question of why the ELLs no longer want to use their native language in school. Regardless, if parents or grandparents in the home speak only the native language, then the students have at least receptive capabilities in that language, and we need to find out about those capabilities and use them as a resource. Some educators believe that the language students use at home is not formal because the parents have not been to school or are not literate, and therefore it will be of little use in helping the students. However, even if the native language is being used in social conversational contexts, it is still important to gather information about it.

Language use patterns should be looked at beginning from birth rather than from the time the ELL enters school. For example, it is important to know whether a child reached the expected milestones at the expected rate. If the parents report that the child did not speak at all in their L1 until after three years of age, it might lead us to ask further questions or have the child's hearing checked.

Another reason we want to determine ELLs' language use patterns prior to their coming to school is that some ELLs may come with limited L1 and L2 academic proficiency. This could be due to insufficient exposure to quality interactions with adults in either language. These students may have been born in the United States and developed some social oral proficiency in English, but, lacking formal instruction in the native language, they would not have developed proficiency in academic language in either language. When they use their native-like social English proficiency, school staff members may believe that they do not need any sort of ESL support. These students get overlooked for any kind of support and are not even considered to be ELL. Chronicle 9.4 illustrates this situation as it is recalled by adults who are former ELLs.

ELLs often are mistaken for monolingual English-speaking students because they drop their home language altogether and claim monolingualism. Some parents and children feel a stigma associated with using a language other than English at home. Other than the fact that this sort of climate can have a significant detrimental effect on the student's cognitive, academic, social, and affective development, it makes it very difficult to gather accurate information about L1 and L2 use. When school staff ask parents or other caregivers what language is used in the home, the answer is inevitably "English!" even though it is clear that the parents are not proficient in English. They have, however, got the message that this is the "correct" answer. As discussed in Chapter 11, the cultural milieu of the school must be such that ELLs' native languages are not only recognized and openly valued but become part of the daily functioning of the school.

A difficult situation emerges when parents who are very limited in English really are using English exclusively at home because of social cultural pressures. Someone may have told parents they should practice their English at home if they ever want their children to learn. Instead of using their well-developed, adult native language, these parents begin to speak in ESL phrases to their children. Not only does the quality of the language used with the children suffer, the quantity is likely to be diminished as well. Students in this kind of home environment do not have the opportunity to solidify structures in L1 and do not have a rich linguistic environment in L2. Speech-language pathologists often receive these students and have to do some detective work to figure out why they are using such unusual structures in English. The mystery is solved once they interview the parents, hear their limited English proficiency, and discover that they were counseled to use only English.

Suggestions for Information Gathering

The easiest and fastest way to gather information about ELLs' oral language and literacy is to administer one of the many language proficiency tests available on the market. However, that would not reflect the complex and multifaceted nature of oral language and literacy and would result in an extremely narrow view of a student's ability to use oral language proficiently and his or her ability to read and write with meaning. Therefore, as a minimal requirement, more extensive information about ELLs' oral language and literacy must be collected. Some of this information naturally will describe the students' proficiency levels, but other information must address the way ELLs use their two languages. Decisions must be made regarding what to assess and how to assess it.

That Was Me!

By a university professor

The university where I teach ran a certification program for paraprofessionals. The program would give participants the credentials they needed to work as paraprofessionals in bilingual programs around the state. The participants in the course I was teaching were all women in their early twenties and had gone back to school while working as paraprofessionals supporting ELLs at a high school. They were all native speakers of Spanish who had been working in different capacities in schools but did not have university training or any kind of certification.

In this class session, we were discussing the stages of L2 acquisition and the importance of knowing when the students acquired each of their languages. We were talking about how some ELLs manage to acquire a bit of English by the time they enter school and somehow give the impression that they are proficient in English when they are not. Over and over these young people kept repeating the same thing:

"That was me!" "I never got extra ESL help at school because I was born here." "We didn't immigrate, so people just assumed we were regular English speakers."

"Me too! We never used English at home, but I learned some from friends, so by the time I went to kindergarten I could speak some. School was always hard and things didn't start making sense until eighth grade, but by then I had missed a lot of stuff. I think that's why high school was so hard. I'm glad I went back to school now, but it would have been nice to know what was happening to me."

"Yeah! They put me in special ed, but then they took me out when I learned more English. I wish I had gotten some help with my English instead of being with the special ed kids."

Questions for discussion:

- Are there ELLs in your school who slip by and are placed in the mainstream without any support when they actually need help in English? What needs to be changed in the system to avoid that?
- Other than the impact on academic performance, what are some likely outcomes (emotional, social, political) of being taken for something you are not?

What to Assess in Oral Language and Literacy

The four domains in L1 and L2: The first condition for learning about ELLs' oral language and literacy is that proficiency in both languages must be considered (Gottlieb, 2006). In addition, to be able to verify exceptionalities across languages, we need to gather information about the two languages in all four domains—listening, speaking, reading, and writing. If we only gather information in English, then we will always have an incomplete picture of what ELLs can do, and we will be guessing about the possible causes of difficulties (Genesee, Paradis, & Crago, 2004; Hamayan & Damico, 1991). Gathering information about some of the less common native languages can be quite challenging. However, the more information we have about ELLs' L1, the easier it will be to identify the cause of the student's difficulties and design an effective intervention. If an informant or an interpreter is used to obtain information about the native language, all the issues discussed in earlier chapters regarding the qualifications of such a liaison and privacy concerns must be heeded.

Conversational and academic language: Both conversational fluency and academic language should be assessed. Students typically develop greater proficiency in one aspect of language usage than in the other. When attempting to describe the ELL's language system, teachers benefit from having this information. These evaluations entail talking to students about everyday social matters as well as observing them in content area classes, and assessing them after they have heard a lecture.

Multiple contexts: The third criterion for collecting valid information about oral language and literacy is that a wide range of contexts in which ELLs use language must be assessed (Gottlieb, 2006). ELLs use language differently and show different levels of proficiency in different contexts. For example, in the ESL classroom, perhaps because students feel relaxed, they may be quite talkative and communicate effectively, whereas in the mainstream classroom they may be anxious and less fluent. Gathering information in different contexts will also ensure that both L1 and L2 are addressed, and that both social and academic language are included.

Discrete aspects and holistic representations of language: Much of the language assessment that happens at school measures the processing of discrete aspects of language, especially in reading. This practice is fraught with difficulties, since a focus on splinter skills often does not yield a valid or authentic picture of an individual's proficiency (Carroll, 1993; Damico, 1991; McDermott & Varenne, 1995; Pinnell, 1989; Tetnowski & Franklin, 2003). Additionally, this assessment is typically done with formal tests that yield a narrow view of what the student is able to do. Thus, it is essential that holistic measures be included in the information gathering. When school staff members assess students on discrete skills, such as the ability to read blends, ELLs may perform well and yet not be able to do the most important thing about reading: make meaning. As another example is, ELLs may know how to decode words on a page in English but have no idea what those words mean. They might as well be decoding nonsense words (Smith, 1983, 1998). The checklist in Table 9.5 can be used to ensure that all aspects of oral language and literacy are being assessed.

How to Assess Oral Language and Literacy

Standardized norm-referenced tests: As long as they are not used exclusively for identification and placement into remedial education and are never solely relied on, there may be a place for standardized norm-referenced tests in the assessment of oral language and literacy when assessing for comparison purposes. However, because of the many problems with the use of these tests with ELLs (Gottlieb, 2006), certain criteria must be met:

1. If a comparison group is being used, that population must be similar to the students being assessed.
2. Assessment must be based on native language or L2 learning standards.
3. Assessment must be based on grade-level, content area expectations.
4. Assessment must make developmental sense.
5. Assessment must reflect the opportunity that students have had to learn.
6. The test performance is analyzed and the scores are interpreted in the context of more natural and authentic assessments.

Table 9.5 Assessing All Aspects of Oral Language and Literacy

	L1				L2			
	L	S	R	W	L	S	R	W
Type of proficiency								
• Conversational fluency								
• Academic language								
Contexts								
• In the general education classroom								
• In the ESL classroom								
• In the bilingual classroom								
• On the playground								
• At home								
• With friends								
Discrete								
• Symbol/sound								
• Vocabulary								
• Grammar								
Holistic								
• Understanding and expressing ideas and feelings								
• Understanding and describing concrete things								
• Understanding and describing abstract concepts								
• Communicating with peers and adults								

Note: L = listening, S = speaking, R = reading, W = writing.

If the standardized test that is being used meets these six criteria, then it may form one piece of a student's profile. Standardized testing should never be the sole measure for any type of instructional or programmatic decision for ELLs. Overreliance on standardized, discrete measures to evaluate student learning, cognitive ability, academic achievement, and teacher effectiveness and to diagnose learning disabilities or language disorders has reduced our capacity to see student growth, recognize divergent thinking, notice subtle changes in attitudes about learning, engage students in higher-level questioning, see progress in ELLs' cross-cultural competence, and recognize students' resiliency. Worse yet, students have no way to see their potential, their areas of strength or growth over time. The families of these students are also bombarded with meaningless scores rather that receive concrete evidence of their children's work and progress in school. Hence, there is a precious need for the use of authentic and perhaps more informal assessment.

Authentic performance assessment: Many of the instructional strategies and classroom activities that teachers use can be rich sources of information for assessing ELLs' areas of growth or difficulty. By using rubrics, checklists, and other tools, teachers can begin to evaluate the work ELLs are producing and the language they are using. As Margot Gottlieb has noted, useful performance assessment requires that "students express their learning in direct ways that reflect real-life situations" (2006, p. 111). These performance measures, because they tend to be more informal and often rely on subjective judgments, must reach some level of reliability. For example, it is important that the same criteria for evaluation be used over time and by different assessors. These measures have some significant advantages over more standardized norm-referenced tests:

- They do not interrupt instruction as they are embedded in the strategies and activities used daily in class.
- They provide immediate feedback that informs and shapes instruction.
- They provide a more comprehensive profile of an L2 student's strengths and areas that need attention.
- They allow students, teachers, and parents to see growth over time.

Performance assessment can be used in two contexts to evaluate ELLs' language and literacy development: in classroom observations and in teacher-student conferences. Classroom observations can be completed by teachers in their own classrooms or by colleagues who sit in for short periods of time. Use of task-specific or skill-specific checklists, anecdotal note taking, and videotaping with subsequent analysis can all supply important information about what students are doing with language and literacy. A list of classroom observation strategies is provided in Table 9.6

Table 9.6 Strategies for Assessing Oral Language and Literacy Through Classroom Observation

Sources of Language	Strategies for Assessment
• Oral language samples across content areas	• Rubrics for listening, speaking, reading and writing
• Writing samples	• Checklist of types of utterances
• Oral reports	• Academic language checklist
• Audio and video recordings	• Rubrics for group interactions
• Student-selected products	• Rubrics for pair work
• Multilingual projects	• Skill-specific checklist
• Artifacts from portfolio over time and across content areas	• Anecdotal records
• Small-group projects	• Informal running records
• Dialogue journals	• Narratives
• Interviews	
• Story telling	

Table 9.7 Interventions for Oral Language and Literacy Development

Social and academic oral language development in L1 and L2	Academic and social literacy development in L1 and L2
Systemic	*Systemic*
• Implement a schoolwide emphasis on having ELLs talk with their families at home in L1 about what they learn at school.	• Provide professional development on literacy strategies to use across the curriculum.
• Use oral language charts for teachers to self-monitor oral language use in classrooms.	• Have administrators emphasize academic language and literacy along with academic content.
• Ask teachers to include language objectives when designing units and lessons.	• Allow time to adapt literacy strategies for use with ELLs in L1 and L2.
• Highlight different collaborative learning structures each month for teachers to try.	• Encourage the coordinated use of graphic organizers that support a variety of text structures (sequence, cause-and-effect, and compare and contrast charts) across grade levels.
• Increase the amount of small-group work.	• Insist on L1 initial literacy instruction at least through grade 3 in multilingual settings.
• Have teachers engage in peer coaching and tally each other's exchanges with students to gather information on who is talking, who is not talking, what languages are being used, how often are girls talking, how often are boys talking, how often is the teacher talking.	• Encourage student-created dual-language writing projects across grade levels and content areas, and display these projects on the school's Web site and library board.
• Speech-language pathologists together with ESL teachers can provide professional development on strategies to help students develop their expressive language.	• Have the school connect with a partner classroom in another country.
	• Ensure that language arts classrooms support mathematics, science, and social studies reading and writing.
	• Place a greater focus on nonfiction reading and writing from the very early grades on.
	• Use multicultural, antibias literature throughout the school for all students.
	• Provide the support of reading specialists throughout the grade levels, not just in the early grades.
	• Encourage parents and family members to read to their children in their native language.
	• Create a home-school reading program that includes books in all the students' languages.
	• Implement a reading program with the support of bilingual high school or university students.
	• Have students read and write every day in every subject.
	• Order multilingual books every school year for the classroom and school libraries and display them prominently.
	• Order multiple-level books on nonfiction topics to support content area texts.
	• Purchase books on CD.

Specific

- Provide students with word banks to use across the curriculum.
- Have students use sentence starters specific to underlying language focus (sequential, compare-contrast, cause and effect, and so on).
- Ask students to talk at home with their parents about what they learned at school.
- Give students time to prepare and process in L1 before talking in L2.
- Organize lunchtime conversation clubs.
- Have parents and community volunteers help out in small-group work to increase conversations.

Specific

- Have teachers capitalize on students' L1 and L2 oral language as a bridge to literacy (such as by creating Language Experience texts).
- Promote student-teacher conferences about ELLs' reading and writing.
- Ask adults to take anecdotal notes about students' interests, strengths, and difficulties in a reading notebook during conferences.
- Use teacher-student dialogue journals in both L1 and L2
- Ask teachers to use visual prompts to preview vocabulary in books and to assess comprehension.
- Use the Language Experience Approach text to teach skills.
- Use learning logs (with dated entries) with all students as a way to assess understanding of content material and to encourage academic writing.
- Ask parents to make their child's oral dictation into a diary of the day's or week's events.
- Implement a reading and writing workshop approach to literacy instruction.
- Ask parents, grandparents, and community members to come into the library or classroom to read in the students' native languages.

Teacher-student conferences provide another opportunity for assessing ELLs' language and literacy development. When students discuss, read, and write about a wide range of topics in a variety of genres, it is useful for teachers to set aside time each week to discuss students' work with them and to listen to them read. Students of all ages and grade levels not only benefit from these conferences, they look forward to these times that have been set aside especially for them. The conference provides an opportunity for students to ask specific questions and seek clarification or guidance about their work. From the teacher's perspective, it provides insight into how the student is processing instruction and how he or she is progressing both in content area acquisition and language proficiency development.

When teachers meet with students, they can keep anecdotal notes about specific issues they have discussed. Teachers can jot down questions the students have and take notes on each student's reading, writing, and personal interests. Teachers can also keep informal running records and take notes on what strategies the students are using and areas they are progressing in (Taberski, 2000). Teachers can use information gathered in these weekly conferences to adjust their whole-class instruction and to determine the content of mini-lessons. Teachers can use the information diagnostically to work strategically with various groups of students and hence differentiate literacy instruction appropriately. Another benefit is that teachers learn about students' interests and can find individualized reading and writing materials and projects for them. The strategies listed in Table 9.6 for classroom observation can also be used to evaluate students' oral language and literacy during conferences.

Comparisons with Peers

Once the school has adopted the practice of collecting authentic language and literacy information from ELLs, it is easier to put ELLs' development of oral language and literacy into a context. It is important that teachers begin to see what "typical" reading, writing, speaking, and listening look and sound like for ELLs at various levels of proficiency in English. Teachers have a sense of what native speakers of English are expected to do at different ages; they need to develop that same sense for ELLs. This sense can be developed by looking at the performance of ELLs within and across grades and proficiency levels, and by looking at individual and group growth in language and literacy longitudinally over time.

This will provide a context in which to interpret the difficulties that some ELLs are having in school. It will also allow staff to compare these ELLs' performance with other ELLs from the same and different language backgrounds who are doing well in school, with monolingual English speaking students who are also having difficulty in school, and with monolingual English-speaking students who are doing well academically. Only then will it possible to know what is typical, so that as a team we can recognize the unusual.

Suggestions for Intervention

A summary of intervention strategies to help support oral language development and literacy in ELLs having academic difficulties is presented in Table 9.7.

Questions for Discussion

1. What do we know about the oral language and literacy development in L1 and L2 of the ELLs we serve?
   1.1. What is the typical pattern of social language development?
   1.2. What is the typical pattern of academic language development?
   1.3. Have the students had instruction that utilized the oral language instruction strategies described in this chapter?
   1.4. Have the students had instruction that utilized the literacy instruction approaches described in this chapter?
   1.5. If ELLs have had the benefit of the oral language and literacy instruction strategies described in this chapter, have those strategies been used across all curricular areas?
   1.6. Do teachers routinely embed authentic, performance-based assessments in instruction?
   1.7. How do teachers apply their understanding of the relationship between students' L1 and L2 to their instructional planning and their selection of instructional approaches and strategies?
2. What do we know about the oral language and literacy development in L1 and L2 of the ELL who is currently having trouble?
   2.1. How can we find out more?
   2.2. How can we establish the validity and reliability of the data we have?
   2.3. What are the student's strengths in the areas of oral language and literacy development?
   2.4. Has the ELL's difficulty been observed in more than one context?
   2.5. What specific interventions are needed?
   2.6. How will we monitor the ELL's progress during the intervention(s)?
   2.7. How will we determine the success of the intervention(s)?

10

Academic Achievement Factors

KEY CONCEPTS

The sixth integral factor focuses on academic achievement, a comprehensive term for the student's performance in all content areas. Because of the close relationship between academic concepts and the language used to process those concepts, interventions must be closely tied to what the student is learning in the classroom and must support content learning.

The sixth integral element to consider when English language learners (ELLs) experience difficulty is their academic achievement. In evaluating ELLs' academic achievement, educators must distinguish between understanding academic content and developing sufficient proficiency to express that understanding in language. This chapter introduces strategies that can be used to make this discrimination. It is also important to look at all content areas to ensure adequate curricular coverage. We present some suggestions for gathering and interpreting information about ELLs' academic achievement and the components of lesson and unit design that should enable ELLs to learn content and concepts while developing academic language in English and their native language. We conclude with suggestions for systemic and specific interventions to help support ELLs' academic performance.

Key Factors in Academic Achievement for ELLs

ELLs' academic success is influenced by all the integral elements discussed in this handbook, but the crux of the matter is how well these students learn what the curriculum is set to teach. For older students, in addition to their responses to current instruction, the ECOS team needs to know how these students performed academically in the past. This information helps the team determine whether the student had the opportunity to learn, and how the student performed at that time with that opportunity. The team also needs to ensure that the learning environment created for ELLs is one that is based on sound theory and on practice that produces effective learning. The learning environment has frequently been shown to be foundational to academic success or failure, from preschool (Magnuson & Waldfogel, 2005) to university education (Schönwetter, Clifton, & Perry, 2002). By learning environment, we mean the whole environment constituted by the school (Calkins, 1997; Wells, 2003). Perhaps because of the emphasis on high-stakes testing in the recent past, much of the concern with academic achievement has centered on the content areas specifically tested (Graves, 2002; Kohn, 2000).

However, in considering the special needs of ELLs, it is imperative to examine all the areas in which any learning is occurring (Coelho, 1994; Kohn, 1998; Miramontes, Nadeau, & Commins, 1997).

Taking into Account All Content Areas: Core Academic Areas, Special Classes, Electives

To develop a good profile of how a student or a group of students is doing, we must look at how well the student or group performs across all curricular areas (Gottlieb, 2006), including, in addition to the core curriculum, the fine arts, industrial technology, drama, and physical education. There are two principal reasons for looking at performance in all content areas. The first reason is that students who are doing poorly in one or two subject areas may be excelling in other areas. An ELL who is having significant difficulties in language arts, social studies, and science may be advancing quite rapidly in English as a second language (ESL) instruction and math, and may be very talented in music. The strengths of that student can tell us as much as the failures do, and provide us with more valuable information.

A complete view of the student makes it easier to come up with specific interventions that take into account many aspects of learning and performance. The interventions that are designed can build on what the student knows and is able to do. Thus, when looking at the performance of particular students, it is important to see if their difficulties are manifest equally across contexts or are limited to particular areas. This information helps the ECOS team identify and use students' strengths to improve performance in areas of academic difficulty. In effect, the individual, social, and cultural capital of the student can be used in designing future programs and strategies of assistance (e.g., Garmezy, 1991; Ogbu & Simons, 1998; Robson, Cook, & Gilliland, 1995; Stanton-Salazar, 1997).

The second reason to monitor ELLs' progress in a variety of content areas is to discern trends across content areas and grade levels (Nguyen, 2006b; Yturriago, 2006b). For example, the team may find that as a group, ELLs do very well in certain content areas and poorly in others. The students may do well in kindergarten through grade 2 in all areas but begin to show dramatic decreases in mathematics and reading achievement in grades 3 and 4. Longitudinal data may show that ELLs who receive support in their native language while learning English reach higher levels of achievement than students whose native language or ESL support is removed after a couple of years. Teachers may notice that ELLs who maintain their native language and culture while learning English remain in school longer than those who do not. Examining trends across content areas and grade levels helps the ECOS team and other school personnel plan strategically in trying to address and even prevent academic difficulties across the curriculum at all grade levels. This type of longitudinal and cross-sectional information yields more effective systemic interventions.

ECOS TEAM ACTIVITY

Invite one or two of the non-core curriculum area teachers (such as an art, physical education, or music teacher) to an ECOS team meeting. Ask them how in their view their subject matter is related to the rest of the curriculum (note that this is about the subject matter, not about the teachers). How integrated is the teaching of those subjects with the rest of the curriculum? To what extent is information from these non-core curriculum areas used in the discussions about ELLs who are having difficulty academically? How can information about ELLs' performance in these special subject areas be incorporated into designing interventions?

When the ECOS team looks at ELLs' academic performance across curricular contexts, it may also learn something from those areas in which ELLs perform well consistently. When identifying the areas in which ELLs excel, it would be of interest to know what those subject area teachers are doing. Are they using particular strategies that are especially useful to ELLs? What do ELLs say about those classes? Why do ELLs say they are successful in those subjects or with those particular teachers? We can capitalize on areas of strength so that successes can be shared with the rest of the school staff.

Language Proficiency versus Knowledge of Concepts

A major concern of general education teachers is how to separate the acquisition of concepts from the ability to talk about those concepts (Gottlieb, 2006b). Teachers need to be sure that ELLs understand the content material independent of their language proficiency. Teachers often ask, "How do I know they get the math that I'm teaching?" "How do I assess what they have learned if they don't speak English and I don't know their language?" How can teachers know that what they are assessing in their classes is not English language proficiency? This becomes even more difficult to figure out in the intermediate, middle, and secondary grades, where the content material becomes more complex and abstract and the language needed to communicate and understand becomes more specialized. These questions indicate the complexity of what ELLs face in school and the specialized knowledge teachers need to meet both the academic content and the language needs of ELLs.

One way to address this complex issue is to make an explicit distinction between academic achievement and language proficiency (Gottlieb, 2006a, 2006b). Having an awareness of the second language (L2) learning process helps teachers understand why ELLs read, write, understand, and speak the way they do in English. With native English speakers, school staffers assume that what students are able to say, read, or write reflects to a great extent what they are thinking. However, ELLs, who are learning academic content in a second language, say, read, and write what their language proficiency allows them to, not necessarily what they know. The speech emergence simulations in Chapter 9 can help clarify this phenomenon. The more proficient students become as readers, writers, and speakers of English in social and academic settings, the closer the match will be between their ability to process concepts and their ability to express understanding and representation of those concepts in English.

The distinction between processing academic concepts and possessing the linguistic means to express those concepts is important for two reasons. The first reason is its relevance to evaluation. One of the biggest challenges with ELLs who do not show high academic achievement is to know whether the poor performance indicates lack of concept attainment or lack of language proficiency. The second reason is its relevance to instruction. Teachers of ELLs need to know how to convey content concepts without depending too heavily on language. We examine the issue of assessment first, followed by a discussion of the best approaches for instruction.

Suggestions for Gathering Information about Academic Achievement

As with literacy and oral language proficiency, the easy way to gather information on ELLs' academic achievement is to administer one of the numerous achievement tests available on the market or, more realistically, to use the scores from the several tests that students must take under the guise of accountability or state and federal requirements. However, results from traditional paper-and-pencil academic achievement tests rarely tell us what ELLs have learned about the specific content material. Rather, these tests tell us about students' English reading comprehension or language proficiency. When these traditional approaches to assessment of academic achievement are used, students with greater proficiency in academic English and those with good memory skills will do well. Others will find it difficult to show what they know. Thus, there is a need to add to the information that standardized tests provide by gathering data through more authentic measures that assess performance more directly.

Standardized Norm-Referenced Testing and Performance Assessment

In gathering academic achievement information about ELLs, the ECOS team must first ask what it is that they want to know about ELLs' academic performance. Does the team want to find out what students know and understand about the content area material (academic achievement) or do they want to know how students are progressing in content area reading, writing, speaking, and listening in either or both of their languages (language proficiency)? Or does the team want information about both of these areas? Information must be gathered from a variety of assessments, both norm-referenced and performance-based, to develop a good profile of ELLs' academic achievement (Gottlieb, 2006a). Let us examine what we can find out from both types of measure.

If standardized academic achievement assessments are used, they must be normed on ELL populations in order to be valid, reliable measures of ELLs' knowledge of the content area being tested. Traditionally, the tests used to assess academic achievement are not normed on ELLs but rather on native speakers of English. The results of such tests may be misleading. They may not provide accurate information about ELLs' content area knowledge and may only show what ELLs cannot do compared with their native English-speaking peers. Another important concern with standardized measures of academic achievement is the effect of cultural bias. Although test designers review their tests for cultural bias, it is impossible to find every instance of bias for every culture represented in a diverse school. Indeed, the whole process of assessment has culturally specific elements. Thus, it is not really possible to eliminate all cultural bias from any test procedure or format. It therefore becomes important to somehow account for the impact of cultural bias when interpreting the results of such tests.

Any standardized norm-referenced measure is likely to include certain contexts, visual aids, and language that will be unfamiliar to ELLs and will interfere with their ability to demonstrate what they know about the academic content presented on the test. If norm-referenced measures in English or the native language are included as part of the data collection, they represent only one piece of the academic achievement puzzle for ELLs. Consequently, that standardized test piece cannot be the biggest or the most important piece of the puzzle (Damico, 1992; Hamayan & Damico, 1991; O'Malley & Valdez-Pierce, 1996; Taylor, 1993).

If the team's purpose is to gather information about what students have learned in academic content areas, then the learning tasks and activities that occur every day in classrooms are a rich source of information. Assessment based on such activities is known as performance assessment (Artiles & Ortiz, 2002; Shea, Murray, & Harlin, 2005). Good teachers observe their students, collect student work in portfolios, have students reflect on their work, and create interesting learning activities in which students can show what they understand and what they are having difficulty with. These teachers ask their students to write and read every day in all of their languages, look at their progress over time, and provide feedback that helps students know where they need to improve and how. They observe how students are working with graphic organizers. All of these activities provide excellent opportunities to assess learning while they serve an instructional purpose.

When teachers learn how to formalize the information they acquire in class, they are able not only to use the data for their own instructional purposes but also to defend their decisions regarding the support and interventions students need. Several publications have practical suggestions on how to collect and report authentic information about ELLs (see, e.g., Gottlieb, 2006 a, b; Hamayan & Damico, 1991; O'Malley & Valdez-Pierce, 1996).

These performance assessment procedures not only yield valuable information about ELLs' academic achievement, they are also effective for instruction. This dual use of materials and procedures for both assessment and instruction is exemplified by the use of graphic organizers (Ewy, 2002) and the widespread use of student portfolios for both assessment and pedagogical purposes (Cambourne & Turbill, 1994; Spandel & Stiggins, 1997). This kind of assessment does not take away from valuable instruction time because it is embedded in the learning cycle itself. Performance assessment measures provide a variety of ways to see students' growth over time and yield information about academic achievement that is comprehensible to students, teachers, parents, and the community.

Obtaining Information in L1 and L2 in All Language Domains

Information on academic achievement, both oral and written, should be gathered in all of the students' languages and in as many content areas as possible (Cummins, 1981; Gottlieb, 2006a). For ELLs who have had any amount of schooling in their native language, this is absolutely essential. Even for ELLs who have not had much instruction in their native language, the insight that can be gained about a student's understanding and processing of concepts is invaluable. In a school where students' native languages play a prominent role (even if no formal instruction is given through those languages), it will become routine to look at information and work samples in students' native languages.

When trying to determine whether a learning difficulty is due to an underlying intrinsic problem, it is important to determine whether the difficulty manifests in expressive or receptive language domains (or both), and in all of the ELL's languages. This information helps the team narrow the likely origin of the difficulties to understanding the academic content or using language to express that understanding. Because a true intrinsic impairment is located at a deeper level of proficiency than the superficial manifestation of L1 or L2, the assessment team should expect a true impairment to manifest in similar ways in both languages (Carroll, 1993; Cummins, 1984; Damico, 1992; Damico & Hamayan, 1991; Damico, Smith, & Augustine, 1996).Teachers who normally incorporate ELLs' L1 into instruction will be able to assess comprehension, for example, even if the students have limited English proficiency. If the teacher reads a story aloud to her students in English, she will be able to assess how much they understood through their sequencing of visual manipulatives while retelling the story in their native language. As well, when teachers give ELLs opportunities to talk, research, and plan in L1 before writing in L2, they begin to see the improvement in English writing over time. When educators view students' languages as resources and apply what they have learned about bilingualism, examples like these will become commonplace. Chronicle 10.1 illustrates what happens when a teacher takes into account an ELL's native language.

Comparisons with Peers

Once the practice of using authentic assessments and collecting students' work across content areas in all of the language domains is established, a rich bank of comparative samples becomes available. The school in general, and the

(text continues on page 165)

CHRONICLE 10.1

How Lucky the L1 Was There!

By a mathematics teacher

The following example illustrates how our perspective on ELLs' academic achievement might change when we have access to information in all of the students' languages.

In my grade 5 English mathematics class, students were furiously writing the answers in English to five math reflections. I noticed that Josue was not producing much and appeared to be struggling a great deal. He paused be-

continued

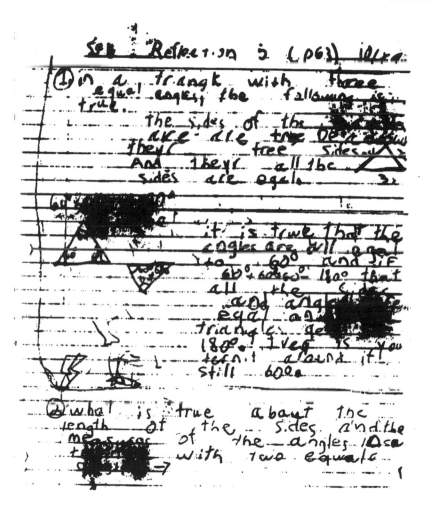

Figure 10-1   Josue's work on questions one and two.

The following is a transcription of the front side of Josue's paper:

1. (Question 1 copied onto page from book) In a triangle with three equal angles, the following is true. *Answer:* the sides of the triangles are are tree becasw theyr tree side And theyr all the sides are egal. / it is true that the angles are all egal to 60° and if 60° + 60° + 60° = 180° that all the sides and angles are egal and triangle gets to 180°. Iven if you ternit around it still 60°.

2. (Question 2 copied onto page from book) What is true about the length of the sides and the measures of the angle. Draw triangles with two equal angles. *Answer: on side 2 of paper below*

tween each word he wrote, and placed his left hand on his forehead as he wrote. This struggle continued for 35 minutes, at which point he had reached the end of the first page. He looked up at the clock and muttered something under his breath as he realized he had only 15 minutes left of class. He flipped his paper over and seemed to be writing with ease and quickly filled the second side of his page. It was astonishing to see the change.

When class was over, students handed in their work, and since my curiosity had been piqued, I couldn't wait to look over this particular student's paper. On the front side of the paper he had written two answers in English to the first reflection question. It was difficult to understand his writing in English,

continued

Figure 10-2. Josue's work on questions two through five.

The following is a translation of Josue's work on the back side of the paper.

(Answer for 2 from front side of this paper)

One of the sides of the triangle is also the length of that side, the shortest distance between the base and the vertex opposite the base is the height of the triangle

3. it's a rectangle in which its 4 angles are right 90° and whose sides have the same length.

4. the side on which the polygon rests, is perpendicular to the height of the polygon.

5. one of the sides of parallelograms, also is the length of that side, the shortest distance between the base and the side opposite to the base is the height of the parallelogram.

but since he had added some diagrams to illustrate his written responses, it helped me to see that the math was correct. Josue had summarized the main points of the lesson as I had done with the overhead projector to the entire class. Something else I noticed about this side of the paper was that there were marks left from the sweat on his hands (Figure 10.1). I was amazed that this very good student took 35 minutes to write the answer to the first question.

As I turned the paper over, I was surprised to see that Josue had easily finished writing his answers to the last four questions, and there were no sweat marks on this side of the page (Figure 10.2). However, he had finished writing the assessment in his native language! I do not know much Spanish, so I asked a colleague to tell me what he wrote. I was thrilled to see that Josue had written quite profound mathematical observations in Spanish! It was clear that those ideas flowed easily from his mind to the page in the last 15 minutes of class. I was glad he had felt comfortable enough in my class to use his L1. If he had not, I would have missed out on his creative mathematical thinking. When we work in class, he can answer very well orally in English, and when given enough time to write, he performs much better.

It dawned on me that there may be other students who, like Josue, are not performing at their best because of some language barrier. From that moment on, I encouraged all my ELLs to take time to plan and think through problems, questions, and reflections in their native language before writing in English. My students write much better in English since I started this practice. It's so lucky that these students have developed their native language to such a high level and that I can make them feel comfortable using it in my class. What would Josue have done after the 35 minutes if he hadn't written in his native language? I would have missed so much of what he was thinking and learning if he hadn't been able to write in his home language!

Questions for discussion:

- What needs to happen for the practice of encouraging ELLs to respond in their L1 to become part of the school routine?
- How would responses in L1 be used for student evaluation, even for the languages with few resources?

(text continued from page 162)
ECOS team specifically, will have collected recorded oral retellings, writing samples, learning logs, anecdotal notes, dialogue journals, dual-language projects, electronic portfolios with photographs, audio recordings, and samples of student writing, among other artifacts. This bank allows the work of ELLs who are experiencing difficulties to be compared with the work of ELLs who are developing typically. It is useful to compare ELLs' work with the work of students from similar linguistic and socioeconomic backgrounds and with similar past educational experiences. Looking at academic work from dissimilar ELLs is also useful. Such an evaluation could show, for example, the impact that formal schooling or the level of L1 development (or socioeconomic status) has on students' academic achievement. Comparing ELLs' work with the work of ELLs with diagnosed learning disabilities may also provide useful insights. When ELLs' work samples are compared with those of typically developing monolingual English students as well as students with learning disabilities, patterns of how disabilities manifest themselves regardless of language background may emerge.

Current and Past Data

Examining past as well as recent information on academic achievement is useful during the evaluation period. This type of longitudinal information provides a sense of how ELLs have progressed over time. If students come from within the school system, it will be easier to look at their electronic portfolios and other documents. If students come from outside the system, all effort must be put into retrieving previous work samples and school records for any new ELLs. If students come from outside the country, then staff often must rely on accounts provided by parents, students, and other family members regarding previous academic performance. Although this source of data is not always ideal and the data cannot be easily verified, it may be the only source of information. In such instances, care must be taken in interpreting the data, which are unverifiable. If general information can be obtained about previous schooling experiences (see Chapter 8), it will provide an important context for students' current performance.

We must also look at the type of programming the students received prior to entering the school, as well as the approach to instruction that was used. If ELLs were in inappropriate programs with little or no support, then the team can assume that a poor learning environment was a major contributor to these students' current academic difficulties. The opposite can also be true. If students come from an enriched ELL program and enroll in a school that provides little or no support for ELLs, their academic performance is likely to falter. Once ELLs receive enriched instruction, it is useful to compare past and present academic performance. Has there been dramatic growth in a short time? Has the student stopped progressing? Is there slow and steady progress? The ECOS team and the framework recommended in this handbook are designed to provide this kind of data collection, interpretation, and comparison.

Evidence of Instruction

In any discussion about a student or group of students who are having difficulties in school, it is essential to focus on the quality of instruction these students have received or are receiving currently (Duckworth, 1997; Freeman & Freeman, 2002). One should first ascertain whether these ELLs have had continuous and full access to the academic curriculum. Opportunity to learn is a key factor in any student's academic achievement, and ELLs are often pulled out of general education classes to such an extent that they end up with an education that has significant holes in it (the Swiss cheese effect of pull-out models).

Even if ELLs have had continuous and full exposure to the curriculum, we need to make sure that the instruction has been such that it has made the learning of new, and usually abstract, concepts accessible. One way to ensure accessibility of content area instruction throughout the school is to make certain everyone who works with ELLs knows specifically what language and content are to be taught at different grade levels. The grade-level expectations and academic curriculum map exist in practically every school district, so the next logical step is to identify the specific procedural language and vocabulary needed for every content area. It is essential for all teachers to realize the necessity of having language objectives for ELLs in every content lesson they teach.

When developing these academic language maps, it helps to look at the language requirements of professionals in different fields. What language do scientists use to communicate their subject matter? What language do historians or mathematicians use in their fields? What kind of reading and writing is required in these fields? Table 10.1 provides an example from the field of science. Once this procedural language or language of thought becomes clear and is written up, staff must articulate what the academic language in-

---

Table 10.1 Establishing an Academic Language Map: An Example from Science

What kind of process or thinking language do scientists use to communicate in their field?

- *Analyzing, summarizing, prioritizing, sequencing, synthesizing, interpreting*

What language tasks do scientists engage in for their work?

- *Speaking: presenting experimental findings to other scientists*
- *Listening: following instructions, understanding procedures*
- *Reading: technical research articles*
- *Writing: lab reports*

---

struction will look like at different grade levels. The standards developed for ELLs at the national level (such as the TESOL standards; TESOL, 2006), the regional level (see the examples from the WIDA Consortium in Appendices G and H), and the district level can be helpful in creating this academic language map. Taking this long-term view of language planning helps ensure that students build their academic language over time from grade to grade (Commins & Miramontes, 2005).

What Happens at Home

The formal educational achievements and socioeconomic background of the parents are an important predictor of academic achievement for all students, regardless of their linguistic or cultural background (Hart & Risley, 2003; Miech, Essex, & Goldsmith, 2001; Ogbu & Simons, 1998; Taylor, 1983). Parents who themselves have had years of formal education have access to the academic content that their children are studying. Those with a higher socioeconomic level have access to material means, books, computers, time, and means of transportation to get to even more resources. Regardless of the economic status or the education level of the parents, however, all families have personal, cultural, cognitive, and professional funds of knowledge that their children can benefit from (Arnold & Doctoroff, 2003; Lareau, 1987; Moll, Amanti, Neff, et al., 1992). Schools must make the effort to tap into these funds of knowledge. The experiences and historical knowledge of ELLs' families as they relate to various content areas must be brought into the classroom and integrated with instruction (Smith, 2006).

Whenever we ask parents to reflect on experiences they have given their children that could support their learning in school, we get a wealth of ideas. One parent talked about the castle he built for his four-year-old daughter out of an old cardboard box and how she played with it all the time. They went to the library and checked out many books about castles. The books were in

---

ECOS TEAM ACTIVITY

As a preliminary step for suggesting interventions, the ECOS team can develop some examples of specific language functions they believe students need in various content areas. As a group, team members can brainstorm examples of process language that scientists use in their field, and examples of the kind of reading, writing, speaking, and listening scientists do. After that, small groups or pairs could do the same work for different content areas. This exercise could be used as a springboard for cross-grade academic language articulation. These language functions could also be part of the interventions that teachers try to support students.

English, and neither father nor daughter could read them, but they looked at the pictures and discussed what they saw. Later, when she entered grade 6, those experiences helped her when the class studied medieval history. He noted that it cost him nothing and it helped her learn. Another parent described hanging her son's drawings (actually, scribbles) on the side of the cabinets in their apartment and how the boy would take visitors by the hand and begin talking about his works of art in his native language. The mother realized that doing that helped the child become confident about speaking to others about what he was thinking. Teachers commented on how eager this child was to share in class and how he was sufficiently confident to ask for help when he did not understand something. The mother was very proud to realize that she had helped her son develop those skills. When ELLs experience difficulties in academics, it is important to find out what sorts of informal learning experiences they have had, and continually encourage parents to see the value of these experiences for their children.

One way to capitalize on ELL families' funds of knowledge is through creating identity texts. In Chapter 9 we discuss the advantages of using dual-language identity texts (Chow & Cummins, 2005; Schecter & Cummins, 2003) to help ELLs develop literacy in both L1 and L2 and as a way to bring their experiences and lives into the classroom. Dual-language projects done orally and in writing can be used across the curriculum and are a wonderful way to engage ELLs' parents, families, and members of the community in their academic learning.

Another way to continue students' learning is by asking ELLs to talk at home about what they are learning in school. This requires few resources but is immensely helpful for students and parents alike (e.g., Calkins, 1997; Taberski, 2000). It is an easy way to maintain a constant flow of communication between home and school. Some families may not have material resources but have other types of linguistic, cultural, and experiential resources that are not being used to full advantage. Schools can do a lot to help ELLs be proud of their cultural backgrounds and of the great resource their parents are in helping them succeed.

Suggestions for Systemic and Specific Interventions

For most students, the main venue for learning academic content is school. Therefore, the curriculum and the way it is taught are the prime candidates for improvement, if improvement is needed, to increase the likelihood that ELLs will learn what they need to learn about the world they live in. System-wide characteristics of effective content area instruction include two elements: first, there must be cross-grade coordination, and second, all teachers must use a framework for teaching new concepts that can best be represented by a cycle of learning. The first element, cross-grade coordination, was discussed briefly earlier in this chapter under "Evidence of Instruction." To summarize, the school must have a curricular map that addresses the language that ELLs need to advance within and across grades for all the content areas. General education teachers must realize that they are language teachers as much as content area teachers as far as ELLs are concerned. They need to be aware of these students' crucial need to learn the language of each content area as they learn the new concepts (Snow, Met, & Genesee, 1989). Preferably, students should have a chance to learn the language of the new concepts before the teacher presents the lesson.

To complete this coordination, time and resources must be reserved for content area experts from all grade levels, both ESL/bilingual teachers and administrators, to come together to work. When teachers use both the curricular expectations and the academic language map in planning instruction, all students benefit, not just ELLs and not just those who are having academic difficulties, because there is a conscious effort by all to focus on content mastery and language development. Having this schoolwide (or district-wide) academic language map allows even teachers with little training in ESL strategies to write language objectives to accompany content objectives for every unit or lesson they teach.

Another way to ensure that ELLs have access to academic content as well as academic language is to organize learning tasks to promote coherent learning. Even the order in which activities are presented to ELLs can have a huge impact on how well they will understand what is being taught. In most pre-K through grade 12 classrooms, instruction typically begins with reading a text in English. In the very early grades, a teacher reads the big book story multiple times before continuing on to the rest of the lesson. In the intermediate grades, instruction begins with the text. Once students have learned the material, activities are introduced, such as experiments, video clips, or simulations. In the later grades, access to the academic content relies almost exclusively on students' ability to independently read and interpret the text. The problem for ELLs is that if instruction is in English, their limited proficiency in the language of the text keeps them from fully understanding what the unit of study is about. They might finally understand what was being studied once the experiment, video clip, manipulatives, or other aids have been used to illustrate the main concepts, but if this occurs near the end of the unit, it will be too late for ELLs. When the order of instruction is rearranged, some of these difficulties are alleviated (see Chronicle 10.2 for an example). Table 10.2 provides an example of a lesson cycle we have used with whole schools and individual teams of teachers to help them organize instruction in a way that optimizes comprehension and participation for ELLs.

The lesson cycle presented in Table 10.2 must be taken into account when implementing any sort of specific intervention as well. Reading, writing, listening, and speaking interventions will not be effective unless they occur

---

Table 10.2 The Lesson Cycle

Preview Phase

- Present key concepts experientially, concretely, or solidify concepts in L1.
- Engage in oral practice; establish collaborative tasks.
- Build a base through shared academic experiences; build on linguistic and cultural experiences.
- Preview key vocabulary through the experiences and visuals.

Instructional Phase

- Introduce text; use a variety of reading materials (in L1 and L2) about the topic.
- Use graphic organizers that reflect the structure of the text and allow students to organize important information from readings; use reading comprehension strategies.
- Begin project or research; engage in questioning, inquiry, problem-based learning, and interviews.

Application Phase

- Use notes and graphics from the comprehension reading strategies as a springboard for writing.
- Prepare small-group presentations, museum displays, expert groups, performances, and debates.
- Engage in discussions, debates, and real-world projects.
- Complete work on product or project from lesson.

Source: Adapted from Karen Beeman and John Hilliard, based on the work of Jeanette Gordon, Illinois Resource Center, Des Plaines, Illinois.

Going from Remediation to Preparation

By an ESL teacher

I used to see my students whenever their homeroom teacher felt they could spare a half-hour away from the "real" instruction going on in the general education classroom. They would bring a homework assignment or a project they were struggling with, and in half an hour I would attempt to bring them to an understanding of the content that their mainstream teacher was unable to achieve in one hour. I was frustrated because the assignments were often way beyond their ability level (spelling words at a fifth-grade level when they were reading at a primer level in English) or grossly inappropriate (write about what you would do if we had a snow day). I never felt like we were getting ahead—we were always playing "catch-up." It was frustrating for me and for the kids. I felt as though I was an overpaid tutor, and the kids started to feel as though they never had any successes.

This year we changed the arrangement. The ELLs are targeted or clustered into specific homerooms and scheduled for protected instructional time with me. I have implemented a pre-teach, teach, and review cycle with the team of teachers I work with. They send their lesson plans to me in advance. After I review their plans, I am able to pre-teach the major concepts and vocabulary before the ELLs experience instruction on that particular topic or skill in the mainstream classroom. That way they are able to draw on the prior experiences they have had with me and utilize the vocabulary I have already introduced and they have practiced. After instruction in the mainstream classroom, the ELLs return to me for a review lesson. I use this time to fill in any gaps in their understanding, clarify concepts, extend concepts, and so on.

This arrangement is working much better than the one we had before. The kids now experience success in the general education classroom. The teachers report that motivation has improved and ELLs are much more willing to participate in small-group activities. ELLs say they feel better about coming to school and that learning in both classrooms makes more sense. I no longer feel as if I am spinning my wheels. The kids are making great gains in achievement, and my principal marvels at how far the kids have come!

Questions for discussion:

- How does the infrastructure of the program affect students? Teachers? Achievement?
- What does the research say about the resource or pull-out configuration for ELLs? For special education students?

within a framework like this lesson cycle for ELLs. Students must start with a meaningful context, then the concepts are introduced through visual aids and related experiences to build background information. Then students practice oral language that has become meaningful, and then they can practice the same language in writing.

This cycle of learning is meant to give school staff a long-term approach to planning instruction. It also allows teachers to make certain they address academic listening, speaking, reading, and writing as well as academic content with all students. Planning in this way gives ELLs access to the content from the beginning of the unit and allows them more opportunities to gain mastery and a deeper understanding of the subject matter.

ECOS TEAM ACTIVITY

Examine the lesson plans provided in Tables 10.3 and 10.4. To what extent are these plans similar to how general education teachers teach their content area lessons? If there are significant differences, what are they? Is there a need to have general education teachers change their approach? If so, what would be a good professional development plan?

Another advantage to planning with this framework is that it allows ESL, bilingual, general education, and special education teachers and others involved in supporting ELLs a way to coordinate their efforts. Perhaps the bilingual teacher presents the information in the preview phase in the students' native language to ensure understanding of the main idea and principle. In the instructional phase, the ESL teacher may present a pre-reading activity in English, and then the general education teacher introduces the text. After students have had time to complete an appropriate during-reading activity, they may return to the bilingual teacher, who will check for understanding and begin the application phase of the lesson cycle with a writing activity using the graphic organizers that students prepared in the previous phases. This is just one example of how educators can share responsibility for ELLs' instruction. Two sample lesson cycle plans, in science and health education, are shown in Tables 10.3 and 10.4.

What is taught is as important as how it is taught. Even if a lesson cycle is followed, a narrowly designed lesson is not as effective as one that gives students a wider scope of the concepts being introduced. If ELLs' instruction has been narrowly designed around a single topic and the students have had to memorize many facts related to this topic, then performance on a test could be misleading, as it may reflect memory more than actual understanding of concepts. For example, in a unit developed around the plants, is it clear what about the topic *plants* is important? What should students focus on? If these questions are not clarified, ELLs (and other students) inevitably will focus on memorizing everything about plants that is presented to them to the best of their ability and as their language proficiency allows. Assessments in this sort of unit of study usually focus on how well students can recall the facts. They take the form of multiple-choice, fill-in, true-false, or short-answer tests. These sorts of assessments are troublesome for ELLs because they must rely on their developing English language proficiency to memorize concepts they are still learning.

In the example plants, the lesson can shift from studying the topic *plants* to studying the principle that *all living things pass through life stages and have basic needs for water, nutrients, protection, and energy in order to survive and grow.* Plants then become an example illustrating this principle, which also applies to the Animal Kingdom. In addition to giving students more substantial knowledge by giving them the principle rather than just the facts, this approach allows students to demonstrate understanding of a con-

(text continues on page 174)

ECOS TEAM ACTIVITY

Examine the lesson plans in Tables 10.3 and 10.4. Create a list of the kind of student work that would be generated throughout the unit. Discuss the quality, amount, and variety of student work that emerges from this approach to instruction and assessment. How does this assist the team in trying to support ELLs who are experiencing difficulties? How does this affect the sort of interventions that are suggested? What could this kind of student work tell you about ELLs' academic achievement?

Table 10.3 Sample Science Lesson (Elementary level)

Underlying principle: All living things pass through life stages and have basic needs for water, nutrients, protection, and energy in order to survive and grow.

Preview Phase	Instructional Phase	Application Phase
Content Objectives • Sequence pictures of the different stages of the plant's life cycle • View a 4-minute planting video clip of the life cycle of a plant from planting to maturity • Preview key vocabulary words from sequencing and from video to place correctly on plant diagram	**Content Objectives** • Predict basic needs plants require based on what humans need • Conduct an experiment (plant 2 beans to collect data on their life cycle, one without basic needs met and the other with needs met)	**Content objectives** • Graph height vs. time of the 2 bean plants • Record plant observations in learning logs • Research other living things and prepare a dual-language poster to display
Language Objectives Use descriptive and sequential language to explain the stages of a plant's life and what it might need to grow	**Language Objectives** • Predict and confirm or refute predictions	**Language Objectives** • Use descriptive scientific language in observing how the plants have changed over time
Strategies • Visuals: video clip of life cycle (4 minutes), sequencing cards, plant diagram with key vocabulary • Predicting/sequencing: prior to viewing video	**Strategies** • Predicting chart for LEA: record student predictions • Teacher-led demonstration: of experiment • Visual: experiment setup on chart paper • Questioning: think-pair-share; which bean will grow better? Why?	**Strategies** • Illustrated learning log: dated entries • Graphing: height and time in days • Poster: display the life cycle related to new living thing with its particular needs highlighted (parents, older students, Internet, L1 resources)
Differentiation • Visual support in video and cards • Provide sequencing vocabulary to encourage oral academic language practice • Preview vocabulary and process in L1	**Differentiation** • Common shared experience: "I predict . . ." (speaking-writing frame) • Multiple-level reading resources in L1 and L2 • Teacher modeling • Visual support throughout lesson	**Differentiation** • Variety of reading level resources • Rehearsal • Research teams • Teacher modeling
Flexible Grouping • Partners: to sequence picture cards and for planting beans • Whole class: view video	**Flexible Grouping** • Partners/small groups: during predictions and experiment • Whole class: teacher demo and LEA • Individual: vocabulary chart with illustration	**Flexible Grouping** • Research teams for posters • Whole class/individual: graphing • Individual: learning log entries
Instructional Assessment • Observation of picture sequencing (before and after video)	**Instructional Assessment** • LEA text of predictions • Anecdotal reading remarks • Student checklist of experiment set-p procedure • Plant life cycle illustrated vocabulary chart	**Instructional Assessment** • Learning log entries about 2 plants over time and how their basic needs affected life stages • Graphs • New life cycle poster rubric • Oral presentation rubric

Source: Adapted from Karen Beeman and John Hillard, based on the work of Jeanette Gordon, Illinois Resource Center, Des Plaines, Illinois

Table 10.4 Sample Health Education Lesson (Intermediate Level)

Underlying principle: The human body has many systems that work together to help it function. The heart and lungs are part of the circulatory system, which provides oxygen-rich blood to the body and removes waste material.

Preview Phase	Instructional Phase	Application Phase
Content Objectives • Locate the position of one's heart and lungs • Feel one's heart pumping and lungs expanding and contracting during respiration • Make observations and conjectures about why the heart rate varies during rest and exercise	**Content Objectives** • Follow the path of the blood from the time it enters the heart until it becomes oxygenated, leaves the heart, and goes to the rest of the body • Use diagram to sequence sentences related to the completed process	**Content Objectives** • Research factors that contribute to a healthy heart and lungs • Create a dual-language Healthy Heart/Healthy Lung brochure for family and community
Language Objectives • Follow oral directions for taking heart rate • Interpret data • Ask and respond to questions	**Language Objectives** • Use descriptive and sequential language to explain how the blood flows through the heart and lungs • Label the parts of the circulatory system • Read vocabulary chart and interpret graphic of heart and lungs • Read circulatory process sentence strips	**Language Objectives** • Use language of cause and effect to explain or write down the factors that contribute to healthy heart/lungs
Strategies • Total Physical Response (TPR): take resting heart rate, jump in place for a few seconds, and take heart rate again • Data collection: keep a chart of the students' heart rates (3 columns: name, resting rate, exercise rate)	**Strategies** • TPR: review key vocabulary • Teacher-led demonstration on overhead diagram • Sentence sequencing: 1 envelope per 2 students • Color coding markers to represent blood on diagram • Sequence graphic organizer	**Strategies** • Graphic organizer used in brainstorming ideas and then collecting health factors during research • Using technology to create brochure • Presentations to peers, parents, siblings
Differentiation • Demonstrate procedure to class (modeling) • Preview vocabulary • Partner work • Academic word bank with visuals	**Differentiation** • Diagram representing heart and lungs given to each student and used as teacher support on the overhead transparency • Text in strips • Partner support • Color coding • Completed visuals as a model	**Differentiation** • Variety of reading level resources • Collaborative research teams • Conferencing to practice presentations
Flexible Grouping • Whole class: demonstration • Partners: timing, pulse taking and recording data	**Flexible Grouping** • Whole-class: during explanation of blood flow • Partners: check with one another during diagram activity and sequencing	**Flexible Grouping** • Research teams of 3-4 students: individual roles on teams; individual explanations to parents, siblings, peers; mentors for homework • Whole class: work on brochure design on computer
Instructional Assessment • Teacher questioning • Check data chart (partner and individuals) • Teacher observation of accurate procedures • Student conjectures in L1 or L2 • Learning logs	**Instructional Assessment** • Teacher observation with checklists • Heart/lung diagram • Completed sequence graphic organizer • Individual questioning during sentence sequencing	**Instructional Assessment** • Completed brochures with rubric • Presentation rubric • Research graphic organizer • Teacher-student conferencing on brochure

Source: Adapted from Danette Meyer, Illinois Resource Center, Des Plaines, Illinois.

(text continued from page 171)
cept rather than merely ability to recall facts. Students can be assessed for their understanding of a principle through more authentic assessments (performance and products) independent of their proficiency in English. Even the facts that are presented during these lessons will be more comprehensible because students have a structure to map these facts onto.

Table 10.5 summarizes the suggestions for effective instructional and assessment strategies for ELLs who are experiencing difficulties.

Table 10.5   Systemic and Specific Intervention Strategies for Teaching Academic Content

---

Systemic Intervention Strategies

Instruction

1. Develop a lesson cycle to be used by all school personnel.
2. Organize instruction to teach underlying principles.
3. Present academic concepts visually and experientially.
4. Actively engage students' L1 as a resource to build background and ensure access to academic concepts.
5. Incorporate reading and writing in L1 into instruction.
6. Use multiple-level reading materials across the curriculum for every unit of study.
7. Use graphic organizers that match text structures in L1 and L2.
8. Articulate content objectives clearly.
9. Articulate language objectives clearly for academic listening, speaking, reading, and writing.
10. Curriculum and materials should incorporate ELLs' linguistic and cultural background and experiences.
11. Provide instruction by teachers with expertise in content areas and ESL/bilingual methods.
12. Develop curriculum maps for all grades.
13. Develop academic language maps for all content areas and all grades.
14. Increase and expand the use of ELLs' L1.
15. Invite parents and community members to come in on a regular basis to assist students in their native languages.
16. Recruit secondary or university students to tutor ELLs in their native languages and English.
17. Create dual-language projects across the curriculum at all grade levels.
18. Conduct meetings with ELL parents to encourage them to use their native language at home and to talk with their children about school in their native language.
19. Obtain funds for professional development for teacher stipends to work on curriculum development and lesson planning in the summer.
20. Create common planning time for teachers to coordinate instruction during the week.

Assessment

1. Collect and organize work samples in portfolios across content areas in L1 and L2.
2. Emphasize product, projects, performance, and process in assessment.
3. Capture L1 and L2 listening, speaking, reading, and writing.
4. Use teacher observation checklists across the curriculum.
5. Use anecdotal notes from teacher-student conferences.
6. Include student self-assessments in the data gathering.
7. Demonstrate progress over time.
8. Present rubrics with clear criteria for work samples.
9. Provide students with multiple ways to show what they know
10. Design clear criteria for all academic projects so that students know what they will be assessed on. Provide examples of excellent work provided so that students have an idea of what they are to do for each assignment.

continued

Table 10.5 *continued*

Specific Intervention Strategies

(Many of the systemic interventions can also be used with specific students in specific contexts. In addition, the following list may be helpful.)

Instruction

1. In lieu of traditional parent-teacher conferences, conduct student-directed portfolio conferences during which the student talks to the parents in the native language about his or her schoolwork.
2. Help the student talk with the student's parents or guardians at home about what the student has learned in school.
3. Find out what life experiences the student has had with the content area material.
4. Use free online multilingual resources with students on a regular basis.
5. Display work in students' languages in the school and on the school's Web site.

Assessment

1. Focus on gathering materials (manipulatives, visuals, charts, maps, graphic organizers, video clips) to use in the preview phase of the lesson cycle in all content areas.
2. Interview students about times they have understood content area material very well. Try to find out what made those experiences so positive, and use the information to improve academic opportunities for ELLs.
3. Ask students to practice talking about their academic portfolio on a regular basis and to fill out self-assessment forms.
4. Review completed standardized tests with the student, doing something like a "think aloud," having the student explain how he or she got to answers to certain items.

Questions for Discussion

1. What do we know about academic achievement in the first and second languages of the ELLs we serve?
    1.1. What is the typical pattern of academic content learning?
    1.2. Have the students had instruction that utilizes the content area instruction strategies described in this chapter?
    1.3. Have the students had instruction that utilizes something similar to the lesson cycle described in this chapter?
    1.4. If ELLs have had the benefit of the instruction strategies described in this chapter, have those strategies been used across all curricular areas and across grades?
    1.5. Do teachers routinely embed authentic, performance-based assessments in instruction?
    1.6. How do teachers apply their understanding of the relationship between students' L1 and L2 to their instructional planning and their selection of instructional approaches and strategies?
2. What do we know about academic content learning in the first and second language of the ELL who is experiencing academic difficulties?
    2.1. How can we find out more?
    2.2. How can we establish the validity and reliability of the data we have?
    2.3. What are the student's strengths in the content area curriculum?
    2.4. Has the ELL's difficulty been validated in more than one context?
    2.5. What specific interventions are needed?
    2.6. How will we monitor the ELL's progress during the intervention(s)?
    2.7. How will we determine the success of the intervention(s)?

11

Cross-Cultural Factors

KEY CONCEPTS

The seventh integral factor is the impact of culture on learning. Because of the multiple determinants of culture and its dynamic nature, and because students are in the process of adapting to a new set of norms and values, interventions must be culturally relevant to the student.

The seventh integral element to consider when an ELL experiences linguistic or academic difficulty is the influence of culture. Since many ELLs come from a cultural background that may be quite different from the culture of school, the ECOS team should try to determine whether the student's difficulties can be explained by those differences. There may be disconnects between the students' first or home culture, the culture of the immigration process, and the culture of the new school and community. Such disconnects can contribute to misunderstandings, miscommunication, and differences in achievement expectations (e.g., Chamberlain & Medeiros-Landurand, 1991; McDermott & Varenne, 1995; Philips, 1983; Suarez-Orozco, 1987). They are yet another hurdle that ELLs must overcome on the way to academic achievement.

Culture is a complex construct, and several factors come into play when a student enters a learning environment that is governed by unfamiliar norms and values. Thus, educators should understand something about culture in general and the school's culture in particular before trying to learn about the students' cultural background. To understand our own and others' norms and values, we need guidelines to help us observe and interpret culturally different behavior. Finally, all educators working with ELLs must learn how to create learning environments that take into account cultural diversity so that ELLs in these contexts are not held back by a myopic view of culture (Agar, 1994).

In this chapter we discuss the key characteristics of culture and the impact of culture on learning. We then suggest ways to gather information about these aspects of culture and ways to identify students' cultural background, and procedures to assess their capacity to function in the current learning environment. The chapter ends with suggestions for drawing the best out of a culturally diverse learning environment. Here we present strategies to create and implement culturally responsive and supportive learning environments systemically and for individual students.

Key Characteristics of Culture

What Constitutes Culture?

Those unfamiliar with the field of ESL and bilingual education might initially list food, festivals, fashion, and the fine arts that represent a group of people when asked what constitutes culture. Those items are the surface aspects of a culture and so are visible to all. Culture, however, is far more complex and deeply penetrating than its superficial manifestations (e.g., Agar, 1994; Hoffman, 1999; Sahlins, 1998). To address this complexity, we use the iceberg metaphor: the most visible forms of culture are just the tip of the iceberg (Figure 11.1). The more important aspects lie beneath the surface (Hamayan, 2006). Limiting our view of another person to just the visible aspects of culture can lead to tokenism and stereotyping (Kibler, 2005). If we do not demand that educators look beyond the immediately visible, biases based on a superficial understanding of others will remain, with negative consequences for learning (McDermott & Varenne, 1995; Trueba, 1988).

Just beyond the visible aspects of culture are those aspects that overtly influence and govern how we interact with one another. They may become visible as we take the time to look and develop interpersonal sensitivity. These aspects of culture are often sources of cultural misunderstandings resulting from miscommunication (e.g., Heath & McLaughlin, 1993; Philips, 1983). Responding to a signal from someone with whom we are interacting without understanding the attitudes and values that motivate and support the other person's behavior can lead to erroneous interpretations of the be-

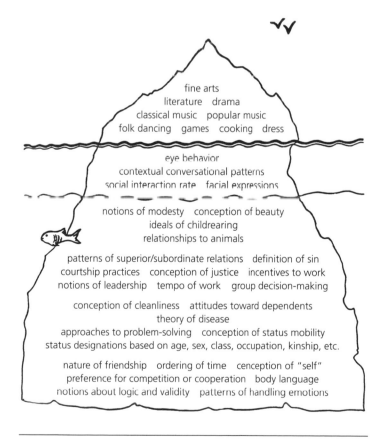

Figure 11.1 The iceberg model of culture
Source: Hamayan, 2006; reprinted from Illinois Resource Center, 1997.

havior and false conclusions (Wax, 1993). The most common example is the different patterns of eye contact considered appropriate in different cultures. In many Anglo-American families, eye contact is used to convey interest, honesty, and respect, but in many other cultures it is considered impolite or even challenging to make direct or prolonged eye contact with someone. In the case of children, such a violation of cultural behavior would be even more egregious. Yet many teachers when reprimanding a student may say, "Look at me when I am talking to you!" They do not realize the misunderstanding to which they are a party if they conclude, based on the student's lack of eye contact, that the student is dishonest or disrespectful or not paying attention. Understanding the role of eye gaze patterns in their own culture and in the student's culture would help teachers better evaluate the student's behavior and so help to inform a more culturally responsive pedagogy.

Other aspects of culture are far below the surface, and although they are often seemingly invisible to those not competent in the culture, these less visible aspects of culture are actually the most important. They provide the context and mechanisms from which culture as an intra-personal and inter-personal entity operates (Hoffman, 1998; McDermott, 1999), and they provide a route to the explanation of observable behaviors. These aspects of culture represent beliefs, attitudes and values and can help provide insight to a student's motivation, expectations, goals and dreams. One of the most frequently discussed examples of the deeper aspects of culture in recent years has been the construct of self as a cultural entity (Hoffman, 1998). An illustration of how this entity is employed and its impact can demonstrate the importance of these deeper aspects of culture.

Over the past 20 years, as anthropologists and educators applied increasingly complex models to the study of culture in educational settings there was a realization that our social and cultural lives and identities in any context, but especially in the context of education, are not static and fixed. Rather, our cultural identities—how we are defined by others and how we define ourselves—change as the expectations, interactions, behaviors, and relationships around us change (Davidson, 1996; McDermott, 1993, 1999). That is, our perceived identity within any given sociocultural context at any given time is a construction based on the input and expectations received and the reactions that we had to this input. As an interpretive lens for viewing the continual changes in student behaviors and the numerous reactions and interactions that occurred in classrooms, the sociocultural account of identity made a great deal of sense. For example, the notion that one's operational identity was not static but was influenced by contextual variables enabled the creation of workable models and explanations for a host of observed behaviors and practices in the classroom (e.g., Lee, 1996; McDermott, 1987; Phelan, Davidson, & Yu, 1993; Spindler & Spindler, 1987). In authentic settings, the concept of fluidity and an emerging identity was consistent with what was observed.

However, there was also a problem. Although identity may emerge as the result of numerous influences, there was no doubt that within the variability, there was still enough consistency to predict how an individual would react to various inputs, given his or her cultural experiences. How, then, could the fluid aspect of identity be reconciled with the stability of identity at the level of the group?

One solution to this problem involved the idea that identity is not merely a manifestation of culture but is partially constructed by a deeper aspect of culture—the "self." As a deep aspect of culture, self is an amalgam of some inherent psychological construct within the person and various social, cultural, and interactive variables that act on that person from outside. In effect, self is a psychosocial construct that is manifested according to various sociocultural variables and can be recognized as identity and in several affective reactions to different cultural variables (Whiting, 1990). As stated by Jen, this makes the self "more than the sum of her social facts" (1997, p. 19). That is, while there is much variability in the manifestation of cultural identity, depending on context, there is still some cultural stability, owing to the deeper aspect of self that is a component of the emergent behavior recognized as one's cultural identity.

This example illustrates two important concepts. First, there are deeper aspects of culture that, while not immediately observable, are important to cultural explanation and understanding. Second, this knowledge and understanding have practical implications. For example, if we are to be effective interpreters of culture as an operational variable in education, we cannot adopt a static view of a student's identity in the classroom. Neither can we assign a fixed social identity or cultural role to the student. We have to recognize that multiple explainable identities may emerge in our students, depending on the context. Consequently, rather than creating oppositional frames such as "us versus them" regarding cultural considerations, we should strive to focus on the characteristics of culture that help establish the fluid, situated, and negotiated character of each individual's identity in a given cultural context (Agar, 1994; Hoffman, 1998; Whiting, 1990).

The deeper aspects of culture are less prone to stereotyping. Educators who seek first to understand their own culture, then the culture of the school, and only then the culture of their students and their students' families according to these nonvisible aspects of culture can expect to move toward more accurate insights (Kibler 1996; 2005). They are more likely to pinpoint cultural mismatches and conflicts, as well as commonalities and similarities, especially if they remember that culture is not limited to race, ethnicity, or language group:

> Beliefs, attitudes and values are at the heart of what is meant by culture. They are also at the heart of concern about individual differences within cultural similarities. Beliefs, attitudes and values have developed out of shared and unique past experiences, and they strongly influence (while being influenced by) behavior and perceptions of the world. (Bennett, 1995)

This definition of culture implies that the important aspects of a person's culture are those elements that are not so easily observed, and that they are often fluid and dependent on the context within which the person is currently operating (Agar, 1994; Hoffman, 1998; Whiting, 1990).

The Multiple Determinants of Culture

Although many educators who work with ELLs tend to think of cultural diversity in terms of ethnicity, race, country of origin, and language, culture goes far beyond those components. This understanding of culture should be expanded to include socioeconomic level, gender, education level, sexual orientation, geographic location, and occupation (Banks, 2001; Salett & Koslow, 1994). All these aspects of culture provide members of the cultural group with unique experiences, which in turn help to shape and influence members' perspectives and interpretation of events. For this reason, educators should keep in mind that large groups of individuals seldom, if ever, conform to the same cultural values, attitudes, and behaviors. Imagine, for example, 100 women gathered for a sale at a store near your house. Within that homogeneous group of 100 individuals (the group under discussion being defined by gender) is a tremendous amount of diversity. No one would argue that all the members of such a group subscribe to the same childrearing practices, the same political beliefs, the same definition of sin, the same concepts of beauty, or the same work ethic.

Educators must guard against the tendency to make similar statements about students who come from the same native country or the same native language background (Kibler, 2005). Indeed, one should not expect that the student will take the same cultural role or engage in the same behaviors when various aspects of the context change. Culture is more complex and more emergent than that. For example, the assumption that everyone from an Asian country eats rice or that all Mexicans like *banda* music are as ridiculous as the assumption that all U.S. Americans eat hot dogs. The unit that we must focus on is the student and his or her immediate family.

Culture as a Dynamic Process

Not only must we avoid generalizations across individuals when dealing with culture, we must also view culture as a dynamic process, not a static concept (Hall, 2001; McDermott, 1999; Wax, 1993). Culture is always changing, subject to the experiences of the individual and his or her interpretation of such experiences. For example, with the growing popularity of cellular telephones, such that family members are able to communicate with one another at any time, many parents allow their children to go places that in the recent past they were not allowed to go unaccompanied by adults. Parents now feel they can monitor their children from a distance, through the telephone, in a way they were unable to in the past. This has led to a change in the degree of responsibility expected of children, the age of independence from parents, the understanding of parents' authority, and a host of other cultural values and beliefs.

In another example, 30 years ago in the United States, many parents expected that their child's elementary schoolteacher would have lunch at their home once during the school year, and the teachers of that era routinely expected to dine at the home of each of their students during the course of the school year. The practice has declined over the years, no doubt because of changes in the work habits and employment of mothers in U.S. society. As well, our expectations of teachers and the relationship between parent and teacher have changed.

Every new experience we have and every new context we encounter may change our perspective slightly, and subsequently may alter the way we interact with our environment prior to that experience. This is especially true of ELLs, who are in the process of discovering novel customs. More than any other students, ELLs experience the dynamism of culture. We must keep that changing nature of students' culture in mind when we are gathering information about it, and we must try to understand ELLs as they are going through the process of adaptation to the new culture (see Chronicle 11.1).

Adapting to a New Culture

The process of adapting to a new culture is long and complex. According to one analysis, people go through seven stages until they reach the highest level of acculturation (Berry, Poortinga, Segall, et al., 1997). In the preliminary stage, the recently arrived immigrant is fascinated by the novelty around him and excited to learn about the new things in his environment. In the second stage the immigrant becomes more aware of the differences, and this is followed by a stage of increased participation, with the clash of the two cultures becoming more apparent. The fourth stage, culture shock, is a stage of emotional overload resulting from the loss of all familiar aspects of the home culture. (Chronicle 11.2 describes the experiences one teacher who went through culture shock.) In the fifth stage, instrumental adaptation, the immigrant must choose a path, either retreating into the home culture, or giving up the home culture altogether in favor of the new one, or adopting parts of the new culture while maintaining some of the home culture. In the sixth stage, integrative adaptation, depending on the choice that was made in the previous stage, the immigrant either experiences a culture split (for the first two choices) or success-

CHRONICLE 11.1

New Culture, New Perspective

By an ESL teacher

Carlo came to me from Italy when he was in fifth grade. I neglected to scout out in the community someone who could provide translation services. I did this typically for every language group represented in my classroom and recorded contact information on a Rolodex placed on my desk, but since Carlo was the only Italian-speaking student in the school, I thought my Spanish was enough to bridge the gulf between Italian and English. Boy, was I wrong! Several weeks went by without incident, and my Spanish was enough to help Carlo out in the beginning . . . until we had a tornado drill. The alarm went off and all the students dutifully walked out of the classroom and into the hallway and began to take their places along the wall and assume the "pretzel" sitting position, with their hands clasped behind their necks and their heads bent down. I looked over at Carlo and he had a look of sheer terror on his face and the next thing I knew he bolted out of the classroom and ran down the hallway heading for the exit doors.

I quickly grabbed another teacher to take over my class and ran down the hall following Carlo, calling his name. Thankfully, once outside he turned around to answer my calls. He was shouting in Italian and crying and motioning for me to come with him and to keep running. I tried my best to calm him down, though I did not know what had happened and what had caused his reaction. I managed to persuade him to come back in the building with me. As we walked through the halls, he noticed that the children had left the hallway and were back in their classrooms hard at work. His pace slowed a bit and his body relaxed only slightly.

We walked to the nurse's office and Carlo lay down on the cot and I sent the building secretary into the teachers' lounge to get him a juice. Next, I set about finding someone I could call who spoke Italian and could translate for me and Carlo on the phone. Finally, a friend of a friend was found and I made the phone call. I explained what had happened in English and confirmed that the man on the other end of the phone could speak fluent Italian and English. Next, I put Carlo on the phone with this man. Immediately, Carlo relaxed. They talked for a few minutes and then Carlo handed the phone to me. The translator told me that Carlo had thought the building was being bombed and that is why he panicked. The translator told him that there was no danger of bombing here in the United States and that this was a tornado drill.

Apparently, Carlo's grandfather had suffered much during the Second World War, and had told many stories of massive bombings to his grandson. Plus, there are no tornadoes in Italy, so Carlo had not been familiar with the concept. That was the last time I neglected to find someone willing to translate for one of my children from a low-incidence language group. Fortunately for Carlo and for me, he stayed in my looped classroom for two years and stayed in the building even longer, so that as he learned English we could stay connected. Years after the incident he could laugh about it, and so could I, but it was very frightening to both of us. Sadly, it could have been prevented easily.

Questions for discussion:

- Could this situation have been avoided? If so, what should the teacher have done?

ful acculturation (for the third choice). In the last stage, structural adaptation, the immigrant reaches the highest level of adaptation and is able to maintain a comfortable balance between his two cultures. Table 11.1 summarizes these stages.

This account suggests that it is possible to reach a level of acculturation that integrates some aspects of both cultures and to feel comfortable in both contexts. Some ELLs may be able to reach that stage of structural adaptation; they maintain their home culture while having acculturated into the new en-

---

CHRONICLE 11.2

Nightmares in Saltillo

By a bilingual special education teacher

At age 20, I decided to travel to Saltillo, Mexico to live there and take college classes. I had been taking Spanish since I was in fifth grade; I was a member of the National Spanish Honor Society and had taken graduate-level Spanish classes as a college freshman. Sadly, all that language instruction failed to prepare me for culture shock. It started innocently enough: one night I had a nightmare and woke up screaming. The next morning my housemates and the members of the family I was living with gave me sidelong glances and good-natured kidding.

To my surprise the same thing happened the very next night. The following morning, the good natured ribbing was replaced with genuine concern. "Are you okay? Is something wrong?" my housemates asked. My housemother made me an extra-special breakfast. To my horror, it happened repeatedly, night after night. Each night the dream was the same—I dreamt that I was covered in bugs and I would be screaming as I tried to brush the bugs off my body. Now the neighbors, who heard the screams, were asking about me.

Word spread throughout my classes that I was having nightmares. My tutor asked me if I was okay. I was perplexed, as I had never had dreams like this before. I was exhausted and feeling as though my behavior was beyond my control. After a week, my housemother sent me to a doctor. The doctor asked me if I was taking any drugs. I wasn't. When he found nothing physically wrong with me, he sent me home, back to the United States. Just as quickly as the nightmares came, they disappeared and never returned.

Since then, I have visited Mexico several times. Those trips have been the highlight of my life and career. I became a bilingual special education teacher and have worked with Spanish-speaking students. I have gotten to know their families and have established close relationships with some of them. I guess at the age of 20, being immersed in another culture was more than I could handle.

As I reflect on this experience, I cannot help but think of some of the families of my students. I realize that they do not have the choice of getting on an airplane and going home to assist them with their culture shock. How difficult it must be for a child who is going through this stage to put on a happy face and come to school, to be bombarded day after day with the strange and foreign culture.

Questions for discussion:

- People experience culture shock in all sorts of ways. Discuss different ways culture shock may be experienced.
- How can people help those with culture shock, short of sending them home?

Table 11.1 Stages of Adaptation for Immigrant Children

Stage	Characteristics	Typical States
Preliminary Phase	Preparation/Anticipation/Migration—Sometimes referred to as the "honeymoon stage" or "initial stage," it includes a time of euphoria, if it is considered a "good" move. A child may be fascinated by everything and excited to learn.	Cooperative, displays a desire to please
Spectator Phase	Occurs when the concept of change overcomes the concept of newness and the reality of the situation sinks in.	Fearful, lonely
Increasing Participation Phase	Sometimes referred to as the "uprooting stage." Survival instincts are awakened and the clash of the two cultures become apparent in all its complexity. "One step forward, two steps back."	Mixture of varying emotions in combination with each other
Culture Shock Phase	Emotional overload. Change in its most profound context resulting from a loss of all familiar signs, symbols, and cues of the original culture, creating a mistrust and fear of the new situation that may not have existed previously. This is a most difficult time, when patience and tolerance are very important and impact all future decision making.	Depressed, frustrated, insecure, withdrawn, hostile; criticizes everything
Instrumental Adaptation Phase	Sometimes referred to as the "adaptation" period. Based on a variety of factors, students choose as ways of dealing with the emotional, educational, and social issues in their lives: • *Encapsulation:* retreating into the first culture. • *Assimilation:* believing that one must give up the original culture in order to fit into the mainstream culture. • *Acculturation:* becoming a part of the mainstream culture while still holding onto the customs and values of the original culture.	Flight/fight/integration
Integrative Adaptation Phase	Sometimes referred to as the "mainstream" phase. Based on their decisions in the previous phase, students experience either a *culture split,* a split between home life (first culture) and school (all aspects of out-of-home) life, or *successful acculturation:* acceptance and integration of parts of both cultures into his/her life and experiences in school.	Fear of embarrassment and lack of acceptance of first culture in mainstream culture
Structured Adaptation Phase	The deepest level of the adaptation experience. The individual grows truly comfortable in the second culture while maintaining a deep and integrated connection with the first culture; typically doesn't happen in the first generation.	Flexibility and appropriate behavior in both cultural contexts

Source: Adapted from Kibler (2005).

vironment. This is not an easy task, as many norms and values from the home culture may clash with those of the school, especially when those norms are from the deeper part of the iceberg (see Figure 11.1). For example, if the home culture views modesty for adolescent girls as important and the dress code that conforms to that notion of modesty is one that requires covering shoulders and arms, but the school culture is more permissive, a young girl may find it difficult to juggle those two norms.

Naturally, not everyone reaches the phase of structured adaptation. In fact, many immigrants who left their home country by choice return to it, at least partly because they could not get over the culture shock (Berry, Segall, Dasen, et al., 2002). ELLs who are going through stages two to four and those who have chosen a nonadaptive path in stages five and six are likely to be in a state of anxiety or discomfort that may stand in the way of optimal learning.

ECOS TEAM ACTIVITY

Team members are to place themselves in unfamiliar situations and are report back to the group on their emotional reactions, coping strategies, and successes or failures. It could be as simple as attending an art gallery for someone who has no interest in art, or for someone who doesn't drive much, it could mean attending a NASCAR race, or eating at a Nigerian restaurant for someone who has never tried food from Africa. The important part of this activity is to encourage everyone to practice getting outside their comfort zone to better understand how it feels to be in a situation of stress or nonfamiliarity. This activity should be repeated more than once to promote the desirability of voluntarily participating in activities outside one's comfort zone. To reward the group for such endeavors, perhaps each meeting could be started with one team member accounting how he or she voluntarily stepped outside the comfort zone and what was learned as a result.

Educators should also consider the resources ELLs have at their disposal to assist them in the process of acculturation. Payne (1998) lists the following resources that make it easier for individuals to adapt to their environment:

- Financial: having the money to buy goods and services.
- Mental: having the cognitive skills and academic achievement to cope with daily life.
- Spiritual: believing in divine purpose and guidance.
- Physical: having physical health and mobility.
- Support systems: having friends, family, and backup resources to access in time of need.
- Relationships and role models: having frequent access to adults who are appropriate and nurturing.
- Knowledge of hidden rules: knowing the unspoken cues and habits of a group.

Many immigrants are likely to not have access to some of these resources. The presence or absence of these resources influences the quality of experiences the ELL may have in the face of acculturation. Information regarding these resources in students' lives can also offer insight as to culturally responsive pedagogy and appropriate interventions to help students navigate the new culture.

The Impact of Culture on Learning

The norms and values that make us who we are influence in two ways how we learn and how efficiently we learn (Hamayan, 2006). First, they provide us with a context for making sense of the world around us. Thus, when we are presented with a new concept, we internalize it in a way that fits our view of the world. When a child who has been taught that animals belong outside of the house and under no circumstance should they be let inside reads a story about pets, she may get very confused and misunderstand the story altogether. Thus, ELLs are faced with learning new concepts, often quite abstract, through a language they are not proficient in. When the lesson to be learned assumes a certain set of norms and values that are shared with the learner, and when the learner has divergent norms and values, additional hurdles materialize for that learner. When there is a mismatch between the student's own cultural context and that of the curriculum, those differences make it difficult for the student to learn the concepts presented in the curriculum.

The second way in which cultural differences affect learning is in the general level of discomfort that students may feel when they cannot see reflections of themselves in the school environment (Kibler, 1996). Students whose ways of doing things are markedly different from the way things are done in school are likely to be on edge and to experience anxiety. Learning takes more effort in a state of agitation and may be impossible (Damico & Damico, 1993a). A student whose notion of a classroom setting is one where the teacher directs everything and students have no choices may feel completely at a loss in a classroom where students determine tasks, activities, and timing (Emery & Csikszentmihalyi, 1981; Garmezy, 1991). A female student who is discouraged or even prohibited from socializing with males who are not immediate family members may feel so uncomfortable with a male teacher that learning is significantly hampered.

The beliefs, attitudes, and values that each of us holds not only shape our perceptions of the world around us, they also make it easier or more difficult for us to build new knowledge (Corsaro & Nelson, 2003; Nieto, 2001). The first step for a school to take is to find out as much as possible about the various cultures and the norms and values that come with that culture, starting with one's own culture. The next section presents suggestions for gathering information about the cultures represented in the school and evaluating students' ability to function in the culture of the school.

Suggestions for Information Gathering and Evaluating Cultural Difference Factors

It is neither expected nor feasible for teachers to know everything about every culture represented in their classrooms. However, educators should attempt to find out as much as they can about the cultures in their classrooms, despite being outsiders to those cultures. They can do this by using the best resources available to them: their students and the students' families. There is one stipulation in gathering information about others' ways of doing things and their values and beliefs: information gathering must be totally free from prejudice and judgment. Norms and values that are different from ours are just that: different, not worse or better.

Some of the knowledge about students' cultures can be built as other information is being gathered, for example, about the student's current and past learning environment, physical and psychological factors, and personal and family factors. However, it is best for this information to emerge from informal discussions with students and their families, from mini research projects that the students themselves undertake, or through dialogue journals that some students keep with their teacher (Peyton & Staton, 1993). As with other information that comes from a context that we are unfamiliar with, a cultural insider, informant, broker, or liaison is needed to provide the appropriate context for interpreting cultural information the student or family offers. Someone who has deep, firsthand knowledge about the native culture as well as a competent understanding of the student's new, non-native culture (typically that of the school) can explain the family's beliefs, attitudes, and values in terms that are comprehensible to others. The cultural liaison can also help initiate meaningful interaction and rapport between the school, home, and community.

The topic of culture is frequently overwhelming. Where does one begin to tap into the identity of a student and his family? How does one organize the information that is obtained, typically in bits and pieces and over a period of time? Table 11.2 provides a categorized list of dimensions of culture that can provide structure to the information obtained. The list in Table 11.2 can also be useful for exploring one's own culture and that of the school.

Table 11.2 Cultural Dimensions Continua

Family Life

Temporary ⇐ ⇒ Permanent
Extended ⇐ Nuclear ⇒ Linear
Emotionally close ⇐ ⇒ Emotionally distant
Matriarchal ⇐ ⇒ Patriarchal

Social Interactions

Physically close ⇐ ⇒ Physically distant
Much eye contact ⇐ ⇒ Little eye contact
Formal ⇐ ⇒ Informal
Symmetrical ⇐ ⇒ Complementary
Demonstrative ⇐ ⇒ Undemonstrative

Education

Highly valued ⇐ ⇒ Not so highly valued
Teaching as prestige ⇐ ⇒ Teaching not prestigious
One teaching style ⇐ ⇒ Varied teaching styles

Work and Achievement

Competition ⇐ ⇒ Cooperation
Work defining person ⇐ ⇒ Work does not figure in one's identity
Survival ⇐ ⇒ Self-actualization

Individuality

Rigid roles ⇐ ⇒ Flexible roles
Independence ⇐ Interdependence ⇒ Dependence
Confrontation ⇐ ⇒ Harmonization
Rebellion ⇐ ⇒ Conformity

Wealth and Materialism

Importance of tangibles ⇐ ⇒ Importance of intangibles
Immediate goals ⇐ ⇒ Lifelong goals

Time

Rigid adherence to time ⇐ ⇒ Flexible adherence to time
Past orientation ⇐ ⇒ Future orientation
Time walks ⇐ ⇒ Time runs
Monochronic ⇐ ⇒ Polychronic

Age

Ages highly segregated ⇐ ⇒ Ages mixed together
Children given choice ⇐ ⇒ Children not given choice
Elderly have vital role ⇐ ⇒ Elderly do not have vital role
Children have critical responsibilities ⇐ ⇒ Not many responsibilities

Space

Individual space clearly marked ⇐ ⇒ Not marked
Generous ⇐ ⇒ Restricted use
Dense cohabitation ⇐ ⇒ Sparse cohabitation
Closed individual space ⇐ ⇒ Open individual space

Communication and Language

Verbal ⇐ ⇒ Nonverbal
Dependent on literacy ⇐ ⇒ Oral

Religious Tenets

Monotheistic ⇐ ⇒ Polytheistic
Spiritualistic ⇐ ⇒ Humanistic
Part of daily life ⇐ ⇒ Distant from daily life

Nature

Industrial ⇐ ⇒ Agricultural
Dominance over ⇐ ⇒ In harmony with
Technologically developed ⇐ ⇒ Technologically simple

ECOS TEAM ACTIVITY

Using the list in Table 11.2 as a guide for various topics to explore, have team members first think about their own norms and values. Divide the list so that each member has two to four dimensions to think about. Then let them share with a partner, and finally have a group discussion. Either concurrently or on another occasion, have team members also think about the culture that is reflected in the curriculum, in the way school is run, and the way that their classrooms are organized and managed. Discuss how similar the individuals' and the school's culture are and where they diverge from one another.

Assessing the Student's Ability to Function in the School Culture

In addition to becoming aware of the norms and values that different students bring with them to the classroom, it is important for teachers to assess ELLs' ability to function within the school culture. Assessing an ELL's capacity to function in the school's current learning environment is essential in order to recommend appropriate interventions for the student experiencing difficulty. Educators should endeavor to determine where the immigrant child is in the process of adaptation to the new, non-native culture. The descriptions provided previously (see Table 11.1) may be useful to give teachers and counselors a sense of the phase of adaptation that the student is passing through. This is not something that can be measured by numbers or ratings; rather, the descriptions can guide educators in exploring the level of comfort of students in the culture of the school.

Suggestions for Systemic Interventions

Systemic interventions that would make the school environment more reflective of the cultural diversity that exists among its student population are something that all schools with diverse populations should put into practice. When a school has students from different cultural backgrounds, be they ethnic, racial, socioeconomic, or other dimensions, it is a shame when teachers and administrators do not use the opportunity to enrich the lives of all their students. Multicultural education is beneficial to all students in the school population, not just those who are immigrants or whose situations put them at risk in school. Multicultural education is fundamentally a perspective that addresses the histories and experiences of people who are typically left out of the curriculum in most U.S. schools (Lee, 1994). Taking this multiple perspective approach can be nothing but an added benefit for all those within that school system. All students need to learn about other cultures, and they need to become skilled in dealing with others whose perspective differs from their own. Additionally, all students need to see the value in diversity and to honor and respect other cultures' perspectives. Another goal of multicultural education that is beneficial for all students is to equip students, parents, and teachers with the tools needed to combat discrimination. Failure to implement multicultural education is akin to promoting monocultural and perhaps discriminatory education.

Multicultural education, although not essential, leads to ideal conditions of instruction for all students; but for ELLs it is indispensable, helping them overcome yet another challenge in their school lives (Tharp, 1999). It is important that teachers connect lessons to students' lives, and that both instruction and the curriculum are contextualized in students' existing experiences in the home, community, and school. The research points consistently to the need for more contextualized instruction (Nieto, 1999). Teachers must show

Table 11.3   Connecting Instruction to Students' Cultures

- Instructional activities begin with what students already know from home, community, and school.
- Instructional activities are designed to be meaningful to students in terms of local community norms and knowledge.
- Understanding of local norms and knowledge is attained by talking to students, parents or family members, and community members and by reading pertinent documents.
- The teacher assists students in connecting and applying their learning to both the home and the community.
- The teacher and students plan jointly to design community-based learning activities.
- Opportunities are provided for parents or families to participate in classroom instructional activities.
- Instruction is varied to include students' preferences, from collective and cooperative to individual and competitive activities.
- Styles of conversation and participation are varied to include students' cultural preferences, such as co-narration, call and response, and choral, among others.

students how abstract concepts are drawn from and applied to the world in general and their world in particular. Relating instruction back to the cultural background and environment that the ELL is most familiar with can make instruction come alive (Kibler, 1996). Assisting students in making those connections strengthens previously learned material, paves the way for acquiring new knowledge, and engages the ELL to take responsibility for learning. Table 11.3 lists some suggestions for making instruction more relevant to students' home contexts and for introducing new concepts in a way that relates to students' perspectives.

Accomplishing these tasks requires a staff that has competency in matters of cross-cultural differences and in ways of making the curriculum and the classroom more diverse. Thus, another systemic intervention that can be implemented is the assessment of the cultural competency of staff and the offering of professional development opportunities to remedy identified areas of weakness. Table 11.4 provides a tool that staff can use to identify their own cultural competencies.

Another systemic intervention involves the use of "cultural therapy" (Spindler & Spindler, 1994). While this approach to addressing the impact of cultural differences involves a focus on the individual and the culture, it can become a routine intervention for culturally different students and for their teachers. As an intervention, cultural therapy encourages examining the complexity of culture as it affects the individual. That is, the deep and deeper aspects of culture—the implicit, tacit, and even unconscious aspects of culture—are brought to awareness and scrutinized for their impact on the individual (teacher or student). Additionally, these aspects of culture are not seen as static and deterministic. Rather, if they can be identified and understood from a practical perspective, they can be modified; the individual need not be a victim of these cultural "constraints". Cultural therapy is proactive and empowering and has been effectively employed over a number of years as an alternative to some less efficacious multicultural practices (e.g., Phelan & Davidson, 1993; Trueba, 1993).

Finally, educators must be mindful of creating opportunities for mutual communication between home and school in ways that communicate value and respect for the families' native culture, as well as providing avenues for parent involvement that are congruent with the parents' culture. Chronicle 11.3 describes how a mismatch between parents' norms and those of the school was resolved.

Table 11.4   Essential Elements of Cultural Proficiency

	1 = Not at all;	2 = Very little;	3 = Somewhat;	4 = A lot

Knowing about Culture

Name the Differences

How well do you . . .

• Describe your own culture and the cultural norms of your school?		1	2	3	4
• Recognize how your culture affects others in the environment?		1	2	3	4
• Understand how the culture of the school affects those whose culture is different?		1	2	3	4

Valuing Diversity

Claiming the Differences

How well do you . . .

• Recognize difference as diversity, rather than as inappropriate responses to the environment?		1	2	3	4
• Accept that each culture considers some values and behaviors more important than others?		1	2	3	4
• Seek opportunities to work with and learn from people whose culture and values may be different than yours?		1	2	3	4

Managing the Dynamics of Diversity

Reframing the Differences

How well do you . . .

• Understand the effect of historic distrust on present-day interactions?		1	2	3	4
• Realize that you may have misjudged another's actions based on your own learned expectations?		1	2	3	4
• Learn effective ways to resolve conflicts among people whose culture and values differ from yours?		1	2	3	4

Adapting to Diversity

Training about Differences

How well do you . . .

• Change the way you have done things to acknowledge the differences present among staff members, students, parents and other community members?		1	2	3	4
• Align programs and practices with guiding principles of cultural proficiency?		1	2	3	4
• Institutionalize appropriate interventions for conflicts and confusion caused by the dynamics of difference?		1	2	3	4

Institutionalizing Cultural Knowledge

Changing for Differences

How well do you . . .

• Incorporate cultural knowledge into the mainstream of the school?		1	2	3	4
• Develop skills for cross-cultural communication among staff?		1	2	3	4
• Integrate into the school's systems information and skills that enable all to interact effectively in a variety of cultural situations?		1	2	3	4

Source: Adapted by John Kibler from Nuri Robins, Lindsey, Lindsey, and Terrell (2002).

I Would Never Let My Child Do That!

By an ESL teacher

Every year the sixth-grade class went to either White Pines or Lorado Taft Field Campus for three days and two nights for outdoor education. Historically, the ELLs had not participated in this fantastic learning experience. Everyone thought that the parents simply did not want their children to go. My colleague Bonnie Miller-Cimo and I hypothesized that the reason parents did not send their children on the outdoor education trip was because they did not know or trust the teachers who were chaperoning the trips. We also figured that this type of educational activity was foreign to them.

As ESL teachers, Bonnie and I had not been relieved of our duties teaching other grade levels to go on these trips. We approached our principal and asked him to allow us to go as chaperones and secure substitutes for our class while we were gone. As the translated paperwork was sent home, we announced that this year, we would be accompanying the ELL students on the trip. Surprise! All of the ELLs signed up. It was a positive experience for the students. For many, it was their first overnight stay away from home. They were able to go horseback riding, take night hikes, identify leaves found in the forest, study the stars at night, and sit around the campfire, with the entire sixth-grade singing songs and telling ghost stories.

At conferences later in the year, the parents told Bonnie and me that since their children were not that comfortable with the mainstream teachers and since they had never heard of such school outings before, they had previously felt it was not suitable for their children to go on the trip. With trusted teachers staying with their children and endorsing the activity as worthwhile, they felt their children could participate.

Questions for discussion:

- How do previous schooling experiences influence participation in current school experiences?
- If ELLs fail to participate in activities that are a part of the curriculum, how can you find out why?
- What can you do to ensure that ELLs are able to participate in all curriculum activities?

Suggestions for Specific Interventions

For individual ELLs whose difficulties in school are thought to have a cultural base, it is essential that a counselor who is sensitive to cross-cultural issues explore the adaptation that the student is going through at the moment. An older student who has adapted successfully may be recruited to be a buddy to that ELL. The pair can share their experiences, and the older student can help the ELL through the process. It is also essential that a teacher get feedback from the ELL regarding the aspects of school life that seem most foreign or most stressful for that student. On that basis, that particular ELL's school environment canbe modified to make it more congruent with his or her cultural norms and expectations. The ELL may also be asked to contribute to the process of making the classroom or school more culturally diverse by adding aspects of his or her culture to the curriculum as well as the physical surroundings. This would confirm the value of the ELL's home culture and would help raise the student's self-confidence.

Questions for Discussion

1. What do we know about our own individual cultures as a staff?
2. What do we know about the culture of our school?
3. What do we know about the culture of the ELLs we serve?
4. What do we know about the culture of the ELL who is currently having difficulties in school?
5. How well are the cultures of the ELLs matched with the culture of the school?
6. To what extent are the cultures of ELLs represented in different facets of school life and in the curriculum?
7. To what extent do we connect with students' home life:
   - In the curriculum?
   - In the way school works?
   - In the way classrooms are managed?

12

Putting It All Together: How Do We Know That What We Are Doing Works?

KEY CONCEPTS

Establishing a system whereby a continuum of services is provided to English language learners with significant difficulties in school is no small feat, but one that is worth investing in. Implementing the interventions that are suggested by extensive information gathering will benefit all students.

Throughout this handbook we have described a process that could help school districts identify and address the varied needs of English language learners (ELLs) who are experiencing difficulties in school. For this process to be most effective, it must be proactive. School problem-solving teams, or ECOS (for Ensuring a Continuum of Services) teams, can use the process described in this handbook for early identification of ELLs who are encountering unusual difficulties in school. In fact, if applied appropriately, the process can help teams to anticipate and even prevent those difficulties that are due to causes extrinsic to the learner. Teachers and other school staff need not wait for students to fail before giving them the support they need to begin experiencing success in school.

In this chapter, we review the elements of the process that can help to ensure that schools provide a continuum of effective services for all ELLs, including those who have a disability. Even if a process is available and in place, it is still necessary to determine when and in what instances the process should be implemented. This requires a kind of circumspection on the part of the individual schools. In the first section of this chapter, we discuss a primary way that such circumspection may occur: how the schools (or even the local educational agencies) can determine how well they are doing with regard to the appropriate placement of ELLs and how the ECOS process can help them improve services. Toward that end, the first section focuses on the need for the individual school to examine its process of service delivery to ELLs, especially how it identifies ELLs as being struggling learners. The rest of the chapter focuses on the services provided to ELLs.

Identification of ELLs with Difficulties in School

Since the identification of ELLs experiencing serious challenges in school is attended by numerous difficulties, schools should check the extent to which ELLs are identified as having a special education need and the way that identification of these students occurs. This review will assist in preventing the two undesirable outcomes too often seen in public schools: overrepresentation and underrepresentation of ELLs in special education.

Checking the Proportion of ELLs in Special Education

One measure that schools can use to ensure that they are appropriately supporting ELLs, both those with and those without disabilities, is the proportion of students who are placed in special education. If the number of ELLs in special education is disproportional to the number of other students in special education, there may be problems with the process of identification and placement. There are two ways to make this determination. The first method entails a cross-student group comparison. With this method, the number of ELL students placed in special education programs in the school or LEA is divided by the total number of ELLs in that school or LEA to derive a percentage of ELLs placed in special education. Then the number of all non-ELLs placed in special education programs in the school or LEA is divided by the total number of non-ELLs in that school or LEA to derive a percentage of non-ELLs placed in special education. A comparison of the two figures should show approximately the same percentage of each group placed in special education. For example, if there are 1,000 ELLs in the LEA and 197 are placed in special education, then 19.7% of ELLs have been placed. When non-ELLs are considered, however, it is a different story. In this example, there are 20,000 non-ELL students in the LEA, but only 2,200, or 11%, of these students are placed in special education. The difference between the placement percentages, 19.7% and 11%, is quite large and suggests a problem of overrepresentation of ELLs in special education.

A second method for determining the proportion of ELLs in special education placement uses within group comparisons. With this method the percentage of students in the school or the LEA representing ELLs is compared with the percentage of ELLs in the entire special education population. The proportion of ELLs in the total population of the school or LEA should be the same as the proportion placed in special education. For example, if ELLs make up 23% of the total school or LEA student population, then approximately 23% of the special education population should also be ELLs. If, as an illustration, only 9% of the ELL population has been placed in special education, there is a real chance of underrepresentation in this example. Since ELLs made up 23% of the total school or LEA population, we would expect a similar percentage in special education.

These methods are useful, but some caveats must be kept in mind when a school begins looking at the over- or underrepresentation of ELLs in special education placement. First, the percentage comparisons are only approximate. Students from lower socioeconomic backgrounds who have received less health care services and perhaps had poorer nutrition may have a slightly greater need for special education services. This difference, however, is generally not large. Second, the disproportionality seen in special education (if it exists) is often seen in the "soft" categories of exceptionality: categories like "language disordered," "learning disabled," "mild emotional disturbance," "mild behavior disordered," "mild developmental delay," "speech and language impaired," and "other health related" most often show the disproportionality. Finally, schools should check for both overrepresentation and underrepresentation of ELLs in special education programs. Providing no services when they are needed is just as problematic as inappropriately providing services that are not needed. Both scenarios exacerbate the problems faced by ELLs.

By gathering information from year to year on the number and percentage of ELLs served in their special education programs, schools can see if they are moving toward a more accurate identification of ELLs with intrinsic learning difficulties (ELL + LD). Unless the school is a specific destination for students with challenges (that is, a side-by-side program or a special education center), the percentages of all subgroups in a school should coincide. The proportion of ELLs in special education programs with respect to the general population should not be significantly higher or lower than the proportion of other groups in the school or school district.

Research suggests that the magnitude of disproportionality changes depending on whether the analysis is conducted at the national, state, district, or school level. Overrepresentation at the national level applies only to African Americans and Native Americans. Although Latinos are not overrepresented nationally, this group is affected in some states and districts. Other factors that can mediate the magnitude of overrepresentation include the size of the district, the proportion of an ethnic group in the district population, the indicators used to measure the problem, and the availability of alternative programs such as bilingual education (Artiles, Higareda, Rueda, et al., 2005). Regardless of the level of analysis, the proportion of ELLs in special education should be no different than the proportion of any other subgroup.

Investigating Misidentification

Once a problem with identification and placement into special education has been identified, how identification and placement occurred should be carefully reviewed to determine possible breakdowns in the methods that are currently being used to identify students with disabilities. There are typically four areas in which breakdown may occur: the assessment instruments used, the interpretations applied to the collected data, placement pressures due to funding issues, and insufficient resources for ELLs.

With regard to the assessment instruments and how they are employed, many problems may arise. Although this issue has been addressed in previous chapters, it is important to revisit some of the concerns in light of the present problem-solving discussion. As previously discussed and detailed elsewhere (e.g., Coles, 1987; Damico, 1991; McDermott, 1993; McDermott & Varenne, 1995) many assessment instruments, especially norm-referenced and standardized tests, are not up to the task of validly and effectively addressing the complexity of human meaning making. These tools may focus on superficial indices of proficiency or may be too decontextualized to give an authentic view of a student's strengths and weaknesses. Some assessments are too narrow or superficial in their focus, and consequently they either overidentify ELLs as having disabilities of some sort or completely miss students who truly are experiencing difficulties due to intrinsic causes. These problems are being increasingly recognized, and there is a change toward more authentic and descriptive assessment procedures (e.g., Artiles & Ortiz, 2002; Fuchs, 2004; Gottlieb & Hamayan, 2006; Hamayan & Damico, 1991; O'Malley & Valdez-Pierce, 1996).

This growing awareness of the problems with formalized testing approaches is one of the reasons why the 2004 reauthorization of the Individuals with Disabilities Education Improvement Act (IDEA) moved away from relying on such of tools for assessment purposes. To ensure the best assessments possible, careful analysis should be conducted regarding the tests used with the ELL population. If assessment instruments are employed, the following questions should be asked of each procedure:

1. Does the instrument directly collect relevant and actual behaviors in the authentic classroom context?
2. Are the actual behaviors focused on and the procedures employed for data collection appropriate, given the ELLs' linguistic, cultural, and experiential diversity?
3. If norms or some other kind of referencing procedure is employed, is it appropriate to this ELL population?

4. Is some flexibility built into the assessment procedure to account for ELLs' diversity during interpretation?

ECOS teams must shift toward a solution-seeking process that looks for possible underlying factors as indices of difficulty, and begin to gather performance data that are more revealing than norm-referenced, standardized test scores. The use of early intervention services, wherein some type of intervention is undertaken before a formal assessment is made, may be the best option to avoid the problems inherent to using formalized tests. The IDEA supports this approach.

The second area of difficulty implicated in the potential misidentification of ELLs involves interpretation of data that have been collected. Even if the information obtained is more authentic, descriptive, performance-based assessment information, once data are collected, they must be carefully analyzed to determine what the patterns of performance actually mean. Do the data show that the ELL has particular strengths and weaknesses? Do these patterns of performance help or hinder classroom or communicative effectiveness? Why do the patterns of weakness or difficulty exist? Are these difficulties due to diversity or disability issues? How would an ELL be affected by one kind of remedial placement versus another? Each of these questions should be a routine part of the interpretive process when focusing on the assessment data. As discussed previously (see Chapter 3), these questions are necessary to complete the explanatory phase of the bi-level analysis paradigm (Damico & Hamayan, 1992). When employed appropriately and completely, these questions enable appropriate data interpretation so that accurate identification and placement may occur. If these interpretive issues are not addressed, however, the result may be insufficient and inappropriate interpretations that lead to misidentification. With regard to addressing these questions, it is critical that all those involved in teaching and assessing ELLs build a solid knowledge base in the areas of bilingualism and second language learning, so that they can apply this knowledge to interpreting the performance of these students. The ECOS team approach is designed to accomplish this objective.

One specific interpretive issue that often results in misidentification of ELLs is the use of discrepancy formulas. Too often, LEAs employ various types of discrepancy formulas when engaging in data interpretation. In many cases, interpretation of deficit becomes a matter of applying the discrepancy formula to determine whether there is a difference between mental age and performance (see Chapters 3 and 4), and no further consideration is given to the validity of the scores or the diversity variables. The 2004 reauthorization of the IDEA particularly targeted discrepancy formulas as problematic, and the legislation and subsequent regulations prohibit state departments of education from requiring that local educational agencies apply discrepancy formulas (see Chapter 4). If school districts abandon these discrepancy formulas, which are riddled with ethical, procedural, and cultural problems, this will move interpretation toward more accuracy. In adopting more authentic means to assess and interpret ELLs, schools move away from the medical model of learning disabilities and accept that no category of disability can be easily diagnosed in any consistently reliable or valid manner. This is especially true for ELLs, who are often functioning in a system that was not designed with them in mind. The infrastructure of monolingual, monocultural schools was not designed to help educators recognize exceptionalities in students from a variety of linguistic, cultural, and socioeconomic backgrounds, and the diagnostic criteria used are subject to the ideologies currently in fashion.

The third area of concern when addressing misidentification involves an organizational variable. School districts must examine biases that are created or reinforced because of the funding structure associated with ELL education and special education. A legitimate (if difficult) question must be asked: Is the school still making decisions about programming based primarily on funding availability or funding categories? For both ethical reasons and issues of equity, school districts must seek to support students' needs whether those needs fall within the realm of funding labels or not. Students should not be placed in special education when they need other, more appropriate services (such as diversity education) just because special education funding is available.

Finally, the LEA and the individual schools must determine whether or not they have sufficient services available for ELLs. A frequent cause of these students' problems in the mainstream or special education classroom is that they are not receiving appropriate services in the first place. Special education then becomes a dumping ground for these otherwise normal learners, and the consequences are often negative and far-reaching. Whether the ECOS team works directly with teachers or advocates for more permanent diversity educational services, if there is misidentification of ELL students with regard to special education, this lack of appropriate services must be considered.

In this handbook we have shown that the many difficulties ELLs experience in school cannot be neatly categorized. The reality of teaching and supporting ELLs is that each student's experience is unique, and thus more creativity and flexibility are needed designing and funding programming for these students. ELLs should not have to wait until their situation becomes desperate enough for them to be considered eligible for support that already exists in their school. The onus is on schools to find ways to intervene in a timely and effective manner, even if the intervention being suggested for a student or group of students has never been implemented in that school before.

Anticipating and Addressing Predictable ELL Difficulties

Once the ECOS team begins gathering information about an ELL or group of ELLs, the team members will engage in a collaborative process for interpreting the information, proposing hypotheses to account for ELLs' difficulties and creating interventions. The team also provides support in implementing interventions. The responsibilities of gathering information and implementing interventions cannot always be left to a small group of individuals or the same group of individuals, or the process will become so cumbersome and draining that it will fall apart. ECOS team members must strike a balance between delegating these responsibilities and supporting those who carry them out.

Identifying Exceptionalities in Diverse Settings

In applying a creative approach to supporting the needs of ELLs, the first step is to shift the orientation from a premature diagnosis ("He is low" or "She is doing poorly in math") to requiring a description of the student's behavior, coupled with evidence of that behavior and, when possible, data on any interventions that have been attempted. The more specific teachers, parents, and others are in describing ELLs' observable behaviors and reactions to interventions, the better able the team will be to hypothesize possible causes and to further intervene in a timely and appropriate manner.

When gathering assessment information, the ECOS team should respond to norm-referenced and other quantitative data with a healthy dose of skepticism, probing to ascertain the true extent of validity and reliability of ELLs' test scores. These quantitative data should never be given more weight than more authentic descriptive and qualitative data. The team must insist on qualitative assessment information (including attempts at intervention) for ELLs who are experiencing difficulties. Rubrics and checklists that enhance reliability and validity and provide a more comprehensive profile of these students' strengths and areas of difficulty should accompany this qualitative information. It is important that ECOS teams look beyond traditional avenues for receiving referrals on students' difficulties. They should seek out teacher recommendations for ELLs who are experiencing difficulties, coordinate the gathering of historical and contemporary data on these students, and assist the teachers in some initial attempts at intervention as an aspect of the assessment process. Once difficulties are identified, teams must validate students' performance across various content areas as well as in diverse settings, including those that are extracurricular or occur in ELL's community and home.

As soon as concerns arise, it is crucial to engage the ELL's parents as collaborators in the information-gathering process through interviews and conversations. Engaging the ELL who is having trouble in school in the information-gathering process by way of conversations, interviews, and dialogue journals is also very beneficial to the solution-seeking process. When addressing the needs of linguistically and culturally diverse learners, it is vital to collaborate with a cultural liaison, who will be able to provide an appropriate context for interpreting the information that is collected. The cultural liaison must be equipped to understand the cultural and linguistic nuances of both the ELL's community and the school culture in order to mediate discussions and explain the nature of the concerns as well as the solution-seeking process.

We have suggested that information be gathered about seven integral factors in students' lives. The seven factors are the learning environment created for ELLs, personal and family issues, physical and psychological factors, previous schooling, oral language and literacy development, academic achievement, and cultural differences. Understanding and addressing these seven integral factors that impact ELLs' success in school will help educators anticipate and address difficulties that are predictable among ELLs. These seven integral factors provide a rich context for understanding learning and achievement among ELLs and will influence how and what data are collected and how they are evaluated and interpreted. The information gathered in relation to the seven factors provides an important context within which instruction in general and interventions specifically are suggested, implemented, and monitored.

Addressing the seven integral factors will help schools begin to change ELLs' learning environment and the instructional approaches, strategies, or techniques that are used to teach them. Once schools focus on these seven integral factors, they can begin removing many of the obstacles that have traditionally kept ELLs from reaching their optimal levels of achievement and their families from gaining access to the school system. Over time, with practice and additional staff development, the ECOS team will be in a position to address situations proactively, before students experience difficulty, rather than only intervening once difficulties arise.

Rejecting Common Myths

For schools to take a proactive approach, staff must reflect on their beliefs regarding how ELLs learn, bilingualism, and academic achievement. Several commonly held misconceptions stand in the way of providing support to ELLs in the most efficient way, and these myths must be explicitly recognized and challenged.. One such myth is that teams must wait until ELLs are fully proficient in English before considering their case. When the ECOS team has reframed the issue as ELL ± LD, there is no reason to wait to provide interventions that will help the student at any stage in the solution-seeking process. Another myth is that the team should rush ELLs into special education programming so that they will get help. ELLs who are experiencing difficulties need specialized support for language and learning that must be provided immediately (ELL – LD) while the team investigates further a possible disability cause (ELL + LD). The last myth that must fall is that ELLs who are experiencing difficulties must be instructed only in English instruction so that they will not get confused. The research and examples presented in this handbook show that ELLs' native languages and cultures are resources for helping these students develop optimal levels of language proficiency in English, academic achievement, and emotional well-being.

Internalizing the Principles of How ELLs Learn

In the process of questioning misconceptions and myths, the ECOS teams will begin to reflect on the principles on which the instruction of ELLs is based. They will no longer find it acceptable to impose research, strategies, infrastructure, or programs that were designed for native English speakers onto ELLs, who come from varied geographic locations and different language, cultural, and socioeconomic backgrounds, with vastly different individual experiences. They will also have acquired the ELL lens through which they can filter information, data, experiences, and interventions so that they can more appropriately address the needs of this unique population of students.

Beyond the ECOS team, all teachers who work with ELLs have an obligation to become familiar with the seven integral factors discussed in this handbook. Trying to maximize the learning environment for ELLs without considering these aspects would reflect an abysmal and unforgiving ignorance that would not be tolerated for any other student population. Any interventions implemented without consideration to these factors may be perceived as educational malpractice, especially if greater care is provided to other student subgroups in the school.

Creating an Enriched Environment for ELLs

In creating an enriched rather than a compensatory environment for ELLs, it is useful to begin with the three-pronged approach provided in *Castañeda v. Pickard.* This would force schools to explicitly begin with a sound theoretical base, ensure that there are adequate resources to implement this sound theory, and conduct periodic review of the program with the intention of continuous improvement. Knowledge and application of laws and regulations specific to the education of ELLs is a critical foundation for any programming or interventions that schools design for ELLs. Schools should go beyond the minimum requirements of the law and seek to ensure they are protecting the civil and human rights of the students they serve.

Teachers

Essential to an enriched learning environment for ELLs is the presence and utilization of expert teachers in the field of ESL/bilingual education. Recruiting and hiring qualified teachers who know the languages and cultures of the ELL population in the school is a priority. When this is not possible, time and resources should go into professional development for existing teachers. A related issue is that of assigning paraprofessionals as ELLs' main teachers. Although paraprofessionals who know the language and culture of the ELLs are a great resource in the schools, noncertified teachers cannot be given the responsibility of initial instruction of these students. Rather, schools must seek out highly motivated, creative, expert teachers to support ELLs so that ELLs can accelerate their learning rather than fall farther behind their peers.

Expanding Professional Expertise

When ECOS team members work together in this solution-seeking process, their professional perspectives will expand, and they will find they are better able to address the new and diverse needs of the students in their schools.

Collectively, they represent an extraordinary amount of knowledge and experiences that ideally will increase over time. For this to happen, the team should establish foundational principles for its operation, its vision, and the roles it will take in the school. One important function of the ECOS team is to build professional bridges within the team and within the school as a way to share and expand professional knowledge The ECOS team will also have to support and create opportunities to clarify and implement the cycle of developing ideas on a variety of topics, hypothesizing possible causes for ELLs' difficulties, creating and implementing interventions, assessing student performance and the success of interventions, and reflecting on their professional practice.

The general education and special education teachers in the school should expand their expertise in the areas of ELLs' first language and literacy development. They should also develop a working knowledge of the second language acquisition process and understand the differences in learning literacy in a second language versus native language literacy development. They should be given opportunities to explore the various cultural dimensions that impact ELLs' performance in school. These teachers will need ongoing support in designing and implementing linguistically and culturally responsive instruction, and in learning about differentiating instruction according to language proficiency levels. They will need guidance in implementing authentic, performance-based assessment and in applying content and language proficiency standards in every area of instruction for ELLs. General education and special education teachers will need strategies for communicating with the parents of ELLs in new and more effective ways. Although the acquisition of this expertise may seem like an intensive and time-consuming process, that is not necessarily the case. A real advantage of the ECOS team approach is that this expertise, like the processes needed to address diversity issues themselves, is inherent in the way that the team is designed to work. By collaborating with teachers in their classrooms, the ECOS team assists the teachers in gradually acquiring much of the knowledge needed.

ESL and bilingual teachers will have to become experts in implementing and coaching others on ESL and bilingual instructional methodology and culturally responsive pedagogy. They must be familiar with the laws and regulations governing the education of ELLs, and must know how to differentiate instruction according to language proficiency levels. Along with designing instruction for ELLs, these ESL/bilingual teachers must feel comfortable designing, implementing, and interpreting the results of authentic, performance-based assessment. They must also be able to apply content and language proficiency standards to lesson design, and they need to know how the seven integral factors can affect ELLs' success in school. Additionally, bilingual teachers and other bilingual staff must develop confidence in their ability to function as cultural interpreters for other staff members and for families. These ESL and bilingual teachers must begin to develop, with the help of special education teachers, a sense of how disabilities affect the learning process and what can be expected of ELLs who are developing normally. The ECOS team framework and the collaboration that it engenders will also assist in this process.

Resources

An enriched learning environment for ELLs includes an abundance of high-quality, age-appropriate academic content area instructional and supplemental materials at a variety of language proficiency and reading levels. These materials should reflect the languages and cultures of the students and can include student-created identity texts as well as purchased resources. In addition to high-quality materials, ELL classrooms must be highly interactive to ensure multiple opportunities for students to practice newly learned language skills. There is no reason for ELLs to be isolated in the school environment even as we seek to give students the specific programming and attention they require. Thus, they need to be fully integrated in nonacademic classes and other school activities; they need to participate in small-group instruction and team-taught classes just as their monolingual English-speaking peers do.

Programmatic and Instructional Issues

If the programming that has been developed for ELLs fails to satisfy federal and state statutory demands, fails to meet the needs of the local community, or fails to include recognized good practices (viewing the ELLs' native languages and cultures as resources and implementing content-based ESL), it should be rectified immediately to create optimal learning environments for these students. Schools should not be limited by existing programs, especially those that are "factory-produced and plastic-wrapped." Rather, schools should seek to provide the range of services ELLs need in terms of both duration and frequency, even if it means creating an innovative program that has not previously existed in the schools.

The ECOS team and school administrators must work together to ensure that classroom instruction includes practices that are based on comprehensibility, increased interaction, and the promotion of higher-order thinking. Assessment practices that are used must include formative, summative, quantitative, qualitative, and performance-based information so that all those who work with ELLs, as well as the students themselves, can have a realistic understanding of what the students know and can do. The most effective and informative assessments are embedded in instruction, include all four language domains, come from all content areas, include self-review and peer review, are in the students' first and second languages and are judged against a rubric.

All aspects of an enriched learning environment for ELLs should work together to help these students gain access to the academic concepts and skills and learn the language necessary to become successful in these classes. Appropriate assessment of the learning that occurs in these enriched learning environments should allow students to show what they know, not just what they are having difficulty learning. When the learning environment is enriched in this way, it is easier to find children who may be experiencing difficulties stemming from more intrinsic causes. When the learning environment is depressed and lacks substance and appropriate methods and materials, many ELLs will look as if they are learning disabled and not making the progress that is expected.

Adopting a Response to Intervention Approach

By adopting a type of response to intervention (RTI) approach in which both systemic and specific interventions are implemented, schools will be better able to assess ELLs' special needs and to provide support to students who are having significant academic difficulties. The ECOS team can provide leadership for this shift to more performance-based, authentic assessment of ELLs' strengths and areas of difficulty. The ECOS team will be engaged in a solution-seeking process that includes proactive information gathering and culturally appropriate interpretation of this information. The team should encourage and support timely application of enhanced instruction that is high quality, effective, consistent, research based, and tailored to the needs of ELLs, as well as facilitating collaboration across disciplines. As discussed in Chapter 4, it is essential to recognize that the application of RTI may be innovative or deceptively stale. Although the overall framework and its three tiers of systematic intervention to determine learning ability and potential are quite promising, if the interventions employed within them are decontextualized and fragmented, if they represent strategies employed far too long in some aspects of special education and remedial reading programs, then nothing will change. If the assessment to determine the response to intervention is based on artificial tasks in contrived situations that only tangentially focus on real meaning-making activities, then nothing will change. It is the obligation of the ECOS team to ensure that any innovation, such as RTI, is truly innovative.

The ECOS team will also periodically implement needs assessments and surveys as a way of assessing current practice and monitoring progress in these new endeavors. Aspects of this innovation should become a part of teacher and administrator performance appraisal, to communicate the importance of institutionalizing these changes in the school culture. The team can review resulting performance appraisals to monitor the extent to which this new approach has been implemented. In order to assess the effectiveness of the changes that have been institutionalized and the interventions that are being implemented with ELLs, it is critical to collect ELL performance data (quantitative and qualitative information on academic language development and academic achievement), along with evidence of systemic and specific interventions, and schedule periodic data-review retreats to scrutinize and interpret the data and evaluate the success rate of interventions, as well as to make recommendations for the short and long term.

Monitoring the Effectiveness of Interventions

As the ECOS team works with individual teachers or groups of teachers, it should meet frequently to monitor the effectiveness of its work. Continual monitoring on an intermittent basis is important, since progress over time is often the criterion used to determine the effectiveness of methods and the proficiency of the ELL. Especially if a kind of RTI is employed, it is necessary to determine what kinds of interventions are employed, whether they are appropriate to the needs of the student, whether they are appropriately and effectively implemented, and whether the intervention resulted in some change or progress in the desirable (and targeted) behaviors of the student. Only if all of these conditions are met can we comment on the learning capacity of the ELL and use the data to help determine the best placement and interventions for this student. For this purpose, monitoring is required. A couple of illustrations may be helpful.

Case 1

A 12-year-old boy whose first language is Spanish has been placed in an English-only classroom. The teacher has expressed concern about how much he understands during social studies lectures and discussions. If this ELL exhibits difficulty comprehending classroom instruction, then observable and documented data should be collected and interventions formulated and monitored.

Observable Difficulties: With that objective in mind, it has been documented that the student does not attend to the actual lectures and the teacher's notes placed on the chalkboard. Rather, his attention is directed elsewhere, and he often draws in his notebook rather than take notes. In three 30-minute class sessions the student raised his hand to respond to only three out of 35 opportunities (8.5% of the time), compared with 63% of the time by three randomly chosen class peers. Additionally, he was not able to respond accurately or appropriately when questions were directed to him during these three sessions. On 14 requests for responses, he responded appropriately in only two instances (both closed-ended questions). This response rate of 14% compares unfavorably with the response rates of three randomly chosen class peers, who responded appropriately to direct questions 79%, 95%, and 100% of the time.

Possible ELL Explanations: Since he has been in the English language classroom only five weeks and in the United States three months, and since he speaks only some conversational English, it is anticipated that he does not have sufficient comprehension of English grammar or the vocabulary of social studies. Moreover, the academic discourse and expectations of how to be an active learner in this classroom are unfamiliar to him.

Interventions: Once the difficulties were documented, several interventions were tried. First a bilingual aide sat with him during a 15-minute homeroom session with a list of vocabulary words that would be used during the social studies lesson. She exposed him to the vocabulary and provided additional information so that he could recognize the English words when they were used and would understood their meaning. Second, with a peer tutor, he jointly prepared a short outline (based on the textbook headings and subheadings) to organize the structure of the social studies lecture. This was done at the end of the previous day's social studies class. Third, the teacher was instructed in several effective sheltered instruction techniques to help increase his comprehension in her classroom (Echevarria, Vogt, & Short, 2004).

Monitoring: The aide and the teacher were asked to keep a journal that required several one-to-two line entries every other day: how well they believed their specific teaching strategies were implemented that day and how well the ELL did in class that day. They were asked to provide some description of behavior rather than just an overall evaluative statement. Additionally, once a week, a member of the ECOS team observed for 10 to 15 minutes during social studies to monitor both the teacher and the ELL. Finally, every two weeks the peer tutor, the aide, and the teacher met with a member of the ECOS team to discuss progress and concerns. This meeting lasted approximately 15 minutes.

Outcomes: Outcomes were determined by comparing the student's performances across the first three sessions (regarding attending, bids for a turn, and correctresponses) with three other sessions approximately 12 weeks later. Additionally, the information in the teacher's and aide's journals was used to triangulate the observational data. The student was found to have made substantial progress (as had the social studies teacher with her strategies), and he was not referred for special education assessment.

Case 2

A six-year-old Filipino girl who did not know English was referred for poor reading ability. Her teacher reported that she could not effectively recognize her letters and that she had little or no phonemic awareness. Additionally, it was reported that she was not a reader and that she avoided any attempts to have her read.

Observable Difficulties: Observations during two round-robin reading sessions documented that she was only able to read 45% of the words on her three assigned pages (compared with 88%, 94%, and 96% of words read by other members of her heterogeneous reading group). Additionally, she tended to guess at unknown words based on their first letters (81% of the time) and often did not even employ the correct first sounds. When given a familiar book that she had been reading with a room-parent, she did try to read. A running record found that she was able to read only 62% of the words correctly and that she either guessed at the others or skipped the words (or whole lines) if she did not know the words or sounds.

Possible ELL Explanations: Given her limited experience with literacy in the Philippines (no prior schooling) and her lack of English language skills, the approaches to reading were not appropriate. Rather than decontextualized phonemic awareness and a round-robin reading approach that provided little mediation while she was learning, more contextualization and assistance based on more meaningful materials should have been employed.

Interventions: Consistent with a modification of reading recovery techniques (Clay, 1985; Pinnell, 1989), three approaches were suggested. First, an older ELL student (a Chinese fifth-grade girl) read aloud to her every day. This was a component of both of their reading programs. Second, with a student teacher she engaged in a joint reading activity for 20 minutes each day. The student teacher was instructed in using Clay's "roaming around the known" strategy to assist the ELL's motivation and confidence. Finally, the teacher engaged in a small-group shared reading activity with this student and two other struggling readers. Alphabetics and the graphophonemic system were not explicitly focused on. Rather, the book and the inherent meaning of the story were stressed as the ELL and the other children read with the teacher.

Monitoring: The student teacher kept a running record of literacy performance (Clay, 1985) during her daily sessions and also observed the teacher once a week during the shared reading time and collected similar running records.

Outcomes: Outcomes were determined by comparing the student's reading performance from the first two round-robin sessions with her reading performances during three shared reading sessions 10 weeks later. Evaluations focused on how many words she could read on the pages, how her fluency had changed, and what meaning-based strategies she exhibited during the shared reading.

There are many ways that various interventions may be employed and monitored to determine effectiveness of intervention. The creative ECOS team and individual teachers are limited only by their own experience and creativity. It is important, however, to have a consistent format from which measurements may be employed and comparisons made. The chart in Table 12.1 can be used to monitor the outcomes of the interventions that the teachers have started to use.

Building Capacity to Anticipate New Difficulties

In time, as ECOS team members work together to build capacity, a creative process of generating innovative programming and interventions will become the norm. Capacity building occurs mainly as teachers and other school professionals learn from each other. As this learning occurs, all team members will find that they incorporate the knowledge sets and skills found in another's specialization into their own repertoire of knowledge and skills. A flexibility of roles will result through the full implementation of the ECOS team as members pair up in nontraditional ways to address the needs of students in their schools. This collaboration will foster dynamic conversations leading to innovative suggestions for both systemic and specific interventions.

With the ever-growing expectations and responsibilities laid on educators, the ECOS team can serve to support the students experiencing difficulties and the teachers who have these students in their classrooms. It is clear that encouraging teaming and collaboration throughout the school is a principal role for the ECOS team because no one individual or program can meet the needs of all students. In these ways the ECOS team can function as a catalyst for change, providing valuable impetus for the more equitable distribution of human, physical, and fiscal resources in schools.

Table 12.1 Monitoring the Outcomes of Interventions

Student: _____   Date(s): _____

Observable Difficulties Listening/Speaking/Reading/Writing	Possible ELL Explanations	Interventions L1 (Primary Language) and L2 (Second Language) [Consider who will implement, training needed, and timelines]	Outcomes [Dates]

Source: Adapted from Theresa Young.

Creating a Context for Assessment

The process and contexts we have been describing in this handbook have been discussed and implemented in part or in alternative versions in various school settings. Discussed as versions of the flexible delivery model, the Iowa model, or the RTI model, these models are all oriented to school-based problem solving and are consistent with ECOS. The framework of RTI (and other models) must be adapted to be beneficial to ELLs. Models used for ELLs should be broader in design and in implementation. In particular, they should stress the innovations necessary for strong contextualized and authentic interventions and should focus on outcomes that truly reflect authentic classroom performance rather than on splinter skills or abilities only tangentially related to the classroom. In the two case studies just presented, this focus is demonstrated.

Whether implementing an RTI approach that is somewhat narrow in scope or a flexible delivery model that broadly attempts to create methods to provide prompt services to different kinds of learners within the limits of the school's resources, it is essential to focus on both the assessment principles and the intervention framework discussed extensively in this handbook. To address the needs of the ELLs, all possible innovations and research-supported practices should be considered as potential sources of implementation.

When an ECOS team embraces an RTI approach or the broader flexible delivery model, a forum is established for contextualized assessment that is appropriate for ELLs as well as other learners in the school. When the team works on interventions and information gathering pertaining to the seven integral factors, this is analogous to Tier 1 interventions in the RTI model. Preparing the inventory of difficulties, brainstorming possible causes, and then creating and implementing interventions that address both extrinsic and intrinsic possible causes corresponds to Tier 2 of the RTI model. When more intensive interventions are required for a group of students above and beyond all of those mentioned the ECOS team will be addressing Tier 3 of the RTI model.

On Tier 3 it is likely that some of the students will require further assessment as part of a full case study. The ECOS team and the processes we have suggested in this handbook ensure a flexible model for further assessment through its cycle of brainstorming, implementing, assessing, and reflecting. Traditionally, ELLs have been given psychological and other assessments out of context and in a language they were still in the process of learning. We hope that the information presented in this handbook has shed light on why this practice is unacceptable. Schools must engage all of students' linguistic, cultural, and cognitive resources when administering any sort of assessment.

These Tier 3 or case study assessments must be carried out bilingually, dynamically, and in a meaningful context. ELLs who go on to a full case study evaluation will take with them all the documentation collected throughout Tier 1 and Tier 2 interventions, as well as information on the seven integral elements. This information provides a rich context for these case study assessments. If students are found at this point to need more intensive special education support, all the L1 and L2 interventions and other information will allow staff to create programming that addresses the ELL's unique linguistic and cultural needs while providing specialized support for the student's particular disabilities.

Benefits for All Learners

Many educators assert that understanding how ELLs learn and the application of such information to a broader student population may have positive effects on the achievement of all students. Much of what we advocate in this handbook makes good sense when laid out in a logical fashion. The same seven extrinsic factors apply to all learners, regardless of their language background. Rather than modifying an existing school system infrastructure to try to fit ELL populations, it may be beneficial to look at recreating our schools so that everyone emphasizes elements such as academic language and literacy development across the curriculum, access to academic concepts and ideas, authentic assessment practices, culturally responsive pedagogy, and school and community links that seek out families' funds of knowledge. Developing school environments that support educators by seeking out their expertise and perspectives allows a school to anticipate and address potential difficulties while encouraging collaboration among professionals. This sort of environment benefits all students, not just ELLs.

Advocating to Change the System

The traditional method used in most schools to identify and serve ELLs with disabilities is rife with problems. In the past, ELLs had to wait to become proficient in English before being considered for any sort of intervention, or they had to wait to fail before their difficulties were considered serious enough to require additional assistance. On the other hand, many ELLs were inappropriately placed in special education programs as a way to "get them some help." Neither approach has been successful in helping ELLs whose difficulties do not fall neatly into categories. Supporting ELLs who are experiencing difficulties in school is a complex process that requires that a continuum of both systemic and specific interventions be employed, not simplistic or short-sighted one-size-fits-all approaches.

Advocacy to change the present system becomes an important activity for the ECOS team as well as all stakeholders. ESL and bilingual teachers must build advocacy into their role as educators as well as their role as liaison to ELLs' families and communities. General education and special education staff members must also take on an advocacy role as they learn more about ELLs and become more flexible in providing support to these students through collaboration with ESL and bilingual teachers. It is clear that schools are becoming increasingly diverse, and the number of ELLs is growing every year. Since all educators have a moral and ethical responsibility to ensure an effective educational program for all ELLs and to secure appropriate methods of intervention for ELLs who are experiencing academic difficulty, advocacy for change must come from all areas of the educational system.

Advocacy may take the form of fellow educators supporting one another, as well as constituents working with policy makers and those who allocate resources in the system, to make certain that ELLs have not only equity but also high-quality of services and resources that will give them permission to dream and allow them to make their dreams a reality. We hope that this handbook is a useful resource in advocating for innovative and creative changes in school systems that will promote optimal learning opportunities for not only ELLs but all students.

Appendix A

Amplified List of Difficulties Typically Experienced by ELLs

1. Omits words or adds words to a sentence. Forgets names of things that he or she knows; has to describe them.

2. Is easily distracted.

3. Has trouble following directions.

4. Can do rote arithmetic problems on paper but has difficulty with math word problems.

5. Avoids writing.

6. Does not transfer learning from one lesson to another. Has to relearn each concept from scratch.

7. Very literal: misses inferences, subtleties, nuances, and innuendoes.

8. Often understands concepts but cannot express this understanding in written symbolic form with paper and pencil or on multiple-choice tests.

9. Learns from watching, not listening.

10. Cannot categorize, classify, or summarize.

11. Cannot provide an oral narrative of a story just read to him/her.

12. Low frustration tolerance. Gives up easily or explodes.

13. Cannot commit multiplication tables to memory.

14. Doesn't grasp cause-and-effect relationships.

15. Doesn't see patterns easily.

16. Poorly organized; desk a mess.

17. Doesn't hear fine differences in words; writes *pin* for *pen*.

18. Understands concepts but can't represent them in written symbolic form.

19. Freezes when asked to perform on demand.

20. Confuses b/d and p/q; confuses order of letters in words.

21. Doesn't hear sequence of sounds in words; writes isolated parts of words: *amil* for animal.

22. Has trouble seeing verbal or visual similarities and differences.

23. Has handwriting difficulty; writes very slowly.

24. Reads without expression.

Appendix B

Chart of Typical Academic Difficulties Encountered by ELLs, to Be Completed with Possible Explanations

Observable Behavior	Possible ELL - LD Explanations	Possible ELL + LD Explanations
1. Omits words or adds words to a sentence. Forgets names of things that he or she knows; has to describe them		
2. Is easily distracted.		
3. Has trouble following directions.		
4. Can do rote arithmetic problems on paper but has difficulty with math word problems.		
5. Avoids writing.		

Observable Behavior	Possible ELL - LD Explanations	Possible ELL + LD Explanations
6. Does not transfer learning from one lesson to another. Has to relearn each concept from scratch.		
7. Very literal: misses inferences, subtleties, nuances, and innuendoes.		
8. Often understands concepts but cannot express this understanding in written symbolic form with paper and pencil or on multiple-choice tests.		
9. Learns from watching, not listening.		
10. Cannot categorize, classify, or summarize.		
11. Cannot provide an oral narrative of a story just heard read aloud.		
12. Low frustration tolerance. Gives up easily or explodes.		

Appendix C

Chart for Generating ELL Interventions in Listening, Speaking, Reading, Writing, and Cultural Impact

Difficulty: Student cannot provide an effective oral narrative of a story just read to him (observed in English)

Possible ELL Explanations	ELL Interventions	
	In L1	*In L2*
Listening The student may not understand many stories because they are in English or because the cultural context of the stories or events is irrelevant or unfamiliar to him.		
Speaking The student understands stories told in English but does not feel comfortable enough in his English-speaking abilities to create a narrative. The student may have developed his social English skills but may not have been taught the academic language of temporal organization (*first, then, next*) to be able to effectively narrate stories. The student may be able to tell stories in his native language after hearing a story in English.		

	ELL Interventions	
Possible ELL Explanations	*In L1*	*In L2*
Reading The story was not at the child's instructional level in English, and so he did not understand enough of the story to retell. He could recount some details that correspond to pictures if he has acquired the vocabulary. Perhaps the child's primary language has a different structure for telling stories, and so his retelling in English sounds "out of order/out of sequence."		
Writing The student may be in the early stages of English language acquisition and is still developing his writing skills. The student may not have been explicitly taught to write in English by someone who knows ESL strategies. The student may be using his first language structures to negotiate writing in the second language; this may make the written text sound "out of sequence" in English. The student may need to develop his writing skills the native language on which to build writing in English.		
Cultural Impact The cultural context of the story may be wholly unknown to the student. For example, the student may come from a culture where people do not keep animals in their houses as pets, and he may be appalled and distracted by a story about pets. This makes it difficult for him to concentrate reading comprehension and on the sequence of the story. Different languages may have storytelling structures that differ from English.		

Appendix D

Difficulty: Student cannot provide an oral narrative of a story that has just been just read to him

Possible Disability Explanations (Observed in student's two languages in academic and social contexts)	Special Education Interventions in L1 and L2
Listening The student may not understand the vocabulary (content or organizational words such as *first, next, last*), story events, inferred information, or narrative structure in L1 and L2. The student may exhibit distractibility.	
Speaking The student may have oral expressive difficulties in both languages with: • formulating ideas into sentences that clearly relay the meaning of the story, • the concept of sequencing in a variety of contexts, not just in story retelling, • the use of cohesive devices (e.g., conjunctions and pronoun references) to connect the story information, • organizing information into story structure.	

Possible Disability Explanations (Observed in student's two languages in academic and social contexts)	Special Education Interventions in L1 and L2
Reading Comprehension Poor comprehension due to inability to employ predictions and efficiently use background information.	
Writing The student may have difficulty spelling in all languages. The student may have difficulties in oral language production that are also evident in written expression, including: • sentence formulation, • sequencing in a variety of contexts, including stories, • use of cohesive devices in both languages (e.g., conjunctions, pronoun references), • organizing the information into story structure.	

Appendix E

Assessment of Needs

Please check your role in the school:

☐ Parent ☐ Former ELL ☐ Current ELL ☐ ESL staff ☐ Bilingual staff
☐ Gen. Ed. staff ☐ Administration ☐ Community Member

Please complete this assessment as best as you can. Express your subjective feelings and impressions. Feel free to use the back of the form for more extensive comments.

Vision: The mission that the school sees as having; the goals that the school has set for itself; the expectations the school has for its students.	
What is:	What should be:

Skills: The knowledge base and the expertise that staff need to possess to accomplish the mission and the goals of the school.	
What is:	What should be:

214

Incentives: The opportunities given to staff to accomplish the mission and goals of the school and the rewards for doing it well.	
What is:	What should be:

Resources: The materials and the resources that are available to staff to accomplish the mission and goals of the school.	
What is:	What should be:

Action Plan: The plan that the school has in place to accomplish its mission and goals.	
What is:	What should be:

Source: Adapted from Ambrose (1987).

Appendix F

A Tool for Gathering Information and Evaluating the Adequacy of the Learning Environment

This checklist has been developed to help schools and districts assess the quality of services they provide to linguistically and culturally diverse students. The checklist can be used for self-evaluation, or it may be used by an outside evaluator through observations and interviews. Research findings on the best practices and key elements for effective instruction of linguistically and culturally diverse students formed the basis for the items in this checklist.

Assess each feature below by circling the appropriate rating.

1 = Not evident at all   4 = Strongly evident   dk = Don't know

STUDENT ASSESSMENT SYSTEM

1. A home language survey is used to identify non-native speakers of English.   1   2   3   4   dk

2. The multiple criteria used to identify and reassess the specialized support services needed by ELLs and those with disabilities are well-defined.   1   2   3   4   dk

3. An assessment of oral and written English language proficiency is conducted annually.   1   2   3   4   dk

4. An assessment of oral and written language proficiency is conducted annually in the students' native languages.   1   2   3   4   dk

5. Assessment is conducted through multiple informal and formal standardized measures.   1   2   3   4   dk

6. The guidelines that outline the assessment process are clearly formalized by district policy.   1   2   3   4   dk

7. Information regarding bilingual students' families and educational backgrounds is collected and used for decisions regarding the specialized services that students need.   1   2   3   4   dk

8. Assessment information is disseminated to all persons working with ELLs.   1   2   3   4   dk

9. ELL assessment is matched to the school- or district-adopted instructional program and curriculum objectives.   1   2   3   4   dk

10. Assessment procedures are adequately modified for ELLs with disabilities.   1   2   3   4   dk

11. Extensive data are gathered prior to referral of ELLs suspected of having special needs.   1   2   3   4   dk

12. ELL evaluations for case studies are conducted by bilingual qualified psychologists or with the assistance of trained interpreters.   1   2   3   4   dk

13. Instruments selected for student assessment are reliable, valid, practical and equitable for the ELL population.   1   2   3   4   dk

ENGLISH AS A SECOND LANGUAGE (ESL) INSTRUCTION

1. ESL curriculum objectives are aligned with those of the school- or district-adopted curriculum   1   2   3   4   dk

2. ESL curriculum objectives are well articulated for content-based oral language and literacy development.   1   2   3   4   dk

3. Instruction in ESL is provided to students on the basis of individual needs as identified through assessment.   1   2   3   4   dk

4. Content-based ESL instruction is provided on a regularly scheduled basis.   1   2   3   4   dk

5. Student-centered teaching strategies represent a variety of methods, approaches, and techniques that respond to individual learning styles.   1   2   3   4   dk

6. Students have ample opportunity for meaningful interaction with peers and the teacher in the ESL classroom.   1   2   3   4   dk

7. Instruction is provided by approved or certificated ESL or bilingual teachers (at the elementary level).   1   2   3   4   dk

8. Instruction is provided by teachers who are proficient in English.   1   2   3   4   dk

9. Instructional materials reflect the curriculum objectives.   1   2   3   4   dk

10. Sufficient instructional and enrichment materials are available for the number of students served.   1   2   3   4   dk

11. The students' interests, experiences and culture are integrated into the instructional program.   1   2   3   4   dk

12. Assessment is matched to the school- or district-adopted instructional program and curriculum objectives.   1   2   3   4   dk

13. Technology is integrated into the curriculum.   1   2   3   4   dk

NATIVE LANGUAGE INSTRUCTION

1. Curriculum objectives are aligned with those of the school/ district approved curriculum.   1   2   3   4   dk

2. Curriculum objectives are clearly defined for literacy development.   1   2   3   4   dk

3. Curriculum (or IEP) objectives are clearly defined for
   a. Social studies   1   2   3   4   dk
   b. Science   1   2   3   4   dk
   c. Mathematics   1   2   3   4   dk

4. Instruction is provided to students on the basis of individual needs as identified through the district assessment plan.   1   2   3   4   dk

5. Instruction is scheduled on a regular basis for
   a. Literacy   1   2   3   4   dk
   b. Social studies, science, and mathematics.   1   2   3   4   dk

6. Student-centered teaching strategies represent a variety of methods, approaches, and techniques that respond to individual learning styles.   1   2   3   4   dk

7. There is ample opportunity for meaningful interaction in the classroom.   1   2   3   4   dk

8. Instruction is provided primarily by approved bilingual teachers.   1   2   3   4   dk

9. Instruction of students with special needs is provided by appropriately trained personnel.   1   2   3   4   dk

10. Modifications and adaptations have been made in instruction to permit ELLs with disabilities to participate in the classroom.   1   2   3   4   dk

11. Instructional materials reflect the curriculum objectives.   1   2   3   4   dk

12. Sufficient instructional and enrichment materials are available for the number of students served.   1   2   3   4   dk

13. The students' interests, experiences and cultures are integrated into the instructional program.   1   2   3   4   dk

14. Technology is integrated into the curriculum.   1   2   3   4   dk

ACADEMIC ACHIEVEMENT

1. Curriculum objectives for ELLs are aligned with school- or district-adopted curriculum and standards for
   a. Social studies   1   2   3   4   dk
   b. Science   1   2   3   4   dk
   c. Mathematics   1   2   3   4   dk

2. Lesson plans reflect school- or district-adopted curriculum goals and objectives for
   a. Social studies   1   2   3   4   dk
   b. Science   1   2   3   4   dk
   c. Mathematics   1   2   3   4   dk

3. Provisions have been made for articulation of objectives for ELLs with disabilities among special education, bilingual/ESL education, and general education.   1 2 3 4 dk

4. Instruction is scheduled on a regular basis for
   a. Social studies   1 2 3 4 dk
   b. Science   1 2 3 4 dk
   c. Mathematics   1 2 3 4 dk

5. Instructional materials that are used reflect the school/district-adopted curriculum (or IEP) objectives and standards for
   a. Social studies   1 2 3 4 dk
   b. Science   1 2 3 4 dk
   c. Mathematics   1 2 3 4 dk

6. Sufficient instructional materials are available for ELLs with disabilities.   1 2 3 4 dk

7. Delivery of the curriculum is well coordinated among all instructional personnel.   1 2 3 4 dk

8. Teaching strategies used in the classroom represent a variety of methods, approaches, and techniques that are meaningful to students in the areas of
   a. Social studies   1 2 3 4 dk
   b. Science   1 2 3 4 dk
   c. Mathematics.   1 2 3 4 dk

9. As students' English language proficiency develops, support services in the academic content areas change accordingly.   1 2 3 4 dk

10. Technology is integrated into the curriculum.   1 2 3 4 dk

STUDENT PROGRESS DOCUMENTATION

1. Provision is made for ongoing assessment of content area concepts in a way that is meaningful to the student in
   a. Social studies   1 2 3 4 dk
   b. Science   1 2 3 4 dk
   c. Mathematics   1 2 3 4 dk

2. ELL progress is documented on an ongoing basis in English language proficiency for
   a. Oral language development   1 2 3 4 dk
   b. Literacy   1 2 3 4 dk

3. ELL progress is documented on an ongoing basis in native language proficiency for
   a. Oral language development   1 2 3 4 dk
   b. Literacy   1 2 3 4 dk

4. Information on ELL progress is communicated among all teachers on a regular basis.   1 2 3 4 dk

5. Information on the progress of ELLs and those with disabilities is communicated to parents on a regular basis in a way that is meaningful to them.   1 2 3 4 dk

6. Information on ELL progress is used to modify instruction on an ongoing basis.   1 2 3 4 dk

7. Grading of ELLs is fair and realistic.   1 2 3 4 dk

8. Documentation of progress is directly aligned with school- or district-adopted curriculum objectives.   1 2 3 4 dk

TEACHER AND STAFF EFFECTIVENESS

1. The teacher conveys clearly to ELLs required classroom tasks, activities and expectations.   1 2 3 4 dk

2. Language is used to promote learning of academic content.   1 2 3 4 dk

3. By constantly monitoring ELLs' performance, the teacher is able to modify the instructional program as needed.   1 2 3 4 dk

4. The teacher has created an instructional environment that promotes interaction among all students.   1 2 3 4 dk

5. The teacher uses effective classroom management strategies for
   a. Time   1 2 3 4 dk
   b. Discipline   1 2 3 4 dk

6. The teacher has created an instructional environment that accommodates the different learning styles of students.   1   2   3   4   dk

7. The teacher allows students the opportunity to participate in setting goals for their own learning.   1   2   3   4   dk

8. The teacher treats students with patience, dignity, and respect.   1   2   3   4   dk

9. The teacher praises students' performance appropriately.   1   2   3   4   dk

10. The teacher incorporates the students' personal interests and experiences into lessons.   1   2   3   4   dk

11. The teacher encourages students to engage in higher-order thinking.   1   2   3   4   dk

12 The teacher maintains high expectations of all students.   1   2   3   4   dk

13. The teacher takes pride in his or her work.   1   2   3   4   dk

14. The teacher shows a willingness to try out new ideas in the classroom.   1   2   3   4   dk

15. The teacher initiates discussion with colleagues regarding instructional issues.   1   2   3   4   dk

16. The teacher seeks ongoing professional development.   1   2   3   4   dk

17. Teachers and staff who serve ELLs with disabilities have appropriate special education support and resources.   1   2   3   4   dk

18. Teachers and staff who serve ELLs with disabilities have been adequately trained to develop and implement IEP goals and objectives.   1   2   3   4   dk

19. Teachers and staff show sensitivity to, and willingness to modify instruction for, ELLs with disabilities.   1   2   3   4   dk

SCHOOL CLIMATE

1. The school is a safe place for teachers and students.   1   2   3   4   dk

2. The school is characterized by an orderly environment.   1   2   3   4   dk

3. The school represents a sense of community.   1   2   3   4   dk

4. Continuous academic and social growth is associated with the school.   1   2   3   4   dk

5. Adequate instructional materials are available to teachers and students.   1   2   3   4   dk

6. Sufficient space allows appropriate instruction for all students.   1   2   3   4   dk

7. The school offers extracurricular activities that are accessible to all students.   1   2   3   4   dk

8. The school environment reflects the cultural backgrounds of all students.   1   2   3   4   dk

9. Administrators exhibit strong leadership skills.   1   2   3   4   dk

10. Goals and expectations are clearly understood by students, teachers, and administrators.   1   2   3   4   dk

11. Administrators are supportive of teachers, students, and parents.   1   2   3   4   dk

12. Administrators promote community involvement.   1   2   3   4   dk

13. Communication is open between administration and staff.   1   2   3   4   dk

14. Administrators provide for group problem-solving among teachers, students and parents as part of the decision-making process in all aspects of education.   1   2   3   4   dk

15. Teachers are motivated to take initiatives for schoolwide projects.   1   2   3   4   dk

16. Administrators afford ongoing staff development opportunities for professional and paraprofessional personnel.   1   2   3   4   dk

17. Students are motivated to learn.   1   2   3   4   dk

18. Pride in students' accomplishments is evidenced throughout the building.   1   2   3   4   dk

19. Cultural diversity is valued in the whole school.   1   2   3   4   dk

20. A sense of mutual respect is evident among all individuals in the school, including those with disabilities.   1   2   3   4   dk

21. ELLs are integrated with the general school body.   1   2   3   4   dk

22. Parents are recognized as resources and are afforded opportunities to participate in numerous school activities.   1   2   3   4   dk

23. Parents are always welcome at the school.   1   2   3   4   dk

24. A good-faith effort is made to recruit teachers who speak the students' languages.   1   2   3   4   dk

Appendix G

Example of English language proficiency standards from the World-Class Instructional Design and Assessment (WIDA) Consortium for Grades 3-5

Domain: SPEAKING — engage in oral communication in a variety of situations for a variety of purposes and audiences

Standards	Level 1 Entering	Level 2 Beginning	Level 3 Developing	Level 4 Expanding	Level 5 Bridging
Social and Instructional	• Ask for assistance with a task or needed supplies	• Ask or provide the meaning of words, phrases, or uses of relevant resources	• Ask questions to seek information or provide opinions, preferences, or wishes	• Ask for or provide clarification of information by restating ideas	• Ask for or provide specific information that confirms or denies beliefs
Language Arts	• Describe self with words and gestures (such as features, clothing, or likes and dislikes)	• Compare self with other familiar persons (such as friends, family members, or movie stars)	• Compare self with characters in literary works	• Compare self with motives or points of view of characters in literary works	• Explain differences between self-motives or points of view and those of characters in literary works
Math	• Repeat new information about **math** processes involving computation with use of manipulatives or realia (e.g., "Here are 3 groups cf 4")	• Rephrase new information about **math** processes involving computation with use of visual support	• Relate new information about **math** processes involving computation to previous experiences	• Explain or discuss uses of information about **math** processes involving computation	• Integrate or synthesize information about **math** processes involving computation to create own problems
Science	• Make collections, organize, and identify natural phenomena (such as leaves, insects, or rocks)	• Describe natural phenomena from real-life examples (e.g., "This leaf has five points")	• Describe the step-by-step process of making and organizing collections of natural phenomena (e.g., "First, I went to the park")	• Compare features of natural phenomena (e.g., "This leaf has five points while this one has two")	• Report on the physical relationships among natural phenomena
Social Studies	• Locate and show places on maps by pointing (e.g., "Here is Delaware")	• Describe locations of places on maps (e.g., "Wisconsin is between Minnesota and Michigan")	• Share locations of places on maps with partners (such as two-way tasks where each student has a map with half of the locations indicated)	• Give directions from place to place on maps using sequential language (e.g., "First, next, finally")	• Give explanations for places on maps (e.g., "I know it's the capital because there is a star")

Appendix H

Example of English Language Proficiency Standards from the World-Class Instructional Design and Assessment Consortium for Grades 6-8

Social Studies

Domain	Level 1 Entering	Level 2 Beginning	Level 3 Developing	Level 4 Expanding	Level 5 Bridging
Listening	• Locate places using a variety of geographic representations (such as globes, maps, aerial photos, or satellite images) from oral commands	• Select appropriate maps to identify regions, countries, or land forms from oral statements	• Select appropriate maps based on oral information about regions, countries, land forms, or highways	• Compare and contrast different types of maps from oral descriptions	• Evaluate the usefulness of different types of maps for different purposes from oral descriptions
Speaking	• Identify historical, governmental, or social figures or events from photographs and illustrations	• Describe historical, governmental, or social figures or events from photographs, illustrations and video	• Role play scenes from historical events or the lives of governmental or social figures from photographs, illustrations, video, and readings	• Reenact historical events or the lives of governmental or social figures based on multi-media	• Participate in plays or give monologues of historical events or people
Reading	• Chart trends based on statements with graphic support (such as changes in crop production or population shifts over a five-year period)	• Compare data based on same year information from text and charts(e.g., "Which state has the most people today?")	• Compare data from year-to-year based on information from text and charts (e.g., "Which crop is produced less today than 5 years ago?")	• Predict data for upcoming years based on information from text and charts (e.g., "If this trend continues, which state will have the most people in 5 years?")	• Interpret data from year to year based on information from grade level text and charts (e.g., "Why do you think X crop has increased over the past 5 years?")
Writing	• Use graphic organizers to produce features of historical periods	• Use graphic organizers to compare features of historical periods	• Use graphic organizers to produce descriptions of historical periods	• Use graphic organizers to produce contrastive summaries of historical periods	• Use graphic organizers to produce historical essays

Source: WIDA. (2006). Reprinted with permission.

Glossary

Academic language The language used for academic content learning at school; the language of academic discussion, of formal writing and the language of texts, for example, the language of math, language arts, science, and social studies. According to research, whereas *English language learners* may develop *social language* in one to three years, it takes five or more years for English language learners to develop sufficient abstract, discipline-specific academic language proficiency.

Acculturation Process of adjusting to and assimilating a new culture. A stage model of cultural adaptation suggests that the individual moves from fascination with the new culture to awareness of differences between the primary and new cultures, to increasing participation in the new culture, to culture shock (in which the clash between the two cultures becomes apparent), to emotional overload, to instrumental adaptation (the individual either retreats into home culture, gives up the home culture altogether, or adopts part of the home culture and part of the new culture), to integrative adaptation (the individual experiences either a culture split or successful integration), to structural adaptation (the individual maintains a comfortable balance between his or her native and new cultural practices).

Additive bilingualism The process describing the acquisition of a second language by an individual or group without loss or displacement of the first language. Additive bilingualism stands in contrast to *subtractive bilingualism.*

Authentic assessment Performance-based assessment of what students know and can do with content and language during actual tasks in real-life contexts. Authentic assessments often stand in contrast to *norm-referenced* standardized *tests.*

Bi-level analysis paradigm An operational framework for implementing *authentic assessment* consisting of an initial phase of descriptive analysis of the difficulties exhibited by an *English language learner*, followed by a detailed explanatory analysis phase. This dual-phase process requires users to describe what language difficulties are observed in the English language learner before determining why the student experiences these difficulties.

Bilingual education An educational program in which instruction is provided in two languages. There are three prototypical kinds of bilingual education: (1) *transitional bilingual education*, (2) *maintenance* or one-way developmental *bilingual education*, and (3) *dual-language* or two-way immersion. These types of bilingual education programs differ in their target populations, goals, program structures, and anticipated outcomes.

Code switching The process of alternating use of two languages during the same conversational event. Although language learners may code switch when they don't know a word in their second language, code switching is more common among highly proficient bilingual speakers.

Common underlying proficiency (CUP) Within a model of language abilities, the deepest level of human processing attribute or capacity that gives rise to all cognitive and linguistic abilities within an individual regardless of the language(s) used. This proposed attribute accounts for the fact that knowledge or skills that have been learned in one language may readily *transfer* to the second language.

Continuum of services framework A framework for assessing the learning difficulties of English language learners, identifying appropriate systemic and specific interventions to address those difficulties, and monitoring the English language learner's response to those interventions. This approach advocates *descriptive analysis* before *explanatory analysis* and the immediate provision of services independent of a formal categorization of the student as having a special education need.

Conversational fluency The highly contextualized language productions used during everyday conversation in face-to-face interaction, also known as *social language*. According to research, it generally takes one to three years for English language learners to develop social language, while it takes much longer to develop the *academic language* necessary for school success.

Descriptive analysis The first stage of analysis in the *continuum of services framework*. During this stage, the ECOS team collects information on the specific difficulties exhibited by the *English language learner* to determine what behaviors and tasks are problems in the classroom. This step of the descriptive analysis yields an *inventory of difficulties*. At the same time, information is collected about characteristics of the student's home and school life.

NOTE: This glossary contains definitions of terms used in specialized ways in the text according to the understood usage in linguistics and education. Italicized words in the glossary entries are defined in this glossary.

Discrepancy model A statistical approach to diagnosis that defines a *learning disability* as a specific discrepancy between intellectual ability (as measured by intelligence tests) and achievement as determined by a *norm-referenced test*. This traditional model stands in contrast to the *response to intervention (RTI) model*, also known as the *dual discrepancy model*, as well as the *continuum of services framework*.

Dual discrepancy model A description of the process that determines if the child responds to scientific, research-based intervention; an example is the *response to intervention model*. This alternative model stands in contrast to the traditional *discrepancy model*.

Dual language education A model or type of *bilingual education* that targets *English language learners* and English speakers who learn together through two languages in integrated classes for at least five years. The goals are bilingualism, biliteracy, academic achievement through two languages, and cross-cultural competence. These programs are also referred to as two-way immersion programs.

Early intervention services Phrase used in the 2004 reauthorization of the Individuals with Disabilities Education Improvement Act (IDEA) that refers to addressing the needs of students and determining the need and eligibility for services on the basis of pre-referral interventions. This service model stands in contrast to *discrepancy models* used to place students into special education.

ELL – LD Abbreviation for *English language learner* without a *learning disability*. The learning difficulties that this student experiences are due to *extrinsic* factors, and not to an *intrinsic* learning disability.

ELL + LD Abbreviation for *English language learner* with a *learning disability*. The learning difficulties that this student experiences are due, at least in part, to an *intrinsic* learning disability.

ELL ± LD Abbreviation for *English language learner* with or without a *learning disability*. Rather than asking whether the ELL has a learning disability or not, the evaluator reframes the question by considering the difficulties the ELL is experiencing as possibly indicative of an underlying *intrinsic* learning disability in addition to the normal manifestations of learning another language, and provide interventions that would support both needs.

English language learners (ELLs) Language minority students in the United States who are learning English. Previously referred to as limited English proficient (LEP) or potential English proficient (PEP) students.

English as a second language (ESL) Referring to programs or classes that target students identified as *English language learners*, with the goal of promoting the language development and social integration of these students.

Ensuring a Continuum of Services (ECOS) Team A team of four or five individuals with expertise in special education and ESL/bilingual education. This team collaborates in information gathering, interpreting information, suggesting interventions (a *continuum of services*), and monitoring the progress of the *English language learners* experiencing difficulties at school.

Explanatory analysis The second stage of analysis in the *continuum of services framework*. In this stage the evaluator seeks to determine the causal factors for the difficulties during the *descriptive analysis*.

Extrinsic Causal variables or factors located outside of the child. Generally accounted for, for example, one of the seven integral factors influencing *English language learners* at school (learning environment, personal and family factors, physical and psychological, previous schooling, oral language and literacy development, academic achievement, cross-cultural factors). Extrinsic factors are to be contrasted with *intrinsic* factors.

Funds of knowledge Areas of expertise that families or communities or cultural groups have developed outside of school (for example, about professional or cultural practices). Educators can tap into and build on these areas of expertise in order to develop students' academic knowledge and skills.

Individualized Education Plan (IEP) Federally-mandated plan for school-based services provided to children with exceptionalities. These services must be developed jointly by the student's family and professional interventionists, based upon multidisciplinary assessment of the student, and include services to enhance the academic development of the student.

Individualized Intervention Tier II within the *response to intervention (RTI)* approach. A Tier II intervention is intended for students who need additional support. These students are typically given individualized intervention plans.

Individuals with Disabilities Education Improvement Act (IDEA) Federal legislation enacted to ensure the rights and provide appropriate and necessary public educational services to students with exceptionalities. Also known as the Individuals with Disabilities Education Act. First passed in 1975 as the Education Act for All Handicapped (PL 94-142) with subsequent re-authorizations (including 2004).

Intensive Intervention Tier III within the *response to intervention (RTI)* approach. A Tier III intervention may be comprised of specialized individualized interventions for students with significant needs. This level of support may involve special education services or may be employed as the last set of specific, one-on-one interventions before placement of the child into special education.

Interventions Strategies used to address a student's observed learning difficulty. See *individualized interventions, intensive interventions, specific interventions, systemic interventions, universal interventions*.

Intrinsic Causal variables or factors located within the child. Generally accounted for by semiotic, cognitive, or linguistic impairments. Intrinsic factors are to be contrasted to *extrinsic* factors.

Inventory of Difficulties (IOD) A compiled list of all the difficulties that a student exhibits. This list can be generated from scratch based on *ECOS team* observations, or it can be based on a previously generated list and revised according to ECOS team observations.

Learning disability   Any of a variety of cognitive, perceptual, language, or mathematical disabilities that lead to difficulties in learning in an academic setting.

Maintenance bilingual education   A model or type of developmental *bilingual education* for *English language learners* and, at times, English speakers who are proficient in the target language. These programs last at least five years. Their goals are bilingualism, biliteracy, academic achievement in two languages, and positive cultural identity development. These programs are also referred to as one-way developmental bilingual programs.

Norm-referenced Test   Standardized test designed to measure a particular skill or knowledge-base wherein student scores are ranked by performance and distributed along a bell curve expressed in percentages, percentiles, or stanines.

Resistant to instruction/intervention   Designation for students who do not respond to instruction in the form of either a *universal intervention* or to *individualized interventions*. These students' *response to intervention* is assessed, and new interventions within the *continuum of services framework* are identified by the *ECOS team* and implemented in practice.

Response to intervention (RTI)   A three tiered framework that seeks to improve the learning environment for all students within the classroom by supporting both teachers and students and keeping track of the students who resist *interventions*. RTI stands in contrast to the *discrepancy model*.

Sheltered instruction   Educational services that offer *English language learners* access to grade-level core content courses taught in English using instructional strategies designed to make the content concepts comprehensible while students are acquiring English. Such programs/classes are sometimes referred to as sheltered English immersion (SEI) or specially designed academic instruction in English (SDAIE). The term sheltered instruction may also be used to describe actual instructional strategies (such as those designed to make content comprehensible to ELLs in the academic mainstream) rather than to a program design.

Social language   The highly contextualized language used for everyday conversation in face-to-face interaction, also known as *conversational fluency*.

According to research, it generally takes one to three years for *English language learners* to develop social language, while it takes much longer for ELLs to develop the *academic language* necessary for school success.

Specific interventions   Teaching designed to assist an individual student overcome or cope with specific identified difficulties in school.

Subtractive bilingualism   The process describing the acquisition of a second language by an individual or group accompanied by loss or displacement of the first language. It is to be contrasted with *additive bilingualism*.

Systemic interventions   Interventions designed to most appropriately address the difficulties *English language learners* encounter in school. These interventions are generally applied systemwide, at the school or district level. It is possible that these systemic interventions may lead to policy changes that affect education at an even more extensive level.

Teacher Assistance Team   School-based problem-solving team designed to combine the knowledge and expertise of the team members in a collaborative fashion to meet the needs of students in general education who are experiencing academic difficulties. Also known as Student Support Teams or Student Services Teams, they are intended to be a general education initiative for problem-solving prior to special education alternatives.

Transfer   Process wherein the knowledge or skills learned in one language is applied in the second language. Transfer can be general such as reading comprehension and strategy use, or specific such as word recognition, vocabulary, and spelling. Transfer can be positive and help the learner (as in the area of cognates), or transfer can be negative and result in errors or interference, as in incorrect word order or false cognates.

Transitional bilingual education   A model or type of bilingual education that targets *English language learners*. The student's primary language is used for some content-area instruction for a limited number of years (generally one to three years in early-exit programs and four to five years in late-exit programs). These programs aim to promote mastery of academic material while students are learning English. As ELLs become proficient in English, they transition from the bilingual program to the all-English academic mainstream.

Universal Intervention   Tier I in the *response to intervention (RTI)* approach. A Tier I or universal intervention is available to all students, for example, in the form of additional mini-lessons during classroom writing instruction for all students.

References

Agar, M. (1994). *Language shock: Understanding the culture of conversation.* New York: William Morrow.

Ahlsén, E. (2005). Argumentation with restricted linguistic ability: Performing a role play with aphasia or in a second language. *Clinical Linguistics & Phonetics, 19*(5), 433–451.

Allington, R. (2001). *What really matters for struggling readers: Designing research-based programs.* Portsmouth, NH: Heinemann.

Allington, R. (2002). *Big brother and the national reading curriculum: How ideology trumped evidence.* Portsmouth, NH: Heinemann.

Alsop, P., & McCaffery, T. (Eds.). (1993). *How to cope with childhood stress: A practical guide for teachers.* Harlow, UK: Longman.

Alvermann, D. (1991). The Discussion Web: A graphic aid for learning across the curriculum. *Reading Teacher, 45,* 92–99.

Ambrose, D. (1987). *Managing complex change.* Pittsburgh, PA: Enterprise Group.

American Federation of Teachers. (1994, July 18). Teachers urge caution of full inclusion, poll finds [ATF news release]. Washington, DC: Author.

American Psychiatric Association. (2000). *Diagnostic and statistical manual of mental disorders* (4th ed., text revision). Washington, DC: Author.

Anastasi, A., & Urbiba, S. (1997). *Psychological testing* (7th ed.). Englewood Cliffs, NJ: Prentice–Hall.

Anderson–Levitt, K. M. (2003). *Local meanings, global schooling: Anthropology and world culture theory.* New York: Palgrave Macmillan.

Armstrong, E. (2005). Language disorder: A functional linguistic perspective. *Clinical Linguistics & Phonetics, 19*(3), 137–153.

Arnold, D. H., & Doctoroff, G. L. 2003. The early education of socioeconomically disadvantaged children. *Annual Review of Psychology, 54,* 517–545.

Artiles, A., Higareda, H., Rueda, R., & Salazar, J. J. (2005). Within–group diversity in minority disproportionate representation: English language learners in urban school districts. *Exceptional Children, 71.*

Artiles, A. J., & Ortiz, A. A. (2002). *English language learners with special education needs: Identification, assessment and instruction.* McHenry, IL: Delta Systems.

Asgedom, M. (2003). *The code: The five secrets of teen success.* New York: Little, Brown.

Aspel, A. D., Willis, W. G., & Faust, D. (1998). School psychologists' diagnostic decision-making processes: Objective-subjective discrepancies. *Journal of School Psychology, 36*(2), 137–149.

Assistance to States for the Education of Children with Disabilities and Preschool Grants for Children with Disabilities. (2006, Aug. 14). Final Regulations. *Federal Register, 71*(156), 46539–46863.

August, D. (2006). How does first language literacy relate to second language literacy development? In E. Hamayan & R. Freeman (Eds.), *English language learners at school: A guide for administrators* (pp. 71–72). Philadelphia: Caslon.

August, D., & Hakuta, K. (1997). *Improving schooling for language minority children: A research agenda.* Washington, DC: National Research Agenda Council and Institute of Medicine, National Academics Press.

August, L. R., & Gianola. B. A. (1987). Symptoms of war trauma-induced psychiatric disorders: Southeast Asian refugees and Vietnam veterans. *International Migration Review, 21,* 820–832.

Bahr, M., Fuchs, D., & Fuchs, L. S. (1999). Mainstream assistance teams: A consultation–based approach to prereferral intervention. In S. Graham & K. Harris (Eds.), *Working together* (pp. 87–116). Cambridge, MA: Brookline Books.

Banks, J. (2001). *Multicultural education: Issues and perspectives.* New York: John Wiley & Sons.

Banks, J. (2005). *Cultural diversity and education: Foundations, curriculum, and teaching* (5th ed.). New York: Allyn & Bacon.

Bartolo, P. A., Dockrell, J., & Lunt, I. (2001). Naturalistic decision-making task processes in multiprofessional assessment of disability. *Journal of School Psychology, 39*(4), 499–519.

Bedore, L. M., Peña, E. D., García, M., & Cortez, C. (2005). Conceptual versus monolingual scoring: When does it make a difference? *Language, Speech and Hearing in Schools, 36,* 188–120.

Bennett, C. (1995). *Comprehensive multicultural education: Theory and practice.* Needham Heights, MA: Allyn & Bacon.

Benton, A. L. (1994). Neuropsychological assessment. *Annual Review of Psychology, 45,* 1–23.

Berger, D. (1977). The survivor syndrome: A problem of nosology and treatment. *American Journal of Psychotherapy, 31,* 238–251.

Berliner, D. C., & Biddle, B. J. (1995). *The manufactured crisis: Myth, fraud and the attack on America's public schools.* Reading, MA: Perseus Books.

Berry, J. W., Poortinga, Y. H., Segall, M. H., & Dasen, P. R. (2002). *Cross-cultural psychology: Research and applications.* New York: Cambridge University Press.

Bhat, P., Rapport, M.J.K., & Griffin, C. C. (2000). A legal perspective on the use of specific reading methods for students with learning disabilities. *Learning Disability Quarterly, 23,* 283–297.

Bialystock, E. (2001). *Bilingualism in development: Language, literacy and cognition.* Cambridge: Cambridge University Press.

Blackburn, C. (1991). *Poverty and health: Working with families.* Buckingham: Open University Press.

Blaxter, M. (1990). *Health and lifestyles.* London: Routledge.

Blosser, J. L. (1990). A strategic planning process for service delivery changes. *Best Practices in School Speech-Language Pathology, 1,* 81–88.

Bode, B. A. (1989). Dialogue journal writing. *Reading Teacher,* April, 568–571.

Bolger, K. E., Patterson, C. J., Thomson, W.W.M., & Kupersmidt, J. B. (1995). Psychosocial adjustment among children experiencing persistent and intermittent family economic hardship. *Child Development, 66,* 1107–1129.

Boocock, S. S. (1972). *An introduction to the sociology of learning.* Boston: Houghton-Mifflin.

Bradley, R. H., & Corwyn, R. F. (2002). Socioeconomic status and child development. *Annual Review of Psychology, 53,* 371–399.

Brinton, B., & Fujiki, M. (1994). Ways to teach conversation. In J. Duchan, L. Hewitt, & R. Sonnenmeier (Eds.), *Pragmatics: From theory to practice* (pp. 59–71). Englewood Cliffs, NJ: Prentice-Hall.

Bronfenbrenner, U. (1979). *The ecology of human development.* Cambridge, MA: Harvard University Press.

Brooks–Gunn, J., & Duncan, G. (1997). The effects of poverty on children. *Future child, 7,* 55–71.

Brophy, J. E., & Good, T. L. (1974). *Teacher-student relationships: Causes and consequences.* New York: Holt Rinehart & Winston.

Brown, R.W. (1973). *A first language: The early stages.* Cambridge, MA: Harvard University Press.

Bruner, J.S. (1981). The social context of language acquisition. *Language and Communication, 1,* 155–178.

Bruner, J. S. (1983). *In search of mind: Essays in autobiography.* New York: Harper-Row.

Bruner, J. S. (1990). *Acts of meaning.* Cambridge, MA: Harvard University Press.

Bruner, J. S. (1996). *The culture of education.* Cambridge: Blackwells.

Bruner, J. S. (2006). *The selected works of Jerome S. Bruner.* Vol. I. *In search of pedagogy.* New York: Routledge.

Bunce, B. (2003). Children with culturally diverse backgrounds. In L. McCormick, D. F. Loeb, & Schiefelbusch, R.L. (Eds.). *Supporting children with communication difficulties in inclusive settings* (2nd ed., pp. 367–408). Boston: Pearson Education.

Bussing, R., Schoenberg, N. E., & Perwien, A. R. (1998). Knowledge and information about ADHD: Evidence of cultural differences among African-American and white parents. *Social Science and Medicine, 64,* 919–928.

Calkins, L., with Lydia Bellino. (1997). *Raising lifelong learners: A parent's guide.* Cambridge, MA: Perseus Books.

Cambourne, B. (1988). *The whole story: Natural learning and the acquisition of literacy in the classroom.* Auckland, NZ: Ashton Scholastic.

Cambourne, B., & Turbill, J. (Eds.). (1994). *Responsive evaluation: Making judgments about student literacy.* Portsmouth, NH: Heinemann.

Campbell, D. T., & Kenny, D. A. (1999). *A primer on regression artifacts.* New York: Guilford Press.

Campbell, J. P. (1996). Group differences and personnel decisions: Validity, fairness, and affirmative action. *Journal of Vocational Behavior, 49*(2), 122–158.

Carlson, V. J., & Harwood, R. L. (1999). Understanding and negotiating cultural differences concerning early developmental competence: The sixth raisin solution. *Zero to Three,* December 1999/January 2000, 20–23.

Carroll, J. B. (1993). *Human cognitive abilities.* Cambridge: Cambridge University Press.

Carroll, J. B. (1997). Psychometrics, intelligence and public perception. *Intelligence, 24,* 25–52.

Chaikind, S., Danielson, L. C., & Brauen, M. L. (1993). What do we know about the costs of special education? A selected review. *Journal of Special Education, 26,* 344–370.

Chalfant, J., & Pysh, M. (1989). Teacher assistance teams: Five descriptive studies on 96 teams. *Remedial & Special Education, 10*(6), 49–58.

Chalfant, J. C., Pysh, M. V., & Moultrie, R. (1979). Teacher assistance teams: A model for within building problem solving. *Learning Disability Quarterly, 2,* 85–95.

Chamberlain, P., & Medeiros–Landurand, P. (1991). Practical considerations in the assessment of bilingual students. In E. V. Hamayan & J. S. Damico (Eds.), *Limiting bias in the assessment of bilingual students* (pp. 111–156). Austin: PRO–ED.

Chamot, A. U., & O'Malley, J. M. (1994). *The CALLA handbook: Implementing the cognitive academic learning approach.* New York: Addison-Wesley.

Chandler, M. K., Dunaway, C., Levine, D., & Damico, J. (2005). *Serving students with language learning disorders collaboratively: A transdisciplinary model.* A miniseminar presented at the annual meeting of the American Speech-Language-Hearing Association, San Diego, CA.

Chase, N. (1999). *Burdened children: Theory, research and treatment of parentification.* Thousand Oaks, CA: Sage.

Cheng, L. L. (1991). *Assessing Asian language performance: Guidelines for evaluating limited-English proficient students* (2nd ed.). Oceanside, CA: Academic Communication Associates.

Cherkes–Julkowski, M., Sharp, S., & Stolzenberg J. (Eds.). (1997). *Rethinking attention deficit disorders.* Cambridge, MA: Brookline Books.

Chow, P., & Cummins, J. (2005). Affirming identity in multilingual classrooms. *Educational Leadership: The Whole Child, 63*(1), 38–43.

Christian, D. (2006). What kinds of programs are available for English language learners? In E. Hamayan & R. Freeman (Eds.), *English language learners at school: A guide for administrators* (pp. 81–83) Philadelphia: Caslon.

Clay, M. (1985). *Early detection of reading difficulties.* Portsmouth, NH: Heinemann.

Clay, M. (1991). *Becoming literate: The construction of inner control.* Portsmouth, NH: Heinemann.

Clay, M. (1998). *By different paths to common outcomes.* York, ME: Stenhouse.

Cloud, N. (1994). Special education needs of second language students. In F. Genesee (Ed.), *Educating second language children: The whole child, the whole curriculum, the whole community* (pp. 243–277). New York: Cambridge University Press.

Cloud, N. 2006. How can we best serve English language learners who do have special needs such as a disability? In E. Hamayan & R. Freeman (Eds.), *English language learners at school: A guide for administrators* (pp. 208–210). Philadelphia, PA: Caslon.

Coelho, E. (1991). *Caribbean students in Canadian schools: Book two.* Markham, ON: Pippin Publishing.

Coelho, E. (1994). *Learning together in the multicultural classroom.* Markham, ON: Pippin Publishing.

Coles, G. (1987). *The learning mystique: A critical look at "learning disabilities."* New York: Pantheon Books.

Collier, V. P. (1987). Age and rate of acquisition of second language for academic purposes. *TESOL Quarterly, 221,* 617–641.

Collier, V. P., & Thomas, W. P. (1997). *School effectiveness for language minority students.* Washington, DC: National Clearinghouse for English Language Acquisition. Available: *www.ncela.gwu.edu/ncbepubs/resource/effectiveness/index.html.*

Collier, V. P., & Thomas, W. P. (2002). *A national study of school effectiveness for language minority students' long–term academic achievement.* Santa Cruz, CA, and Washington, DC: Center for Research on Education, Diversity and Excellence. Available: *www.crede.ucsc.edu/reserach/llaa/1.1_final.html.*

Collins, H. M. (1998). Socialness and the undersocialized conception of society. *Science, Technology, & Human Values, 23,* 494–516.

Commins, N. (2006). What are the critical features of programs for English language learners? In E. Hamayan & R. Freeman (Eds.), *English language learners at school: A guide for administrators* (pp. 99–101). Philadelphia: Caslon.

Commins, N. L., & Miramontes, O. B. (2005). *Linguistic diversity and teaching.* Mahwah, NJ: Erlbaum.

Cook, G. I., Marsh, R. L., & Hicks, J. L. (2003). Halo and devil effects demonstrate valenced-based influences on source-monitoring decisions. *Conscious Cognition, 12*(2), 257–278.

Corsaro, W. A., & Nelson, E. (2003, July). Children's collective activities and peer culture in early literacy in American and Italian preschools. *Sociology of Education, 76,* 209–227.

Cousins, J. H., Power, T. G., & Olvera-Ezzell, N. (1993). Mexican-American mothers' socialization strategies: Effects of education, acculturation, and health locus of control. *Journal of Experimental Child Psychology, 55,* 258–276.

Covington, M. V. (1992). *Making the grade: A self-worth perspective on motivation and school reform.* New York: Cambridge University Press.

Crago, M., & Paradis, J (2003). Two of a kind? Commonalities and variation in languages and language learners. In Y. Levy & J. Schaeffer (Eds.), *Language competence across populations: Towards a definition of specific language impairment* (pp. 97–110). Mahwah, NJ: Erlbaum.

Crandall, J., with Stein, H., & Nelson, J. (2006). What kinds of knowledge and skills do mainstream teachers, English as a second language teachers, bilingual teachers, and support staff need to implement an effective program for English language learners? In E. Hamayan & R. Freeman (Eds.), *English language learners at school: A guide for administrators* (pp. 169–178). Philadelphia: Caslon.

Crawford, A. N. (1994). Communicative approaches to second language acquisition: From oral language development into the core curriculum and L2 literacy. In C. F. Leyba (Ed.), *Schooling and language minority students: A theoretical framework* (2nd ed., pp. 79–131). Los Angeles: Evaluation, Dissemination, and Assessment Center, California State University.

Crawford, J. (2006). What does a valid and reliable accountability system for English language learners need to include? In E. Hamayan & R. Freeman (Eds.), *English language learners at school: A guide for administrators* (pp. 6–9). Philadelphia: Caslon.

Cronbach, L. J. (1957). The two disciplines of scientific psychology. *American Psychologist, 12,* 671–684.

Cronbach, L. J. (1975). Beyond the two disciplines of scientific psychology. *American Psychologist, 30,* 116–127.

Crowe, L. (2003). Comparison of two reading feedback strategies in improving the oral and written language performance of children with language-learning disabilities. *American Journal of Speech-Language Pathology, 12,* 16–27.

Culotta, B. (1994). Representational play and story enactments: Formats for language intervention. In J. Duchan, L. Hewitt, & R. Sonnenmeier (Eds.), *Pragmatics: From theory to practice* (pp. 105–119). Englewood Cliffs, NJ: Prentice-Hall.

Cummins, J (1981). The role of primary language development in promoting educational success for language minority students. In *Schooling and language minority students* (pp. 3–49). Sacramento, CA: California Department of Education.

Cummins, J. (1984). *Bilingualism and special education: Issues in assessment and pedagogy.* Clevedon, UK: Multilingual Matters.

Cummins, J. (1996). *Negotiating identities: Education for empowerment in a diverse society.* Sacramento, CA: California Association for Bilingual Education.

Cummins, J. (2000). *Language, power and pedagogy: Bilingual children in the crossfire.* Clevedon, UK: Multilingual Matters.

Cummins, J. (2006). How long does it take for an English language learner to become proficient in a second language? In E. Hamayan & R. Freeman (Eds.), *English language learners at school: A guide for administrators* (pp. 59–61). Philadelphia, PA: Caslon.

Dahl, K. L., Scharer, P. L., Lawson, L. L., & Grogan, P. R. (1999). Phonics instruction and student achievement in whole language first-grade classrooms. *Reading Research Quarterly, 34,* 312–341.

Damico, J. S. (1987). Addressing language concerns in the schools: The SLP as consultant. *Journal of Childhood Communication Disorders, 11*(1), 17–40.

Damico, J. S. (1991). Descriptive assessment of communicative ability in limited English proficient students. In E. V. Hamayan & J. S. Damico (Eds.), *Limiting bias in the assessment of bilingual students* (pp. 157–218). Austin: PRO-ED.

Damico, J. S. (1992). Performance assessment of language minority students. *Proceedings of the National Research Symposium on Limited English Proficient Students' Issues: Focus on Evaluation and Measurement* (pp. 137–172). Washington, DC: OBEMLA.

Damico, J. S. (1993). Establishing expertise in communicative disorders: Implications for the speech-language pathologist. In D. Kovarsky, M. Maxwell, & J. Damico (Eds.), *Language interaction in clinical and educational settings. ASHA Monographs, 30,* 92–98.

Damico, J. S. (2003). The role of theory in clinical practice: Reflections on model building. *Advances in Speech-Language Pathology, 5,* 57–60.

Damico, J. S. (2006). *Shared reading with the exceptional child.* Portland, OR: National CEU. Available: *http://modavox.com/nationalceu.*

Damico, J. S., Damico, H., & Nelson, R. (2003). Impact of mixed instruction on meaning making in literacy. Poster presented at the Annual meeting of the American Speech-Language-Hearing Association, Chicago.

Damico, J. S., & Damico, S. K. (1993a). Language and social skills from a diversity perspective: Considerations for the speech-language pathologist. *Language, Speech, and Hearing Services in Schools, 24,* 236–243.

Damico, J. S., & Damico, S. K. (1993b). Mapping a course over different roads: Language teaching with special populations. In J. W. Oller, Jr. (Ed.), *Methods that work: A smorgasbord of language teaching ideas* (2nd ed., pp. 320–331). New York: Newbury House.

Damico, J. S., & Hamayan, E. V. (1991). Implementing appropriate assessment in the real world. In E. V. Hamayan & J. S. Damico (Eds.), *Limiting bias in the assessment of bilingual students* (pp. 303–318). Austin, TX: PRO–ED.

Damico, J. S., & Hamayan, E. V. (1992). *Multicultural language intervention: Addressing culturally and linguistically diverse issues.* Chicago: Riverside.

Damico, J. S., & Nelson, R. L. (2005). Interpreting problematic behavior: Systematic compensatory adaptations as emergent phenomena in autism. *Clinical Linguistics and Phonetics, 19*(4), 405–418.

Damico, J. S., Nelson, R. L., & Bryan, L. (2005). Literacy as a sociocultural process. In M. Ball (Ed.), *Clinical sociolinguistics* (pp. 242–249). Oxford: Blackwell Publishers.

Damico, J. S., & Nye, C. (1990). Collaborative Issues in multicultural populations. *Best Practices in School Speech-Language Pathology, 1,* 127–139.

Damico. J. S., Müller, N., & Ball, M. J. (2004). Owning up to complexity: A sociocultural orientation to Attention deficit hyperactivity disorder. *Seminars in Speech and Language, 25*(3), 277–285.

Damico, J. S., Oller, J. W., and Storey, M. E. (1983). The diagnosis of language disorders in bilingual children: Pragmatic and surface–oriented criteria. *Journal of Speech and Hearing Disorders, 48,* 285–294.

Damico, J. S., & Simmons-Mackie, N. N. (2003). Qualitative research and speech-language pathology: Impact and promise in the clinical realm. *American Journal of Speech Language Pathology, 12,* 131–143.

Damico, J. S., Smith, M., & Augustine, L. L. (1996). Multicultural populations and childhood language disorders. In M. Smith and J. S. Damico (Eds.), *Childhood language disorders* (pp. 272–299). New York: Thieme Medical Publishers.

Davidson, A. L. (1996). *Making and molding identity in schools: Student narratives on race, gender, and academic engagement.* Albany: SUNY Press.

De Jong, E. (2006). How do you decide what kind of program for English language learners is appropriate for your school? In E. Hamayan & R. Freeman (Eds.), *English language learners at school: A guide for administrators* (pp. 90–92). Philadelphia: Caslon.

Delpit, L. (1988). The silenced dialogue: Power and pedagogy in educating other people's children. *Harvard Educational Review, 58,* 78–95.

Dionisio, M. (1994). Teaching reading strategies in a "remedial" reading class. In C. Weaver (Ed.), *Reading process and practice: From socio-psycholinguistics to whole language* (2nd ed., pp. 537–543). Portsmouth, NH: Heinemann.

Duckworth, E. (1987). *"The having of wonderful ideas" and other essays on teaching and learning.* New York: Teachers College Press.

Duckworth, E. (1997). *Teacher to teacher: Learning from each other.* New York: Teachers College Press.

Dudley-Marling, C. (2000). *A family affair: When school troubles come home.* Portsmouth, NH: Heinemann.

Dudley-Marling, C., & Paugh, P. (2004). *A classroom teacher's guide to struggling readers.* Portsmouth, NH: Heinemann.

DuFour, R., & Baker, R. (1998). *Professional learning communities: Best practice for enhancing student achievement.* Bloomington, IN: National Education Service.

Dunaway, C. (2004). Attention deficit hyperactivity disorder: An authentic story in the schools and its implications. *Seminars in Speech and Language, 25*(3), 27–275.

Durkheim, E., & Coser, L. A. (1984). *The division of labor in society.* New York: Fred Press.

Echevarria, J., & Short, D. (2003). *The effects of sheltered instruction on the achievement of limited English proficient students.* Washington, DC: Center for Applied Linguistics. Available: *www.cal.org/crede/si.htm.*

Echevarria, J., Vogt, M. E., & Short, D. (2004). *Making content comprehensible to English learners: The SIOP model* (2nd ed.) Boston: Pearson/Allyn & Bacon.

Edelsky, C. (1999). On critical whole language practice: Why, what, and a bit of how. In C. Edelsky (Ed.), *Making justice our project* (p. 736). Urbana, IL: National Council of Teachers of English.

Edelsky, C., Altwerger, B., & Flores, B. (1990). *Whole language: What's the difference?* Portsmouth, NH: Heinemann.

Education Alliance at Brown University. (2006). *The knowledge loom.* Providence, RI: Brown University.

Ehren, B. J., & Nelson, N. W. (2005). The responsiveness to intervention approach and language impairment. *Topics in Language Disorders, 25,* 120–131.

Elias, M. J., & Dilworth, J. E. (2003). Ecological/developmental theory, context-based best practice, and school-based action research: cornerstones of school psychology training and policy. *Journal of School Psychology, 41*(3), 293–297.

Elley, W. B. (1997). In praise of incidental learning: Lessons from some empirical findings on language acquisition. *CELA List of Reports, 4.9,10002,* Albany, NY: Center on English Learning and Achievement.

Emery, O. B., & Csikszentmihalyi, M. (1981). The socialization effects of cultural role models in ontogenetic development and upward mobility. *Child Psychiatry and Human Development, 12*, 3–18.

Entwisle, D. R., Alexander, K. L. & Olson, L. S. (1997). *Children, schools, and inequality.* Boulder, CO: Westview Press.

Epstein, J. (2001). *School, family, and community partnerships: Preparing educators and improving schools.* Boulder, CO: Westview Press.

Erickson, F. (1987). Transformation and school success: The politics and culture of educational achievement. *Anthropology and Educational Quarterly, 18*, 335–357.

Ewy, C. A. (2002). *Teaching with visual frameworks: Focused learning and achievement through instructional graphics co–created by students and teachers.* Thousand Oaks, CA: Corwin Press.

Fabiano, L., & Goldstein, B. (2005). Phonological cross-linguistic effects in bilingual Spanish-English speaking children. *Journal of Multilingual Communication Disorders, 3*(1), 56–64.

Fadiman, A. (1997). *The spirit catches you and you fall down. A Hmong child, her American doctors, and the collision of two cultures.* New York: Noonday Press.

Feeley, T. H. (2002). Comment on halo effects in rating and evaluation research. *Human Communication Research, 28*(4), 578–586.

Fielding, N. G., & Fielding, J. L. (1986). *Linking data.* Beverly Hills, CA: Sage.

Five, C. L. (1995). Ownership for the special needs child: Individual and educational dilemmas. In C. Dudley-Marling & D. Searle (Eds.), *Who owns learning? Questions of autonomy, choice, and control* (pp. 113–127). Portsmouth, NH: Heinemann.

Fletcher, J. M., Denton, C. A., Fuchs, L. S., & Vaughn, S. R. (2005). Multi-tiered reading instruction: Linking general education and special education. In S. O. Richardson & J. W. Gilger (Eds.), *Research-based education and intervention: What we need to know* (pp. 21–44). Baltimore: International Dyslexia Association.

Fletcher, J. M., Francis, D. J., Shaywitz, S. E., Lyon, G. R., Foorman, B. R., Stuebing, K. K., & Shaywitz, B. A. (1998). Intelligent testing and the discrepancy model for children with learning disabilities. *Learning Disabilities Research & Practice, 13*(2), 186–203.

Flick, U. (1992). Triangulation revisited: Strategy of validation or alternative? *Journal for the Theory of Social Behavior, 27*, 175–198.

Flynn, J. R. (2000). The hidden history of IQ and special education: Can the problems be solved? *Psychology, Public Policy, and Law, 6*(2), 191–198.

Fradd, S. H. (1993). *Creating the team to assist culturally and linguistically diverse students.* Tucson, AZ: Communication Skill Builders.

Fradd, S. H., & Weismantal, M. J. (1989). *Meeting the needs of culturally and linguistically diverse students: A handbook for educators.* Boston: College-Hill Press.

Freeman, D. (1998). *Doing teacher research: From inquiry to understanding.* Boston: Heinle & Heinle.

Freeman, D. E., & Freeman, Y. S. 2001. *Between worlds: Access to second language acquisition* (2nd ed.). Portsmouth, NH: Heinemann.

Freeman, D., & Freeman, Y. (2003). Teaching English learners to read: Learning or acquisition? In G.G.

García (Ed.), English *Learners reaching the highest level of English proficiency* (pp. 34–54). Newark, NJ: International Reading Association.

Freeman, Y., & Freeman, D. (2002). *Closing the achievement gap: How to reach limited formal schooling and long-term English learners.* Portsmouth, NH: Heinemann.

Freijo, T. D., & Jaeger, R. M. (1976). Social class and race as concomitants of composite halo in teachers' evaluative rating of pupils. *American Educational Research Journal, 13*(1), 1–14.

Friend, M., & Cook, L. (1992). The ethics of collaboration. *Journal of Educational and Psychological Consultation, 3*(2), 181–184.

Friend, M., & Cook, L. (1996). *Interactions: Collaboration skills for school professionals.* White Plains, NY: Longman.

Frick, P. J., & Lahey, B. B. (1991). The nature and characteristics of attention-deficit hyperactivity disorder. *School Psychology Review, 20*, 163–173.

Freppon, P., & Dahl, K. (1991). Learning about phonics in a whole language classroom. *Language Arts, 68*, 190–197.

Fuchs, D., & Fuchs, L. S. (1994). Inclusive school movement and the radicalization of special education reform. *Exceptional Children, 60*, 294–309.

Fuchs, D., Fuchs, L. S., & Compton, D. L. (2004). Identifying reading disabilities by responsiveness to instruction: Specifying measures and criteria. *Learning Disabilities Quarterly, 27*, 216–228.

Fuchs, D., Mock, D., Morgan, P. L., & Young, C. (2003). Responsiveness-to-intervention: Definitions, evidence, and implications for the learning disabilities construct. *Learning Disabilities Research & Practice, 18*, 157–171.

Fuchs, L. S. (2002). Three conceptualizations of "treatment" in a responsiveness-to-treatment framework for LD identification. In R. Bradley, L. Danielson, & D. P. Hallahan (Eds.), *Identification of learning disabilities: Research to practice* (pp. 521–529). Mahwah, NJ: Erlbaum.

Fuchs, L. S. (2003). Assessing intervention responsiveness: Conceptual and technical issues. *Learning Disabilities Research & Practice, 18*, 172–186.

Fuchs, L. S. (2004). The part, present, and future of curriculum-based measurement research. *School Psychology Review, 33*, 188–192.

Garbarino, J., Kostelny, K., & Dubrow, N. (1991). *No place to be a child.* San Francisco: Jossey-Bass.

García, E. (2005). *Teaching and learning in two languages: Bilingualism and schooling in the United States.* New York: Teachers College Press.

García, E. (2006). What is the role of culture in language learning? In E. Hamayan & R. Freeman (Eds.), *English language learners at school: A guide for administrators* (pp. 61–62). Philadelphia: Caslon.

García, G. G. (Ed.). (2003). *English learners: Reaching the highest level of English literacy.* Newark, DE: International Reading Association.

García, S. B., & Ortiz, A.A. (1988). Preventing inappropriate referrals of language minority students to special education. *Occasional Papers in Bilingual Education. NCBE New Focus, No. 5.* Silver Springs, MD: National Clearinghouse for Bilingual Education.

Garmezy, N. (1991). Resiliency and vulnerability to adverse developmental outcomes associated with poverty. *American Behavioral Scientist, 34,* 416–430.

Geekie, P., Cambourne, B., & Fitzsimmons, P. (1999). *Understanding literacy development.* Staffordshire, UK: Trentham Books.

Genesee, F. (2003). Rethinking bilingual acquisition. In J.M. deWaele (Ed.), *Bilingualism: Challenges and directions for future research* (pp. 158–182). Clevedon, UK: Multilingual Matters.

Genesee, F. (2006). How do English language learners acquire a second language at school? In E. Hamayan & R. Freeman (Eds.), *English language learners at school: A guide for administrators* (pp. 65–66). Philadelphia: Caslon.

Genesee, F., Lindholm–Leary, K., Saunders, W., & Christian, D. (2005.) English language learners in US schools: An overview of research findings. *Journal for Education for Students Placed at Risk, 10*(4), 365–385.

Genesee, F., Lindholm–Leary, K. J., Saunders, W., & Christian, D. (2006). *Educating English language learners: A synthesis of empirical evidence.* New York: Cambridge University Press.

Genesee, F., Paradis, J., & Crago, M. B. (2004). *Dual language development and disorders: A handbook on bilingualism and second language learning.* Baltimore: Paul H. Brookes.

Gersten, R., & Woodward, J. (1994). The language-minority student and special education: Issues, trends, and paradoxes. *Exceptional Children, 60*(4), 310–322.

Giangreco, M. F. (1994). Effects of a consensus building process on team decision-making: Preliminary data. *Physical Disabilities: Education and Related Services, 13*(1), 41–56.

Giangreco, M. F. (2000). Related services research for students with low-incidence disabilities: Implications for speech-language pathologists in inclusive classrooms. *Language, Speech and Hearing Services in Schools, 13*(3), 230–239.

Gibson, K. (1989). Children in political violence. *Social Science Medicine, 28,* 659–667.

Gilbert, J. K. (2005). *Constructing worlds through science education.* New York: Routledge.

Gnys, J. A., Willis, W. G., Faust, D. (1995). School psychologists' diagnoses of learning disabilities: A study of illusory correlation. *Journal of School Psychology, 33*(1), 59–73.

Goffman, E. (1964). *Stigma: Notes on the management of spoiled identity.* New York: Simon & Schuster.

Goldstein, B. A. (Ed.). (2004). *Bilingual language development and disorders in Spanish-English speakers.* Baltimore: Paul H. Brookes.

Goodman, K. (1982). *Language, literacy, and learning.* London: Routledge.

Goodman, K. (2001). *On reading. A common-sense look at the nature of language and the science of reading.* Portsmouth, NH: Heinemann.

Goodman, K. (Ed.). (2006). *Examining DIBELS: What it is and what it does.* Brandon, VT: Vermont Society for the Study of Education.

Gordon, R.G., Jr. (Ed.). (2005). *Ethnologue: Languages of the world* (15th ed.). Dallas, TX: Summer Institute of Languages International.

Gottlieb, M. (2006a). *Assessing English language learn-ers: Bridges from language proficiency to academic achievement.* Thousand Oaks, CA: Corwin Press.

Gottlieb, M. (2006b). How should you assess the academic achievement of English language learners? In E. Hamayan & R. Freeman (Eds.), *English Language Learners at School: A Guide for Administrators* (pp. 123–125). Philadelphia: Caslon.

Gottlieb, M., & Hamayan, E. (2006). Assessing oral and written language proficiency: A guide for psychologists and teachers. In G. B. Esquivel, E. Lopez, S. Nahari, & A. Brice (Eds.), *Handbook of multicultural school psychology.* Mahwah, NJ: Erlbaum.

Graves, D. H. (2002). *Testing is not teaching: What should count in education.* Portsmouth, NH: Heinemann.

Graves, M. F., & Fitzgerald, J. (2003). Scaffolding reading experiences for multilingual classrooms. In G. G. García (Ed.), *English learners reaching the highest level of English proficiency* (pp. 96–124). Newark, NJ: International Reading Association.

Greene, J. (1997). A meta-analysis of the Rossell and Baker review of the bilingual education research. *Bilingual Research Journal, 21,* 103–122.

Grosjean, F. (1998). Studying bilinguals: Methodological and conceptual issues. *Bilingualism: Language and Cognition, 1 (1),* 131–149.

Gunderson, L., & Siegel, L. S. (2001). The evils of the use of IQ tests to define learning disabilities in first- and second-language learners. *Reading Teacher, 55*(1), 48–55.

Gutiérrez, K., Baquedano-Lopez., & Tejeda, C. (1999). Rethinking diversity: Hybridity and hybrid language practices in the third space. *Mind, Culture, & Activity: An International Journal, 6*(4), 286–230.

Gutiérrez-Clellen, V. F., & Peña, E. (2001). Dynamic assessment of diverse children: A tutorial. *Language, Speech, and Hearing Services in Schools, 32,* 212–224.

Gutkin, T. B. (1990). Consultative speech-language services in the schools: A view through the looking glass of school psychology. *Best Practices in School Speech Language Pathology, 1,* 57–65.

Gutkin, T. B., & Nemeth, C. (1997). Selected factors impacting decision in prereferral intervention and other school-based teams: Exploring the intersection between school and social psychology. *Journal of School Psychology, 35*(2), 195–216.

Hakuta, K. (1986). *Mirror of language: The debate on bilingualism.* New York: Basic Books.

Hakuta, K., Butler, Y., & Witt, D. (2000). *How long does it take English learners to attain proficiency?* University of California Linguistic Minority Research Institute Policy Report 2000–1. Berkeley: University of California Linguistic Minority Research Institute.

Hall, E. T. (2001). *The hidden dimension.* New York: Double Day.

Hamayan, E. (1994). Language development of low–literacy students. In F. Genesee (Ed.), *Educating second language children: The whole child, the whole curriculum, the whole community* (pp. 278–300). New York: Cambridge University Press.

Hamayan, E. (2006). What is the role of culture in language learning? In E. Hamayan & R. Freeman (Eds.), *English language learners at school: A guide for administrators* (pp. 62–64). Philadelphia: Caslon.

Hamayan, E., & Damico, J. (Eds.). (1991). *Limiting bias*

in the assessment of bilingual students. Austin, TX: Pro Ed.

Hamayan, E., & Freeman, R. (2006). How do English language learners acquire a second language at school? In E. Hamayan & R. Freeman (Eds.), *English language learners at school: A guide for administrators* (pp. 68–71). Philadelphia: Caslon.

Harry, B., & Klingner, J. (2006). *Why are so many minority students in special education? Understanding race and disability in schools.* New York: Teachers College Press.

Hart, B., & Risley, T. R. (2003). *Meaningful differences in the everyday experience of young American children.* Baltimore: Paul H. Brookes.

Haycock, K. (1998). *Good teaching matters.* Washington, DC: Education Trust.

Heath, S. B., & McLaughlin, M. (1993). *Identity and inner city youth: Beyond ethnicity and gender.* New York: Teachers College Press.

Heider, F. (1958). *The psychology of interpersonal relations.* New York: John Wiley & Sons.

Hilliard, J., & Hamayan, E. (2006). How do you plan for language development? In E. Hamayan & R. Freeman (Eds.), *English language learners at school: A guide for administrators* (pp. 94–06). Philadelphia: Caslon.

Hoffman, D. M. (1998). A therapeutic moment? Identity, self, and culture in the anthropology of education. *Anthropology & Education Quarterly, 29,* 324–346.

Hoffman, D. M. (1999). Culture and comparative education: Toward decentering and recentering the discourse. *Comparative Education Review, 43,* 464–488.

Holm, A., & Dodd, B. (1999). Differential diagnosis of phonological disorder in two bilingual children acquiring Italian and English. *Clinical Linguistics & Phonetics, 13*(2), 113–129.

Huyck, E. E., & Fields, R. (1981). Impact of resettlement on refugee children. *International Migration Review, 15,* 246–254.

Illinois Resource Center. (1997). *The iceberg model of culture.* Des Plains, IL: Author.

Illinois Resource Center. (1999). *Learning English: The Stages.* Des Plains, IL: Author.

Illinois Resource Center. (2000). *Evaluation of instructional services for bilingual students.* Des Plaines, IL: Author.

Individuals with Disabilities Education Improvement Act, PL 108-466. (2004). 20 USC 1400.

International Reading Association. (2001). *Second language literacy instruction: A position statement of the International Reading Association.* Newark, DE: Author.

Jack, G. (2000). Ecological influences on parenting and child development. *British Journal of Social Work, 30,* 703–720.

Jen, G. (1997). Who's to judge? *New Republic,* April 21, pp. 18–19.

Jerald, C. D. (2003). *All talk no action: Putting an end to out-of-field teaching.* Washington, DC: Education Trust.

Jimenez, R. T., García, G. E., & Pearson, D. P. (1996). The reading strategies of bilingual Latina/o students who are successful English readers: Opportunities and obstacles. *Reading Research Quarterly, 31*(1), 90–112.

Jitendra, A. K., & Rohena-Diaz, E. (1996). Language assessment of students who are linguistically diverse: Why a discrete approach is not the answer. *School Psychology Review, 25*(1), 40–56.

Johnson, G. M. (2004). Constructivist remediation: Correction in context. *International Journal of Special Education, 19,* 72–88.

Johnson, K. (1989). *Trauma in the lives of children.* London: Macmillan.

Joyce, B., & Showers, B. 2002. Designing training and peer coaching: Our needs for learning. Alexandria, VA: ASCD.

Justice, L. M. (2006). Evidence-based practice, response-to-intervention, and the prevention of reading difficulties. *Language, Speech, and Hearing Services in Schools, 37,* 284–297.

Kame'enui, E., Fuchs, L.S., Good, R. Francis, D., O'Connor, R., & Simmons, D. (2006). The adequacy of tools for assessing reading competence in primary grades: A decision-making framework and review of prominently used tests. *Educational Researcher, 35,* 3–11.

Kaminski, R. A., & Good, R. H. (1998). Assessing early literacy skills in a problem solving model: Dynamic indicators of basic early literacy skills. In M. S. Shinn (Ed.), *Advanced applications of curriculum-based measurement* (pp. 113–142). New York: Guilford.

Kasten, W. (1998). One learner, two paradigms: A case study of a special education student in a multiage primary classroom. *Reading & Writing Quarterly, 14,* 335–354.

Katz, S. R. (1999). Teaching in tensions: Latino immigrant youth, their teachers and the structures of schooling. *Teachers' College Record, 100* (4), 809–840.

Kay–Raining Bird, E., Cleave, P.L., Trudeau, N., Thordardottir, E, & Sutton, A. *Bilingual children with Down syndrome: A longitudinal study.* Manuscript submitted for publication.

Kibler, J. (1996). Latino voices in children's literature: Instructional approaches in teacher training and staff development. In J. LeBlanc Flores (Ed.), *Children of la frontera: Binational efforts to serve Mexican migrant and immigrant students.* Washington, DC: ERIC Clearinghouse on Rural Education and Small Schools.

Kibler, J. (2005). How does one develop an intercultural perspective? *International Forum of Teaching and Studies, 1.*

Kiernan, B., & Swisher, L. (1990). The initial learning of novel English words: Two single-subject experiments with minority-language children. *Journal of Speech, Language and Hearing Research, 33,* 707–716.

Klasen, H. (2000). A name, what's in a name? The medicalization of hyperactivity revisited. *Harvard Review of Psychiatry, 7*(3), 334–344.

Knoff, H. A. (1983). Investigating disproportionate influence and status in multidisciplinary child study teams. *Exceptional Children, 49*(4), 367–370.

Kock, D. L. (1997). *Teacher Assistance Teams: A case study of best practices at the elementary school level.* Unpublished doctoral dissertation, Illinois State University.

Kohn, A. (1998). *What to look for in a classroom . . . and other essays.* San Francisco: Jossey-Bass.

Kohn, A. (2000). *The case against standardized testing. Raising the test scores, ruining the schools.* Portsmouth, NH: Heinemann.

Kohnert, Y. (2004). Processing skills in early sequential bilinguals. In B. Goldstein (Ed.), *Bilingual language development and disorders in Spanish-English speakers* (pp. 53–76). Baltimore: Paul H. Brookes.

Koskinen, P. S., Gambrell, L. B., Kapinus, B., & Heathington, B. S. (1988). Retelling: A strategy for enhancing students' reading comprehension. *The Reading Teacher, May,* 892–897.

Kozol, J. (1988). *Rachel and her children: Homeless families in America.* New York: Random House.

Kozol, J. (1992). *Savage inequalities: Children in America's schools.* New York: Harper Collins.

Krashen, S. (1982). *Principles and practices in second language acquisition.* Oxford, UK: Pergamon Press.

Krashen, S. (1996). Under attack: The case against bilingual education. Culver City: Language Education Associates.

Krashen, S. (2001). Does "pure" phonemic awareness training affect reading comprehension? *Perceptual and Motor Skills, 93,* 356–358.

Krashen, S. (2003). Three roles for reading for minority-language children. In G. G. Garcia (Ed.), *English learners reaching the highest level of English literacy* (pp. 55–70). Newark, DE: International Reading Association.

Krashen, S. (2004). *The power of reading.* Westport, CT: Libraries Unlimited.

Krashen, S., & Terrell, T. (1983). *The natural approach: Language acquisition in the classroom.* Hayward, CA: Alemany Press.

Kritikos, E. P. (2003). Speech–language pathologists' beliefs about language assessment of bilingual/bicultural individuals. *American Journal of Speech-Language Pathology, 12,* 73–91.

Lacey, P., & Lomas, J. (1993). *Support services and the curriculum: A practical guide to collaboration.* London: Fulton.

Laing, S. P., & Kamhi, A. (2003). Alternative assessment of language and literacy in culturally and linguistically diverse populations. *Language, Speech, and Hearing Services in Schools, 34,* 44–55.

Lambert, W. E. (1974). Culture and language as factors in learning and education. In F. E. Aboud & R. D. Mead (Eds.), *Cultural factors in learning and education.* Proceedings of the Fifth Western Washington Symposium on Learning, Bellingham, WA.

Lanauze, M., & Snow, C. (1999). The relation between first- and second-language writing skills: Evidence from Puerto Rican elementary school children in bilingual programs. *Linguistics and Education, 4,* 323–339.

Lareau, A. (1987). Social class differences in family-school relationships: The importance of cultural capital. *Sociology of Education, 60,* 73–85.

Lau, R. R. (1982). Origins of health locus of control beliefs. *Journal of Personality and Social Psychology, 31,* 322–334.

Lave, J., & Wenger, E. (1991). *Situated learning: Legitimate peripheral participation.* New York: Cambridge University Press.

Leary, M. R. (1990). Anxiety, cognition and behavior: In search of a broader perspective. In M. Booth-Butterfield (Ed.), *Communication, cognition, and anxiety* (pp. 39–44). Newbury Park, CA: Sage.

Lee, E. (1994). Taking multicultural anti–racist education seriously and Justice: An interview with Enid Lee. *Rethinking our classrooms: Teaching for equity and justice.* Milwaukee, WI: Rethinking Schools.

Lee, S. (1996). *Unraveling the "model minority stereotype": Listening to Asian American students.* New York: Teachers College Press.

Levitt, E.E. (1980). *The psychology of anxiety.* Hillsdale, NJ: Erlbaum.

Lightbown, P., & Spada, N. (2003). *How languages are learned.* Oxford, UK: Oxford University Press.

Lindholm-Leary, K. (2006). What are the most effective kinds of programs for English language learners? In E. Hamayan & R. Freeman (Eds.), *English language learners at school: A guide for administrators* (pp. 84–85). Philadelphia: Caslon.

Lubinski, D. (2000). Scientific and social significance of assessing individual differences: Sinking shafts at a few critical points. *Annual Review of Psychology, 51,* 405–444.

Lucas, T., Henze, R., & Donato, R. (1990). Promoting success of Latino language minority students: An exploratory study of six high schools. *Harvard Educational Review, 60,* 315–340.

Lupart, J. L. (1998). Setting right the delusion of inclusion: Implications for Canadian schools. *Canadian Journal of Education/Revue canadienne de l'education, 23,* 251–264.

Lupart, J .L., McKeough, A., & Yewchuk, C. (1996). *Schools in transition: Rethinking regular and special education.* Scarborough, ON: Nelson.

Lum, C. (2002). *Scientific thinking in speech and language therapy.* Mahwah, NJ: Erlbaum.

MacIntyre, P. D., & Gardner, R. C. (1991). Methods and results in the study of foreign language anxiety: A review of the literature. *Language Learning, 41,* 85–117.

Macksoud, M. S., & Aber, J. L. (1996). The war experiences and psychosocial development of children in Lebanon. *Child Development, 67,* 70–88.

Maeroff, G. I. (1993). *Team building for school change.* New York: Teachers College Press.

Magnuson, K. A., & Waldfogel, J. (2005). Early childhood care and education: Effects on ethnic and racial gaps in school readiness. *The Future of Children, 15,* 169–196.

Manning, M., Kamii, C., & Kato, T. (2005). Dynamic Indicators of Basic Early Literacy Skills (DIBELS): A tool for evaluating student learning? *Journal of Research in Childhood Education, 20,* 81–96.

Marchman, V., & Martínez-Sussman, C. (2002). Concurrent validity of caregiver/parent report measures of language for children who are learning both English and Spanish. *Journal of Speech, Language, and Hearing Research, 45*(5), 983–997.

Marler, B. (2006). How can we best serve "newcomers," students who come with interrupted formal schooling and from educational backgrounds that are very different from those in the United States? In E. Hamayan & R. Freeman (Eds.), *English language learners at school: A guide for administrators* (pp. 214–215). Philadelphia: Caslon.

Marvin, C. (1990). Problems in school-based speech-language consultation and collaboration services: Defining the terms and improving the process. *Best*

Practices in School Speech–Language Pathology, 1, 37–48.

Marzano, R. (2003). *What works in schools: Translating research into action*. Alexandria, VA: Association for Supervision and Curriculum Development.

Maslow, A., & Lowery, R. (Eds.). (1998). *Toward a psychology of being* (3rd ed.). New York: John Wiley & Sons.

McCabe, A. (1989). Differential language learning styles in young children: The importance of context. *Developmental Review, 9,* 1–20.

McCabe, A. & Peterson, C. (Eds.). (1991). *Developing narrative structure*. Hillsdale, NJ: Erlbaum.

McCormick, T. W. (1988). *Theories of reading in dialogue: An interdisciplinary study*. New York: University Press of America.

McDermott, R. (1993). The acquisition of a child by a learning disability. In S. Chaiklin & J. Lave (Eds.), *Understanding practice* (pp. 269–305). New York: Cambridge University Press.

McDermott, R. (1997). Achieving school failure: An anthropological approach to illiteracy and social stratification. In G.D. Spindler (Ed.), *Education and cultural process. Anthropological* approaches (2nd ed., pp. 173–209). Prospect, IL: Waveland Press.

McDermott, R. (1999). Culture is not an environment of the mind. *The Journal of Learning Sciences, 8,* 157–169.

McDermott, R., & Varenne, H. (1995). Culture *as* disability. *Anthropology & Education Quarterly, 26*(3), 324–348.

McLaughlin, B., & McLeod, B. (1996). *Educating all our children: Improving education for children from culturally and linguistically diverse backgrounds*. Impact Statement/Final Report on the Accomplishments of the National Center for Research on Cultural Diversity and Second Language Learning. Submitted to the U.S. Department of Education.

McLaughlin, M. J., Fuchs, L. S., & Hardman, M. (1999). Individual rights to education and students with disabilities: Some lessons from U.S. policy. In H. Daniels & P. Garner (Eds.), World Yearbook (pp. 24–35). London: Kogan Page.

McMaster, K. L., Fuchs, D., & Fuchs, L. S. (2006). Research on peer-assisted learning strategies: Peer mediation's promise and limitations. *Reading and Writing Quarterly, 22,* 5–25.

McNamara, B. E. (1998). *Learning disabilities: Appropriate practices for a diverse population*. Albany, NY: State University of New York Press.

McNeil, L. M. (2000). *Contradictions of school reform: Economic costs of standardized testing*. New York: Routledge.

McNeilly, L. G., & Coleman, T. J. (2000). Language disorders in culturally diverse populations: intervention issues and strategies. In T. J. Coleman (Ed.), *Clinical management of communication disorders in culturally diverse children* (pp. 157–172). Boston: Allyn & Bacon.

Miech, R., Essex, M. J., & Goldsmith, H. H. (2001). Socioeconomic status and the adjustment to school: The role of self-regulation during early childhood. *Sociology of Education, 74,* 102–120.

Miramontes, O., Nadeau, A., & Commins, N. (1997). *Re-structuring schools for linguistic diversity: Linking decision making to effective programs*. New York: Teachers College Press.

Moll, L., Amanti, C., Neff, D., & Gonzalez, N. (1992). Funds of knowledge for teaching: using a qualitative approach to connect homes and classrooms. *Theory into Practice, 31*(1): 132–41.

Montgomery, J. K. (1990). Building administrative support for service delivery changes. *Best Practices in School Speech-Language Pathology, 1,* 75–80.

Müller, N. (2003). Multilingual communication disorders: Exempla et desiderata. *Journal of Multilingual Communication Disorders, 1 (1),* 1–12.

Murphy, D. M. (1996). Implications of inclusion for general and special education. *The Elementary School Journal, 96,* 469–492.

Nagy, W. E., McClure, E. E., & Mir, M. (1997). Linguistic transfer and the use of context by Spanish-English bilinguals. *Applied Psycholinguistics, 18*(4), 431–452.

National Institutes of Health. (2004). *National Diabetes Education Program*. Available: http://ndep.nih.gov/campaigns.htm.

Nessel, D. D., & Jones, M.B. (1981).*The Language Experience approach to reading: A handbook for teachers*. New York: Teachers College Press.

Nguyen, D. (2006a). How do you decide what kind of program for English language learners is appropriate for your school? In E. Hamayan & R. Freeman (Eds.), *English language learners at school: A guide for administrators* (pp. 92–94). Philadelphia: Caslon.

Nguyen, D. (2006b). How do you use data on student performance about the implementation of your program for English language learners? In E. Hamayan & R. Freeman (Eds.), *English language learners at school: A guide for administrators* (pp. 129–131). Philadelphia: Caslon.

Nieto, S. (1999). *The light in their eyes: Creating multicultural learning communities*. New York: Teachers College Press.

Nieto, S. (2002). *Language, culture and teaching: Critical perspectives for teacher education*. 26th Annual Charles DeGarmo Lecture. Presented at the AERA meeting, New Orleans. Kennesaw, GA: Society of Professors of Education.

Norris, J.A. (1988). Using communicative reading strategies to enhance reading strategies. *The Reading Teacher, 47,* 668–673.

Nuri Robins, K., Lindsey, R., Lindsey, D. & Terrell, R. (2002). *Culturally proficient instruction: A guide for people who teach*. Thousand Oaks, CA: Corwin Press.

Ogbu, J. U., & Simons, H. (1998). Voluntary and involuntary implications for education. *Anthropology & Education Quarterly, 29*(2), 155–188.

Ollendick, T. H., Weist, M. D., Borden, M. C., & Greene, R. W. (1992). Sociometric status and academic, behavioral, and psychological adjustment: A five year longitudinal study. *Journal of Clinical Psychology, 60,* 80–87.

Oller, D. K., & Eilers, R. E. (2002). *Language and literacy in bilingual children*. Clevedon, UK: Multilingual Matters.

O'Malley, J. M., & Valdez-Pierce, L. (1996). *Authentic assessment for English language learners: Practical approaches for teachers*. New York: Addison-Wesley.

Ontario Association of Speech-Language Pathologists and Audiologists. (2005). *Effective collaborative practices for speech-language pathologists: A resource guide.* Toronto, ON: Author.

Orelove, F. P., & Sobsey, D. (1996). *Educating children with multiple disabilities: A transdisciplinary approach* (3rd ed.). Baltimore: Paul H. Brooks.

Ortiz, A. A., García, S. B., Holtzman, W. H., Jr., Polzoi, E., Snell, W. E., Jr., Wilkinson, C. Y., & Willig, A. C. 1(985). *Characteristics of limited English proficient Hispanic students in programs for the learning disabled: Implications for policy, practice and research.* Austin, TX: University of Texas, Disabled Minority Research Institute on Language Proficiency.

Ortiz, A. A., García, S. B., Wheeler, D., & Maldonado–Colon, E. (1986). *Characteristics of English Language Learners served in programs for the speech and language disabled: Implications for policy, practice and research.* Austin, TX: University of Texas, Disabled Minority Research Institute on Language Proficiency.

Owan, T.C. (Ed.). (1985). *Southeast Asian mental health: Treatment, prevention, services, training, and research.* Washington, DC: U.S. Government Printing Office.

Paley, V.G. (1994). Every child a story teller. In J.F. Duchan, L.E. Hewitt, & R.M. Sonnenmeier (Eds.), *Pragmatics: From theory to practice* (pp. 10–19). Englewood Cliffs, NJ: Prentice-Hall.

Paradis, J. (2005). Grammatical morphology in children learning English as a second language: Implications of similarities with specific language impairment. *Language, Speech and Hearing in Schools, 36*, 172–187.

Paradis, J., Crago, M., Genesee, F., & Rice, M. (2003). Bilingual children with specific language impairment: How do they compare to their monolingual peers? *Journal of Speech, Language and Hearing Research, 46*, 1–15.

Parish, R., & Arends, R. (1983). Why innovation programs are discontinued. *Educational Leadership, 4*, 62–65.

Parrish, T. B., & Chambers, J.G. (1996). Financing special education. *The Future of Children, 6*, 121–138.

Payne, R. (1998). *A framework for understanding poverty.* Highlands, TX: RFT Publishing.

Pearson, P. D., & Duke, N. K. (2000). Improving the reading comprehension of America's children: 10 research principles. *Reading Research Quarterly, 35*, 202–224.

Pearson, P. D., & Samuels, S. J. (1980). Editorial. *Reading Research Quarterly, 15*, 429–430.

Pearson, B. Z., Fernánez, S., & Oller, D. K. (1993). Lexical development in bilingual infants and toddlers: Comparison to monolingual norms. *Language and Learning, 43 (1)*, 93–120.

Pearson, B. Z., Fernánez, S., & Oller, D. K. (1995). Cross-language synonyms in the lexicons of bilingual infants: One language or two? *Journal of Child Language, 22(2)*, 345–368.

Penfield, J. (1987). ESL: the regular teachers' perspective. *TESOL Quarterly, 21*, 21–39.

Perkins, M. R. 2005. Pragmatic ability and disability as emergent phenomena. *Clinical Linguistics and Phonetics, 19*, 367–378.

Perkins, D. F., & Fogarty, K. (1999). Active listening: A communication tool. December 1999. *http://edis.ifas.ufl.edu/HE361*

Perozzi, A. J. (1985). A pilot study of language facilitation for bilingual language-handicapped children: Theoretical and intervention implications. *Journal of Speech and Hearing Disorders, 50*, 403–406.

Perozzi, A. J., & Sanchez, M.L.C. (1992). The effect of instruction in L1 on receptive acquisition of L2 for bilingual children. *Language, Speech and Hearing in Schools, 23*, 348–352.

Peyton, J. K., & Staton, J. (1993). *Dialogue journals in the multilingual classroom: Building language fluency and writing skills through written interaction.* Norwood, NJ: Ablex.

Phelan, P., & Davidson, A.L. (Eds.). (1993). *Renegotiating cultural diversity in American schools.* New York: Teachers College Press.

Phelan, P., Davidson, A. L., & Yu, H. C. (1993). Students' multiple worlds: Navigating the borders of family, peer, and school cultures. In P. Phelan & A.L. Davidson (Eds.), *Renegotiating cultural diversity in American schools* (pp. 52–88). New York: Teachers College Press.

Philips, S. (1983). *The invisible culture.* New York: Longman.

Pinker, S. (1994). *The language instinct: How the mind creates language.* New York: Harper Collins.

Pinnell, G. S. (1989). Reading recovery: Helping at-risk children learn to read. *The Elementary School Journal, 90*, 160–183.

Poplak, S. (1980). "Sometimes I'll start a sentence in English y termino en español": Toward a typology of code switching. *Linguistics, 18*, 581–618.

Portes, P. R. (1999). Social and psychological factors in the academic achievement of children of immigrants: A cultural history puzzle. *American Educational Research Journal, 36(3)*, 489–507.

Potocky–Tripodi, M. (2002). *Best practices for social work with refugees and immigrants.* New York: Columbia University Press.

Prelock, P.A. (2000). Multiple perspectives for determining the roles of speech-language pathologists in inclusionary classrooms. *Language, Speech and Hearing Services in Schools, 31 (3)*, 213–218.

Reese, L., Garnier, H., Gallimore, R., & Goldenberg, C. (2000). Longitudinal analysis of the antecedents of emergent Spanish literacy and middle-school English reading achievement of Spanish-speaking students. *American Educational Research Journal, 37(3)*, 633–662.

Quinn, A. E. (2001). Moving marginalized students inside the lines: Cultural differences in classrooms. *English Journal, March, 44–50.*

Reid, R., Maag, J. W., & Vasa, S. F. (1994). Attention deficit hyperactivity disorder as a disability category: A critique. *Exceptional Children, 60*, 198–214.

Reid, B. M., Secord, W. A., & Damico, J. S. (1993). Strategies for the integration of collaborative theory into practice. *The NSSLHA Journal, 20*, 32–42.

Rist, R. (1970). Student social class and teacher expectations: The self-fulfilling prophecy in ghetto education. *Harvard Educational Review, 40*, 411–451.

Robson, M., Cook, P., & Gilliland, J. (1995). Helping children manage stress. *British Educational Research Journal, 21*, 165–174.

Rogoff, B. (1990). *The cultural nature of human development.* New York: Oxford University Press.

Rolstad, K., Mahoney, K., & Glass, G. (2005). Weighing the evidence: A meta-analysis of bilingual education in Arizona. *Bilingual Research Journal, 29:1.*

Roseberry-McKibbin, C., Brice, A., & O'Hanlon, L. (2005). Serving English language learners in public school settings: A national survey. *Language, Speech, and Hearing Services in Schools, 36,* 48–61.

Routman, R. (2003). *Reading essentials: The specifics you need to teach reading well.* Portsmouth, NH: Heinemann.

Ruiz-de-Velasco, J., & Fix, M. (2000). *Overlooked and underserved: Immigrant students in U.S. secondary schools.* Washington, DC: Urban Institute.

Rutter, M., & Madge, N. (1976). *Cycles of disadvantage.* London: Heinemann.

Sacks, P. (1999). *Standardized minds: The high price of America's testing culture and what we can do to change it.* Cambridge, MA: Perseus.

Saenz, L., Fuchs, L. D., & Fuchs, D. (2005). Effects of peer-assisted learning strategies on English language learners: A randomized controlled study. *Exceptional Children, 71,* 231–247.

Sahlins, M. (1999). Two or three things that I know about culture. *Journal of the Royal Anthropology Institute, 5,* 399–421.

Salameh, E., Håkansson, G., & Nettelbladt, U. 2004. Developmental perspectives on bilingual Swedish-Arabic children with and without language impairment: A longitudinal study. *International Journal of Language and Communication Disorders, 39(1),* 65–92.

Salett, E. P., & Koslow, D. R. (1994). *Race, ethnicity and self.* Washington, DC: National Multicultural Institute.

Samway, K. D., & McKeon, D. (1999). *Myths and realities. Best practices for language minority students.* Portsmouth, NH: Heinemann.

Sanchez-Lopez, C. 2006. How can we distinguish between a language difficulty and a learning disability? In E. Hamayan & R. Freeman (Eds.) *English language learners at school. A guide for administrators* (pp. 206–207). Philadelphia: Caslon.

Sanchez-Lopez, C., & Young, T. 2003. *Continuum of interventions for English Language Learners experiencing difficulties.* Paper presented at the Twenty-Seventh Annual Statewide Conference for Teachers of Linguistically and Culturally Diverse Students, Oak Brook, Ill.

Schecter, S. R., & Cummins, J. (Eds.). (2003). *Multilingual education in practice: Using diversity as a resource.* Portsmouth, NH: Heinemann.

Schiller, B. (2001). *The economics of poverty and discrimination.* Englewood Cliffs, NJ: Prentice Hall.

Schon, D. A. (1987). *Educating the reflective practitioner: Toward a new design for teaching and learning in the professions.* San Francisco: Jossey-Bass.

Schönwetter, D. J., Clifton, R. A., & Perry, R. P. (2002). Content familiarity: Differential impact of effective teaching on student achievement outcomes. *Research in Higher Education, 43,* 625–655.

Schulze, P. A., Harwood, R. L., Goebel, M. J., & Schubert, A. M. (1999). Cultural influences on mothers' developmental expectations for their children. Poster presented at the Biennial Meeting of the Society for Research in Child Development, Albuquerque, NM.

Schwarzer, R. (Ed.). (1986). *Self-related cognition in anxiety and motivation.* Hillsdale, NJ: Erlbaum.

Seccombe, K. (2002). "Beating the odds" versus "changing the odds": Poverty, resilience, and family policy. *Journal of Marriage and Family, 64,* 384–394.

Shea, M., Murray, R., & Harlin, R. (2005). *Drowning in data? How to collect, organize, and document student performance.* Portsmouth, NH: Heinemann.

Simmons-Mackie, N. N., & Damico, J.S. (2003). Contributions of qualitative research to the knowledge base of normal communication. *American Journal of Speech-Language Pathology, 12,* 144–154.

Sinclair, R. L., & Ghory, W. J. (1987). Becoming marginal. In H. T. Trueba (Ed.), *Success or failure? Learning and the language minority student* (pp. 169–184). Cambridge, MA: Newbury House.

Sirin, S. R. (2005). Socioeconomic status and academic achievement: A meta-analytic review of research. *Review of Educational Research, 75(3),* 417–453.

Skrtic, T. M. (1991a). The special education paradox. *Harvard Educational Review, 6(2),* 148–206.

Skrtic, T. M. (1991b). *Behind special education: A critical analysis of professional culture and school organization.* Denver, CO: Love.

Slavin, R., & Cheung, A. (2003). *Effective reading programs for English language learners: A best evidence synthesis.* Baltimore: Johns Hopkins University, Center for Research on the Education of Students Placed at Risk.

Slavin, R., & Cheung, A. (2005). A synthesis of research on language of reading instruction for English Language Learners. *Review of Educational Research, 75,* 247–281.

Smaje, C. (1995). *Health, "race" and ethnicity: Making sense of the evidence.* London: King's Fund Institute.

Smith, F. (1983). Twelve easy ways to make learning to read difficult. *Essays into literacy: Selected papers and some afterthoughts* (pp. 12–25). Exeter, NH: Heinemann Educational Books.

Smith, F. (1998). *The book of learning and forgetting.* New York: Teachers College Press.

Smith, F. (2003). *Unspeakable acts, unnatural practices: Flaws and fallacies in scientific reading instruction.* Portsmouth, NH: Heinemann.

Smith, F. (2004). *Understanding reading* (6th ed.). Mahwah, NJ: Erlbaum

Smith, P. (2006). How do English language learners acquire a second language at school? In E. Hamayan & R. Freeman (Eds.) *English language learners at school: A guide for administrators* (pp. 66–88). Philadelphia: Caslon.

Snow, C., Burns, M. S. & Griffen, P. (1998). *Preventing reading difficulties in young children.* Washington, DC: National Academies Press for the National Research Council.

Snow, M. A., Met, M., & Genesee, F. (1989). A conceptual framework for the integration of language and content in second/foreign language instruction. *TESOL Quarterly, 23,* 201–217.

Spandel, V., & Stiggins, J. J. (1997). *Creating writers. Linking writing assessment and* instruction (2nd ed.). New York: Longman

Spindler, G.D.D. (1997). *Education and cultural Process:*

Anthropological approaches. Prospect Heights, IL: Waveland Press.

Spindler, G.D.D., & Spindler, L. (1987). Cultural dialogue and schooling in Schoenhausen and Roseville: A comparative analysis. *Anthropology and Education Quarterly, 18,* 3–16.

Spindler, G.D.D. & Spindler, L. (1994). *Pathways to cultural awareness: Cultural therapy with teachers and students.* Thousand Oaks, CA: Sage.

Stanton-Salazar, R. D. (1997). A social capital framework for understanding the socialization of racial minority children and youths. *Harvard Education Review, 67,* 1–40.

Stecker, P. M., Fuchs, L. S., & Fuchs, D. (2005). Using curriculum-based measurement to improve student achievement: Review of research. *Psychology in the Schools, 42,* 795–820.

Steinhauer, P. D. (1998). Developing resiliency in children from disadvantaged populations. In *Canada Health Action Plan: Building on the legacy.* Vol. 1. *Children and youth.* Saint–Foy, PQ: Editions Multi-Montes.

Stern, M. P., Pugh, J. A., Gaskill, S. P., & Hazuda, H. (1982). Knowledge, attitudes, and behavior related to obesity and dieting in Mexican Americans and Anglos: The San Antonio Heart Study. *American Journal of Epidemiology, 115,* 917–928.

Sternberg, R. J., & Grigorenko, E. L. (2002). Difference scores in the identification of children with learning disabilities: It's time to use a different method. *Journal of School Psychology, 40 (1),* –65–83.

Stevenson, M. (1995). The power of influence: Effecting change by developing ownership. In C. Dudley-Marling & D. Searle (Eds.), *Who owns learning? Questions of autonomy, choice, and control* (pp. 128–141). Portsmouth, NH: Heinemann.

Stow, C., & Dodd, B. (2005). A survey of bilingual children referred for investigation of communication disorders: A comparison with monolingual children referred in one area in England. *Journal of Multilingual Communication Disorders, 3*(1), 1–24.

Strauss, S. L. (2001). An open letter to Reid Lyon. *Educational Researcher,* June/July. 26–33

Suarez-Orozco, M. M. (1987). Towards a psychosocial understanding of Hispanic adaptation to American schooling. In H. T. Trueba (Ed.), *Success or failure: Learning and the language minority student* (pp. 156–158). Cambridge, MA: Newbury House.

Suarez-Orozco, M. M. (1995). The cultural patterning of achievement motivation: A comparative study of Mexican, Mexican immigrant, and non-Latino white American youths in schools. *International Migration Review, 28,* 748–794.

Swan, M., & Smith, B. (Eds.). (2001). *Learner English: A teacher's guide to interference and other problems* (2nd ed.). Cambridge: Cambridge Handbooks for Language Teachers.

Taberski, S. (2000). *On solid ground: Strategies for teaching reading K–3.* Portsmouth, NH: Heinemann.

Taylor, D. (1983). *Family literacy. Young children learning to read and write.* Portsmouth, NH: Heinemann.

Taylor, D. (1991). *Learning denied.* Portsmouth, NH: Heinemann.

Taylor, D. (1993). *From a child's point of view.* Portsmouth, NH: Heinemann.

Teachers of English to Speakers of Other Languages (TESOL). (2006). *PreK–12 English Language Proficiency Standards.* Alexandria: TESOL, Inc.

Tetnowski, J. A., & Franklin, T. C. (2003). Qualitative research: Implications for description and assessment. *American Journal of Speech-Language Pathology, 12*(2), 155–165.

Tett, L., & Crowther, J. (1998). Families at a disadvantage: Class, culture and literacies. *British Educational Research Journal, 24,* 449–460.

Tharp, R. (1999). *The five standards for effective pedagogy.* Berkeley, CA: University of California, Santa Cruz, Center for Research on Education, Diversity and Excellence.

Thomas, C. C., Correa, V. I., & Morsink, C. V. (1995) *Interactive teaming: Consultation and collaboration in special programs* (2nd ed.). Englewood Cliffs, NJ: Prentice-Hall.

Thomas, W., & Collier, V. 2002. *A national study of school effectiveness for language minority students' long term academic achievement.* Santa Cruz, CA: Center for Research in Education, Diversity and Excellence, University of California, Santa Cruz. Available: *http://www.crede.ucsc.edu.*

Thordardottir, E., Rothenberg, A., Rivard, M.-E., & Naves, R. (2006). Bilingual assessment: Can overall proficiency be estimated from separate measure of two languages? *Journal of Multilingual Communication Disorders, 4*(1), 1–21.

Tizard, J., Schofield, W. N., & Hewison, J. (1982). The Haringey shared reading project. *British Journal of Educational Psychology, 52,* 1–15.

Tomlinson, S. (1985). The expansion of special education. *Oxford Review of Education, 11,* 157–165.

Trelease, J. (2001). *The read-aloud handbook* (5th ed.). New York: Penguin Books.

Trousdale, A. M. (1990). Interactive storytelling: Scaffolding children's early narratives. *Language Arts, 67,* 164–173.

Trueba, H. T. (1988). Culturally–based explanations of minority students' academic achievement. *Anthropology & Education Quarterly, 19,* 270–287.

Trueba, H. T. (1993). Cultural therapy in action. In H.T. Trueba, C. Rodriguez, Y. Zou, & J. Cintron (Eds.), *Healing multicultural America: Mexican immigrants rise to power in rural California* (pp. 155–168). London: Falmer Press.

Ukrainetz, T. A. (2006). The implications of TRI and EBP for SLPs: Commentary on L. M. Justice. *Language, Speech, and Hearing Services in Schools, 37,* 298–303.

UNESCO. (1996). *World education report 1996.* Paris: Author.

U.S. Department of Education. (2001). *Twenty third annual report to Congress on the implementation of the Individuals with Disabilities Education Act.* Washington, DC: Author.

U.S. Department of Veterans Affairs. (2006, July 20). Facts about PTSD. Washington, DC: National Center for Post Traumatic Stress Disorder. www.ncptsd.va.gov/facts/index.html.

Vaughn, S. R., & Fuchs, L. S. (2003). Redefining learning disabilities as inadequate response to treatment: Rationale and assumptions. *Learning Disabilities Research and Practice, 18,* 137–146.

Vitevitch, M. S., & Rodríguez, E. (2005). Neighborhood

density effects in spoken word recognition in Spanish. *Journal of Multilingual Communication Disorders, 3*(1), 64–73.

Vogt, M. E. (1991). An observation guide for supervisors and administrators: Moving toward integrated reading/language arts instruction. *The Reading Teacher, 45,* 206–211.

Vygotsky, L. S. (1978). *Mind in society: The development of higher psychological processes.* Cambridge, MA: Harvard University Press. [Originally published in Russian in 1930]

Walker, J. I., & Cavenar, J. O. (1982). Vietnam veterans: Their problems continue. *Journal of Nervous and Mental Disease, 170*(3), 174–180.

Wax, M. (1993). How culture misdirects multiculturalism. *Anthropology and Education Quarterly, 24,* 99–115.

Weissbourd, R. (1996). *The vulnerable child: What really hurts America's children and what we can do about it.* Reading, MA: Addison-Wesley.

Weisz, J. R., Suwanlert, S., Chaiyasit, W., et al. (1988′). Thai and American perspectives on over- and under-controlled child behavior problems: Exploring the threshold model among parents, teachers, and psychologists. *Journal of Nervous and Mental Disease, 181,* 401–408.

Welch, M., Sheridan, S. M., Wilson, B., Colton, D., & Mayhew, J. C. (1996). Site-based transdisciplinary educational partnerships: Development, implementation, and outcomes of a collaborative professional preparation program. *Journal of Educational and Psychological Consultation, 7*(3), 223–249.

Wells, G. (1986). *The meaning makers: Children learning language and using language to learn.* Portsmouth, NH: Heinemann.

Wells, G. (1990). Talk about text: Where literacy is learned and taught. *Curriculum Inquiry, 20,* 369–405.

Wells, G. (1998). Some questions about direct instruction: Why? To whom? How? And when? *Language Arts, 76,* 27–35.

Wells, G. (2003). *Dialogic inquiry: Toward a sociocultural practice and theory of education.* Cambridge: Cambridge University Press.

Wentzel, K. R., & Wigfield, A. (1998). Academic and social motivational influences on students' academic performance. *Educational Psychology Review, 10*(2), 155–175.

Werner, E., & Smith, R. (1992). *Overcoming the odds: High-risk children from birth to adulthood.* Ithaca, NY: Cornell University Press.

Westby, C. (1997). There's more to passing than knowing the answers. *Language, Speech and Hearing Services in Schools, 28, July,* 274–287.

Westby, C., & Vining, C. B. (2002). Living in harmony: Providing services to Native American children and families. In D. E. Battle (Ed.), *Communication disorders in multicultural populations* (3rd ed., pp. 135–178). Woburn, MA: Butterworth-Heinemann.

White, K. R. (1982). The relationship between socioeconomic status and academic achievement. *Psychological Bulletin, 91*(3), 461–481.

Whiting, J.W.M. (1990). Adolescent rituals and identity conflicts. In J. W. Stigler, R. A. Shweder, & G. Herdt (Eds.), *Cultural psychology: Essays on comparative human development* (pp. 357–365). Cambridge: Cambridge University Press.

Whitmore, R. (1987). *Living with stress and anxiety.* Manchester, UK: Manchester University Press.

Wiener, J., & Davidson, I. (1990). The in–school team: A preventive model of service delivery in special education. *Canadian Journal of Education, 15*(4), 427–444.

Wiley, T., & Wright, W. (2004). Against the undertow: Language–minority education policy and politics in the "age of accountability." *Educational Policy, 18*(1), 142–168.

Wilkinson, C. Y., & Ortiz, A. A. (1986). *Characteristics of limited English proficient learning disabled Hispanic students at initial assessment and at reevaluation.* Austin, TX: Handicapped Minority Research Institute on Language Proficiency.

Wilkinson, R. G. (1996). *Unhealthy societies: The afflictions of inequality.* London: Routledge.

Wilson, W. F., Wilson, J. R., & Coleman, T. J. (2000). Culturally appropriate assessment: Issues and strategies. In T. J. Coleman (Ed.), *Clinical management of communication disorders in culturally diverse children* (pp. 101–112). Boston: Allyn & Bacon.

Wine, J. D. (1980). Cognitive attentional theory of test anxiety. In I.G. Sarason (Ed.), *Test anxiety: Theory, research, and applications* (pp. 349–385). Hillsdale, NJ: Erlbaum.

Winter, K. (1999). Speech and language therapy provision for bilingual children: Aspects of the current service. *International Journal of Language and Communication Disorders, 34*(1), 85–98.

Winter, K. (2001). Number of bilingual children in speech and language therapy: Theory and practice of measuring their representation. *International Journal of Bilingualism, 5*(4), 465–495.

Woodward, H. (1994). *Negotiated evaluation: Involving children and parents in the process.* Portsmouth, NH: Heinemann.

World–Class Instructional Design and Assessment (WIDA) Consortium. (2006). *English language proficiency standards.* Madison, WI: Wisconsin Center for Education Research, University of Wisconsin-Madison.

World Health Organization. (2002). *International Classification of Diseases (ICD–10).* Geneva: Author.

Wright, J. (2005, Summer). Five interventions that work. *NAESP [National Association of Elementary School Principals] Leadership Compass, 2*(4), 1, 6.

York–Barr, J., & Rainforth, B. (1997). *Collaborative teams for students with severe disabilities: Integrating therapy and Educational Services* (2nd ed.). Baltimore: Paul E. Brookes.

Young, T., & Westernoff, F. (1999). Reflections of speech and language pathologists and audiologists on practices in a multicultural, multilingual society. *Journal of Speech-Language Pathology and Audiology, 23*(1), 24–30.

Yturriago, J. (2006a). What can you can tell parents of English language learners about language use at home? In E. Hamayan & R. Freeman (Eds.), *English language learners at school: A guide for administrators* (pp. 51–52). Philadelphia: Caslon.

Yturriago, J. (2006b). How do you use evidence on program effectiveness to inform policy? In E. Hamayan & R. Freeman (Eds.) *English language learners at school: A guide for administrators* (pp. 27–28). Philadelphia: Caslon.

Index

Page numbers followed by an *f* or *t* indicate figures and tables.